Mastering VMware NSX® for vSphere®

Elver Sena Sosa

Published simultaneously in Canada

ISBN: 978-1-119-51354-4
ISBN: 978-1-119-51351-3 (ebk)
ISBN: 978-1-119-51353-7 (ebk)

Manufactured in the United States of America

Library of Congress Control Number: 2019956689

V10018255_032620

About the Authors

Elver Sena Sosa is a Data Center Solutions Architect who specializes in Software Defined Data Center technologies. Over the past 20 years, Elver has driven the presales, design, and deployment of projects throughout APAC, EMEA, and APAC. Elver has been the go-to partner for helping VMware evangelize NSX, vSAN, and VCF, VMware's Software Defined products and solutions. Elver is a skilled communicator who enjoys sharing his experience on the interdependencies of technology to audiences around the world. Elver has continued working in SDDC with his company, Hydra 1303, Inc, where he published his first book, the NSX exam study guide, *VCP6-NV Official Cert Guide*, and the YouTube vSAN Architecture 100 series.

Trey McMahon is based out of Richmond, Virginia, and is a Cloud Data Engineer on the Hydra 1303 team. Trey has been in networking since 1997, writing authorized courses and exams for Cisco, developing instructor readiness programs and labs for EMC and Cisco, teaching network engineering in over 30 countries, and supporting VMware customer enablement. These days at Hydra 1303, he specializes in cloudy things.

Zac Smith is a lead Data Center Solutions Engineer at Hydra 1303. He specializes in providing automated data center solutions. Zac has been in the IT industry for 20 years and has been a part of many enterprise solution designs and deployments. Zac has also been involved in writing numerous courses for VMware and Cisco, as well as providing partner and customer enablement sessions on a global scale.

About the Technical Editor

Shane Weinbrecht has been in the technology industry for the past 20 years, working as a systems administrator for enterprise companies such as IBM and The Adidas Group; for the past 10 years, he has been on the vendor side currently employed by Nutanix as a senior systems engineer covering healthcare. Most importantly, Shane is happily married and the proud father of two amazing boys and enjoys spending time with his family and friends, photography, Obstacle Course Racing, and Krav Maga.

Acknowledgments

A special thanks goes to Luciana de Padua, a key member of our team here at Hydra 1303 that we rely on for . . . well, everything. She sets a high bar for excellence with her ninja-level PKS and NSX-T skills, positive energy, and ability to make all of this fun, while loving what she does. Always in demand, both by VMware internally and our direct customers, she's never in one time zone for very long. This book wouldn't have been written if we didn't have Lu leading Hydra 1303's European engagements throughout the process.

Thanks also to the talented editors at Wiley Publishing: Tom Cirtin, Kim Cofer, Shane Weinbrecht, Kathyrn Duggan and Athiyappan Lalith Kumar. Your suggestions were consistently dead on and helped to improve the clarity every time.

Contents at a Glance

Contents

Introduction

The advantages of server virtualization in data centers are well established. From the beginning, VMware has led the charge with vSphere. Organizations migrating physical servers to virtual immediately see the benefits of lower operational costs, the ability to pool CPU and memory resources, server consolidation, and simplified management.

VMware had mastered compute virtualization and thought, "Why not do the same for the entire data center?" Routers, switches, load balancers, firewalls . . . essentially all key physical networking components, could be implemented in software, creating a Software-Defined Data Center (SDDC). That product, VMware NSX, is the subject of this book.

In 1962, Sir Arthur Clarke published an essay asserting three laws. His third law stated, "Any sufficiently advanced technology is indistinguishable from magic." If you're not familiar with NSX, the abilities you gain as a network administrator almost seem like magic at first, but we'll dive into the details to explain how it all works. It doesn't matter if you don't have a background in vSphere. There are plenty of analogies and examples throughout, breaking down the underlying concepts to make it easy to understand the capabilities of NSX and how to configure it.

The way NSX provides network virtualization is to overlay software on top of your existing physical network, all without having to make changes to what you have in place. This is much like what happens with server virtualization. When virtualizing servers, a hypervisor separates and hides the underlying complexities of physical CPU and memory resources from the software components (operating system and application), which exist in a virtual machine. With this separation, the server itself just becomes a collection of files, easily cloned or moved. An immediate benefit gained is the time and effort saved when deploying a server. Instead of waiting for the order of your physical servers to arrive by truck, then waiting for someone to rack and stack, then waiting for someone else to install an operating system, then waiting again for network connectivity, security, installation, and configuration of the application . . . you get the picture. Instead of waiting on each of those teams, the server can be deployed with a click of a button.

NSX can do the same and much more for your entire data center. The agility NSX provides opens new possibilities. For instance, a developer comes to you needing a temporary test server and a NAT router to provide Internet connectivity. The admin can use NSX to deploy a virtual machine (VM) and a virtual NAT router. The developer completes the test, the VM and NAT router are deleted, and all of this occurs before lunch. NSX can do the same thing for entire networks.

The same developer comes to you in the afternoon requesting a large test environment that mimics the production network while being completely isolated. She needs routers, multiple subnets, a firewall, load balancers, some servers running Windows, others running Linux: all set up with proper addressing, default gateways, DNS, DHCP, and her favorite dev tools installed and ready to go. It's a good bet that setting this up in a physical lab would take a lot of time and may involve several teams.

With NSX, that same network could be deployed by an administrator with a few clicks, or even better, it can be automated completely, without having to involve an administrator at all. VMware has a product that works with NSX called vRealize Automation (vRA) that does just that. It provides our developer with a catalog portal, allowing her to customize and initiate the deployment herself, all without her needing to have a background in networking.

If you're a security admin, this might seem like chaos would ensue, with anyone being able to deploy whatever they want on the network. NSX has that covered as well. As a security administrator, you still hold the keys and assign who can do what, but those keys just got a lot more powerful with NSX.

Imagine if you had an unlimited budget and were able to attach a separate firewall to every server in the entire network, making it impossible to bypass security while significantly reducing latency. Additionally, what if you didn't have to manage each of those firewalls individually? What if you could enter the rules once and they propagate instantly to every firewall, increasing security dramatically while making your job a lot easier and improving performance. It's not magic; that's the *S* in NSX.

The *N* in NSX is for networking, the *S* is for security. The *X*? Some say it stands for eXtensibility or eXtended, but it could just as well be a way to make the product sound cool. Either way, the point is that both networking and security get equal treatment in NSX, two products in one. At the same time, instead of these additions adding more complexity to your job, you'll find just the opposite. With the firewall example or the example of the developer deploying the large test network, as a security administrator, you set the rules and permissions and you're done. Automation takes care of the tedious legwork, while avoiding the typical mistakes that arise when trying to deploy something before having your morning coffee. Those mistakes often lead to even more legwork with more of your time drained troubleshooting.

Wait, the title of the book says NSX-V. What does the *V* for? Since NSX is tightly integrated with vSphere, its legal name is NSX for vSphere, but we'll just refer to it as NSX for short. NSX-V has a cousin, NSX-T, with the *T* standing for transformers. In a nutshell, that product is made to easily integrate with environments using multiple hypervisors, Kubernetes, Docker, KVM, and OpenStack. If all that sounds like a lot to take in, not to worry, we'll save that for another book.

Welcome to NSX.

What Does This Book Cover?

Chapter 1: Abstracting Network and Security We often learn how to configure something new without really understanding *why* it exists in the first place. You should always be asking, "What problem does this solve?" The people armed with these details are often positioned to engineer around new problems when they arise. This chapter is a quick read to help you understand why NSX was created in the first place, the problems it solves, and where NSX fits in the evolution of networking, setting the stage for rest of the book's discussions on virtualization.

Chapter 2: NSX Architectures and Requirements This chapter is an overview of NSX operations. It details the components that make up NSX, their functions, and how they communicate. Equally important, it introduces NSX terminology used throughout the book, as well as virtualization logic.

Chapter 3: Preparing NSX In this chapter, you will find out everything you need to have in place before you can deploy NSX. This includes not only resources like CPU, RAM, and disk space, but it also covers ports that are necessary for NSX components to communicate, and prepping your ESXi hosts for NSX.

Chapter 4: Distributed Logical Switch It's helpful if you are already familiar with how a physical switch works before getting into the details of a Distributed Logical Switch. Don't worry if you're not. In this chapter, we'll look at how all switches learn, and why being distributed and logical is a dramatic improvement over centralized and physical. You'll also find out how NSX uses tunnels as a solution to bypass limitations of your physical network.

Chapter 5: Marrying VLANs and VXLANs On the virtual side, we have VMs living on VXLANs. On the physical side, we have servers living on VLANs. Rather than configuring lots of little subnets and routing traffic between logical and physical environments, this chapter goes into how to connect the two (physical and logical), making it easy to exchange information without having to re-IP everything.

Chapter 6: Distributed Logical Router In Chapter 4, we compared a physical switch and a Distributed Logical Switch. We do the same in this chapter for physical routers vs. Distributed Logical Routers, covering how they work, how they improve performance while making your job easier, and the protocols they use to communicate.

Chapter 7: NFV: Routing with NSX Edges In this chapter, we talk about network services beyond routing and switching that are often provided by proprietary dedicated physical devices, such as firewalls, load balancers, NAT routers, and DNS servers. We'll see how these network functions can be virtualized (Network Function Virtualization, or NFV) in NSX.

Chapter 8: More NFV: NSX Edge Services Gateway This chapter focuses on the Edge Services Gateway, the Swiss Army knife of NSX devices, that can do load balancing, Network Address Translation (NAT), DHCP, DHCP Relay, DNS Relay, several flavors of VPNs, and most importantly, route traffic in and out of your NSX environment.

Chapter 9: NSX Security, the Money Maker When it's said that NSX provides better security, you'll find out why in this chapter. Rather than funneling traffic through a single-point physical firewall, it's as if a police officer were stationed just outside the door of every home. The NSX Distributed Firewall provides security that is enforced just outside the VM, making it impossible to bypass the inspection of traffic in or out. We also look at how you can extend NSX functionality to incorporate firewall solutions from other vendors.

Chapter 10: Service Composer and Third-Party Appliances This chapter introduces Service Composer. This built-in NSX tool allows you to daisy-chain security policies based on what is happening in real time. You'll see an example of a virus scan triggering a series of security policies automatically applied, eventually leading to a virus-free VM. You'll also learn how to tie in services from other vendors and explain the differences between guest introspection and network introspection.

Chapter 11: vRealize Automation and REST APIs Saving the best time-saving tool for last, this chapter covers vRealize Automation (vRA), a self-service portal containing a catalog of what can be provisioned. If a non-admin needs a VM, they can deploy it. If it needs to be a cluster of VMs running Linux with a load balancer and NAT, they can deploy it. As an admin, you can even time bomb it, so that after the time expires, vRA will keep your network clean and tidy by removing what was deployed, automatically. You will also see how administrative tasks can be done without going through a GUI, using REST APIs.

Additional Resources

Here's a list of supporting resources that augment what is covered in this book, including the authorized VCP6-NV NSX exam guide, online videos, free practice labs, helpful blogs, and supporting documentation.

VCP6-NV Official Cert Guide (NSX exam #2V0-642) by Elver Sena Sosa:

`www.amazon.com/VCP6-NV-Official-Cert-Guide-2V0-641/dp/9332582750/ref=sr_1_1?keywords=elver+sena+sosa&qid=1577768162&sr=8-1`

YouTube vSAN Architecture 100 Series by Elver Sena Sosa:

`www.youtube.com/results?search_query=vsan+architecture+100+series`

Weekly data center virtualization blog posts from the Hydra 1303 team:

`www.hydra1303.com`

Practice with free VMware NSX Hands-on Labs (HOL):

`www.vmware.com/products/nsx/nsx-hol.html`

VMUG – VMware User Group:

`www.vmug.com`

VMware NSX-V Design Guide:

`www.vmware.com/content/dam/digitalmarketing/vmware/en/pdf/products/nsx/vmw-nsx-network-virtualization-design-guide.pdf`

VMware authorized NSX classes (classroom and online):

`mylearn.vmware.com/mgrReg/courses.cfm?ui=www_edu&a=one&id_subject=83185`

How to Contact the Publisher

If you believe you've found a mistake in this book, please bring it to our attention. At John Wiley & Sons, we understand how important it is to provide our customers with accurate content, but even with our best efforts, an error may occur.

In order to submit your possible errata, please email it to our Customer Service Team at `wileysupport@wiley.com` with the subject line "Possible Book Errata Submission."

Chapter 1

Abstracting Network and Security

In this chapter, we will examine the evolution of Data Center Networking and Security from the 1990s to the present in order to better understand how network virtualization in today's data centers provides solutions that reduce costs, greatly improve manageability, and increase security.

Most IT professionals are familiar with server virtualization using virtual machines (VMs). A virtual machine is purely software. An abstraction layer creates a way to decouple the physical hardware resources from that software. In doing so, the VM becomes a collection of files that can be backed up, moved, or allocated more resources without having to make changes to the physical environment.

We will delve into how VMware NSX is the next step in data center evolution, allowing virtualization to extend beyond servers. Routers, switches, firewalls, load balancers, and other networking components can all be virtualized through NSX. NSX provides an abstraction layer that decouples these components from the underlying physical hardware, which provides administrators with new solutions that further reduce costs, improve manageability, and increase security across the entire data center.

IN THIS CHAPTER, YOU WILL LEARN ABOUT:

- The evolution of the modern data center
- How early networks created a need for data centers
- Colocation: the sharing of provider data centers
- Challenges in cost, resource allocation, and provisioning
- VMware server virtualization
- VMware storage virtualization
- VMware NSX: virtual networking and security

Networks: 1990s

The 1990s brought about changes to networking that we take for granted today. We shifted from the original Ethernet design of half-duplex communication, where devices take turns sending data, to full duplex. With full duplex, each device had a dedicated connection to the network that allowed us to send and receive simultaneously, while at the same time reducing collisions on the wire to zero (see Figure 1.1). The move to full duplex effectively doubled our throughput.

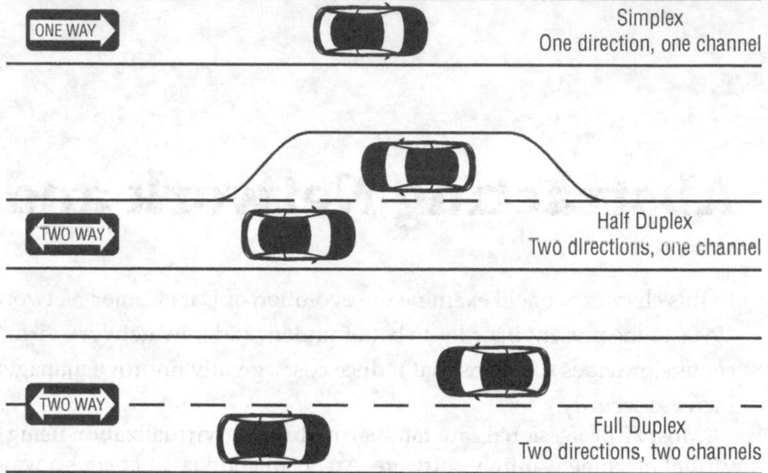

FIGURE 1.1 Simplex, half duplex, and full duplex compared

100 Mbps Ethernet connections became possible and the technology was given the unfortunate name Fast Ethernet, a label that has not aged well considering that available 100 GB ports of today are 1000 times faster than the '90s version of "Fast."

The '90s also ushered in our first cable modems, converging data and voice with VoIP, and of course, the Internet's explosion in popularity. As Internet businesses started to boom, a demand was created for a place to host business servers. They needed reliable connectivity and an environment that provided the necessary power and cooling along with physical security. They needed a data center. Although it was possible for an organization to build its own dedicated data centers, it was both costly and time-consuming, especially for online startups booming in the '90s.

Colocation

An attractive solution, especially for startups, was colocation. Many providers offered relatively inexpensive hosting plans, allowing businesses to move their physical servers and networking devices to the provider's ready-made data center. With colocation, organizations were essentially renting space, but they still maintained complete control over their physical devices (see Figure 1.2). The organization was still responsible for installing the operating system, upgrades, and backups. The only real difference was that the location of their compute resources had changed from locally hosted to the provider site.

FIGURE 1.2 Colocated space rented in provider data centers

The Internet boom of the '90s meant that due to web computing, a massive amount of data was being generated, which created a need for storage solutions such as Fibre Channel, iSCSI, and NFS. One major benefit in having these resources together in a data center was centralized management.

Not all data centers looked as impressive in the '90s as they do today. Google's first data center was created in 1998, and was just a 7 × 4 foot cage with only enough space for 30 servers on shelves.

Workload-to-Server Ratio

The general design choice at the time was that each server would handle a single workload in a 1:1 ratio. To support a new workload, you bought another server, installed an operating system, and deployed it. There were numerous issues with this plan.

Inefficient Resource Allocation

There was no centralized management of CPU and memory. Each server was independent and had its own dedicated resources that could not be shared. This led to one of two choices:

- The simplistic approach was to allocate servers with a fixed amount of CPU and RAM, giving wide berth for future growth. This strategy meant that resources were largely underutilized. For example, servers on average used less than 20 percent of their CPU.
- The alternative was to micromanage the resources per machine. Although compute resources were better utilized, the administrator's time was not. Spikes in usage sometimes created emergency situations with applications failing due to a lack CPU or memory.

The Long Road to Provisioning

Rolling out a new server involved numerous teams: the infrastructure team would install the server; the network team would allocate an IP subnet, create a new VLAN, and configure routing; the server team would install the operating system and update it; the database team would establish a database for the workload, and the team of developers would load their applications; and finally, the security team would modify the firewall configuration to control access to and from the server (see Figure 1.3). This process repeated for every new workload.

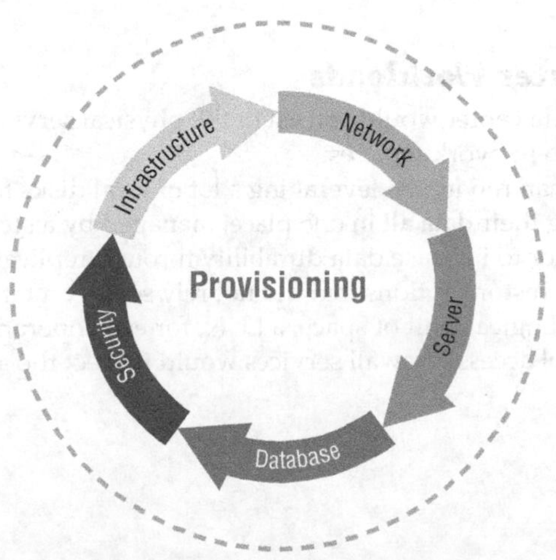

FIGURE 1.3 Traditional provisioning involves numerous teams and is time-consuming.

The time to fully provision a new workload, from the moment the server was purchased to the point where the application was ready to use, could often take months, greatly impacting business agility. Hand in hand with the slow rollouts was cost. When dealing entirely in the physical realm with hardware, it's almost impossible to automate the process. Many teams had to be directly involved and, typically, the process could not move forward until the tasks of the previous team had been completed.

Data Centers Come of Age

As companies grew, many reached a point where colocation was no longer cost-effective due to the amount of rented space required, and they built out their own data centers. Some organizations were unable to take advantage of colocation at all due to compliance regulations, and they built their own data centers for this reason (see Figure 1.4).

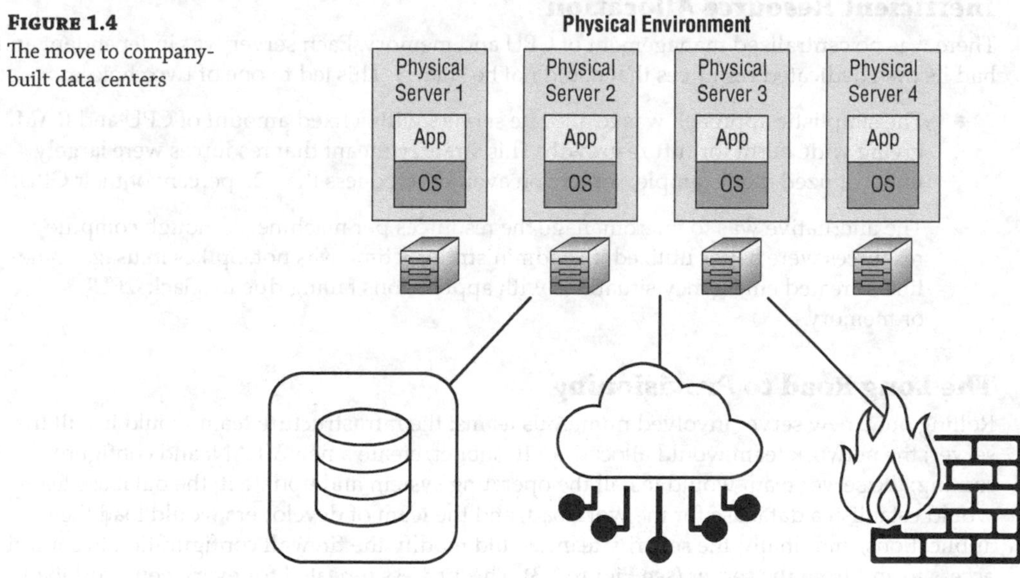

FIGURE 1.4 The move to company-built data centers

Data Center Workloads

A typical data center would consist of the physical servers, each with its own operating system connected to network services.

Rather than relying on leveraging a lot of local disks for permanent storage, most enterprises liked having their data all in one place, managed by a storage team. Centralized storage services made it easier to increase data durability through replication and to enhance reliability with backup and restore options that did not rely solely on tape backups. The storage team would carve out a Logical Unit of space, a LUN, for each operating system.

To control access, firewall services would protect the applications and data.

Workloads Won't Stay Put

Having centralized resources and services only solved part of a problem. Although being in one place made them easier to control, so much still could only be accomplished manually by personnel. Automation allows the organization to be much more agile; to be able to quickly react when conditions change. Data centers during the '90s lacked that agility.

Consider this analogy. Imagine you are the civil engineer for what will someday be Manhattan, New York. You design the layout for the roads. Going from design to a fully functional road will take considerable time and resources, but an even greater issue is looming in the future. The grid design for Manhattan was developed in 1811 (see Figure 1.5). The design supported the 95,000 residents of the time and took into consideration growth, but not enough to cover the 3.1 million people who work and live there now. The point is that trying to alleviate traffic congestion in New York is very difficult because we lack the ability to move the roads or to move the traffic without making the problem worse. Any time we are dealing with the physical world, we lack agility.

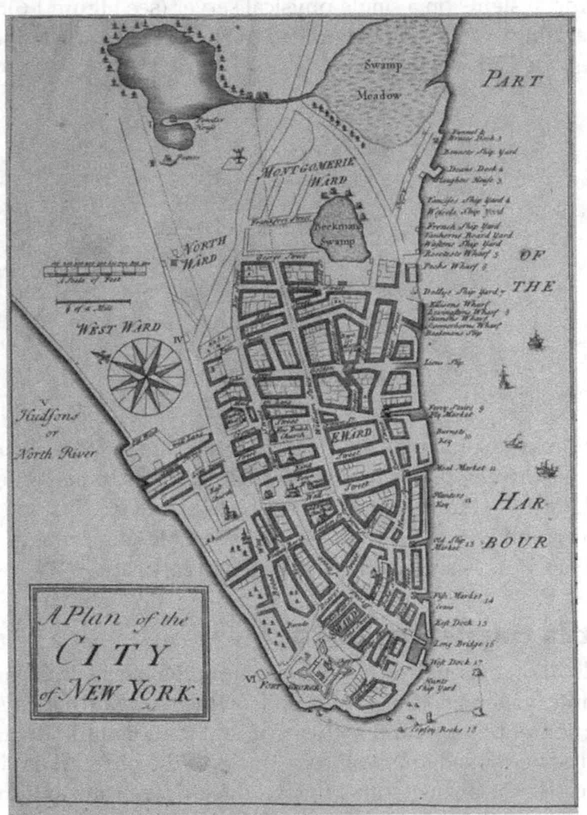

FIGURE 1.5
Manhattan city grid designed in 1811

The data centers of the '90s were heavily reliant on dedicated physical devices. If congestion occurred in one part of the data center, it was possible that a given workload could be moved to an area of less contention, but it was about as easy as trying to move that city road. These data center management tasks had to be done manually, and during the transition, traffic was negatively impacted.

VMware

In 2005, VMware launched VMware Infrastructure 3, which became the catalyst for VMware's move into the data center. It changed the paradigm for how physical servers and operating systems coexist. Prior to 2005, there was a 1:1 relationship: one server, one operating system.

Virtualization

VMware created a hypervisor (what we now refer to as ESXi) that enabled installing multiple operating systems on a single physical server (see Figure 1.6). By creating an abstraction layer, the operating systems no longer had to have direct knowledge of the underlying compute services, the CPU and memory.

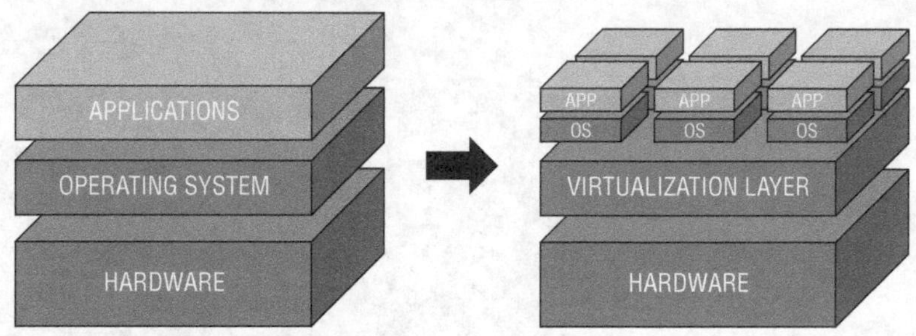

FIGURE 1.6 The hypervisor is a virtualization layer decoupling software from the underlying hardware.

The separate operating systems are what we now call virtual machines. The problem of trying to decide between provisioning simplicity and micromanaging resources immediately disappeared. Each virtual machine has access to a pool of CPU and memory resources via the abstraction layer, and each is given a reserved slice. Making changes to the amounts allocated to a virtual machine is something configured in software.

What Is Happening in There?

Virtualization decoupled the software from the hardware. On the software side, you had the operating system and the application; on the hardware side, you had the compute resources. This bifurcation of physical and software meant that on the software side, we finally had agility instead of being tied to the railroad tracks of the physical environment (see Figure 1.7).

Consider the analogy of a physical three-drawer metal filing cabinet vs. a Documents folder on your laptop (Figure 1.8). They may both contain the same data, but if the task is to send all your records to your lawyer, sending or copying the contents of the papers within the metal filing cabinet is a giant chore. In comparison, sending the files from your Windows Documents folder may take a few clicks and 45 seconds out of your day.

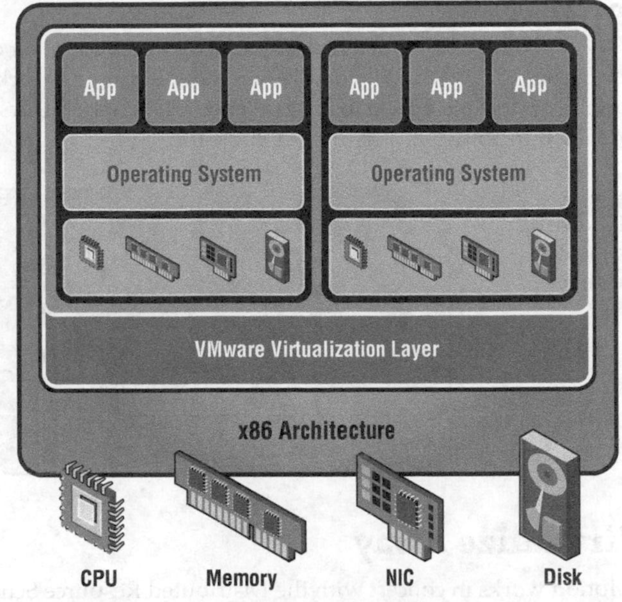

FIGURE 1.7 Virtualization creates an abstraction layer that hides the complexities of the physical layer from the software.

FIGURE 1.8 Physically storing data

The point is we can easily move things in software. It is a virtual space. Moving things in physical space takes vastly more effort, time, and almost always, more money. VMware's decoupling of the two opened a whole new world of possibilities.

Portability

A key VMware feature that really leveraged the decoupling of physical and software is vMotion (see Figure 1.9). With vMotion, we can move a running workload to a different physical host. But portability and the option to move workloads is only the first step. Once an entity is wholly contained in software, you can automate it.

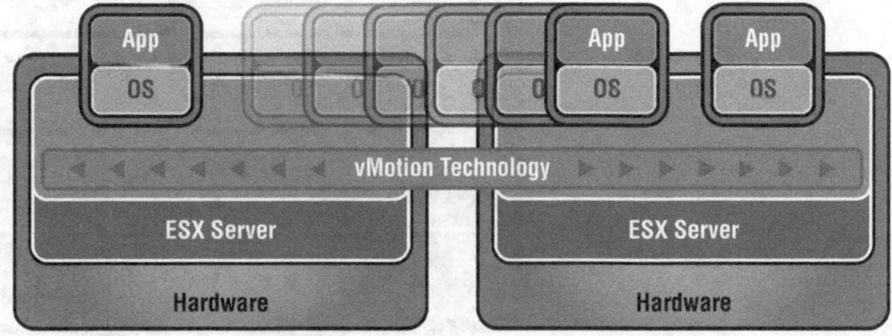

FIGURE 1.9 VMware vMotion is a benefit that would not be possible without virtualization.

Virtualize Away

vMotion works in concert with the Distributed Resource Scheduler (DRS). The DRS actively monitors the CPU and memory resource utilization for each virtual machine. If multiple virtual machines located on the same physical server spike in CPU or memory usage to the point where there is a contention for these resources, DRS can detect the issue and automatically leverage vMotion to migrate the virtual machine to a different server with less contention (see Figure 1.10).

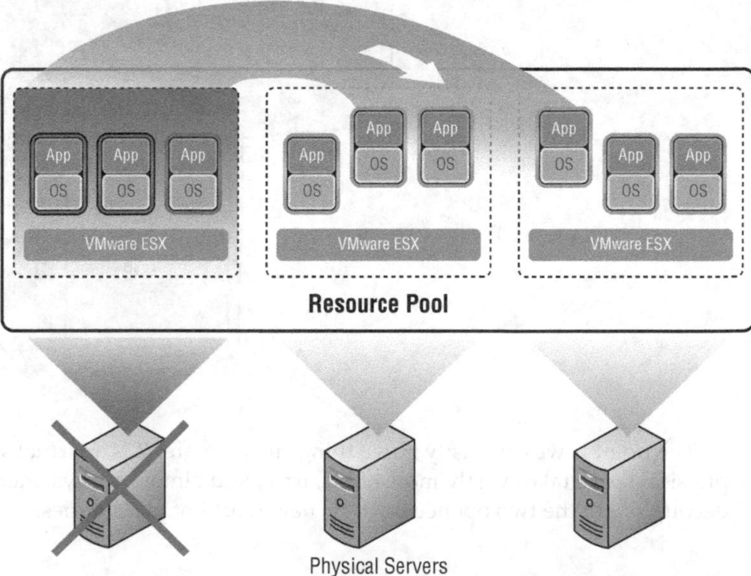

FIGURE 1.10 In the event of a physical host failing, the workload can be moved to other hosts in the cluster.

Another way VMware takes advantage of portability is to provide a means for disaster recovery. It does so with the VMware High Availability (HA) feature. Think of HA as a primary and backup relationship, or active and passive. For example, suppose you have a physical server with eight virtual machines and HA is enabled. If the server loses all power, those virtual machines would be automatically powered up on a different physical server. A physical server with an ESXi hypervisor is referred to as a host.

These key VMware features—HA, DRS, and vMotion—are the building blocks of VMware's Software Defined Data Center solution.

Extending Virtualization to Storage

Virtualizing compute was a game changer in data centers, but VMware realized that it didn't have to stop there. Traditional storage could be virtualized as well. They took the same idea they used in abstracting compute to abstract the storage to be available across all physical servers running the ESXi hypervisor.

The traditional way of allocating storage involved having the storage team create a LUN and configuring RAID. VMware's alternative is the vSAN product (see Figure 1.11). Instead of manually carving out a LUN and RAID type, the administrator configures a policy. The policy is then used to determine the amount of storage needed for a given application.

FIGURE 1.11
Allocating storage

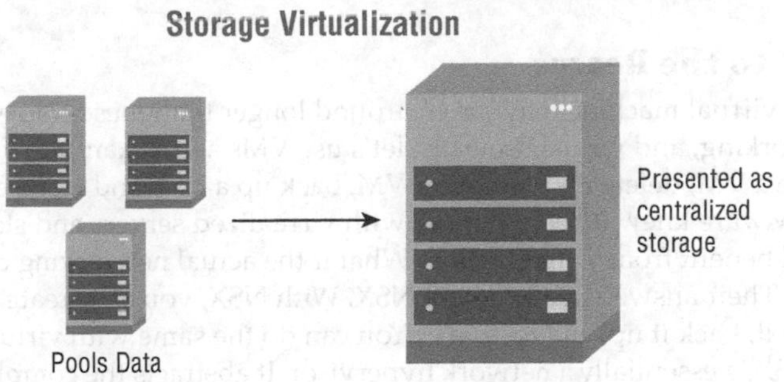

From the perspective of the application and virtual machine, the complexities of dealing with the physical network to access the storage are factored out. It is as simple as accessing local storage on a laptop.

Virtual Networking and Security

Recall the diagram of the general data center architecture from the '90s we started with in the beginning of the chapter (Figure 1.1). We've discussed how VMware has virtualized the operating systems so that they can share a single physical server, and we just mentioned how VMware extended the virtualization concept to storage (see Figure 1.12).

VMware recognized the value in the Software Defined Data Center strategy and decided to apply it to networking and security services as well, giving us even more flexibility and new ways of doing things that previously were impossible.

FIGURE 1.12
Virtualization can now go beyond only servers.

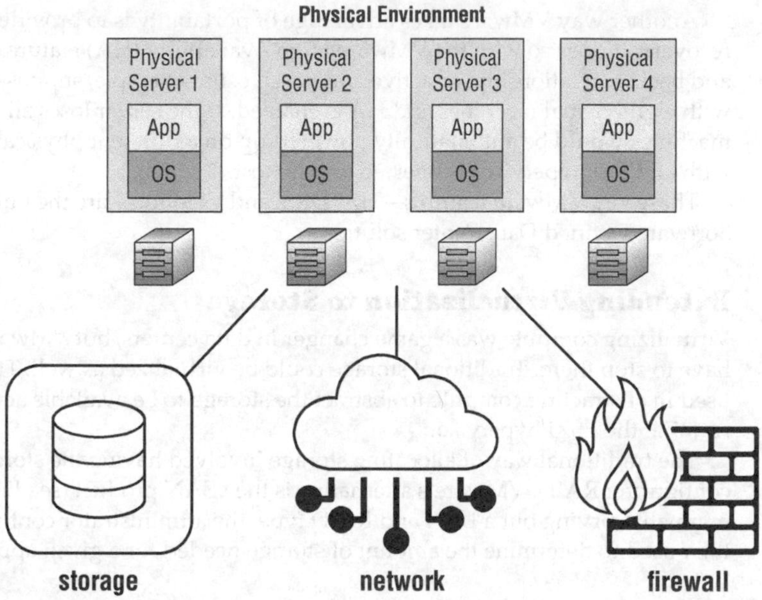

NSX to the Rescue

Since virtual machines have been around longer than these concepts of virtual storage, virtual networking, and virtual firewalls, let's use VMs as an example of what is now possible. You can create a VM, delete a VM, move a VM, back up a VM, and restore a VM.

VMware knew it had a winner with virtualized servers and started to question what else could benefit from virtualization. What if the actual networking components were virtualized as well? Their answer was VMware NSX. With NSX, you can create a virtual network, delete it, move it, back it up, and restore it. You can do the same with virtual firewalls and load balancers.

NSX is essentially a network hypervisor. It abstracts the complexity of the underlying physical network, and it overlays on top of your physical network (see Figure 1.13). You don't need to change how your physical network is currently being used. Since NSX runs on top of the physical network as an abstraction layer, it doesn't affect workloads you may decide to keep on the physical network. It coexists, but it also greatly simplifies and creates new options for the workloads running on your virtual machines.

In terms of security, NSX does something that no other vendor can provide. Other vendors have created virtual machines that provide firewall services, but NSX moves this functionality into the kernel itself and it is distributed across all your ESXi hosts (see Figure 1.14).

This strategy has two major advantages:

- The first is resource utilization.

  A typical firewall that is examining every packet will take a performance hit, especially when the amount of traffic is high, and you have configured an access list with lots and lots of rules. By moving it into the kernel, it is no longer an outside operation and the amount of resources required—even when dealing with literally millions of traffic flows with an enormous list of rules—is still negligible.

- There's also not a bandwidth hit.

  To inspect internal traffic in data centers without NSX, it needs to be routed to the firewall and then routed back out the same interface. This is known as *hairpinning*. Hairpinning is eliminated with an NSX distributed firewall because it is not an external entity. It is part of the kernel itself; therefore, the same firewall is present on every physical ESXi host.

Figure 1.13
NSX is a hypervisor for the network.

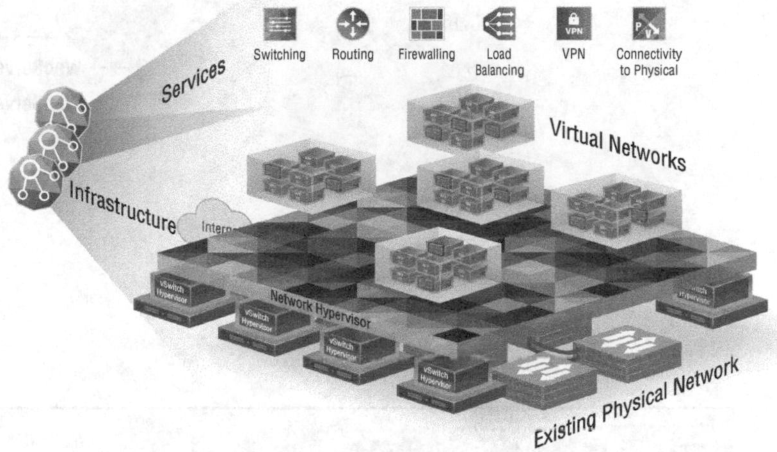

Figure 1.14
Traditional security relies on external security.

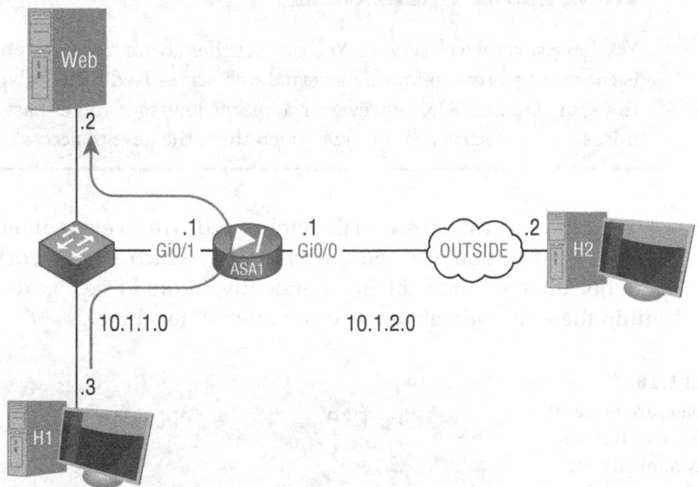

That leads us to the top feature of this firewall design. Your existing physical firewall is very capable of keeping the bad guys out, of being the guard between your network and the outside world. What it is less great at doing is acting as a guard with your internal, VM-to-VM traffic (see Figure 1.15).

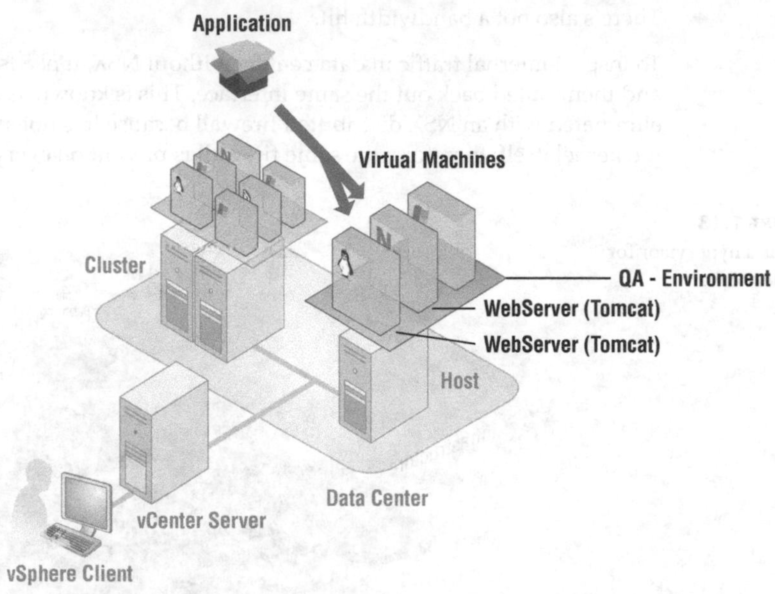

FIGURE 1.15
NSX microsegmentation moves the security rules to the VMs, securing all traffic in or out.

Real World Scenario

THINK ABOUT THIS EXAMPLE

You have several web servers. You protect them from the malicious actions of the outside world. But is there ever a reason for one internal web server to directly talk to another internal web server on the same subnet? No. However, if a hacker manages to get past your initial security and compromises one web server, you've just given them the keys to access the rest.

The NSX firewall is essentially embedded within every interface on every virtual machine. This means that you have *microsegmentation,* which allows workloads to be completely isolated from one another and to be independently secured (see Figure 1.16). You've got protection, even within the same subnet, to any other internal machine.

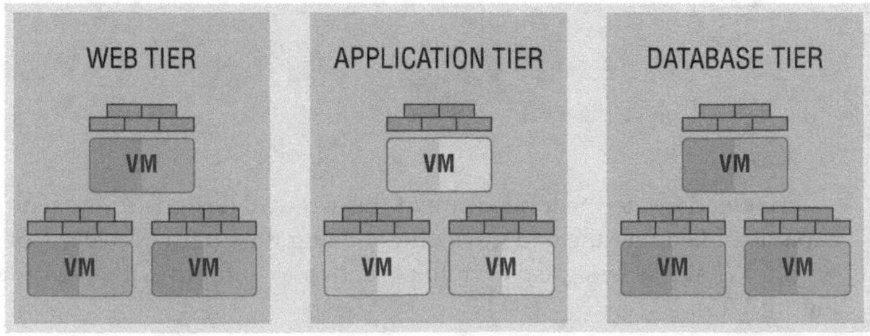

FIGURE 1.16
Workloads are isolated from one another, with security applied to the VM interfaces.

The Bottom Line

SDDC Virtualization Software Defined Data Centers are possible due to decoupling physical hardware from software. VMware changed the game by first virtualizing compute resources. VMware virtual machines are operating systems that have been separated from the physical server by a hypervisor abstraction layer, called ESXi.

Master It VMware extended the same concepts to the other major infrastructure services including storage, networking, and security. What is the name of the hypervisor abstraction layer that VMware developed for networking and security?

NSX Prerequisites NSX re-creates traditional physical network components such as routers, switches, ports, and firewalls in software. You manage the vSphere team for your organization and are considering NSX. Which additional physical components are required before NSX can be deployed? (Choose all that apply.)

Master It

1. Firewall virtual appliance
2. Distributed Resource Scheduler (DRS)
3. SDDC-compatible servers
4. None

NSX Kernel-Embedded Firewall By moving firewall services to the kernel, which of the following is *not* true?

Master It

1. An embedded firewall only increases resource utilization by a negligible amount.
2. Bandwidth is conserved due to the elimination of hairpinning.
3. Firewall rules are distributed and are the same on every ESXi host.
4. VM-to-VM traffic is easier to secure.

Chapter 2

NSX Architecture and Requirements

In this chapter, we will review the architecture of NSX to understand better how network virtualization is accomplished and compare this to how it has been handled traditionally. It is important to understand the architectural components, their functions, and how they interoperate with each other before diving into features and options we will cover later throughout the book.

NSX depends on VMware vCenter and vSphere Distributed Switches to work across multiple ESXi hosts. These provide the foundation necessary for NSX to build upon. By integrating with vCenter, NSX doesn't have to be managed separately. We will see that management is further simplified using predefined administration roles with Role-Based Access Control.

NSX allows virtual networks to be created on top of an existing physical network. We will discuss how this is accomplished and find that implementing it requires little to no changes to the physical network. This means that getting the benefits of NSX doesn't mean having to alter your existing infrastructure or invest in new hardware. NSX leverages the existing network by creating a virtual overlay network.

IN THIS CHAPTER, YOU WILL LEARN ABOUT:

- Management, control, and data planes of operation
- Centralized management via NSX Manager
- NSX Manager fault tolerance features and behavior
- The 1:1 relationship between vCenter and NSX Manager
- NSX Virtual Switch: Born from the vSphere Distributed Switch
- Ready-made vSphere installation bundles to deploy NSX
- Improving data optimization and security through the IOChain
- NSX Controllers providing the control plane
- Bulletproofing the control plane with NSX Controller clusters
- Slicing NSX Controller tasks and responsibilities
- NSX Controller roles

- NSX Edge: DLRs and ESGs
- Choosing the right size of your ESG virtual machine
- Role-Based Access Control for your NSX team
- NSX providing a feature-rich overlay network
- Replication modes for handling BUM traffic

NSX Network Virtualization

VMware NSX provides network virtualization. Like a VMware hypervisor, which abstracts the underlying physical compute and memory, network virtualization is essentially a hypervisor abstracting the physical network. The physical network is still connecting the physical devices, but the L2 through L7 network services are reproduced in software (see Figure 2.1), including all the components and functions you normally associate with networking: routing, switching, firewalls, load balancing, NAT, DHCP, QoS, and access lists.

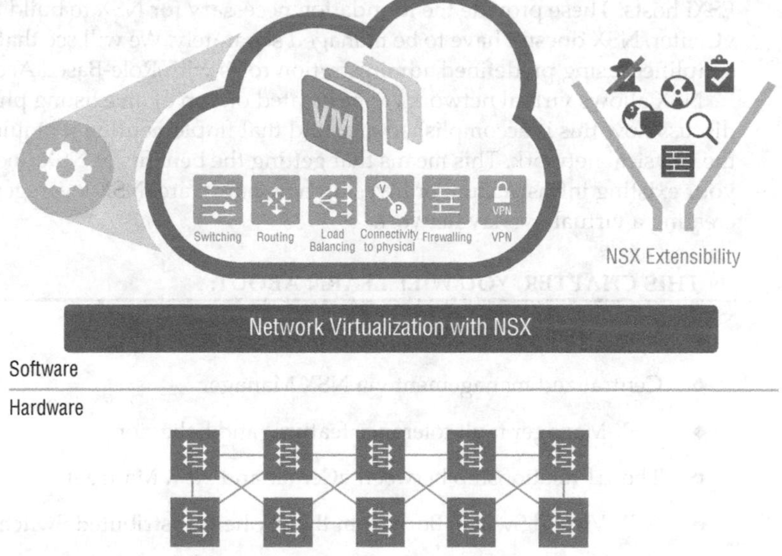

FIGURE 2.1 Network virtualization decoupling network functions from the physical hardware

Having all these network functions wholly contained in software provides flexibility with these services that would be impossible on dedicated hardware devices. Provisioning can often be as simple as a few clicks.

Planes of Operation

With traditional networking, there are three planes of operation (management, control, and data) all contained within a single device (see Figure 2.2).

FIGURE 2.2 Traditional three planes of operation found in each networking device

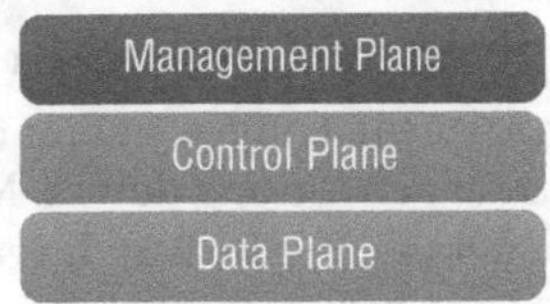

For example, a router has a management plane, which provides a configuration point to enter commands via a Command Line Interface (CLI) or to select options using a Graphical User Interface (GUI). A routing protocol like Open Shortest Path First (OSPF) would be configured here. The routing protocol allows that router to exchange routing information with other routers. As an analogy, you could think of the management plane as a company boardroom where the goals of the organization are defined.

Continuing with the analogy, the control plane would be like a department supervisor at the company (see Figure 2.3). Supervisors are given their goals from management, but it's up to the supervisors to determine how to best get the job accomplished. The control plane is where learning occurs and decisions are made. In the case of the router, it has collected information from other routers and determined the best interface to exit to reach each destination and put that into a routing table.

FIGURE 2.3 Network planes of operation compared with company job roles

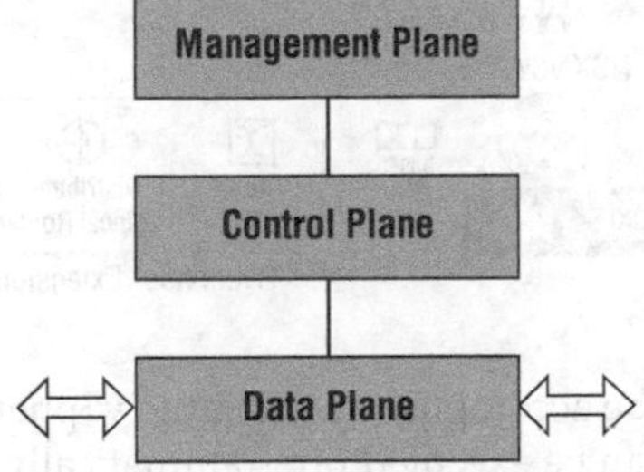

But the supervisors don't do the heavy lifting. They instruct the workers to complete the tasks. This is what happens in the data plane, which is concerned with forwarding the traffic out of the interface that was learned and decided by the control plane.

In traditional networking, this process is repeated for every device (see Figure 2.4). Every router and every switch makes its own decisions on where to forward traffic based on the intelligence it has gathered in the control plane.

FIGURE 2.4 Each networking device in traditional networking making decisions independently

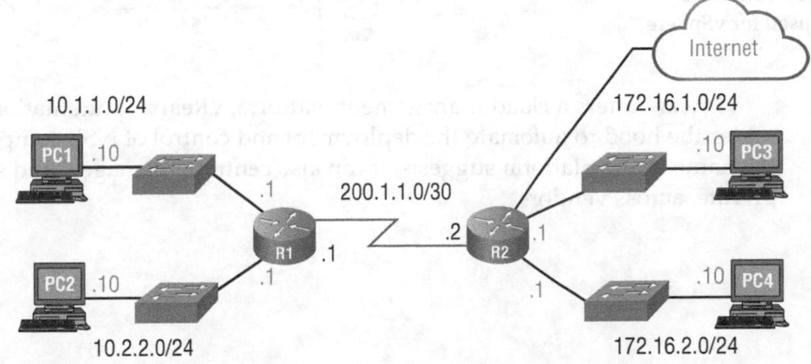

NSX Manager Role and Function

With NSX, the management, control, and data planes are separate instead of being housed together in each virtual networking device. Management is centralized from a single point, the VMware NSX Manager (see Figure 2.5). It is a virtual appliance used to provision, configure, and monitor NSX virtual network devices such as logical routers, switches, firewalls, and load balancers. Because it's centralized, it obviates the need to log in to each virtual component separately.

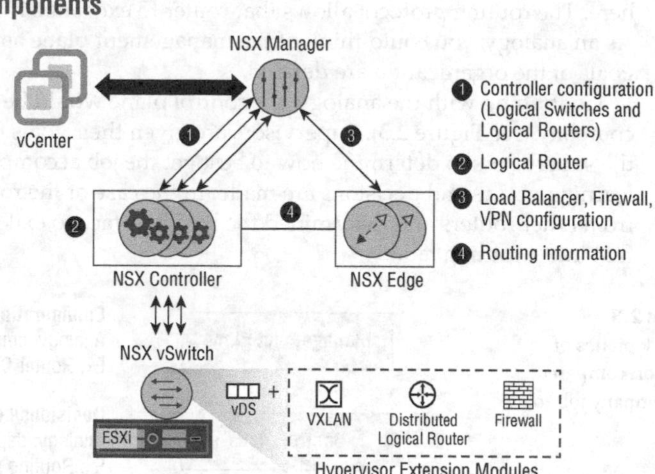

FIGURE 2.5 NSX architecture

Accessing the NSX Manager can be accomplished using the vSphere Web Client to make manual changes, or the same tasks can be executed programmatically using REST APIs (see Figure 2.6). REST APIs allow objects that can be accessed through a URL to be created or modified. Consider the time and effort required to move or re-create a physical network. In comparison, a single administrator could automate the re-creation of an entire network of virtual routers, switches, firewalls, and the like at another site with minimal effort by scripting the tasks with REST APIs. However, it's not necessary to be a programmer to accomplish this.

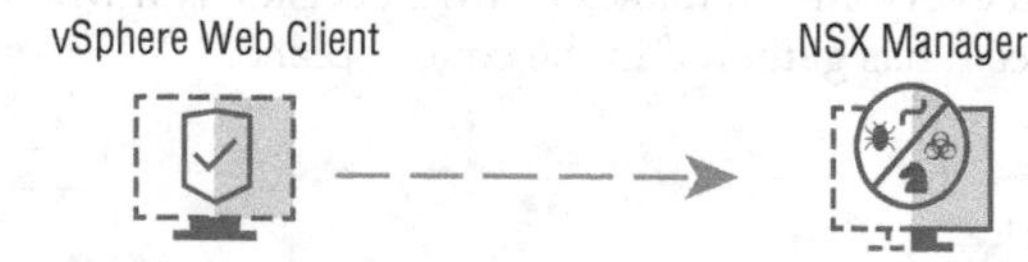

FIGURE 2.6 Accessing NSX Manager using the same web client used for vSphere

VMware offers a cloud management platform, vRealize Automation, which uses REST APIs under the hood to automate the deployment and control of NSX components (see Figure 2.7). As the name of the platform suggests, it can also centrally manage cloud services, both public and private, across vendors.

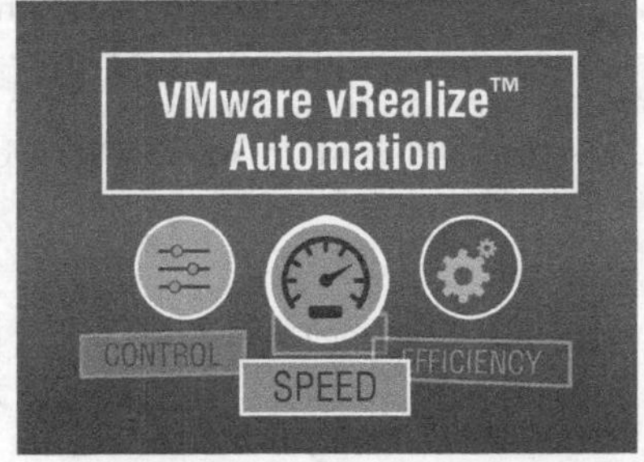

FIGURE 2.7 Deploying and controlling NSX components through automation

NSX Manager is a virtual machine installed on an ESXi host, which is packaged as an Open Virtual Appliance (OVA) file. The benefit of installing it as an OVA is that it will be assigned a unique identifier known as a UUID. Having a unique identifier is essential in a cross-vCenter environment, which allows multiple sites to each have a separate NSX Manager.

In these instances, there is a primary NSX Manager and one or more secondary NSX Managers (see Figure 2.8). The primary NSX Manager can create universal firewall rules, universal logical routers, universal logical switches, and the like whose services are available to all sites.

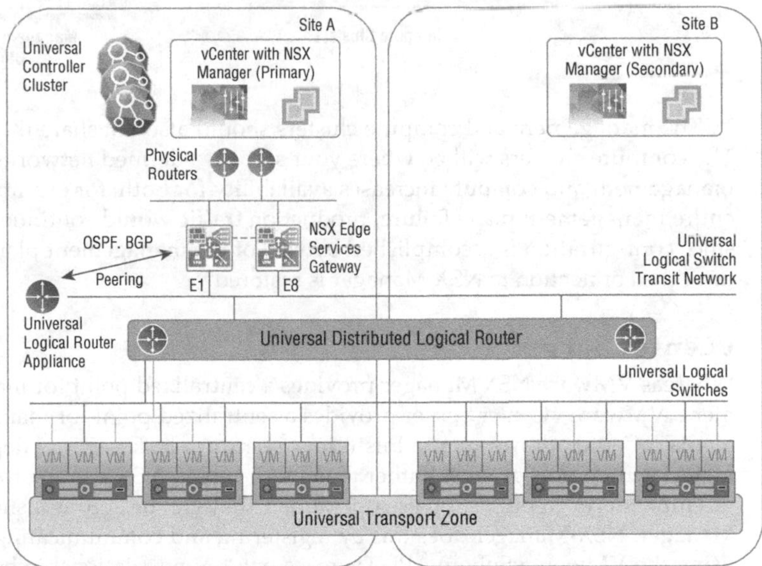

FIGURE 2.8 Primary NSX Manager at Site A managing secondary NSX Manager at Site B

ESXi Hosts

VMware recommends that you deploy NSX Manager on a management cluster of at least three ESXi hosts that is separate from the compute cluster and configured with VMware High Availability (HA) and VMware Distributed Resource Scheduler (DRS). HA is achieved by deploying members of the cluster in an active/standby configuration. If the active component fails, the standby takes over and continues to provide the services. DRS can be configured to use an anti-affinity rule that ensures that the active and standby components are always installed on different hosts to increase availability (see Figure 2.9). That way, even if an entire host were to fail, NSX Manager would still be available with a standby becoming active. NSX Manager doesn't have HA and DRS built in; instead, it relies on ESXi's HA and DRS features.

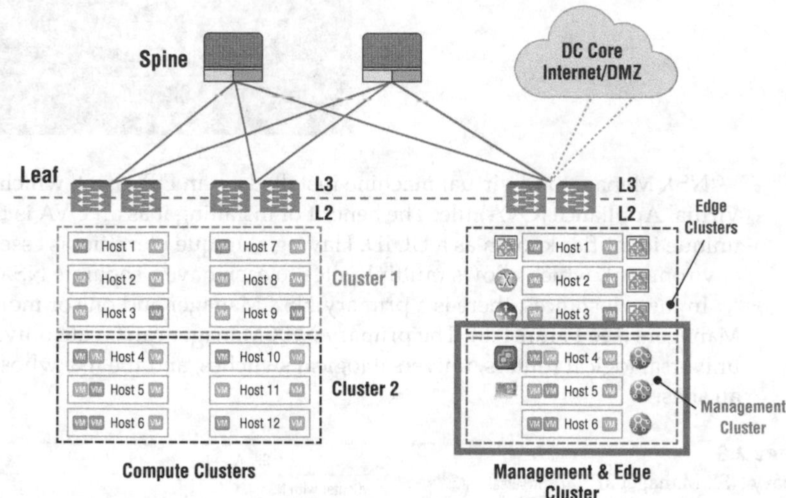

FIGURE 2.9 Compute clusters separated from management clusters, increasing availability

The management and compute clusters should also not share the same IP address space. The compute clusters will be where your software-defined networks are deployed. Separating management and compute increases availability for both; for example, even in the event of entire management plane failure, production traffic would continue to be forwarded. However, since configuration is accomplished by way of the management plane, no changes could made until the connection to NSX Manager is restored.

vCenter Server

Whereas VMware NSX Manager provides a centralized point for managing an NSX environment, VMware vCenter Server provides a centralized point for managing vSphere environments. vCenter allows an administrator to perform tasks such as deploying VMs and creating logical switch port groups. Rather than requiring an NSX administrator to separately log in to vCenter Server to perform these operations, they can be accomplished directly from NSX Manager. NSX Manager does this by registering and communicating with vCenter Server using the VMware vSphere API. There's a one-to-one relationship between NSX Manager and vCenter Server, with one NSX Manager only connected to one vCenter Server (see Figure 2.10). This holds true even in a Cross-vCenter environment over multiple sites. For every instance of NSX Manager, there is one vCenter Server. Once the NSX Manager registration with a vCenter Server is completed, the registration cannot be changed to communicate with a different vCenter Server. Instead, a new NSX Manager would have to be deployed to register with a new vCenter Server and the former NSX Manager deleted.

FIGURE 2.10
NSX Manager can only be registered to one vCenter Server.

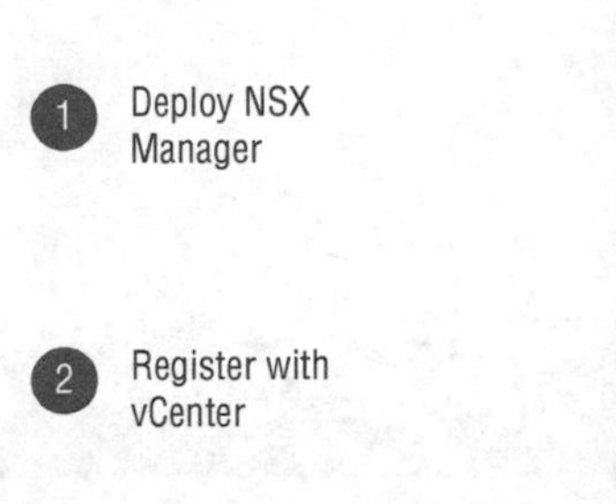

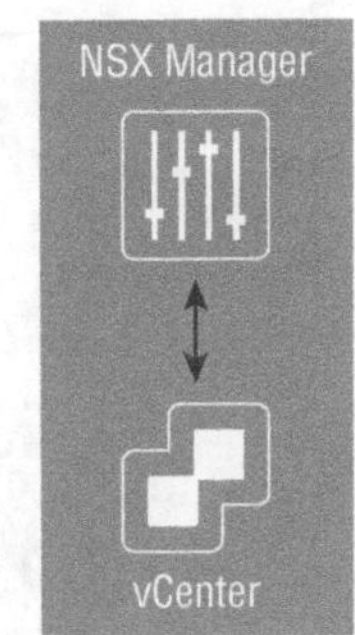

vSphere Distributed Switch

Prior to vSphere Distributed Switches (VDSs), a vSphere administrator would typically configure individual virtual switches on a per-ESXi host basis (see Figure 2.11). The vSphere administrator would then have to coordinate with network infrastructure administrators so that the configuration of VLANs was consistent. After deployment, both teams would need to be involved in troubleshooting and monitoring the data center.

FIGURE 2.11
Individual vSphere Standard Switches

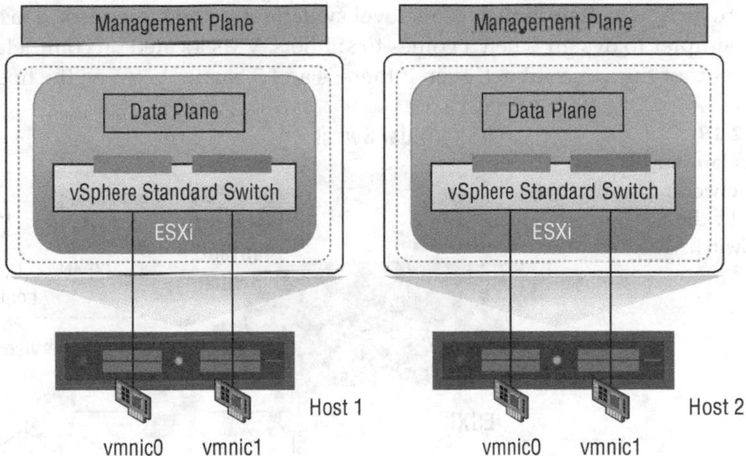

VMware vSphere Enterprise Plus includes a vSphere Distributed Switch (VDS), which works across multiple ESXi hosts (see Figure 2.12). The VDS is also shipped with a vSAN license. The VDS allows the management of VM networking and the configuration settings like virtual switch port configuration and port group naming to be accomplished centrally. It treats the vSphere network as a collective resource by setting up switching that can span the data center. Communication from a VM on one host to a VM on another host doesn't require coordination with the infrastructure team. Configuration is simplified and can be done centrally across multiple ESXi hosts. This aggregation provides the foundation for enabling Software-Defined Network configurations, which is where NSX comes in.

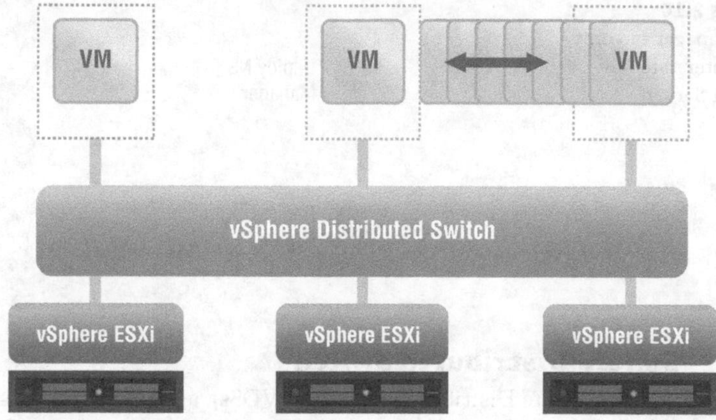

FIGURE 2.12 A vSphere Distributed Switch spanning several ESXi hosts

The NSX data plane is provided by the VMware NSX Virtual Switch, which is based on the vSphere Distributed Switch, but with additional components that allow virtual networking services to be enabled such as logical switching (VXLAN), logical routing, and logical firewall (see Figure 2.13). The complexities of the physical network are abstracted by the NSX Virtual Switch, which provides access-level switching in the hypervisor. This makes the virtual network simpler to design when it comes to subnets. VMs located on completely different hosts can be part of the same subnet, even if there is an L3 barrier between the hosts on the physical network.

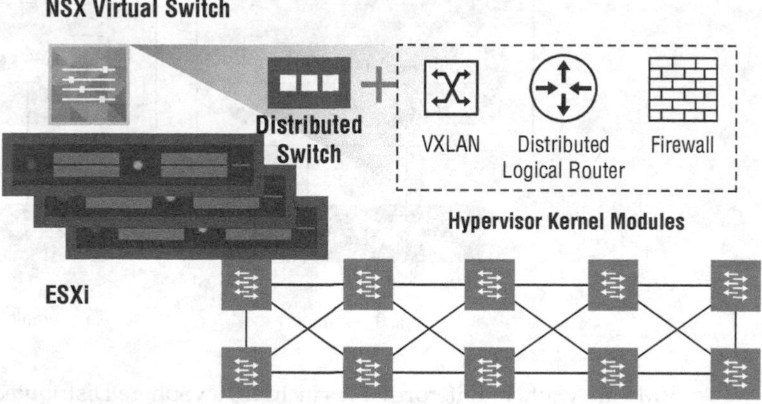

FIGURE 2.13 The data plane for the overlay network, provided by the NSX Virtual Switch

For example, if several ESXi hosts were connected by an underlying physical network with a router between each pair of hosts, in the physical network, these routers would define the boundaries of L2 domains. A subnet could only span a single host. However, with the physical network treated as if it were one giant switch, then the L2 domain, an IP subnet, could potentially stretch from end to end of the data center. A VM on ESXi host 1 could communicate with a VM on ESXi host 8 with simplified addressing (see Figure 2.14). They can be assigned to the same subnet. And with the abstraction of the physical hardware, there's no need to coordinate with the infrastructure team, requesting that they create matching VLANs. End-to-end communication within the NSX environment can be implemented solely by the NSX administrator.

Figure 2.14
VMs on separate hosts but members of the same 10.1.1.0 subnet

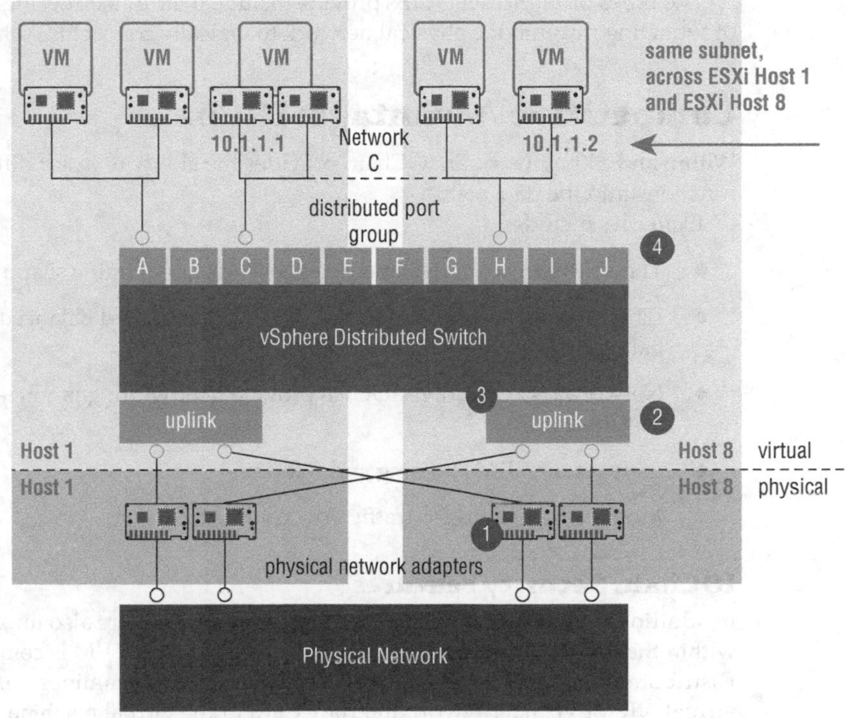

NSX VIBs

The kernel modules that are added to the NSX Virtual Switch to enable virtual networking services, the necessary configuration files, installation scripts, and agents for internal communications are packaged into vSphere Installation Bundles, or VIBs (see Figure 2.15). These compressed packages are the building blocks that allow you to customize the ESXi hosts and create the NSX virtual environment. VMware Certified VIBs are created and tested by VMware, so you're not having to manually collect individual files and worry about compatibility. Everything within the bundles is designed to work together, and for security, the VIBs are digitally signed.

Figure 2.15
vSphere Installation Bundles used to create the NSX virtual environment

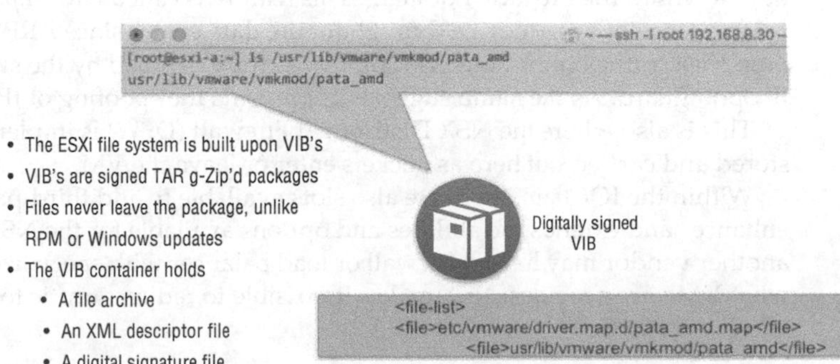

The types of services the VIBs provide include distributed routing, VXLAN bridging (a form of tunneling through the physical network to logically connect ESXi hosts), and logical firewalls.

Competitive Advantage: IOChain

Within an ESXi network, an IOChain provides the ability to insert different quality control functions into the data path.

Examples include:

- The ability to do ingress and egress bi-directional traffic shaping to mitigate congestion
- Link Aggregation Control Protocol (LACP) and Load Balanced Teaming (LBT) to load balance traffic
- Network I/O Control (NIOC) to provide bandwidth guarantees for VMs as well as for system traffic
- Support for VLAN tagging and filtering
- Monitoring options for traffic flow control

IOChain Security Features

In addition to quality control functions, security services are also implemented as IOChains within the kernel. These are automatically applied when a VM is connected to a logical switch. A Distributed Virtual Filter (DVFilter) is an access list that examines traffic entering and leaving the virtual NIC or virtual Network Interface Card of the virtual machine.

A switch security (swsec) module examines packets to learn the IP and MAC address of the VM. Additionally, it listens for Address Resolution Protocol broadcasts that come from the VM. In a physical network, those ARP broadcasts are picked up from the wire and sent up the stack of every device within the same subnet. This means that even if a device is not the intended receiver of the message, it still consumes CPU. With NSX, these ARP broadcasts are handled much more intelligently. Rather than allowing the broadcast to be propagated and impacting the performance of the other devices, the switch security module redirects the message to the NSX Controller only. The Controller learns all the IP/MAC mappings and can return the requested information to the VM without needing to blast the request out as a broadcast to every other device within the broadcast domain. This feature is called *ARP suppression*. It improves the performance of every device throughout the data center since ARP normally generates a lot of broadcast traffic on the network. Another feature handled by the switch security module is NSX IP Spoofguard. As the name suggests, it prevents the spoofing of IP addresses.

This is also where the NSX Distributed Firewall (DFW) is implemented. Firewall rules are stored and carried out here as packets enter or leave the VM.

Within the IOChain, there are also slots available to add third-party services, which greatly enhances and extends the abilities and options available for the NSX environment. For example, another vendor may have a firewall or load balancer with specialized features that are beyond what VMware provides. NSX makes it possible to redirect traffic to those third-party appliances (see Figure 2.16).

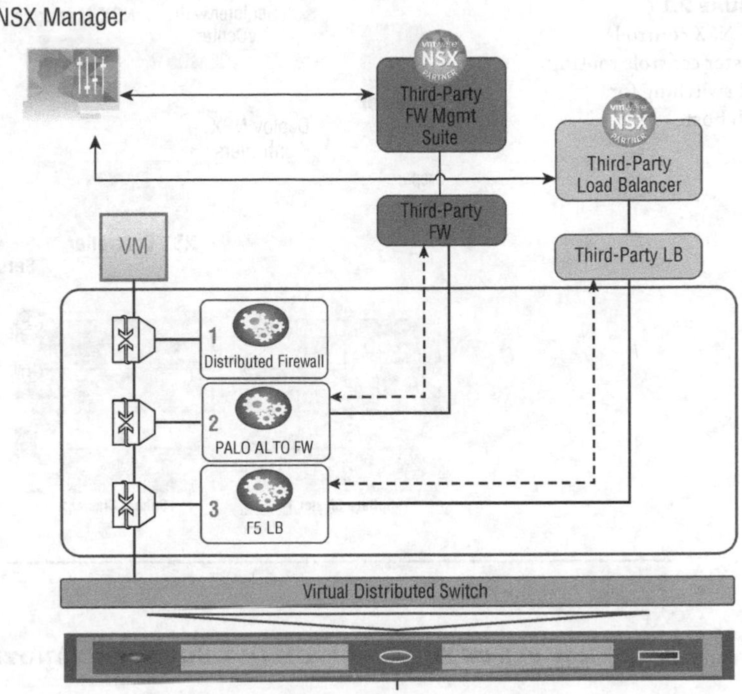

FIGURE 2.16 IOChain with customizable slots for adding third-Party functions

NSX Controllers

As a quick review of the NSX planes of operation, the management plane (for configuration) is created and handled by the NSX Manager. The data plane (for forwarding traffic) is implemented in the NSX Virtual Switch. But what about the control plane (for learning/decision making)? The control plane is found in the aptly named NSX Controller cluster. The Controller cluster is responsible for managing the switching and routing kernel modules (see Figure 2.17). It learns and maintains information related to every ESXi host, the Distributed Logical Routers, and the logical switches, which are also referred to as VXLANs. Based on the information it receives, it's able to make the decisions for routing, for switching, and the like. But more importantly, it's able to then distribute this information to every ESXi host and ultimately make its way into their kernels. From its stored information, it's able to return the mappings of IP to MAC addresses requested as a result of ARP suppression, for example. This optimizes the performance of the data center, with all ARP traffic being handled in software instead of being blasted out as a broadcast in hardware.

Not only do the controllers collect this information, but more importantly, they propagate the information to the other ESXi hosts, which ultimately makes its way into the respective kernels of the hosts. This distribution of forwarding, security, and quality control is what allows actions on traffic to be taken directly without having to exit the host, get the required information, return to the host, and then finally forward packets.

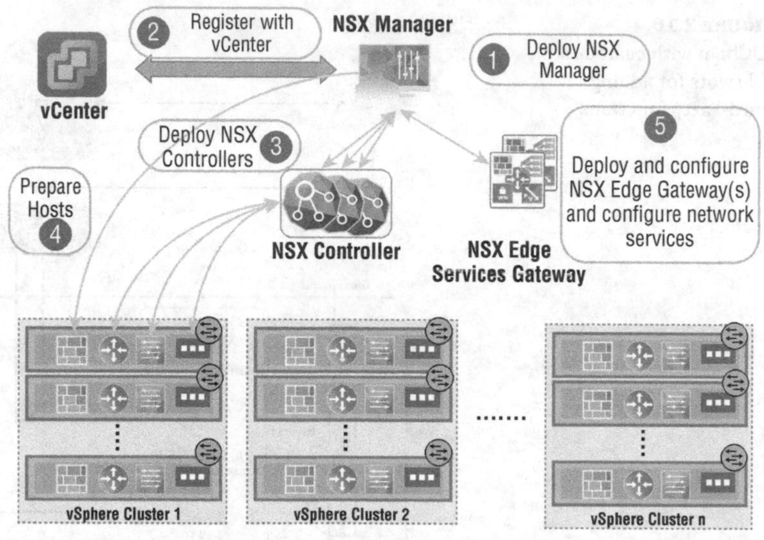

FIGURE 2.17 The NSX controller Cluster controls routing and switching for each host.

Real World Scenario

AN EXAMPLE OF ROUTING FROM ONE SUBNET TO ANOTHER

In an environment other than NSX, you could have two VMs in the same ESXi host, but if they are on different subnets, the traffic would be routed out of the host to a router, the path would be looked up in the routing table, and then the packet would be routed back to the same host but sent to the other subnet. This is referred to as hairpinning. It adds latency and takes up additional bandwidth and CPU. However, NSX distributes the routing information to the individual hosts, so the traffic from VM to VM on the same host can be handled without needing to exit the host.

NSX Controller Clustering

The NSX Controller is in the form of a VM. When deploying NSX Controllers in production, it's recommended that there should be three in a cluster, but that each VM should reside on a different ESXi host (see Figure 2.18). One reason for this is fault tolerance. If an entire host were to fail, the remaining two controllers would continue to function and would take on the workloads of the failed host. Another reason is scalability. Part of the NSX Architecture design for scalability is to ensure that all NSX Controllers are active at any given time, so that they can share the workload.

NSX Controller Roles

The mechanism for doing this is called *slicing* or *sharding*. The three controllers will have elections to decide which will be the master NSX Controller instance for a particular role. Controller 1 might be the master for the logical switching (VXLAN) role, and Controller 2 might be the master for the logical routing role. The same is done for other NSX services.

The masters for the roles are responsible for dividing the workload into slices and then assigning which controller will handle which slices (see Figure 2.19).

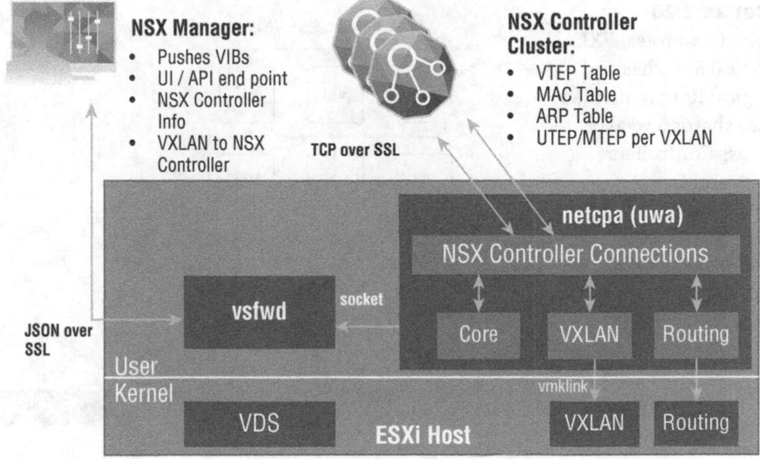

FIGURE 2.18 NSX Controllers deployed three to a cluster, each on a different host

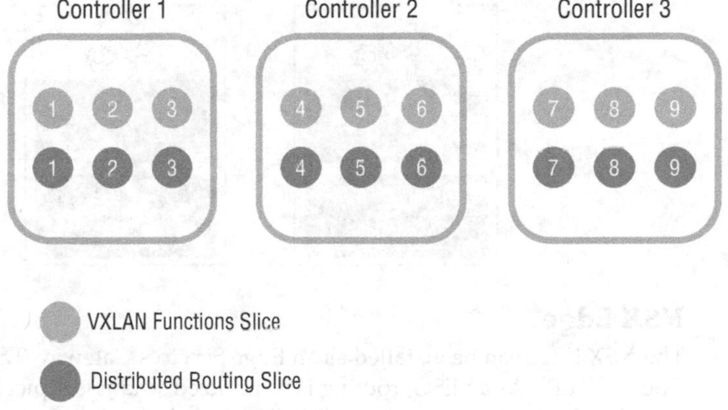

FIGURE 2.19 Dividing the workload into slices/shards, assigned across the three controllers

Let's say that Controller A is the master controller for logical routing, and it has divided the workload into six slices. It would assign slice 1 to itself, slice 2 to Controller B, and slice 3 to Controller C. Slices 4, 5, and 6 would be handed out in the same way, to Controllers A, B, and C, respectively. When a request comes in on logical router shard 3, for example, it is directed to Controller C (see Figure 2.20).

Each master is also responsible for keeping track of the other controllers to determine if a controller has failed. If this happens, the master of each role would redistribute those affected shards to the remaining controllers. The election of the master for each role is done by a majority vote. It's for this reason that we start with three controllers in a cluster. Being an odd number, it's enough to break a tie, so always deploy an odd number of controller instances for this reason.

Reslicing/resharding will occur any time there is a change in the number of controllers. This means the slices will be reallocated when:

- An NSX Controller is created
- An NSX Controller is deleted
- An NSX Controller fails

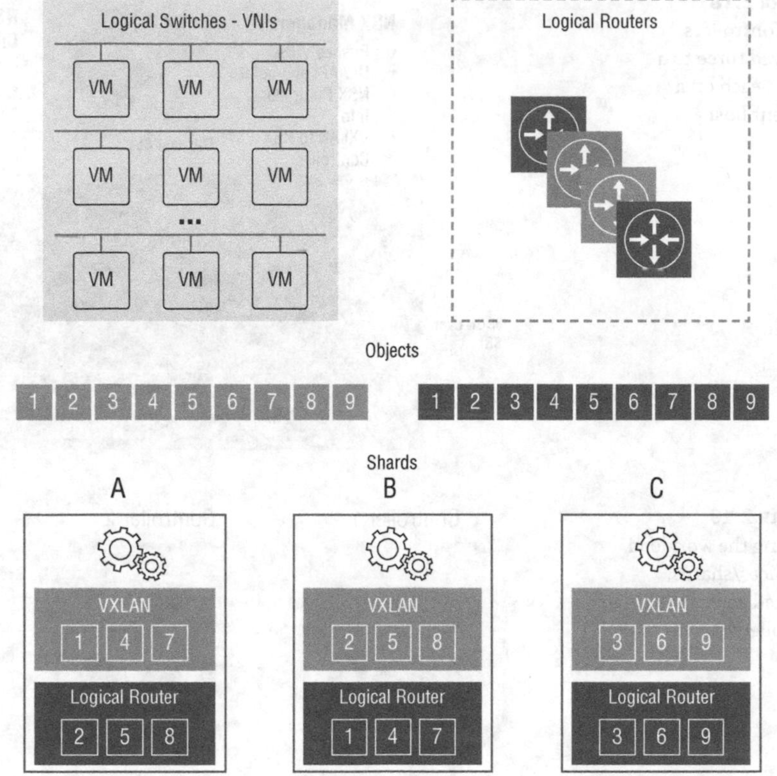

FIGURE 2.20 Job of two roles, VXLAN Logical Switches and Logical Router, divided into shards and allocated across Controllers A, B, and C

NSX Edge

The NSX Edge can be installed as an Edge Services Gateway (ESG) or as a Distributed Logical Router (DLR). As an ESG, routing is centralized, and it is typically used for routing traffic in and out of your virtualized network. This is referred to as North-South traffic (see Figure 2.21). For example, traffic between a VM and the Internet would be considered North-South. An ESG shares similarities with a traditional router or firewall. Each ESG can have up to 10 vNIC interfaces.

FIGURE 2.21 NSX Edge routes traffic between your virtual and physical networks.

With a DLR, routing is distributed and is primarily used for forwarding East-West traffic. This is traffic from VM to VM within your data center. Because the routes are distributed into the kernels of each ESXi host, there's no need to cross the network to find out the route to reach the other VM. The host already has the answer, greatly improving performance. When it comes to logical interfaces (LIFs) on a DLR, there can be up to 999 on each, plus one for management.

The NSX Edge Services Gateway (see Figure 2.22) provides several logical networking services that can be provisioned on demand, including:

- Firewall
- Network Address Translation (NAT)
- Routing
- L2 and L3 VPNs
- DHCP and DNS relay
- Load Balancing

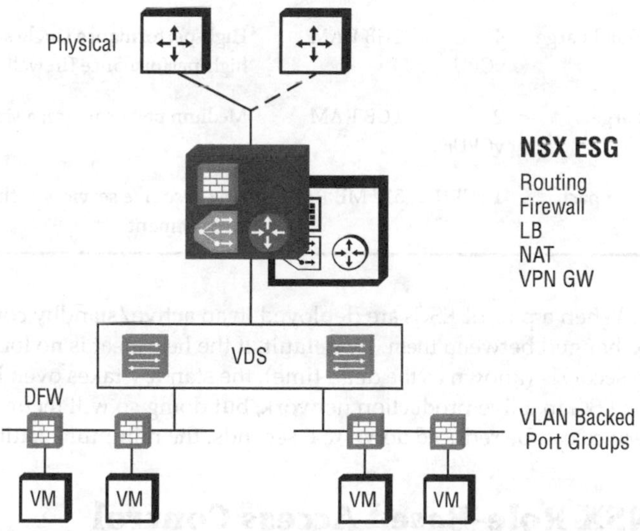

FIGURE 2.22
NSX Edge services

The firewall can work alongside the Distributed Firewall (DFW), with the ESG firewall focusing on North-South traffic in and out of your virtualized network and the DFW dealing with East-West traffic within your data center.

For address translation, the NSX Edge supports both source NAT and destination NAT.

For routers to exchange routes dynamically, a routing protocol is necessary. The NSX Edge supports iBGP, eBGP, and OSPF. Static routing is also available to manually configure routes.

Site-to-site IPSec Layer 2 and Layer 3 VPN services allow data centers that are spread out geographically to extend their domains. Remote access VPNs using SSL are also supported.

DHCP and DNS Relay services intercept requests from within your virtualized network and forward them to a DHCP or DNS server within the physical network.

The NSX Edge provides a Load Balancing service to dynamically spread a workload over a server farm cluster.

The NSX Edge is a VM. You can have two Edge VMs: one in active mode, the other in standby. Another design choice for the NSX Edge is Equal Cost Multi-Path (ECMP) mode. This allows up to eight Edge VMs acting as DLRs. This provides higher bandwidth and faster convergence; however, the only service available with this option is routing.

ESG Sizing

ESGs can be deployed in four different sizes: Compact, Large, Quad Large, and X-Large. The larger the size, the more vCPUs and RAM required, as shown in Table 2.1.

TABLE 2.1: Sizes of ESGs

SIZE	vCPU	RAM	USE CASE
X-Large	6 vCPUs	8 GB RAM	High performance, combining multiple services, firewall, load balancing, and routing
Quad Large	4 vCPUs	1 GB RAM	High-performance single service such as ECMP DLRs or as a high-performance firewall
Large	2 vCPUs	1 GB RAM	Medium performance; a single service or for a small data center
Compact	1 vCPU	512 MB RAM	Low-resource services such as a DHCP/DNS relay or lab/test environment

When a pair of ESGs are deployed in an active/standby configuration, a heartbeat signal is exchanged between them. By default, if the heartbeat is no longer heard by the standby ESG for 15 seconds (known as the dead time), the standby takes over. It's possible to upgrade the size of the ESG in a live production network, but doing so will incur downtime. The outage of the ESG service can be reduced down to 6 seconds, the minimum setting for the dead time.

NSX Role-Based Access Control

Role-Based Access Control (RBAC) is assigning access to resources on the basis of someone's role in the organization. Groups are created for each role, and permissions are assigned to each group. By making a user a member of a group, they are granted those assigned permissions.

NSX Manager has several pre-built RBAC roles, including Auditor, NSX Administrator, Security Administrator, and Enterprise Administrator (see Figure 2.23).

FIGURE 2.23 RBAC pre-built roles for assigning access to NSX

Auditor

Can't make configuration changes

Can only view the system

NSX Administrator

Can perform all tasks related to deploying and administering an NSX Manager instance

Examples: can install virtual appliances, can configure port groups

Security Administrator

Can configure security policies and view the reporting and auditing information in the system

Examples: define firewall rules, configure NAT, configure load balancing

Enterprise Administrator

Has all of the rights of the NSX Administrator

Has all of the rights of the Security Administrator

Security Engineer

Can't prepare hosts

Can't manage user accounts

Can perform all security tasks

Can have read access to some networking features

Examples: define firewall rules, configure policies

Network Engineer

Can't access security features

Can perform all networking tasks

Examples: routing, switching, DHCP

Security and Role Administrator

Has all of the rights of a Security Engineer

Can also manage user accounts

A user can only have one role. Assigning a user to a role will grant them access to use the Networking & Security plug-in found in the vSphere Web Client and to access the NSX Manager. It's recommended with RBAC to only grant permissions to groups, not individual users. This makes permission management simpler and in some cases is required for compliance.

Overlay and Underlay Networks

NSX allows virtual networks to be created on top of an existing physical network. The virtual network is referred to as the *overlay*, and the physical network is the *underlay*. Most organizations looking to upgrade their networks prefer the ability to leverage their current network (a brownfield deployment) and don't have the luxury of being able to simply create a brand-new network from scratch (a greenfield deployment). This is where NSX really shines. For the most part, adding a virtual NSX overlay requires little to no changes to the physical underlay. This means avoiding that fork-lift upgrade while still getting all the benefits that NSX brings to the table.

Overlay networks, or VXLANs, provide an architecture that allows this virtual-physical dichotomy to coexist. The Virtual Extensible LAN (VXLAN) network virtualization technology was created as a joint effort by VMware, Cisco, and Arista, but soon after, other vendors came on board to support it, including Dell, Citrix, Juniper, Huawei, and Red Hat, to name a few. It was later documented in RFC 7348 by the Internet Engineering Task Force.

Essentially, VXLAN is a tunneling protocol (see Figure 2.24). It allows for a network segment on one host to be extended to other hosts by tunneling through the physical network. For example, a VM may exist on ESXi host A on the 10.1.1.0 subnet. Another VM exists on host D, and it is also on the 10.1.1.0 subnet. Prior to VXLANs, this would require a set of Layer 2 physical switches connecting the hosts together to all be configured to carry the same VLAN from end-to-end. If any routers were used to connect the hosts, the Layer 2 VLAN segment was severed by the Layer 3 router. Coordination of creating VLANs and probably having to change the physical topology was necessary. In addition, broadcasts on that particular VLAN had to span the entire data center.

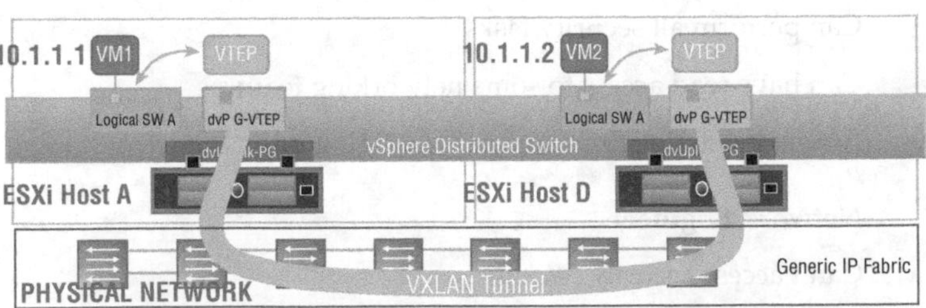

FIGURE 2.24
VXLANs tunnel through the physical network to allow traffic to other hosts.

VXLANs give the ability to tunnel through the physical network regardless of the complexities. Every ESXi host could be connected by only routers, and it would not matter. VLANs configured on switches in the physical network would not matter. This greatly simplifies the architecture since the physical network essentially is treated as a transport pipeline.

To provide the tunneling, an extra 50 bytes is added to an Ethernet frame (see Figure 2.25). Because of this, VMware recommends increasing the Maximum Transmission Unit (MTU) frame size to at least 1600 bytes. This is one thing that would need to potentially be changed in the physical environment. All the physical routers and switches would need to also support this minimum, but this is a very minor change and can be implemented in production without affecting traffic.

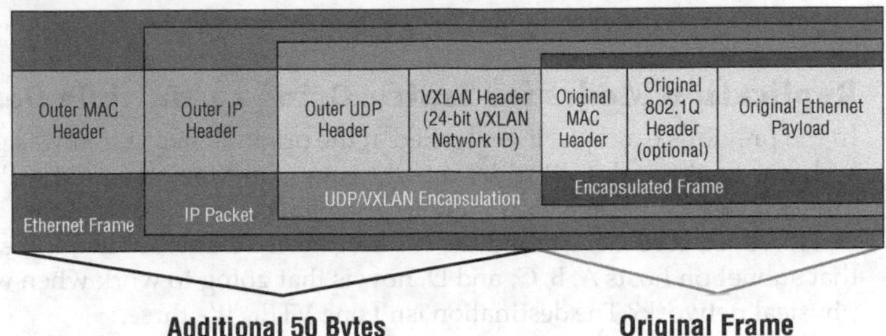

FIGURE 2.25 A 50-byte header containing VXLAN information is added to the front of a frame to be forwarded to another host.

Each ESXi host will have a VXLAN Tunnel Endpoint (VTEP). As an analogy, think of New York City as the physical network. The subway provides tunnels through the city. If you want to get from the Empire State Building to Times Square, all you need to know is the destination subway stop (see Figure 2.26). With VXLANs, you just need to know the IP address of the VTEP (subway stop) of the destination ESXi host (Times Square).

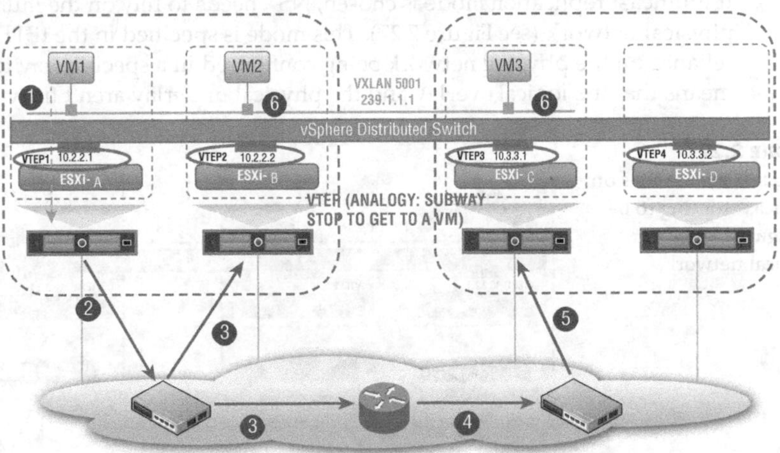

FIGURE 2.26 VTEPs are the tunnel endpoint IP addresses assigned to each host.

Each VTEP is configured as a separate VMKernel interface on the hosts and is assigned an IP address. When a packet leaves a VM on ESXi-Host1 destined for a VM on ESXi-Host3, the hypervisor of Host1 encapsulates the packet, adding the 50-byte header that contains the source and destination VTEP IP addresses. This is then forwarded out of the host into the physical network. The physical network knows how to reach each VTEP and treats the packet like any other. Once it gets to the destination host, the frame is decapsulated and the 50-byte outer header is stripped off. What's left is the original Ethernet frame, which the host then forwards to the destination VM.

NSX is agnostic to the underlay network topology. It only has two requirements: 1) IP connectivity and 2) an MTU size of at least 1600 bytes. For any network architect considering network upgrade options, this incredibly short and easy requirements list means that NSX can be immediately integrated.

Replication Modes for Traffic Going to Multiple Destinations

In the previous example, if we looked at the original packet that was generated by the source VM, we would find its IP address as the source and the other VM's IP address as the destination. This is a unicast packet, with a single destination.

However, consider a broadcast to all VMs on a single subnet. If there were VMs belonging to that subnet on hosts A, B, C, and D, how is that going to work when we send it through the physical network? The destination isn't one VTEP, it's three.

It's handled by replicating the packet, and there are three replication modes: unicast, multicast, and hybrid. By default, the logical switch within the host will inherit the mode configured for the entire transport zone (the group of ESXi hosts that can all communicate with one another). However, if desired, this can be overridden by manually making the change on the virtual switch.

Multicast Mode

If multicast replication mode is chosen, NSX needs to rely on the multicast routing abilities of the physical network (see Figure 2.27). This mode is specified in the IETF specifications, but this reliance on the physical network being configured in a specific way to handle multicast traffic means that the logical overlay and the physical underlay aren't truly decoupled.

Figure 2.27
Multicast mode relies on multicast routing to be configured in the physical network.

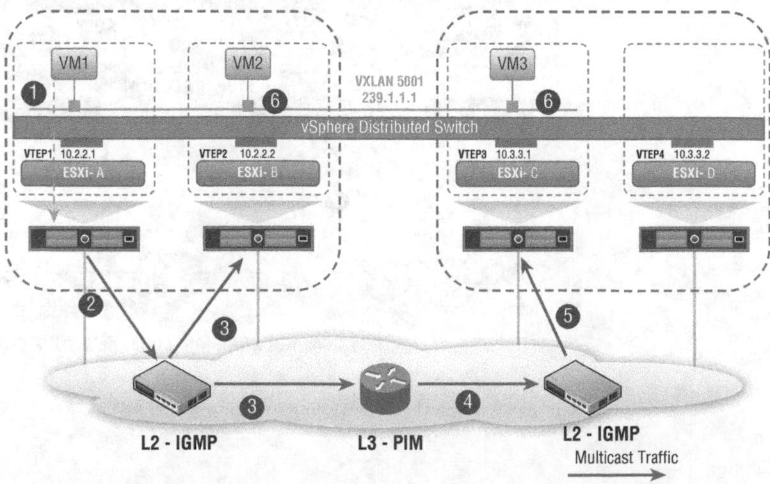

Unicast Mode

Unicast mode allows for a true decoupling of the overlay and underlay. Based on the IP addresses of the VTEPs for each host, some VTEPs may belong to the same subnet. These ESXi hosts are seen as a single group. For example, group 1 might include ESXi hosts A and B (see Figure 2.28). They are addressed 10.2.2.1 and 10.2.2.2, respectively. They belong to the same subnet. Hosts C and D are addressed 10.3.3.1 and 10.3.3.2, respectively. They are in a separate group and share a subnet. For each group/subnet, a single ESXi host is chosen to be the Unicast Tunnel End Point (UTEP) for the group. The UTEP's job is to replicate the broadcast packet to all the hosts within its own group.

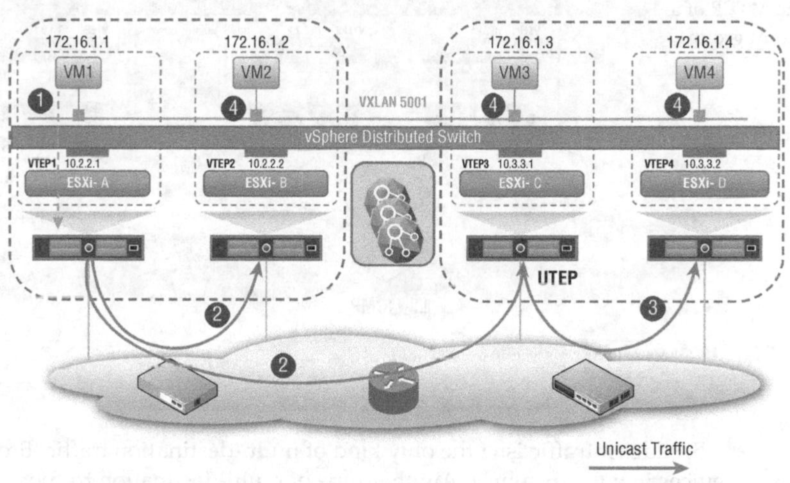

Figure 2.28 Unicast mode does not require the physical network to be configured for multicast routing.

VM1 on host A sends a broadcast. The broadcast is intended for every device on the 172.16.1.0 network. Host D has a VM with the address 172.16.1.4. Within the host group of A and B, say that host B is chosen as the UTEP. And within the host group of C and D, say host C is picked as the UTEP.

The packet flow would look like this: VM1 on host A, 172.16.1.1 sends a broadcast. Host A knows this is a multi-destination packet and sends it to host B. If other hosts existed in its group, host B would replicate the packet to those that have VMs in the same 172.16.1.0 subnet.

Host A also sends the packet to the other group's UTEP, host C. Host C, knowing that host D contains at least one VM in the 172.16.1.0 subnet, replicates the packet to host D where the VM4 172.16.1.4 receives it.

Hybrid Mode

As the name implies, hybrid mode is a hybrid between unicast and multicast modes. If a host needs to replicate a broadcast packet to other hosts in the same group, it uses one solution. But if the host needs to replicate the broadcast packet to hosts belonging to a different group, it uses a second solution.

Solution 1: When Replicating a Packet to Other Hosts in Your Same Group The first group in our example consists of hosts A and B (in subnet 10.2.2.0). When host A needs to replicate a packet to B, its solution is to send it as an L2 multicast. If other hosts were part of the same group, they would also receive it.

Solution 2: When Replicating a Packet to Other Hosts Belonging to a Different Group When host A (in subnet 10.2.2.0) needs to replicate a packet to C and D (in subnet 10.3.3.0), its solution is to send it as a unicast only to the Multicast Tunnel Endpoint for that group, host C (10.3.3.1)—see Figure 2.29. Then host C is responsible for replicating it to the other hosts in its group as an L2 multicast. In this example, it would multicast it to host D.

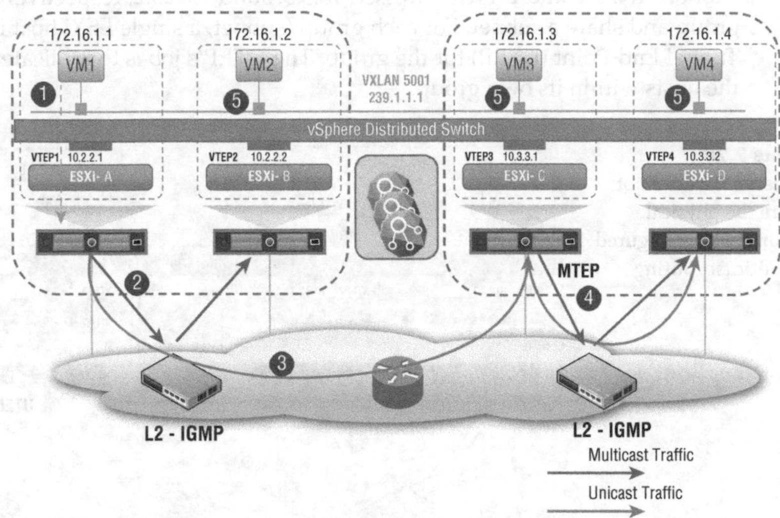

FIGURE 2.29 Hybrid mode multicasting to members of the same group, unicasting to the MTEP of a different group

Broadcast traffic isn't the only kind of multi-destination traffic. Broadcasts are intended for all devices in a given subnet. Another type of multi-destination traffic is an unknown unicast. This is what happens when a switch receives a frame with a destination MAC address but has no idea to which port to send it, so it floods it out all ports, and therefore it becomes multi-destination traffic. Another type of multi-destination traffic is a multicast. This traffic iintended for a specific group. For example, if you are familiar with the OSPF routing protocol, it works by sending information to other OSPF routers without bothering anyone else. When you configure OSPF, it automatically joins the OSPF group.

These different types of multi-destination traffic (broadcast, unknown unicast, and multicast) are sometimes referred to as BUM traffic. In the previous examples given, the initial traffic generated by the VM was in the form of a broadcast, but if the examples were unknown unicasts or multicasts, they would be handled identically depending on the chosen replication mode.

The Bottom Line

Planes of Operation Traditional network devices operate autonomously, having the management, control, and data planes all contained within each. NSX moves the management plane to NSX Manager and the control plane to NSX Controllers.

Master It What NSX component provides the data plane?

1. NSX Data Appliance
2. NSX Virtual Switch

3. ESXi Host
4. NSX Edge

NSX Controllers Instead of an active/backup design, each NSX Controller in a cluster is always active. This is so that they can slice and share the workloads.

Master It When deploying NSX Controllers in production, how many should a cluster contain?

Software-Defined Data Center Terminology It's commonly thought that most data center traffic is between the data center and outside networks, when in reality, it is from one VM to another within the data center. Both types of traffic have specific SDDC terms to describe each.

Master It East-West traffic refers to:

1. Traffic within the data center
2. Traffic between the data center and outside networks
3. Traffic between the virtual and physical networks

Chapter 3

Preparing NSX

In this chapter, we will go over the prerequisites that need to be taken care of before deploying NSX, including having specific ports open for NSX components to communicate along with DNS for name resolution.

We will then look at how to determine the CPU, RAM, and disk space resources needed to match the needs of your organization. You will see that it is also helpful to have the IP addresses you plan to use for NSX determined ahead of time along with the IP addresses of your existing NTP and DNS servers.

The primary focus of the chapter will be on deploying NSX, which can be done manually or automated with APIs. You will see how to deploy the NSX Manager, associate it with vCenter, and prepare the clusters to provide NSX services.

IN THIS CHAPTER, YOU WILL LEARN ABOUT:

- Required TCP and UDP ports for NSX communication
- CPU, memory, and storage minimums for an NSX design
- HA for NSX Manager failover and DRS for choosing a new home
- Addressing information to have ready prior to deployment
- Deploying NSX Manager
- Pairing NSX Manager with a vCenter Server
- Integrating single sign-on services
- Going big: Cross-vCenter NSX Design
- Universal objects in Cross-vCenter
- Primary and secondary NSX Managers to maintain 1:1 relationships
- Prepping your hosts for NSX
- Cross-vCenter universal transport zone

NSX Manager Prerequisites

NSX Data Center for vSphere (NSX-V) can be configured manually through the vSphere Web Client or command-line interface or programmatically using a REST API. A REST API allows developers to send requests and receive responses using the HTTP protocol. Since virtually every programming language supports HTTP, programmers can use their language of choice to execute the same tasks that can be performed manually, such as provisioning, configuring, backing up, restoring, and deleting NSX components including logical routers, logical switches, logical firewalls, and logical load balancers.

Open Ports and Name Resolution

In order for the NSX Data Center to function properly, several TCP and UDP ports need to be open (see Figure 3.1).

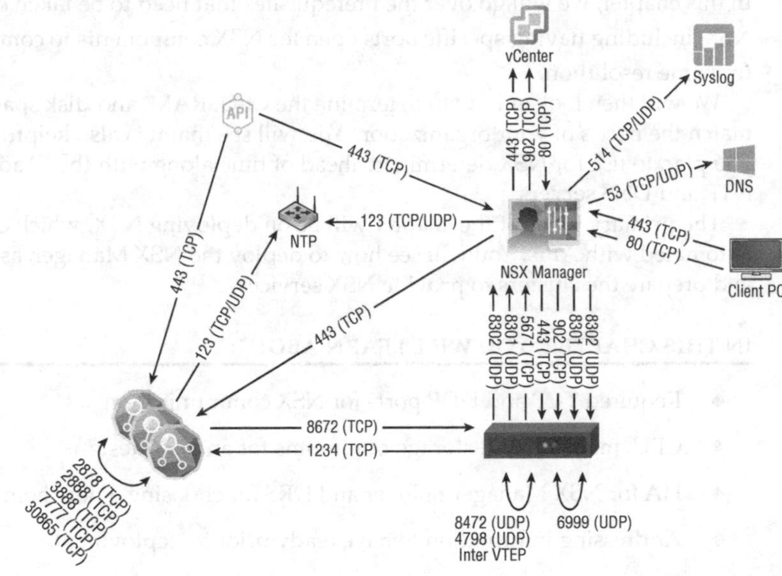

FIGURE 3.1 TCP and UDP ports needed for NSX communication

TCP 80, 443, 5671, 1234, 2878, 2888, 3888, 7777, 30865, 902, 48656, 53, 514, and 123.

UDP 53, 514, 4789, 6999, 8301, 8302, and 123.

These allow communication with the NSX Manager, NSX Controller, vCenter Server, ESXi hosts, DNS Server, Syslog Server, NTP Time Server, and VXLAN Tunnel End Points (VTEPs).

To manage NSX, both forward and reverse name resolution is required. The reason for this is that when ESXi hosts are added to vSphere by name, NSX Manager must be able to resolve the names to in order to communicate with the hosts. Likewise, the hostname of the NSX Manager will be used by other components, so the name and its IP address must be known by the DNS servers.

Minimum Resource Requirements for NSX Data Center Appliances

The major NSX appliances including the NSX Manager, NSX Controller, NSX Edge, and Guest Introspection each need memory, CPU, and disk space (see Figure 3.2).

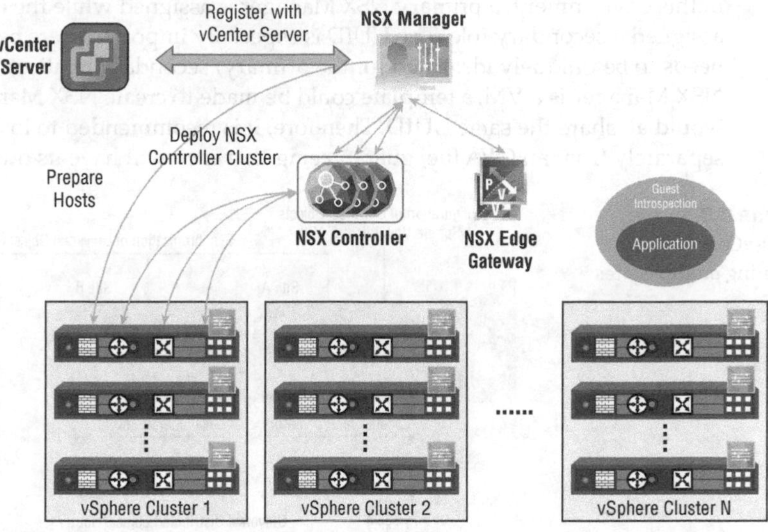

FIGURE 3.2 Major NSX components requiring resources

The NSX Manager requires 16 GB of memory, four virtual CPUs, and 60 GB of disk space. Each NSX Controller (there will be three) needs 4 GB of memory, four vCPUs, and 28 GB of disk space. Guest Introspection offloads security services like anti-virus and anti-malware agent processing to a dedicated security appliance on each ESXi host. The advantage is that the agents don't need to run and take up resources on each Virtual Machine guest OS. Guest Introspection requires two GB of memory, 2 vCPUs, and 5 GB of disk space.

The resource requirements for the NSX Edge depends on the chosen form factor.

NSX EDGE FORM FACTOR	MEMORY	VCPU	DISK SIZE
Compact	512 MB	1	1 disk 584 MB and 1 disk 512 MB
Large	1 GB	2	1 disk 584 MB and 1 disk 512 MB
Quad Large	2 GB	4	1 disk 584 MB and 1 disk 512 MB
X-Large	8 GB	6	1 disk 584 MB and 1 disk 256 MB

vSphere HA and DRS

NSX Manager is a virtual machine. It comes packaged as an Open Virtual Appliance (OVA) file, which can be downloaded online from VMware's website. This file is compressed, which allows for faster downloads. When attempting to import an OVA file, the vSphere Web Client will validate it first to ensure compatibility.

Another advantage of installing NSX Manager from an OVA file is that it will automatically be assigned a Universally Unique Identifier (UUID). This is especially important with Cross-vCenter NSX installations. With a Cross-vCenter NSX design, there are multiple vCenter Servers (see Figure 3.3). The one-to-one relationship between vCenter Servers and NSX Managers means that an NSX Manager can only be paired with a single vCenter Server. To centralize management in this environment, a primary NSX Manager is assigned while the other NSX Managers are assigned a secondary role. The UUID is especially important here because each NSX Manager needs to be uniquely identified for the primary/secondary relationship to be created. Since the NSX Manager is a VM, a template could be made to create NSX Manager copies, but the copies would all share the same UUID. Therefore, it is recommended to install each NSX Manager separately from an OVA file, guaranteeing that each will have its own UUID.

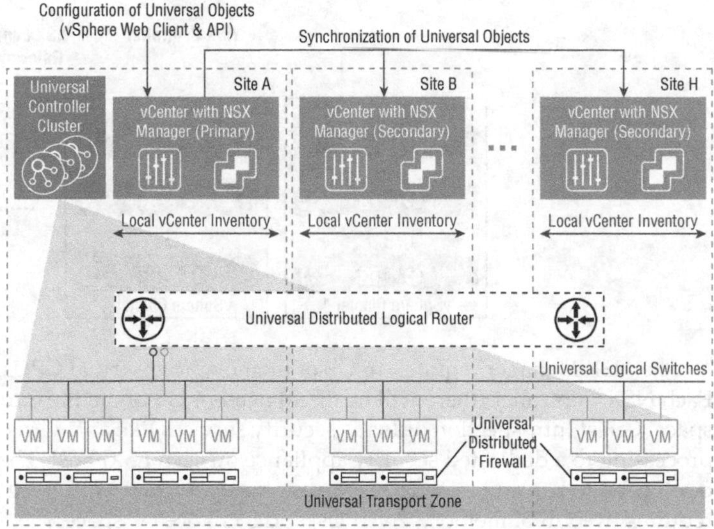

FIGURE 3.3
Cross-vCenter design spanning multiple sites

Instead of deploying NSX Manager on a single ESXi host, it is recommended to install it on a management cluster that has been configured with vSphere High Availability (HA) and Distributed Resource Scheduler (DRS). Ideally, the management cluster should be separate from the compute cluster. Separating management from compute means that even if every host in the management cluster were to fail, compute workloads moving through the network would remain unaffected (see Figure 3.4).

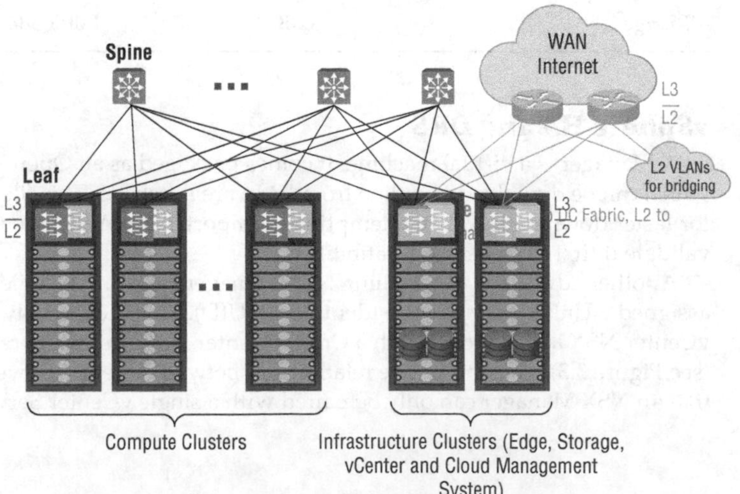

FIGURE 3.4
Separate compute and management clusters

HA pools the VMs and the hosts they reside on into a cluster. If a host fails, the VMs on that host are restarted on a different host in the cluster. For HA to work, it requires shared storage. Shared storage allows for the NSX Manager to be restarted on a different host if the host it is active on fails.

DRS chooses the appropriate host within the cluster on which to install the NSX Manager and improves service levels by guaranteeing that NSX Manager will have the proper amount of resources. DRS combined with HA ensures that in the event of a host failover, the appliance is moved to the next best host in the cluster, based on available resources for each remaining host.

IP Addressing and Port Groups

NSX Manager can be configured with IPv4, IPv6, or both (dual-stack). In most cases, IPv4 will be selected. Before initiating the installation of NSX Manager, have the following information on hand:

- NSX Manager IP address
- NSX Manager default gateway
- NTP server IP address
- DNS server IP address
- Domain search list

For NSX Manager to communicate with other components, it will need to be assigned to a management traffic distributed port group.

To create a distributed port group:

1. Click the Home icon and select Networking (see Figure 3.5).

FIGURE 3.5 Home ➤ Networking

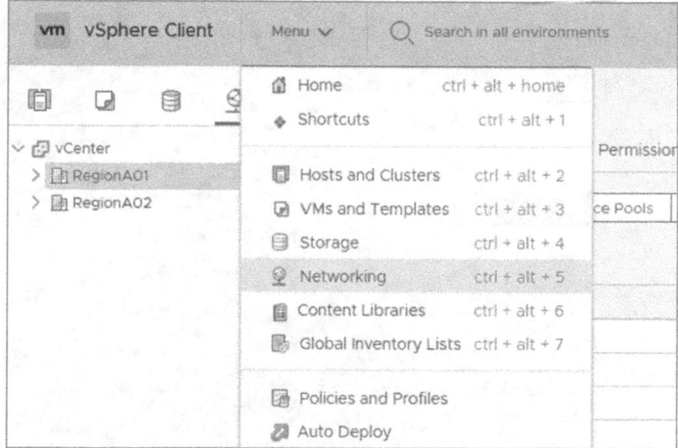

2. Right-click the data center.
3. Select Distributed Switch – New Distributed Switch from the menu and give it a descriptive name such as **RegionA1-VDS-Mgmt**.

   The settings will default to four uplinks, with Network I/O Control enabled, and a default port group.

4. Enter a port group name such as **Mgmt-PG**.

   The number of uplinks you choose depends on your design. Typically, the number of uplinks is equal to the number of physical NICs associated with the VDS.

5. Each port group is created to carry a different type of traffic. It's recommended that the checkbox for Default Port Group be unchecked so that every port group is explicitly defined for each traffic type.

Installing the Client Integration Plug-in

To check to see if the Client Integration Plug-in is installed, enter the URL for the vSphere Web Client in a browser. Firefox is recommended. On the login page, if you do not see a download link for the plug-in, it means that it is already installed.

Otherwise, click Download Client Integration Plug-in.

Installing NSX Manager

NSX Manager is installed by deploying an OVA, which can be found online. The easiest way to find the NSX OVA file is to do an Internet search of the phrase "Download VMware NSX."

1. Log in to the vSphere Web Client.
2. Click Home and select VMs And Templates.

   The left section is the Navigator panel, which includes inventory objects such as the data center.

3. Right-click the data center and select Deploy OVF Template (see Figure 3.6).

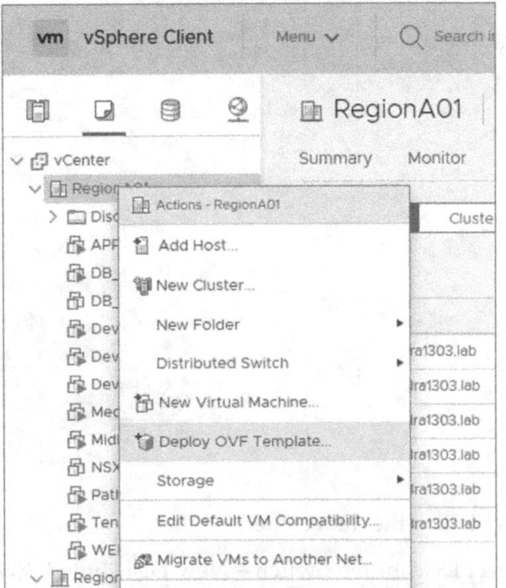

FIGURE 3.6
Deploy OVF Template

4. Choose Local File and then Browse to find the downloaded OVA file.

   You will be prompted to assign a unique name for NSX Manager as well as a deployment location. By default, the name shown will match the name of the OVA. The default location will be based on the inventory object you right-clicked to initiate the Deploy OVF Template wizard.

5. Select a name and location.

   The resource page of the wizard is where you select the management cluster. This is where the OVA will be deployed. You will get a chance to review your choices and accept the VMware license agreement.

6. Select a resource.

   The Select Storage page is where you select the location to store the files for the deployed template. The virtual disk format can be Thin Provision, Thick Provision Lazy Zeroed, or Thick Provision Eager Zeroed, as explained in the following table:

Thick Provision Lazy Zeroed	This format is the default. With thick provisioning, you reserve space for the virtual disk.
Thick Provision Eager Zeroed	Another Thick Provision format, it also reserves space for the virtual disk.
Thin Provision	If saving storage space is desired, it allows the storage space to start out small, using only enough for initial operations.

7. Select Storage.

LAZY ZEROED VS. EAGER ZEROED

The difference between Lazy and Eager Zeroed is that Lazy Zeroed does not erase any data on the physical disk when the virtual disk is first created. It instead does this on demand when data is first written from the VM. Eager Zeroed erases the remaining data immediately upon the creation of the virtual disk, which takes longer compared to the other formats.

8. When prompted for a VM Storage Policy, keep the default (None) unless storage policies are needed and enabled. Select the datastore that will store the configuration file and the virtual disk files.

   The Source Network column lists the network(s) defined in the OVA, like the Management Network. Map the source network to the management port group by selecting it under the Destination Network column.

9. Select Networks.

10. In the Customize Template section, enter and confirm passwords for the CLI Admin user and for CLI Privilege Mode.

    Network properties are also defined here, including the hostname for the VM, the IP address, subnet mask, default gateway, DNS servers, NTP servers, and the option to enable SSH.

11. You will see a summary of the configuration. Click Finish to deploy NSX Manager. Once the deployment is complete, right-click NSX Manager and power it on.

Associating NSX Manager to vCenter

Only one NSX Manager can be registered with a vCenter Server, and this 1:1 relationship applies even in a Cross-vCenter design. To register NSX Manager to vCenter:

1. Open a web browser and log in to NSX Manager using its IP address or FQDN:

    `https://<NSX-Manager-IP-Address>` or `https://<NSX-Manager-FQDN>`

    The default admin username is simply admin. The password is what you configured when the NSX Manager was deployed. You can also use any account assigned Enterprise Administrator privileges.

2. From the NSX Manager home page, select Manage vCenter Registration (see Figure 3.7).

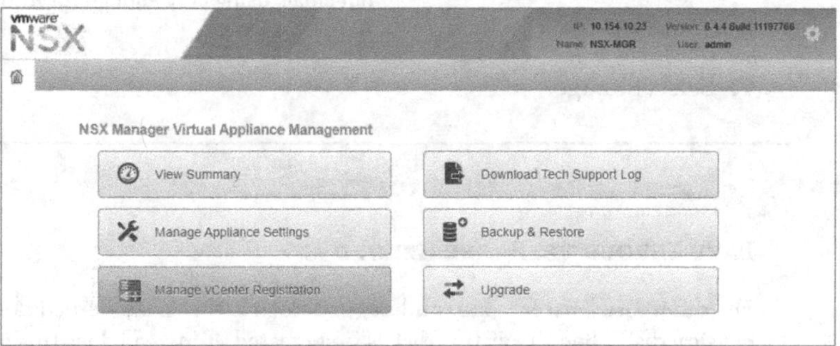

FIGURE 3.7 Manage vCenter Registration

3. In the vCenter Server pane, click Edit to enter the vCenter Server's hostname, along with username and password login information to access.

    The recommendation for the username is administrator@vsphere.local, not the root account (see Figure 3.8).

4. When prompted to proceed with the SSL certificate, click Yes and then confirm that the vCenter Server status is Connected.

5. Close the browser window to the vSphere Web Client (if it is open) and log in again.

    By going to Home, you should see a new icon: Networking & Security.

6. Click it to verify that NSX is deployed and communicating with vCenter Server (see Figure 3.9).

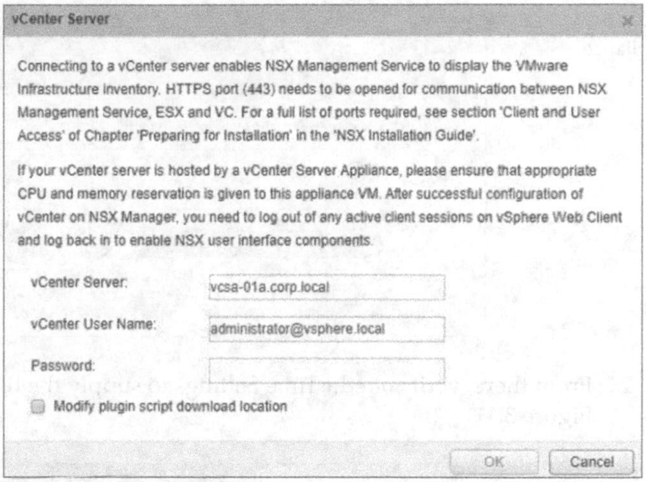

FIGURE 3.8
vCenter Server name and login

vCenter Server

Connecting to a vCenter server enables NSX Management Service to display the VMware Infrastructure inventory. HTTPS port (443) needs to be opened for communication between NSX Management Service, ESX and VC. For a full list of ports required, see section 'Client and User Access' of Chapter 'Preparing for Installation' in the 'NSX Installation Guide'.

If your vCenter server is hosted by a vCenter Server Appliance, please ensure that appropriate CPU and memory reservation is given to this appliance VM. After successful configuration of vCenter on NSX Manager, you need to log out of any active client sessions on vSphere Web Client and log back in to enable NSX user interface components.

vCenter Server: vcsa-01a.corp.local

vCenter User Name: administrator@vsphere.local

Password:

Modify plugin script download location

OK Cancel

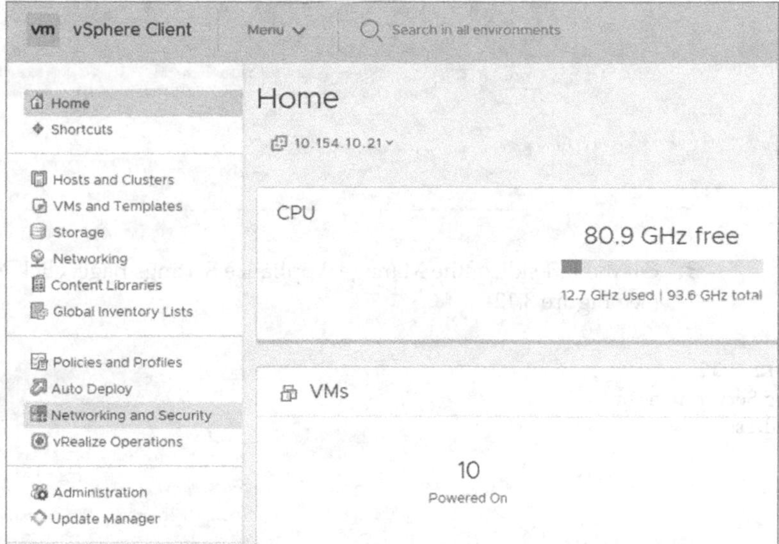

FIGURE 3.9
vSphere Web Client

Adding AD/LDAP to NSX

Instead of NSX and vSphere independently authenticating users, security is improved with a single sign-on (SSO). Integrating the SSO service with NSX allows NSX to authenticate users from Active Directory (AD) and Lightweight Directory Access Protocol (LDAP).

The SSO service and NSX must be in sync to function, which means that a Network Time Protocol (NTP) server has to be specified. It is recommended that SSO and NSX Manager use the same NTP server.

To have NSX point to the IP address of the NTP server, follow these steps:

1. Log in to the NSX Manager virtual appliance and select Manage Appliance Settings (see Figure 3.10).

FIGURE 3.10
Manage Appliance Settings

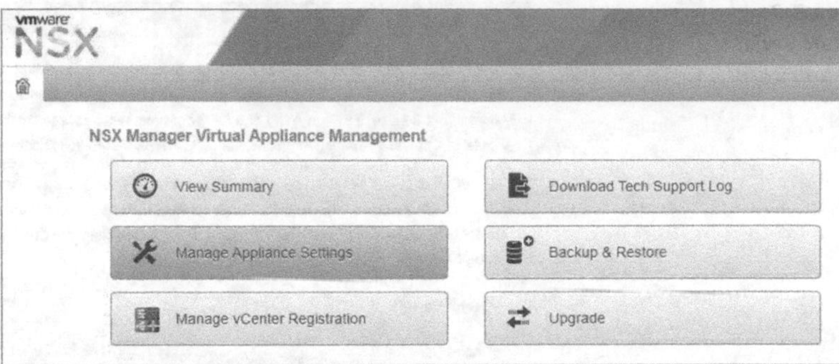

2. From there, verify or edit Time Settings to supply the IP address of the NTP server (see Figure 3.11).

FIGURE 3.11
NTP Time Settings

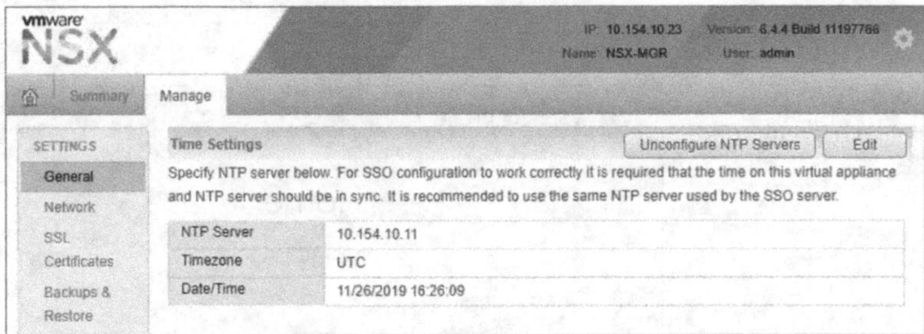

3. On the left side of the Manage Appliance Settings page, click NSX Management Service (see Figure 3.12).

FIGURE 3.12
Syslog Server name or IP address

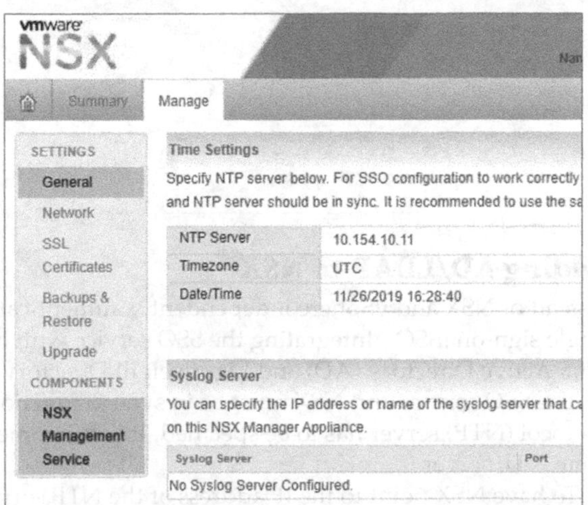

Lookup Service URL

Under Lookup Service URL, click the Edit button and enter either the name or IP address of the lookup service (AD or LDAP server) along with port number 443. Configure the SSO admin username and password and verify that the status of the Lookup Service shows Connected.

Deploying NSX Controllers

The three-node NSX Controller cluster provides all the control plane operations for logical switching and logical routing in NSX. Additionally, it tracks and maintains information regarding hosts, Distributed Logical Routers (DLRs), and VXLANs.

NSX Controller Placement

Before deploying the controller cluster, have the networking information ready, including the IP pool for the cluster, the default gateway, and the IP address range:

1. Log in to the vSphere Web Client.
2. Click Home and select Networking And Security.
3. Select Installation And Upgrade (see Figure 3.13).

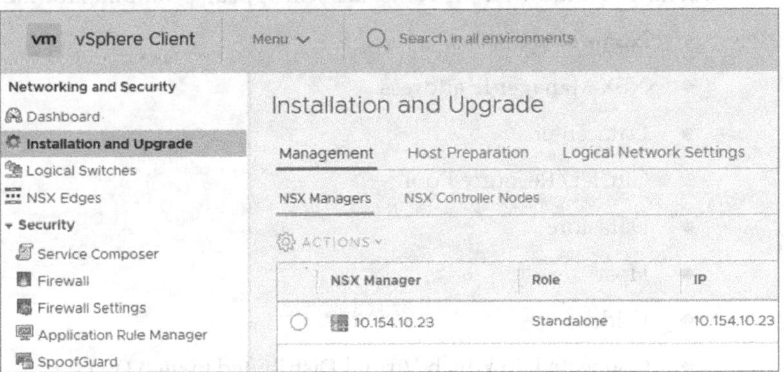

Figure 3.13
Installation and Upgrade

Under the Management tab, there are two sub-tabs: NSX Managers and NSX Controller Nodes.

4. Select NSX Controller Nodes (see Figure 3.14).
5. Click the +Add icon (see Figure 3.15).

FIGURE 3.14
NSX Controller Nodes

Management Host Preparation Logical Network Settings
NSX Managers NSX Controller Nodes
+ ADD DELETE SUPPORT LOGS ACTIONS

Name	Controller Node	NSX Manager	Mana
Controller_01	192.168.110.31 controller-1	192.168.110.42	19

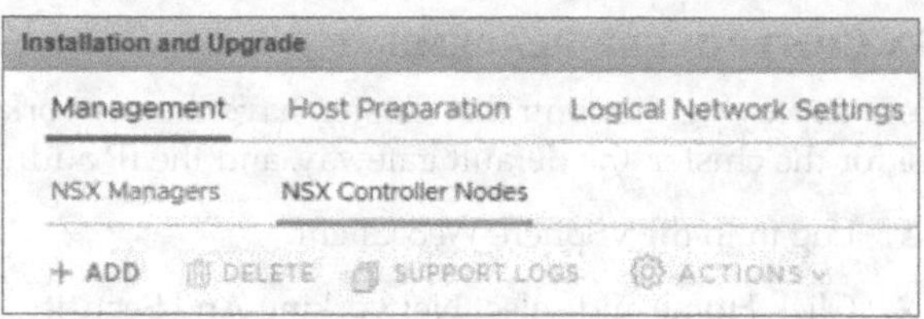

FIGURE 3.15
Add a Controller Node

ADDING THE CONTROLLER

A settings window for the controller will appear, prompting for the following information:

- Name of controller
- NSX Manager IP address
- Datacenter
- Cluster/Resource Pool
- Datastore
- Host
- Folder
- Connected To Which Virtual Distributed Switch (VDS)
- IP Pool
- Password

CONTROLLER PASSWORD RULES

For the controller password to be accepted, it must conform to these rules:

- At least 12 characters
- At least one special character
- At least one number
- At least one uppercase letter
- At least one lowercase letter

The deployed controller should show as Connected. Once verified, deploy the other two controllers following the same steps. We recommend that the Distributed Resource Scheduler (DRS) be configured for the three controllers with the anti-affinity rule. The anti-affinity rule ensures that the controllers are deployed to different hosts. This increases the availability of the controllers if one host fails.

Linking Multiple NSX Managers Together (Cross-vCenter NSX)

NSX Cross-vCenter provides solutions for connectivity between NSX domains located in different data centers or within a single site (see Figure 3.16). Layer 2 can be extended across these domains, despite being separated by Layer 3 boundaries. This means that you can use the same logical switches across multiple NSX environments and could even have a vCenter Server associated with NSX Manager located in a different site. Application security policies are also extended, which avoids having to re-create the same policies at the second site and maintains security consistency.

FIGURE 3.16
Cross-vCenter design

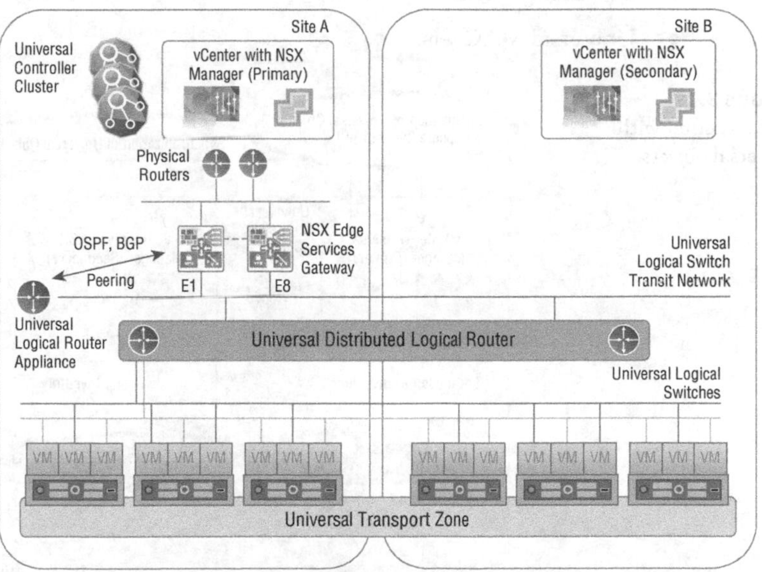

Cross-vCenter NSX provides a foundation of site-to-site connectivity and security that allows for design options that were previously unavailable for active workloads running across data center sites to improve resource utilization through pooling, merge companies after an acquisition, and provide automated solutions for disaster recovery, disaster avoidance, and data center migrations.

Multi-site Consistency with Universal Components

IP address space can be shared across sites, simplifying your design. Applications can keep the same IP addresses even when moved from one site to the other due to migration or recovery.

Since security is managed centrally, it is maintained for the application without the need to sync with the other site. By allowing IP space and security to span across all vCenter instances, VMs can long-distance vMotion across these boundaries, maintaining the same consistent security policy with the same IP addressing without the need for manual changes.

Universal components allow Cross-vCenter NSX to extend across domains (see Figure 3.17):

- A universal transport zone spans the organization.
- Universal logical switches are attached to the universal transport zone.
- VMs connect to the universal logical switches.
- Universal logical routers connect to the universal logical switches for dynamic routing.
- Universal Controller Cluster (UCC) provides the control plane for Cross-vCenter NSX, maintaining information about the universal logical switches and routers.
- Universal firewall rules.
- Universal security groups.
- Universal IP sets.
- Universal MAC sets.

FIGURE 3.17
Cross-vCenter with universal objects

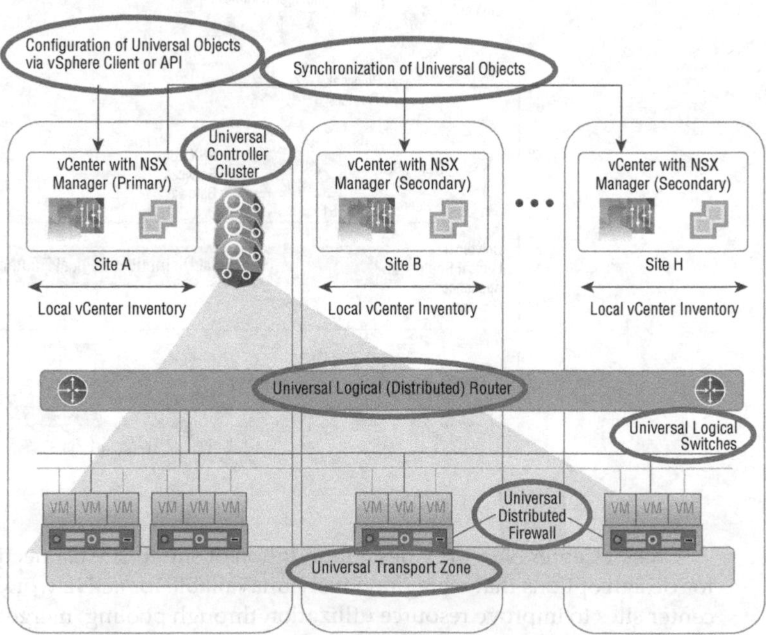

Universal objects are close in function to their local counterparts, like distributed logical switches, firewalls, and routers. The difference is that they can span multiple vCenter Servers.

Primary and Secondary NSX Managers

With Cross-vCenter NSX, there is still a 1:1 relationship between NSX Manager and the vCenter Server. Only one NSX Manager can be primary in this design. The rest of the NSX Managers are secondary. In total, there can be up to eight pairs of NSX Manager/vCenter Server relationships: one pair for the primary and seven pairs of secondaries. The primary NSX Manager is responsible for creating universal objects and deploying the Universal Controller Cluster as well as creating local objects.

The Universal Controller Cluster provides the control plane for the entire Cross-vCenter NSX environment. Secondary NSX Managers do not have their own controller cluster. They rely on the UCC even to create local objects. However, only the primary NSX Manager can create and manage universal objects. The Universal Synchronization Service (USS) runs on the primary NSX Manager and uses it to replicate universal objects to the secondary NSX Managers. The Universal Controller Cluster must be deployed in the same site as the primary NSX Manager. To maintain consistency, the USS runs every 30 seconds but can also be triggered manually. The synchronization checks for differences between the primary and the secondaries. If a difference is detected, USS will synchronize the secondaries to match the primary.

ENHANCED LINK MODE WITH CROSS-vCENTER NSX

Enhanced Link Mode is an option that allows all vCenter Servers, NSX Managers, and universal NSX objects to be managed from a single vCenter Server. Otherwise, each NSX Manager must be managed individually through its corresponding vCenter Server.

DEPLOYING NSX CONTROLLERS ON THE PRIMARY NSX MANAGER

Regardless of the size of the deployment, the only supported option is to have a cluster of three controllers:

1. With the vSphere Web Client, log in to the vCenter Server registered with the NSX Manager that will be primary.
2. Click Home and select Networking & Security.
3. Select Installation And Upgrade.
4. Under the Management tab and NSX Managers sub-tab, choose the NSX Manager that you wish to be primary (see Figure 3.18).

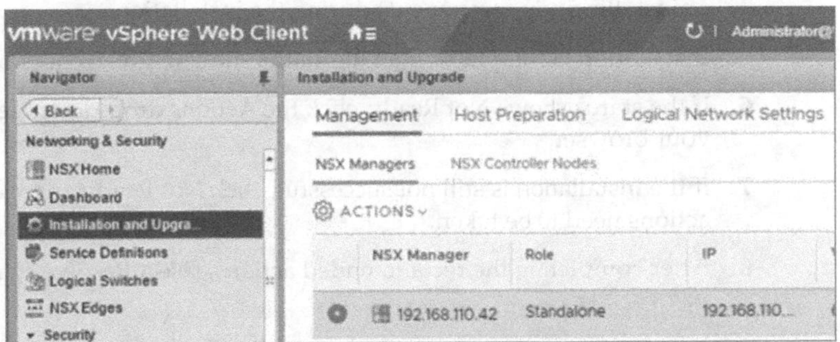

FIGURE 3.18 Selecting the primary NSX Manager

5. Click the NSX Controller Nodes sub-tab and select Add.
6. Enter the appropriate controller settings as previously mentioned, including the name of the controller, IP address, data center, port group, and so forth.

Preparing ESXi Clusters for NSX

Host preparation involves using the NSX Manager to install NSX kernel modules on ESXi hosts that are members of the vCenter clusters. This creates the control and management planes for NSX. The kernel modules provide the host with distributed routing, VXLAN support, and a distributed firewall. Once the necessary components have been implemented on the cluster, adding another host to the cluster will automatically trigger the installation of the same required components on the new host.

Determining Which Clusters to Prepare

All hosts must be attached to the same vSphere Distributed Switch (VDS):

1. With the vSphere Web Client, log in to the vCenter Server registered with the NSX Manager that will be primary.
2. Click Networking & Security.
3. Select Installation And Upgrade and choose Host Preparation (see Figure 3.19).

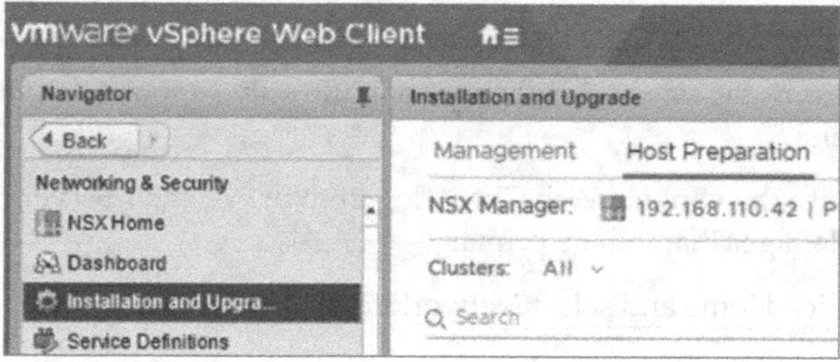

Figure 3.19 Host Preparation

4. Select the cluster. Click the Actions drop-down and choose Install.
5. Monitor the installation progress, but do not make changes such as deploying or uninstalling any components during the installation.

   Installation is complete when the status shows a green check mark.
6. If the status shows Not Ready, click the Actions drop-down, select Resolve, and refresh your browser.
7. If the installation is still not successful, click Not Ready and view the errors to find what actions need to be taken.
8. After completing the recommended actions, select Resolve again.

Configuring VXLAN from the Primary NSX Manager

VXLAN allows Layer 2 switching across ESXi hosts, even if there are Layer 3 domains between hosts in the physical network. When the cluster of ESXi hosts is mapped to a distributed switch, the VMkernel interface is created on each host. Configuring VXLAN will create a new distributed port group on the distributed switch:

1. With the vSphere Web Client, log in to the vCenter Server registered with the NSX Manager that will be primary.
2. Click Networking & Security.
3. Select Installation And Upgrade, and then choose Host Preparation.
4. Click the cluster in the left pane and click Not Configured next to VXLAN in the right pane.
5. In the Configure VXLAN Networking section, specify the management VDS and the VLAN for the overlay network, set an MTU size of at least 1600, create an IP pool, and configure the VMKNIC teaming policy.

The number of VTEPs is automatically set to match the number of dvUplinks on the distributed switch.

Assigning a Segment ID Pool for the Primary NSX Manager

Each ESXi host will have a VXLAN Tunnel Endpoint (VTEP). The tunnels created between VTEPs are VXLAN segments, which can be identified with segment IDs. These IDs are automatically assigned from a segment ID pool, which you must define.

It's important to make sure that the universal segment ID pools don't overlap with pools configured on other NSX Managers:

1. With the vSphere Web Client, log in to the vCenter Server registered with the NSX Manager that will be primary.
2. Click Networking & Security.
3. Select Installation And Upgrade, and then choose Logical Network Settings.
4. Under the Segment IDs section, click Edit.
5. Enter a range of Segment IDs. For example, 5000–5999.

Assigning the NSX Manager as Primary

The primary NSX Manager is responsible for the controller cluster, with any additional NSX Managers acting as secondaries. To assign the primary:

1. With the vSphere Web Client, log in to the vCenter Server registered with the NSX Manager that will be primary.
2. Click Home and select Networking & Security.

3. Select Installation And Upgrade.
4. Under the Management tab and NSX Managers sub-tab, choose the NSX Manager that you wish to be primary.
5. Click the Actions drop-down and select Assign Primary Role.

ASSIGNING A RANGE FOR UNIVERSAL SEGMENT IDs ON THE PRIMARY NSX MANAGER

The universal segment ID pool is used to automatically assign IDs when logical network segments are created. This automatic assignment is to ensure that VXLAN Network Identifiers (VNIs) are non-overlapping and are consistent across all the secondary NSX Managers:

1. Use the vSphere Web Client to log in to the primary NSX Manager.
2. Click Home and select Networking & Security.
3. Select Installation And Upgrade.
4. Choose Logical Network Settings and click Edit next to Segment IDs.
5. Enter a range for the universal segment IDs. For example, 900000–909999.

Creating a Universal Transport Zone on the Primary NSX Manager

A universal logical switch can only reach as far as the defined universal transport zone, and only one universal transport zone can be created. When the universal transport zone is configured on the primary NSX Manager, it will be replicated to all the secondaries, which defines the span of the vSphere clusters within the transport zone:

1. With the vSphere Web Client, log in to the vCenter Server registered with the NSX Manager that will be primary.
2. Click Home and select Networking & Security.
3. Select Installation And Upgrade.
4. Under the Logical Network Settings tab, choose the Transport Zones submenu (see Figure 3.20).

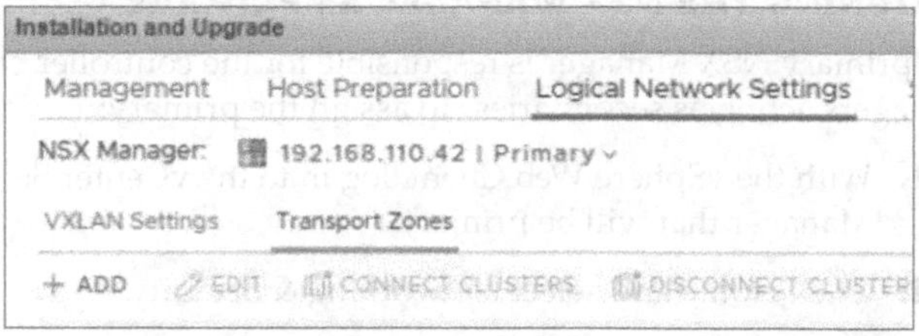

FIGURE 3.20
Transport Zones

5. Click +Add.
6. Provide a descriptive name such as **UniversalTransportZone**.
7. Enable Universal Synchronization so that the universal transport zone will be replicated to the secondary NSX Managers.

   For the control plane mode, there are three options:

Multicast	Multicast on physical network used for VXLAN control plane
Unicast	VXLAN control plane handled by NSX Controller Cluster
Hybrid	Offloads local traffic replication to physical network

8. Choose a mode that is best suited for your deployment.
9. Select the clusters to add to the universal transport zone.

vSphere Distributed Switches Membership

Universal logical switches span all vCenter Servers. Adding a logical switch to a universal transport zone converts the logical switch to a universal logical switch:

1. With the vSphere Web Client, log in to the vCenter Server registered with the NSX Manager that will be primary.
2. Click Home and select Networking & Security.
3. Select Logical Switches (see Figure 3.21).

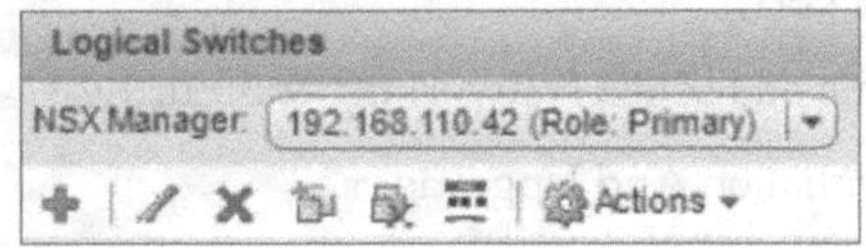

FIGURE 3.21 Logical Switches

4. Click the + icon to bring up the New Logical Switch window.
5. Provide a name for the logical switch (see Figure 3.22).
6. Click the Change link, select the universal transport zone, and pick your preferred replication mode: multicast, unicast, or hybrid.

The option to Enable IP Discovery allows you to minimize the flooding of ARP traffic between VMs connected to the same logical switch. You will find that this option cannot be disabled when creating a universal logical switch. However, once created, it's possible to disable IP discovery using an API.

Another option to consider is to Enable MAC Learning. When selected, each vNIC will dynamically build a table mapping MAC addresses to the VLANs on which they reside using Reverse ARP (RARP) for every entry. This is especially helpful if your vNICs are configured as trunks to carry VLAN traffic.

FIGURE 3.22
Logical Switch naming and replication mode

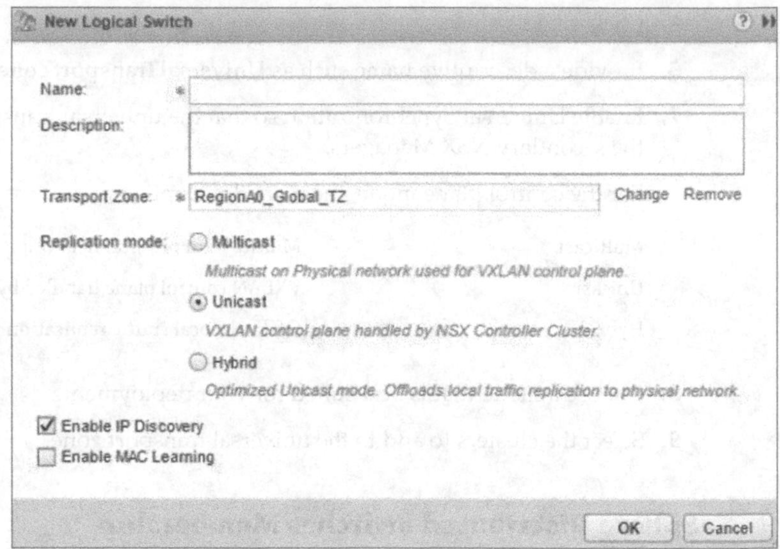

Adding Secondary NSX Managers

Although universal objects cannot be created from secondary NSX Managers, they are able to use all the universal objects, such as universal logical routers and switches. Keep in mind that there is a 1:1 relationship between NSX Managers and vCenter Servers. Therefore, each NSX Manager needs to be registered with a unique vCenter Server:

1. With the vSphere Web Client, log in to the vCenter Server registered with the primary NSX Manager.
2. Click Home and select Networking & Security.
3. Select Installation And Upgrade.
4. Under the Management tab and NSX Managers sub-tab, choose the primary NSX Manager.
5. Click Actions and select Add Secondary Manager (see Figure 3.23).

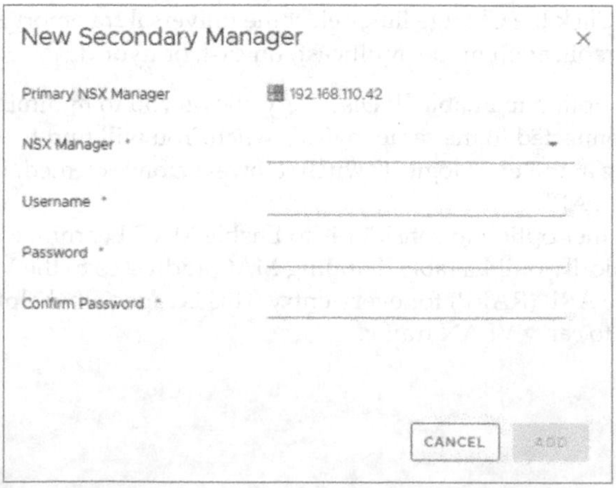

FIGURE 3.23
Add Secondary Manager

New Secondary Manager
Primary NSX Manager 192.168.110.42
NSX Manager *
Username *
Password *
Confirm Password *
CANCEL ADD

6. Enter the IP address that will be used for the secondary NSX Manager along with a username and password. If, however, the primary NSX Manager is configured with IPv6, use a hostname instead of an IPv6 address.
7. Verify that the registration was successful by looking under the Role column.

   It should indicate that it is Secondary instead of Standalone. If this remains unchanged, try logging out of the web client and then log back in again.
8. If the controller status shows Disconnected, refresh the web client and it should change to Normal.

The Bottom Line

Deploying NSX Manager When deploying the NSX Manager, rather than cloning an existing instance, it is recommended to deploy it from an OVA file.

Master It The primary reason for deploying from an OVA file is so that NSX Manager gets its own what?

Deploying an NSX Controller A secure password must be configured when deploying an NSX Controller.

Master It Which of the following is not a listed requirement for the NSX Controller password to be accepted?

1. At least one uppercase letter
2. At least one lowercase letter
3. At least one special character
4. At least eight characters
5. At least 12 characters

Connectivity between Multiple vCenter Domains Cross-vCenter can allow multiple data centers to be managed from a central point.

Master It Your Cross-vCenter design will include one primary NSX Manager and four secondary NSX Managers. How many vCenter Servers are required to support this configuration?

Chapter 4

Distributed Logical Switch

If you're new to NSX, but coming from the networking world, you know what a physical switch is and does. In case you're not entirely sure, a switch is a device that dynamically learns the MAC addresses of endpoints like servers, routers, printers, and hosts. It records which port is used when traffic sourced from these endpoints enters the switch and then uses that information to directly forward traffic out the correct port.

For example, PC A connected to port 3 with the MAC address 1C-1B-0D-11-11-11 sends traffic to its default gateway (see Figure 4.1). The switch records the MAC address and the associated port number in its MAC table. With this stored information, any future traffic destined for this PC will be directly switched to port 3 without having to bother any other device connected to the switch. This intelligent switching of traffic from one port to another is why it's called a switch.

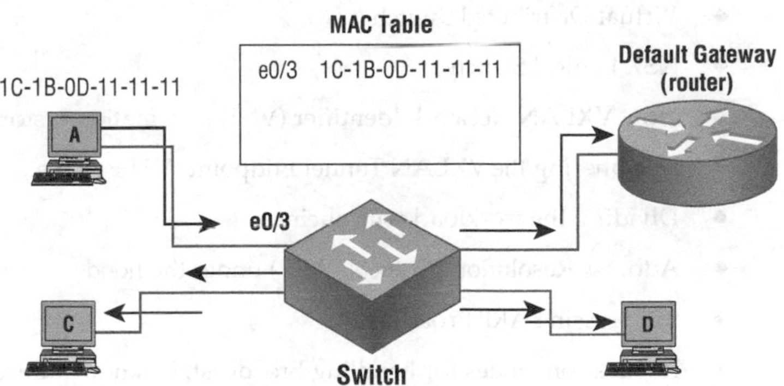

FIGURE 4.1 Switch dynamically learning MAC addresses and ports

Here's a quick overview of switch operations:

1. Initially, the MAC table is empty.
2. PC A on port 3 sends traffic to the default gateway.
3. The switch caches the MAC address of PC A and its source port.
4. Since the switch has not yet learned the default gateway's MAC and port, the frame is flooded out all ports except port 3.
5. When the default gateway responds, its MAC and port will be recorded in the MAC table and all traffic between the two going forward will be directly switched.

In the days before switches (and their predecessors, bridges), we used hubs, which had no intelligence. They simply repeated the traffic out all ports, with the exception of the ingress port, taking up bandwidth and CPU of every connected device. If the switch shown in Figure 4.1 were to be replaced with a hub, there would be no MAC table construct since hubs do not have the ability to store MAC addresses. All traffic would be flooded to every device with every transmission.

However, a switch quickly learns the MAC addresses of the devices along with the ports to reach them. If PC A sent a 20GB .MP4 file to PC D, no other device connected to the switch would have their resources affected.

IN THIS CHAPTER, YOU WILL LEARN ABOUT:

- Traffic shaping
- Port groups
- Network Interface Card (NIC) teaming
- Mitigating Layer 2 attacks
- vSphere Standard Switch (vSS) Standard Switch (vSS)
- Virtual eXtensible LANs (VXLANs)
- Virtual Distributed Switch (vDS)
- NSX Logical Switch
- How VXLAN Network Identifier (VNI) information is stored
- Deciphering the VXLAN Tunnel Endpoint (VTEP) table
- Dividing the workload with slicing
- Address Resolution Protocol (ARP) under the hood
- Suppressing ARP broadcasts
- Replication modes for handling Broadcast, Unknown unicast, and Multicast (BUM) traffic
- Deploying a Logical Switch

vSphere Standard Switch (vSS)

VMware has three types of virtual switches: the vSphere Standard Switch (vSS), the virtual Distributed Switch (vDS), and the Logical Switch. This can be confusing at first, so we will examine each to get a better understanding.

The vSS works much like a physical switch (see Figure 4.2). Virtual machines connected to it can communicate with one another, and it will forward traffic based on learned MAC addresses. What sets this apart from the other two types of VMware virtualized switches is that it functions on a single ESXi host.

FIGURE 4.2
A vSS can only span a single ESXi host.

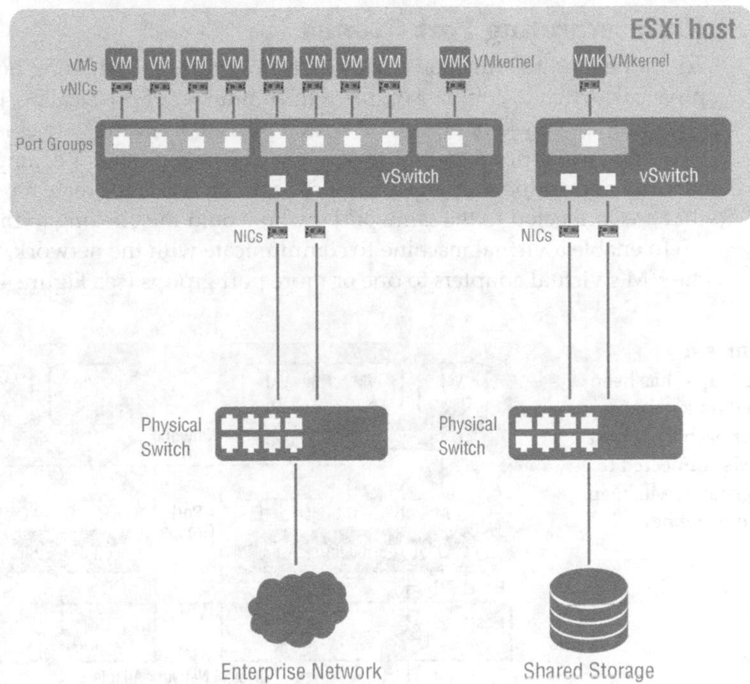

A vSS is automatically created by default when ESXi is installed, and each vSS is managed independently on each ESXi host. Like a physical switch, it can also be optimized with traffic shaping, configurable security features, and NIC teaming.

Traffic Shaping

Traffic shaping helps to avoid congestion by effectively managing available bandwidth. As an administrator, you can configure average rate, peak bandwidth, and burst size for a port group. Any VM belonging to that port group will have its traffic shaped according to the limits you define (see Figure 4.3).

FIGURE 4.3
Traffic shaping is a mechanism for controlling a VM's network bandwidth.

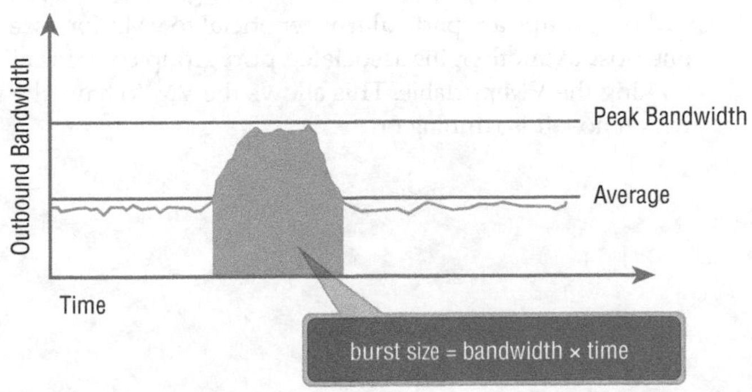

Understanding Port Groups

To understand the function of a port group, begin by imagining ports on a virtual switch. A physical switch in comparison has a fixed number of physical ports; but with a virtual switch, you could have 100 or even 1000 virtual ports. Port groups are essentially templates that allow us to create virtual ports that share a policy. The policy can, for example, enforce rules regarding security and traffic shaping. The most common use is to create a port group for each VLAN. VMs that are connected to the same port group would then belong to the same subnet.

To enable a virtual machine to communicate with the network, you are essentially connecting the VM's virtual adapters to one or more port groups (see Figure 4.4).

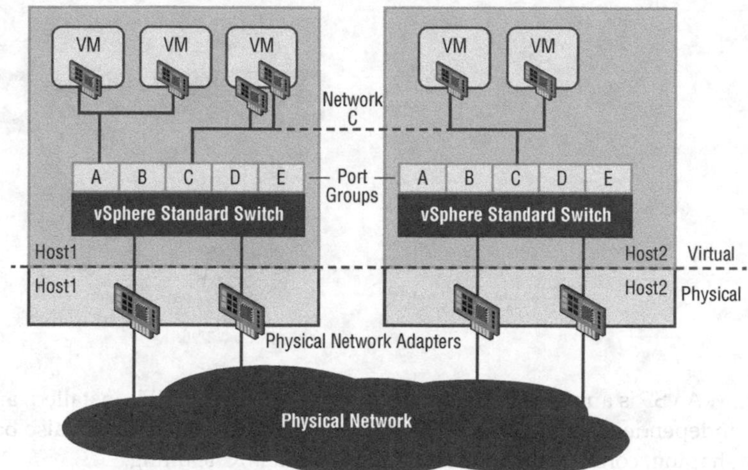

FIGURE 4.4
Port group C has been created on a separate vSS for each ESXi host. All VMs connected to port group C will be in the same subnet.

Each port group is identified by a network label. Whether or not to assign a VLAN ID is optional. You can even assign the same VLAN ID to multiple port groups. For example, let's say you had a set of VMs all on the same subnet, but you wanted the first half of the VMs to use one set of physical adapters to exit the ESXi host in an active/standby configuration, while the second half uses the same physical adapters, but with active and standby reversed. By varying the active/standby status across the two groups, you've improved link aggregation and failover.

Port groups are particularly beneficial to vMotion (see Figure 4.5). When migrating a VM from one host to another, the associated port group contains all the settings for the switch port, making the VM portable. This allows the VM to have the same type of connectivity regardless of which host it is running on.

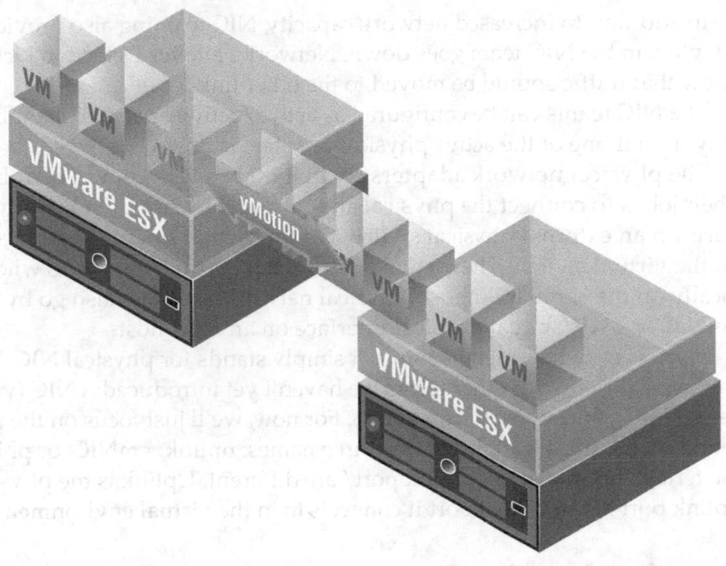

FIGURE 4.5 vMotion not only migrates the virtual machine, but the VM's port group settings such as the IP subnet it belongs to as well.

NIC Teaming

NIC teaming is a feature that allows you to connect a virtual switch to multiple physical network adapters on the ESXi host so that together as a team, they can share the load of traffic between physical and virtual networks (see Figure 4.6). Load balancing increases throughput, and there are several ways to optimize exactly how the load balancing decisions are made and traffic is distributed.

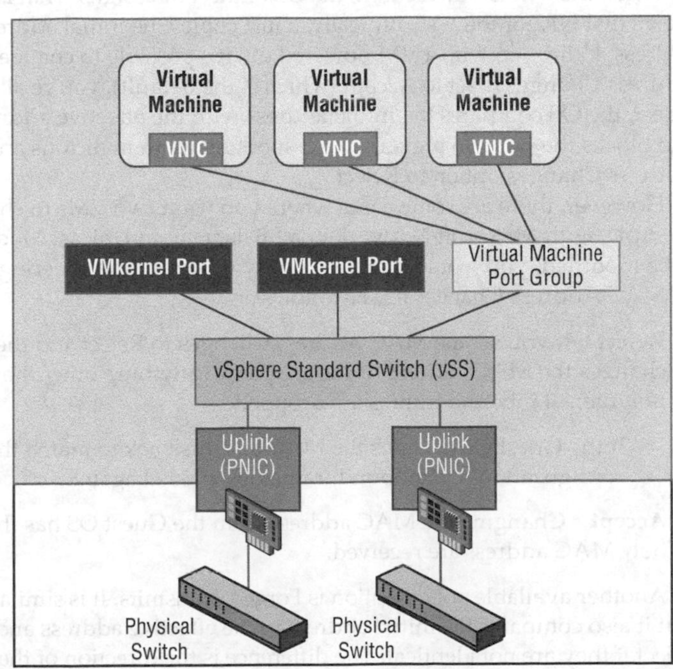

FIGURE 4.6 Connecting the virtual switch to two physical NICs on the ESXi host provides the ability to enable NIC teaming to share the traffic load or provide passive failover.

In addition to increased network capacity, NIC teaming also provides failover. If one of the adapters in the NIC team goes down, Network Failover Detection kicks in to let the ESXi host know that traffic should be moved to the other link.

The NIC teams can be configured as active/active or active/standby. An adapter in standby is only used if one of the active physical adapters is down.

The physical network adapters on an ESXi host are known as uplinks (again, see Figure 4.6). Their job is to connect the physical and virtual networks. On the physical side, they connect to ports on an external physical switch. On the virtual side, they connect to virtual uplink ports on the virtual switch. The virtual switch doesn't use the uplinks when forwarding traffic locally on the same ESXi host. Physical network adapters also go by a couple of other names: vmNIC or pNIC, a real physical interface on an ESXi host.

pNIC is easy to remember since it simply stands for physical NIC. The term vmNIC is often confused at first with other terms we haven't yet introduced: vNIC (virtual NIC), vmkNIC (VM kernel NIC), and vPort (virtual Port). For now, we'll just focus on the physical network adapter found on the ESXi host. It goes by three names: uplink, vmNIC, or pNIC. Also keep in mind that the terms "uplink" and "uplink port" are different. Uplink is the physical network adapter, and uplink port is the virtual port it connects to in the virtual environment.

Ensuring Security

To mitigate Layer 2 attacks such as MAC spoofing and traffic sniffing, several security options are available for the vSphere Standard Switch. One policy option is called MAC Address Changes. When enabled, it allows the guest OS of a virtual machine to define what MAC address it will use for inbound traffic. The initial address of the VM is defined in the `.vmx` configuration file (a VMX file is the primary configuration file for the virtual machine) and acts as the Burned In Address (BIA).

When the VM is powered on, the OS of the VM assigns what is called the *effective address* to the virtual NIC of the VM. Typically, it just copies the initial address and makes it the effective address. However, with a VM powered off, it's possible to change the MAC address. If MAC Address Changes is set to Accept (which is the default), you're allowed to edit it. If it's set to Reject, the OS compares the initial address with the effective address, sees that they are different, and blocks the port. To prevent MAC spoofing (both malicious and otherwise), set the MAC Address Changes option to Reject.

However, there are some cases where you want two VMs to share the same MAC address; for example, with Microsoft Network Load Balancing in Unicast Mode. To allow the MAC address to be modified, you would want the policy to Accept the differing address.

MAC Address Changes are as follows:

Reject If you set the MAC Address Changes to Reject and the guest operating system changes the MAC address of the adapter to anything other than what is in the `.vmx` configuration file, all inbound frames are dropped.

If the Guest OS changes the MAC address back to match the MAC address in the `.vmx` configuration file, inbound frames are passed again.

Accept Changing the MAC address from the Guest OS has the intended effect. Frames to the new MAC address are received.

Another available policy option is Forged Transmits. It is similar to MAC Address Changes in that it also compares the initial address to the effective address and can be configured to Accept or Reject if they are not identical. The difference is the direction of the traffic. The MAC Address Changes policy examines incoming traffic. The Forged Transmits policy examines outgoing traffic.

Forged Transmits are as follows:

Reject Any outbound frames with a source MAC address that is different from the one currently set on the adapter are dropped.

Accept No filtering is performed, and all outbound frames are passed.

A third policy option to combat Layer 2 attacks is Promiscuous Mode. Typically, a virtual network adapter for a guest OS can only receive frames that it's meant to see. This includes unicasts, broadcasts, and multicasts. But say, for instance, that you wanted to monitor traffic between two VMs. The switch will do its job and directly switch traffic only between the two VMs. Your sniffer wouldn't be able to capture that traffic. However, if the guest adapter used by the sniffer is in Promiscuous Mode, it can view all frames passed on the virtual switch, allowing you to monitor traffic between the VMs. Unlike the other two security policies mentioned, Promiscuous Mode is disabled by default.

Promiscuous Mode works as follows:

Reject Placing a guest adapter in Promiscuous Mode has no effect on which frames are received by the adapter.

Accept Placing a guest adapter in Promiscuous Mode causes it to detect all frames passed on the vSphere standard switch that are allowed under the VLAN policy for the port group that the adapter is connected to.

Virtual Distributed Switch (vDS)

Recall that vSphere Standard Switches are configured individually per host and only work within that host. By comparison, a virtual Distributed Switch (vDS) is configured in vCenter and then distributed to each ESXi host (see Figure 4.7). One of the most salient benefits is centralization. The vDS provides a centralized interface that you can use to configure, monitor, and manage switching for your virtual machines across the entire data center instead of requiring you to configure each switch individually.

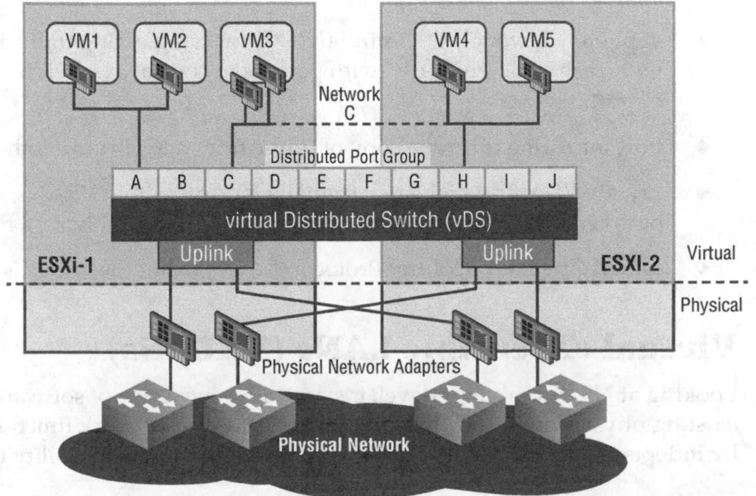

FIGURE 4.7 The vDS is created and managed centrally but spans across multiple hosts.

The key difference between the vSS and the vDS is the architecture. A vSphere Standard Switch Standard Switch contains both the data plane and management plane. You may recall from an earlier chapter that the data plane is responsible for switching traffic to the correct port, whereas the management plane is all about providing instructions for the data plane to carry out. Since both planes are housed together in a vSS, each switch has to be maintained individually.

The architecture of a vDS is different. Each individual switch forwards data via the data plane, but here the management plane is not bundled in. It's centralized, separate from the vDS. This architecture means that instead of having independent switches per host, the vDS abstracts all of the host-level switches into one giant vDS that can potentially span across every ESXi host in the data center.

Centralized configuration also means that it's simpler to maintain and less prone to configuration mistakes. Imagine doing something as simple as adding a port group label to 50 vSphere Standard Switches on 50 ESXi hosts. The chances that you may accidentally misspell the port group label on a few are fairly good, not to mention the time it will take to complete. With a centralized configuration, you define the port group only once and it gets pushed to every host. In addition, centralization also makes troubleshooting easier and less time-consuming.

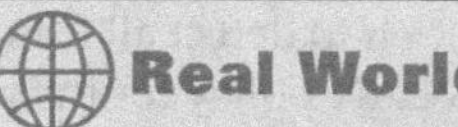

ACQUIRING A VIRTUAL DISTRIBUTED SWITCH

In order to implement a virtual Distributed Switch, you must either purchase an Enterprise Plus vSphere license or purchase NSX-V, which also includes the vDS. Be aware that the ESXi host versions must be equal to or greater than the vDS version, so these may need to be updated.

Simplified management is not the only benefit with vDS. Virtual Distributed Switches also provide features that go beyond the capabilities of a vSphere Standard Switch including:

- Health checks of all uplink connections to detect misconfigurations between the physical switch and the port groups
- vSphere Network I/O Control (NIOC) for categorizing traffic into network resource pools with each pool configured with policies to control bandwidth for the different types of traffic
- Port mirroring to send a copy of traffic from one port to another
- Private VLANs, which are essentially VLANs within VLANs, that can filter traffic between devices on the same subnet, despite not involving a router
- Link Aggregation Control Protocol (LACP) to bundle vmNICs together for load balancing

Virtual eXtensible LANs (VXLANs)

Looking at NSX from a high-level, it's basically an overlay of software that sits on top of your existing physical network (the underlay), abstracting network functions traditionally provided by independently operating devices. This gives enormous flexibility to control and manage what's going on in the overlay, far beyond what was previously possible. The physical network then only needs to provide the plumbing, acting as a simple pipe that physically carries traffic from host to host.

Using the NSX overlay removes a lot of the complexities we see in traditional underlay (physical) environments. Configurations on core data center devices go from hundreds of pages down to 20 or less in many cases.

It also allows us to have, for example, VM1 on ESXi host 1 to be on the same segment, same subnet as VM5 on ESXi host 2. If all your hosts were interconnected with physical *switches*, the extension of a single subnet across hosts is easy to imagine since switches allow you to extend a subnet. But what if a host had to send traffic through a physical *router* to reach another host? (See Figure 4.8.)

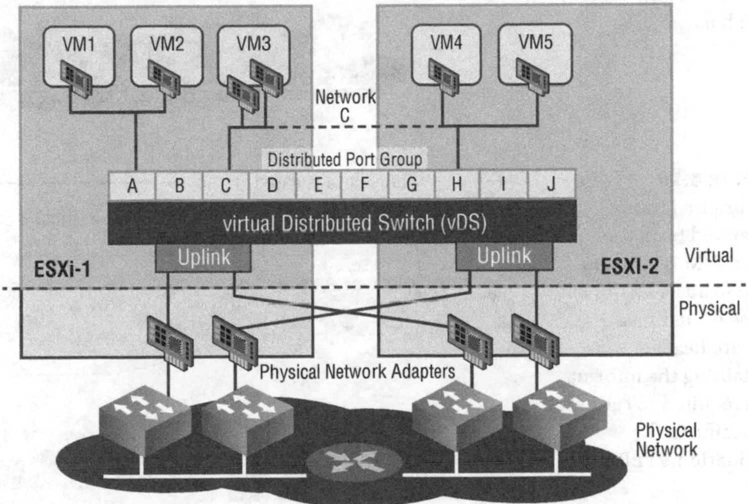

FIGURE 4.8
Traffic from ESXi-1 to ESXi-2 in this topology must now traverse a Layer 3 boundary: a router.

Switches can extend a network segment, but routers terminate segments. Routers create Layer 2 boundaries. Therefore, every interface on a router belongs to a different subnet/segment. For example, you could not have the IP 10.1.1.1 /24 configured on one interface and 10.1.1.2 /24 on another interface of the same router. A router's job is to connect different segments (different subnets) and to determine the best path to reach remote segments.

NSX doesn't care if the physical network is made up of routers or switches interconnecting the ESXi hosts. Instead, the way host-to-host connectivity works is through tunneling. Recall the subway analogy from Chapter 2. The physical network is treated like a subway that NSX uses to get from building to building (host to host). Each ESXi host has a subway stop, which is simply a tunnel endpoint. These are referred to as a Virtual Tunnel Endpoints (VTEPs). See Figure 4.9.

Tunneling is simply taking the traffic we want to send, breaking it into pieces, and encapsulating it inside an Ethernet frame by adding an additional header containing the "subway stop" information. Once the traffic is received at the destination tunnel endpoint, the header is stripped off and the packet decapsulated. What's left is the original frame that was sent from the source. The VXLAN header adds an additional 50 bytes of overhead to the Ethernet frame (see Figure 4.10). The default Maximum Transmission Unit (MTU) size for an Ethernet header is 1500 bytes. To accommodate the larger frames used for VXLAN traffic, the MTU size should be configured to support 1600 bytes at a minimum.

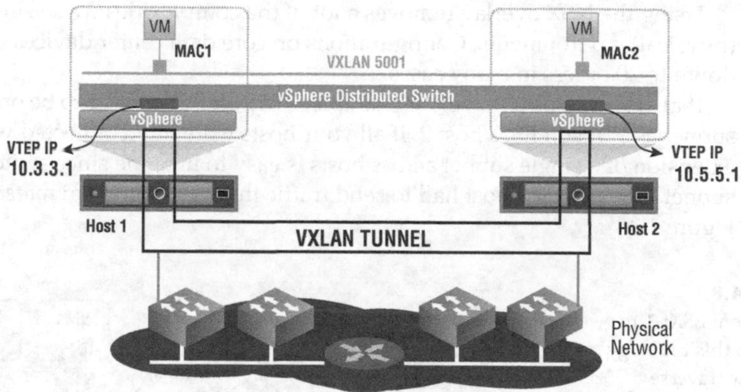

FIGURE 4.9 Two VMs on the same subnet but located on different hosts communicate directly regardless of the complexity of the underlying physical network by tunneling to the VTEP of the remote ESXi host.

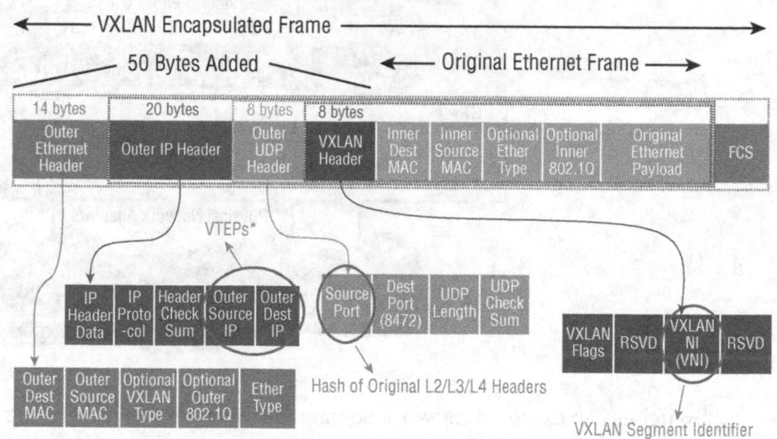

FIGURE 4.10 The original frame generated from the source VM is encapsulated inside a VXLAN frame by adding a 50-byte header containing the information required to tunnel the traffic to the destination VTEP.

Jumbo frames are simply Ethernet frames that carry more than a 1500-byte payload. When using jumbo frames on the virtual side, the underlay also needs to account for this. For this reason, it is recommended to use an MTU 9214 or 9216 byte size, depending on vendor support for your underlying physical devices. Also be aware that some devices require a reboot for the new MTU size to take effect (Cisco switches, Palo Alto firewalls, etc.). Therefore, some planning is required.

Each network physical adapter on an ESXi host gets a VTEP assigned to it. It is the VTEP that is responsible for both encapsulating traffic as it exits an ESXi host and for decapsulating traffic that is received. The VTEP is a special VM kernel interface that has its own IP address (see Figure 4.11).

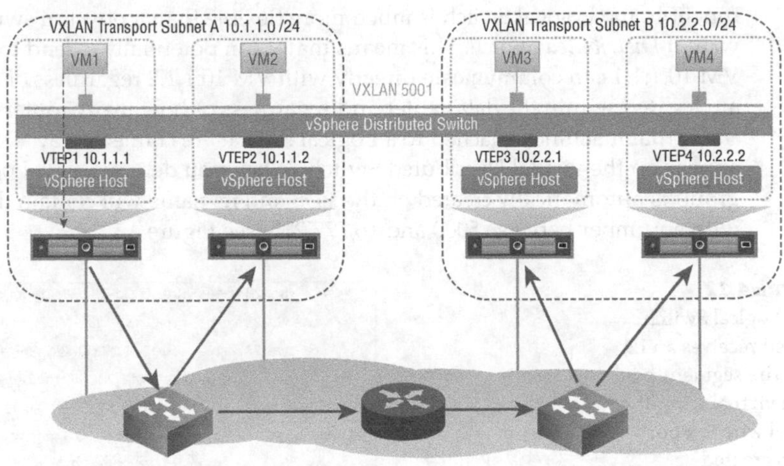

FIGURE 4.11 Using the analogy of a subway stop, for VM1 to send traffic to VM3, the traffic is tunneled to stop 10.2.2.1, the IP of the VTEP on the third ESXi host.

The host has a table indicating which VTEP address (which "subway stop") should be used when sending traffic to a remote VM. That IP information is included in the VXLAN header. VXLAN traffic is identified with UDP port 8472 for any NSX installation starting with version 6.2.3.

If you are familiar with VLAN tagging, the idea is very similar. VLAN tagging is another example of encapsulation. Its job is to encapsulate frames and add a VLAN ID so that when a remote switch receives a tagged frame, it knows to send the frame out ports that belong to the same VLAN. Once the destination VLAN has been determined, the packet is decapsulated, discarding the header, and the destination device receives the unaltered frame sent by the source.

VXLAN is an encapsulation technique that was originally developed by VMware, Cisco, and Arista and was eventually documented in RFC 7348 to standardize an overlay encapsulation protocol. It allows you to extend a Layer 2 domain through Layer 3 boundaries (routers).

Employing Logical Switches

With NSX, you can spin up a Layer 2 network just as easily as a virtual machine. Because the physical network infrastructure is decoupled from the logical VXLAN overlay network, the endpoints connecting to the L2 segment can be anywhere in your data center when using a Logical Switch in NSX

From the perspective of the ESXi host, a Logical Switch is a port group on a vDS. Without a vDS, you can't create a Logical Switch. The term itself can be confusing, especially if you are trying to contrast it with a physical switch. A physical switch can carry many VLANs. The traffic from each VLAN is a different subnet. A Logical Switch instead is more like a single subnet (a single VLAN.) It makes more sense that a Logical Switch would only represent a single VLAN rather than attempting to emulate a single physical switch supporting thousands of VLANs because it is virtual. In the physical world, you wouldn't necessarily purchase a dedicated switch for every VLAN. There is often some consolidation to lower cost. Since the Logical Switches are entirely virtual, cost is not a factor, so it's simpler to create one for each workload. In terms of function, the Logical Switch is much more flexible than a physical switch because it lives on a virtual *Distributed* Switch. This means that it can potentially extend to all ESXi hosts. Therefore, VM 10.1.1.1 can communicate directly with VM 10.1.1.2 regardless of where their respective hosts are located within the data center and regardless of how many routers separate them.

Virtual machines attached to a Logical Switch are connected by VXLAN virtual wires. These appear on the virtual Distributed Switch. When you deploy a new Logical Switch in NSX, a port group is automatically created on the vDS and its name will contain the word *virtualwire* along with a number between 5000 and 16,777,215 (see Figure 4.12).

FIGURE 4.12 Each Logical Switch created receives an ID from the segment pool and a virtual wire. The virtual wire is a port group created on the vDS.

These segment IDs are defined in a pool with a range defined. A typical pool might be set with a range from 5000 to 6000. For example: vxw-dvs-311-**virtualwire**-sid-**5001**-app. In the virtual environment, instead of referring to this number as a VLAN ID, it's called a VXLAN Network Identifier (VNI) Network Identifier (VNI). Keep in mind that the Logical Switch is like a single VLAN that only exists in the virtual environment and is labeled with a VNI number. If you have a background in networking, you already are aware that a VLAN is a single subnet. The same idea applies here. Each VNI represents a different subnet.

If the term *Logical Switch* is still a point of confusion, substitute the word "Overlay" for "Logical" here. It is an *Overlay* Switch. It only exists in the NSX overlay and it represents a single L2 segment, but with the added ability to extend across the entire data center. Physical switches not only lack that extensibility, they also must play by the rules of VLANs. For example, in a VLAN header, the VLAN ID field is 12 bits, which gives a maximum of 4096 combinations (see Figure 4.13).

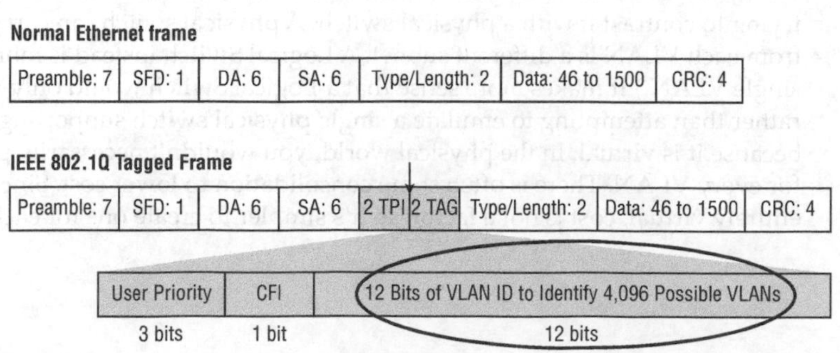

FIGURE 4.13 The VLAN ID field is 12 bits long, which indicates that over 4000 VLAN IDs can be created from the 12-digit combinations of ones and zeros.

The *Overlay Switch* uses VNIs, which gives us over 16 million numbers to choose from, meaning that theoretically, you could have over 16 million subnets. For almost all enterprise networks, they will never even come close to the 4000+ VLAN limitation. However, for service providers with thousands of customers, it's a different story. VLAN IDs and VNIs are close cousins, but VNIs are much more scalable.

Consider another benefit of a Logical Switch over its physical counterparts. If you have 100 physical switches and want to add a new Layer 2 domain, all 100 must be configured individually to support it. With NSX, adding that new Layer 2 domain only requires creating a new Logical Switch, and it only needs to be done once. It is just as simple to delete a Layer 2 domain. As an administrator, if you needed any two VMs in your data center to communicate directly ad hoc, a Logical Switch can be quickly and easily created to provide that connectivity and can, just as quickly and easily, be torn down when the job is complete.

After a Logical Switch is created, all members of the same Transport Zone have access to it. A Transport Zone is simply a collection of VTEPs that can share VNI information. The VTEP knows which VMs are located on each ESXi host and what segments the VMs are attached to. The information is shared with every VTEP in the same Transport Zone (see Figure 4.14).

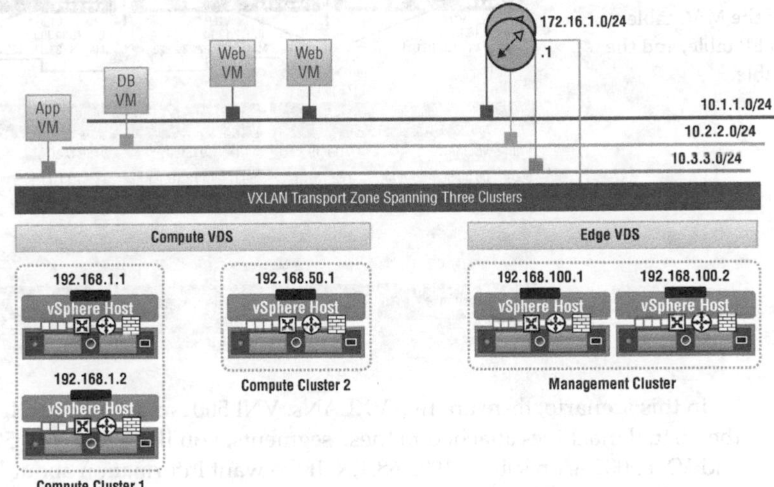

FIGURE 4.14 Each VTEP, indicated here with an IP address starting with 192.168.X.X, can be viewed as a door to an ESXi host.

Transport Zones were originally created to support different overlay encapsulation types. Each encapsulation type would use a different zone. With NSX-V, a decision was made to only use one encapsulation type: VXLAN. Most implementations will use a single transport zone. The exception is when using a Universal Transport Zone that only comes into play with Cross-vCenter, which allows us to tie multiple vCenter Servers together.

Three Tables That Store VNI Information

To communicate at Layer 2, a Layer 2 address (a MAC address) is needed. Not only do your VMs have MAC and IP addresses, but the VTEPs do as well. On a physical switch, an attached server sends its first frame, and the switch records the MAC address, its associated port, and the VLAN it belongs to in its MAC table. This information is maintained in the table for 300 seconds (5 minutes). During that time, if the switch receives any traffic destined for the server's MAC address, it knows exactly which switch port the server is plugged into. Armed with this information, the switch can forward the traffic directly to the server and only the server. MAC tables on physical switches map learned MAC addresses to physical ports. With a Logical Switch, there are no physical ports, so the MAC table in NSX behaves a bit differently.

Collecting VNI Information

In NSX, three tables hold Virtual Network Information: the VTEP table, the MAC table, and the Address Resolution Protocol (ARP) table. The function and behavior of each is easier to understand with an example (see Figure 4.15).

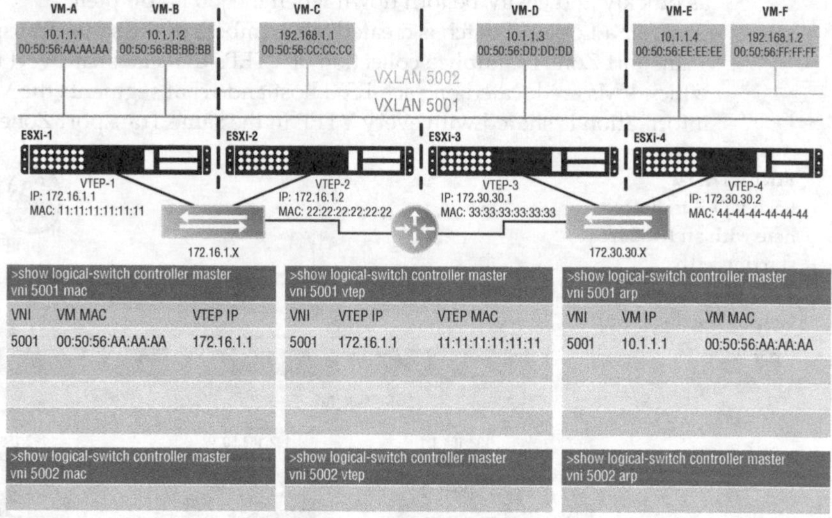

FIGURE 4.15 VM-A is attached to VXLAN 5001. When it is powered on, information about VNI 5001 is then populated in three tables: the MAC table, the VTEP table, and the ARP table.

In this scenario, there are two VXLANs: VNI 5001 and VNI 5002. If you take a closer look at the virtual machines attached to these segments, you'll see that VNI 5001 is on subnet 10.1.1.X and VNI 5002 is on subnet 192.168.1.X. If we want information about VNI 5001, we can use these three CLI commands to look at the MAC, VTEP, and ARP tables:

```
show logical-switch controller master vni 5001 mac
show logical-switch controller master vni 5001 vtep
show logical-switch controller master vni 5001 arp
```

Assuming all the VMs were powered off, the tables would be empty.

We then power on VM-A. VTEP-1 takes note and populates its local MAC table with the MAC address of VM-A (00:50:56:AA:AA:AA) and the VNI segment it is attached to (VNI 5001) along with the VTEP's own IP (172.16.1.1). The VTEP is like a door to the host, and it's aware of all VMs that live behind that door. The mapping here of VM-MAC to VTEP-IP is so that other VMs know which door to go to in order to get to VM-A. We can view the MAC table with the following command:

```
show logical-switch controller master vni 5001 mac
```

Traffic coming from another VM on a different host would need to know the IP of the door (VTEP) to go through to reach VM-A. The answer is 172.16.1.1, the VTEP IP. However, the IP address isn't enough. We would also need to know the Layer 2 (MAC) address of the VTEP. That information isn't stored in the MAC table; it's stored in the VTEP table. An example is shown in the middle column of Figure 4.15.

There, you will see for VNI 5001 the mapping of the VTEP IP to the VTEP MAC address. We can view the VTEP table for VNI 5001 with the following command:

```
show logical-switch controller master vni 5001 vtep
```

In the last column of Figure 4.15, you see the IP address of VM-A and that it is associated with VNI 5001. Just like it was necessary to know the Layer 2 address associated with the VTEP's IP address, the same applies to the IP address of the VM itself. The mapping here is built by Address Resolution Protocol (ARP). We'll get into the details of that process coming up, but for now, just be aware that for a packet to be sent to VM-A, we need to know both its Layer 3 (IP) and Layer 2 (MAC) addresses. The ARP table can be viewed with the following command:

```
show logical-switch controller master vni 5001 arp
```

Centralized MAC Table

The VNI information collected by the VTEP is sent to the NSX Controller cluster. The Controller cluster then shares the information with every VTEP on each ESXi host within the same Transport Zone. Since every VTEP is doing the same, the Controller cluster is able to collect and disperse all of the VNI information for the entire Transport Zone, ultimately meaning that if every VTEP in the data center falls within the same Transport Zone, each has all the information it needs to know exactly where every VM is located and how to get there (see Figure 4.16).

FIGURE 4.16
VTEPs send their local VNI information to the Controller cluster, where it is distributed to the other VTEPs in the same Transport Zone.

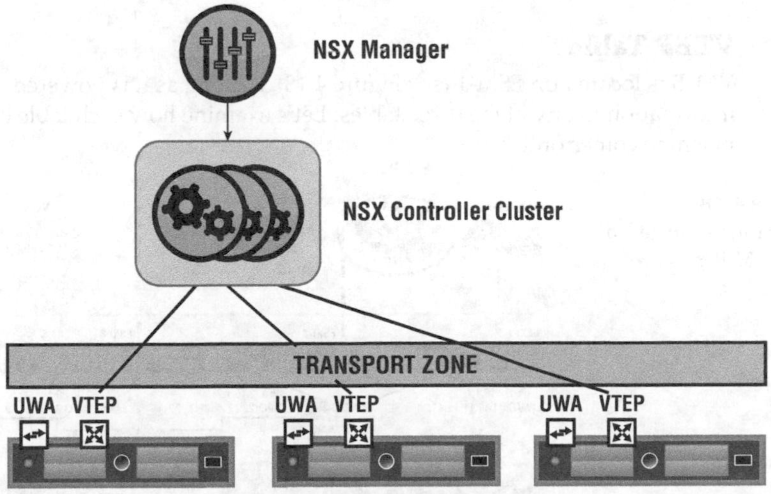

With the tables populated, let's walk through the process again. We want to send a packet to VM-A. We know that VM-A's IP address is 10.1.1.1. Looking at the ARP table (see Figure 4.17), we see that the MAC address associated with 10.1.1.1 is 00:50:56:AA:AA:AA. This MAC address can be found behind one of the VTEPs. The MAC table is checked, and we find that the MAC of

VM-A (00:50:56:AA:AA:AA) is behind VTEP 172.16.1.1. We want to send the packet to the correct VTEP, but all we have is the IP address so far. To find its associated MAC address, we examine the VTEP table. There we find that the MAC address associated with VTEP 172.16.1.1 is 11:11:11:11:11:11.

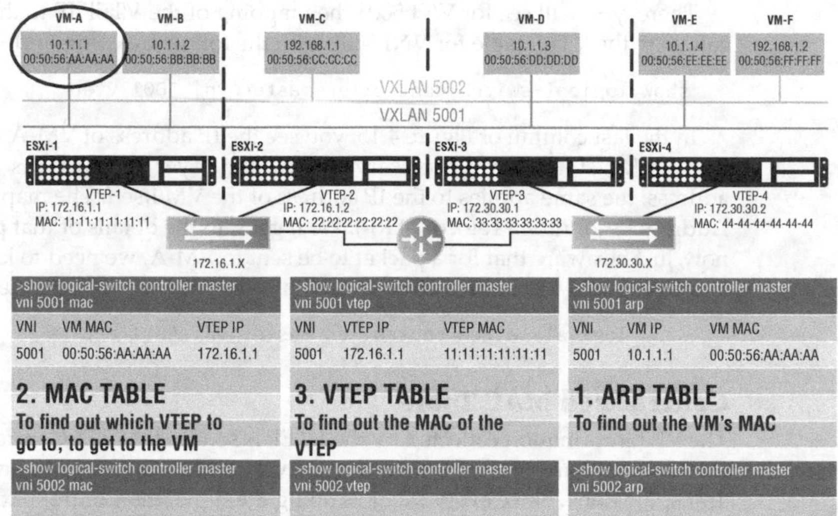

FIGURE 4.17 Walkthrough to find the VNI information needed to send traffic to VM-A

Now that you know the purpose of each table, let's power on another VM and see what changes.

VTEP Table

VM-B is located on ESXi-1 (see Figure 4.18). As long as it is powered down, we have no related information in any of the three tables. Let's examine how each table changes once the virtual machine comes online.

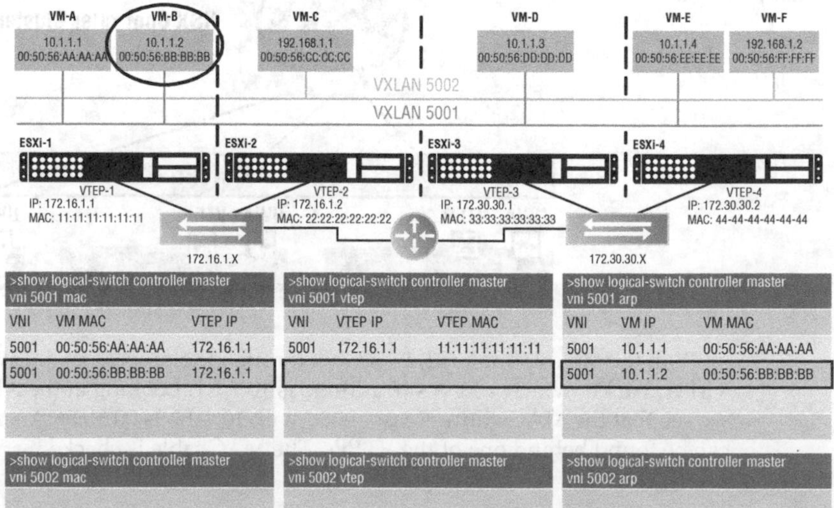

FIGURE 4.18 VNI information added when VM-B is powered up

Looking at the MAC table (first column), we see that the VTEP recorded VM-B's MAC address and entered its own VTEP IP (172.16.1.1).

Looking at the ARP table (third column), we see that the VTEP recorded the IP and MAC of VM-B.

But, why isn't there any new information added for the VTEP table (second column)? The reason is that both VM-A and VM-B sit behind the same door, VTEP-1 (172.16.1.1). This table simply records the IP-to-MAC mapping of the VTEP. Since this mapping (172.16.1.1=11:11:11:11:11) was recorded previously, there's nothing new to add to the table.

Now, let's power on VM-D and check the tables again (see Figure 4.19).

FIGURE 4.19 VNI information added when VM-D is powered up

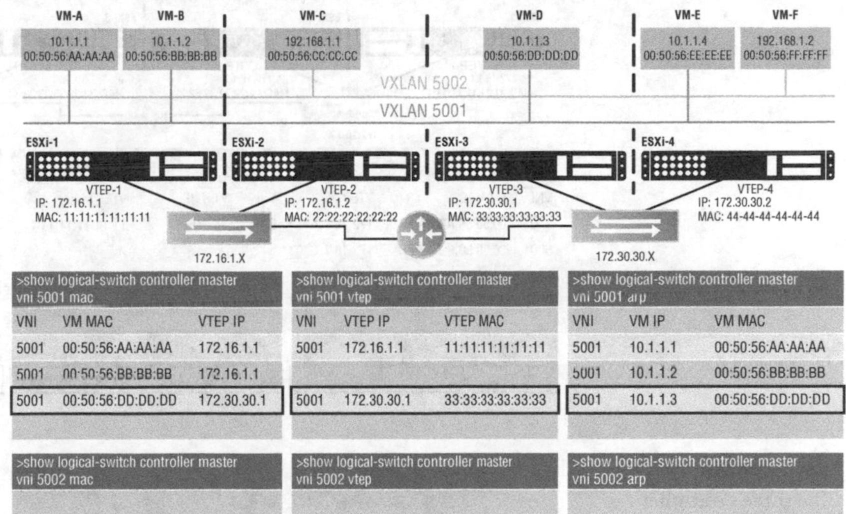

The MAC table (first column) records which VTEP (172.30.30.1) is the door to VM-D (00:50:56:DD:DD:DD).

This time, the VTEP table (second column) has new information. The reason is that VM-D isn't located on ESXi-1 like the previous two VMs. It is on ESXi-3, behind VTEP-3 (172.30.30.1). The previously recorded VTEP entries were for ESXi-1's VTEP-1 (172.16.1.1).

The VTEP table records the associated VTEP-3 MAC address (33:33:33:33:33:33). If VM-A (10.1.1.1) were to communicate with VM-D (10.1.1.3), it's on the same segment/subnet from VM-A's perspective. VTEP-1 must send the traffic through the physical router shown in the middle to reach VTEP-3. Even though we are crossing a Layer 3 boundary, this is the magic of having an overlay. The network as seen from the virtual side is simpler. VM-D is just another VM on the same segment; but in reality, the traffic is being tunneled through the physical network, exiting one tunnel endpoint (VTEP-1) to leave the virtual environment and re-entering the virtual environment on a different host using another tunnel endpoint (VTEP-3).

The ARP table has VM-D's IP-to-MAC mapping.

Now that you have a better understanding of the process, let's power on one more VM and see what changes.

We power on VM-F (see Figure 4.20).

Examine the first column, showing the MAC table. A key thing to note here is that this new information is not stored in the VNI 5001 MAC table, it's stored in the VNI 5002 MAC table. Why not just have one big MAC table like we see in physical switches? It's all about dividing the work and distributing it among the nodes. Remember that the information gathered locally is then sent to the Controller cluster. These three nodes have the same job description, but they divide the work into slices, each taking a slice that corresponds to a different VNI. One slice is all the information gathered for VNI 5001; another slice is the information for VNI 5002. In the example shown in Figure 4.21, Controller 2 is responsible for the tables of VNI 5001, 5004, and 5007. This includes the tables for ARP, MAC, and VTEP.

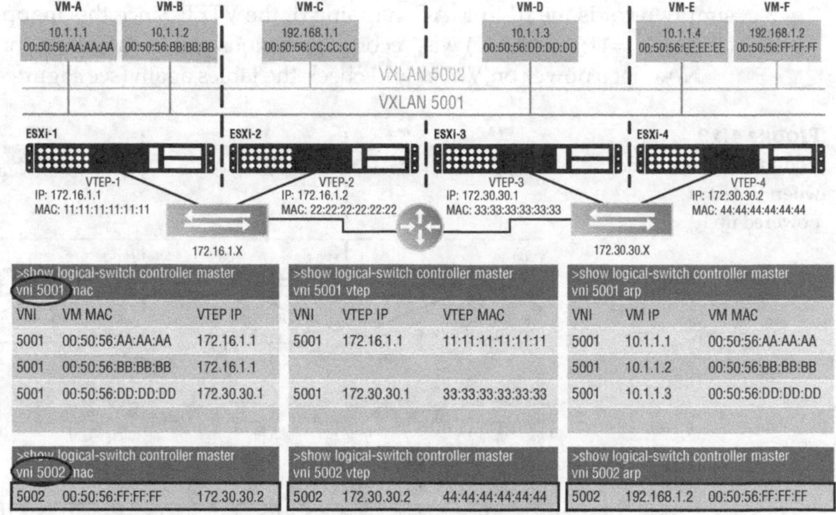

FIGURE 4.20 Powering on VM-F adds VNI information to a new table.

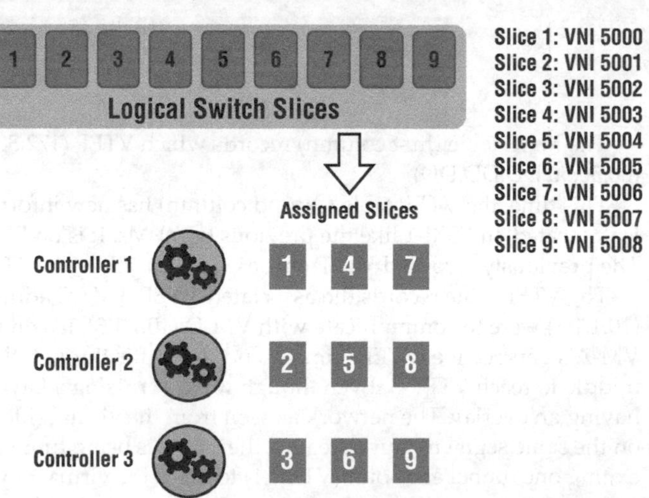

FIGURE 4.21 The three Controller nodes divide the workload of tracking VNI information.

Ultimately, it all gets propagated to every ESXi host, but the task of collecting and distributing the VNI information is made more efficient by defining which controller keeps track of what information. Additionally, if one of the nodes in the Controller cluster were to fail, the slices for the failed node would be reassigned to the remaining nodes.

We Might as Well Talk about ARP Now

Address Resolution Protocol is used to discover the MAC address (Layer 2) of an endpoint when you already know the IP address (Layer 3). That information is then stored in the previously mentioned ARP table. But how does ARP work to make the discovery?

First, let's look at how a packet travels from point A to B in a physical network and see where ARP fits into the mix; then we'll look at how it works within NSX.

When a PC wants to send a packet, there's not a lot of decision-making going on. It simply needs to figure out whether the destination is local or remote (see Figure 4.22).

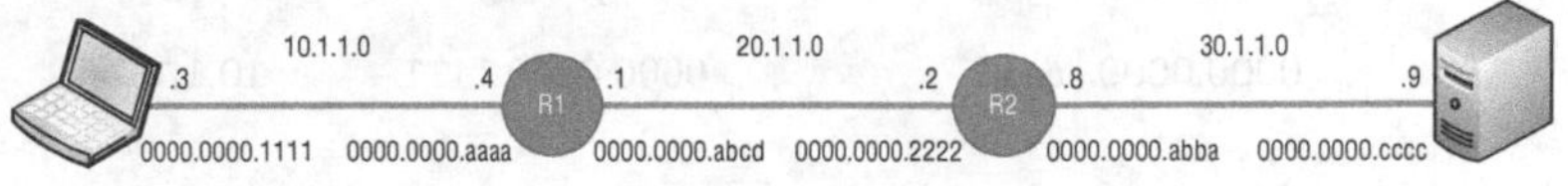

FIGURE 4.22 The PC, 10.1.1.3/24, wants to send packets to the server, 30.1.1.9/24.

This is where the subnet mask comes in. If the PC's IP address is 10.1.1.3 with a mask of /24 (255.255.255.0), the mask indicates a match on the first three octets, the first 24 bits. Any destination that starts with 10.1.1.X is local. Everything else is remote.

For example, from the perspective of PC 10.1.1.3, a server with the address 30.1.1.9 would be remote. Since the destination is remote, the PC needs to forward the packet to its default gateway. *Gateway* is simply an older term for router. Your default "router" is your gateway out of the local subnet. For the PC's traffic to reach the server, it must leave the local subnet. In this example, R1 is the PC's default gateway, 10.1.1.4.

Before your PC sends the frame to the gateway, *all* source and destination fields for both Layer 2 and Layer 3 headers need to be filled in. You can't send a packet with partially filled in headers. For Layer 3, that's easy to determine for the PC. The source IP belongs to the PC itself, 10.1.1.3. The destination IP is the server receiving the data, 30.1.1.9. The source MAC address is immediately known because it also belongs to the PC. The only piece missing is the destination MAC address, but this is *not* the MAC address of the server, your final destination. It is the MAC address to get across the local link. It is the MAC address of your default gateway.

LAYER 2 HEADER		LAYER 3 HEADER	
___________	0000.0000.1111	10.1.1.3	30.1.1.9
dest mac	source mac	source IP	dest IP

Filling In the L2 and L3 Headers

We may have to traverse several data links (local links) to get to the destination. In the Figure 4.22 diagram, we have three links to cross: the link from the PC to R1, the link from R1 to R2, and the final link from R2 to the server.

This is where ARP comes in to help. The PC knows the IP address of its default gateway on the local link but has no clue what MAC address that router is using (see Figure 4.23). To send the packet across the local link, it must also learn the default gateway's MAC address.

It essentially broadcasts the message, "Whoever has the IP address 10.1.1.4, please tell me your MAC address." Being a broadcast, it is picked up by every device on that subnet. However, only the device with that IP, which in this case is R1, responds with a unicast. "Yes, I'm 10.1.1.4 and my MAC address is 0000.0000.aaaa."

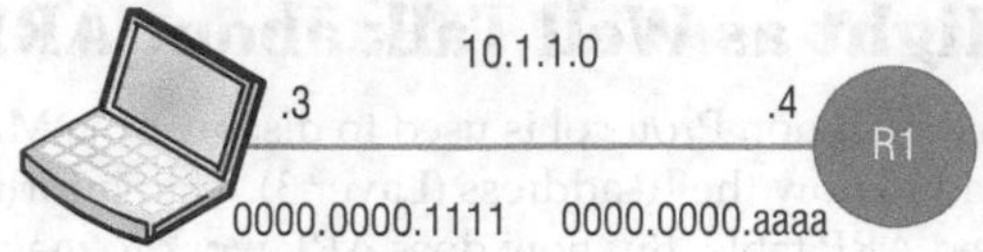

FIGURE 4.23 The PC knows the default gateway IP address 10.1.1.4 through DHCP or manual configuration.

The PC keeps this information in ARP cache for 4 hours (14400 seconds).

Now the final field (the destination MAC) can be filled in and the packet is sent to R1:

LAYER 2 HEADER		LAYER 3 HEADER	
0000.0000.aaaa	0000.0000.1111	10.1.1.3	30.1.1.9
dest mac	source mac	source IP	dest IP

R1 knows to pick it up from the wire because it sees its own MAC address as the destination MAC. After doing a Frame Check Sequence (FCS) calculation to make sure the packet has not been changed or corrupted, the router breaks off the Layer 2 header altogether and sends the remainder up to Layer 3, the network layer:

LAYER 3 HEADER	
10.1.1.3	30.1.1.9
source IP	dest IP

What remains is the Layer 3 header. The router looks at the destination IP to determine if the destination network is a known route in its routing table. In this example, say we have a routing protocol running on both routers, allowing them to learn all the routes, including network 30.1.1.0. Look back to Figure 4.22 to see the end-to-end network.

The routing table on R1 would show that the next hop toward network 30.1.1.0 is 20.1.1.2 (R2). In the example shown in Figure 4.24, assume that there is an entry and that the next hop to get there is R2: 20.1.1.2.

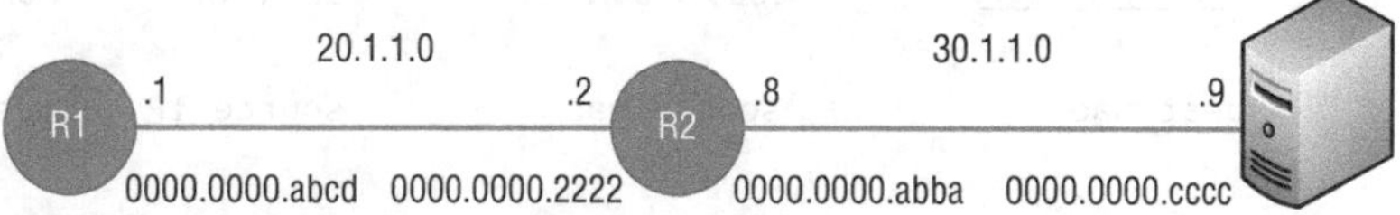

FIGURE 4.24 Once R1 (the PC's default gateway) receives the packet, it checks its routing table to see if there is an entry to know how to get to the destination network, 30.1.1.0.

To get across this data link, though, we need to rebuild a new Layer 2 header with the source being R1's MAC address and the destination being R2's MAC address. The Layer 3 header remains unchanged, with the PC as the source and the server as the destination.

LAYER 2 HEADER		LAYER 3 HEADER	
______________	0000.0000.abcd	10.1.1.3	30.1.1.9
dest mac	source mac	source IP	dest IP

We have the same issue as before. R1 knows that the next hop IP address is 20.1.1.2, but it has no idea what R2's associated MAC address is. So again, it ARPs. "Whoever has the IP address 20.1.1.2, please tell me your MAC address." R2 responds with, "Yes, I'm 20.1.1.2 and my MAC address is 0000.0000.2222."

R1 fills out the remaining field (destination MAC) in the Layer 2 header, which allows it to cross the local link:

LAYER 2 HEADER		LAYER 3 HEADER	
0000.0000.2222	0000.0000.abcd	10.1.1.3	30.1.1.9
dest mac	source mac	source IP	dest IP

R2 receives the frame and picks it up from the wire since it sees its own MAC address as the destination at Layer 2.

The same process is repeated for the final link to the server. R2 checks its routing table to see if it can reach network 30.1.1.0 and finds that it is directly connected. It then goes through the same ARP process as in previous steps to determine the MAC address of the server, 30.1.1.9 (see Figure 4.25).

FIGURE 4.25 The destination network, 30.1.1.0, is directly attached.

The Layer 2 header is stripped off, the routing table is checked to see if it has a route to 30.1.1.0, and then seeing that 30.1.1.0 is directly connected, R2 rebuilds a new Layer 2 header with the server's MAC address, 0000.0000.cccc, as the destination and R2's MAC address, 0000.0000.abba, as the source.

The server receives the frame and sends the data all the way up the stack to Layer 7.

That's how it works in the physical networking world. Now let's see how NSX improves on the idea.

Switch Security Module

ARP broadcast traffic can consume a lot of resources. It's not only bandwidth; CPU resources are consumed when sending requests and also when recording the information received. To lessen the impact, NSX Logical Switches can suppress ARP flooding between VMs that are connected to the same Logical Switch. This feature can be disabled per Logical Switch. If you wanted VNI 5001 to have ARP suppression functionality and 5002 to not have it, as an administrator, that option is provided by the Switch Security module of the Logical Switch. Although it can be disabled, the ability to suppress ARP broadcasts is a key feature in NSX that helps to scale in large domains.

Using a previous topology, let's say that VM-A (10.1.1.1) needs to send traffic to VM-E (10.1.1.4). They both are connected to the same Logical Switch: VNI 5001. Examining the diagram in Figure 4.26, you'll see that they are both on VXLAN 5001, subnet 10.1.1.X, the same local link.

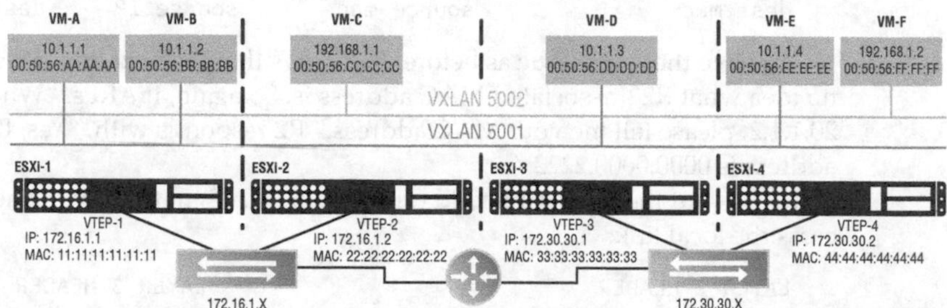

FIGURE 4.26 VM-A needs to send packets to VM-E.

VM-A has no idea it's a virtual machine. It behaves the same as a physical PC. From VM-A's perspective if we are assuming it has a subnet mask of 255.255.255.0, it's on the 10.1.1.X network. It is attempting to send traffic to 10.1.1.4 and by applying the mask, it sees that there's a match. Both the source and destination are on the same 10.1.1.X network. Although it knows the destination IP of VM-E, 10.1.1.4, it has no clue what VM-E's MAC address is, so it sends an ARP request as a broadcast.

The Switch Security module of the Logical Switch intercepts the broadcast and checks to see if it has cached the requested ARP information. If it already has an ARP entry for the destination, it immediately sends that information to VM-A as a unicast and the broadcast is suppressed, not taking up bandwidth or CPU of any other VM. If the ARP information for the target is not found, the Logical Switch sends a direct ARP query to the Controller cluster. If the Controller cluster has the VM IP-to-MAC binding, it replies to the Logical Switch with the ARP information, which then forwards that response to VM-A.

Initially, there would be no ARP information stored on the Controller cluster about VM-E. When the Controller cluster doesn't have the ARP entry, the ARP request is rebroadcast by the Logical Switch. At this point, all of the VMs on the 10.1.1.X subnet would receive the ARP request, but only VM-E would respond since the message specifies that it is intended for 10.1.1.4. The response is then noted by the Switch Security module, since one of its jobs is to specifically listen in on all ARP conversations. It's equally nosey when it comes to DHCP conversations. Once the Switch Security module has the ARP mapping for VM-E, it notifies the Controller cluster.

At this point, both the Controller cluster and the Switch Security module have the ARP information for VM-E, but what about VM-A? When the initial ARP request was generated from VM-A, included in that request was VM-A's own information regarding its IP address and its MAC address. This information is passed from the Switch Security module to the Controller cluster as well. This means that the Controller cluster and Switch Security module at this point have all the ARP mapping information needed for both VM-A and VM-E, triggered from a single ARP request generated by VM-A.

Understanding Broadcast, Unknown Unicast, and Multicast

When a physical switch receives a unicast, say to 00-00-0C-11-22-33, it checks its MAC table to see if an entry exists for that MAC address, and if so, it indicates which exiting port it should use to forward the frame. With NSX, instead of an exiting port, it would indicate which VTEP to send it to. However, when a physical switch receives a broadcast, there is no mapped port in the MAC table. Instead, it floods the broadcast out all ports in the same VLAN, except for the port it came in on. Remember that a broadcast is essentially addressed to all nodes in that L2 domain. Multicasts are just a subset of broadcasts and are also flooded.

But what if you have an unknown unicast? Let's say that the traffic is destined for 00-00-11-22-33-44, but there isn't an entry for that MAC address in the table yet. The switch doesn't drop the traffic; it floods it the same as it does with broadcasts and multicasts. When other devices in that L2 domain see the frame cross their wire, they won't pick it up because the destination MAC address isn't theirs. The mail isn't addressed to them, so to speak, and therefore they don't touch it. Only the device with a matching MAC address will pull it from the wire and process the frame.

Layer 2 Flooding

All three of these frame types—Broadcast, Unknown unicast, and Multicast (BUM traffic for short)—are treated the same way by the switch. The traffic is flooded. Flooding is another way to say that the traffic is replicated. When two VMs on different hosts communicate directly, the traffic is exchanged between the two tunnel-endpoint VTEP IP addresses without any need for flooding. But when traffic needs to be sent to all other VMs that are connected to the same Logical Switch, this is BUM traffic. It is still considered BUM traffic and is subject to flooding if the VMs are connected to the same Logical Switch but are found on different ESXi hosts. Any BUM traffic that is originated from a VM on one host needs to be replicated to all remote hosts that are connected to the same Logical Switch.

Replication Modes

How this traffic is replicated depends on what we discussed at the end of Chapter 2, "NSX Architecture and Requirements," regarding replication modes. We pointed out that there are three options: Multicast Mode, Unicast Mode, and Hybrid Mode (see Figure 4.27).

We're bringing it up again since this chapter is all about switching, and the different replication modes affect how the Logical Switch will handle replicating broadcasts, unknown unicasts, and multicasts instead of simply flooding like physical switches do. Now that we've gone into more depth regarding switching behavior, you might want to peek back at those paragraphs covering replication modes in Chapter 2. They should be easier to digest now that you have a broader understanding of how the modes fit in NSX operation.

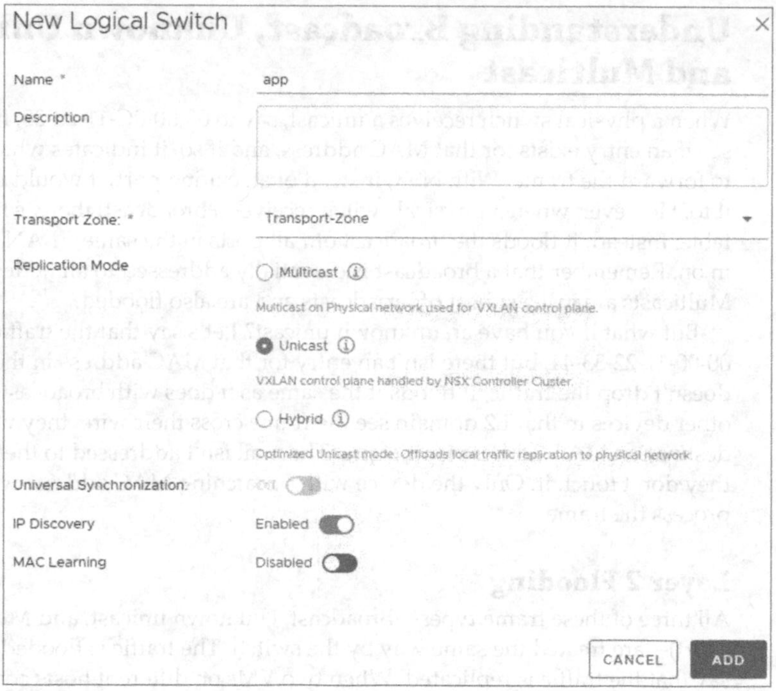

FIGURE 4.27 Selecting a Replication Mode (Multicast, Unicast, Hybrid) when creating a new Logical Switch

Deploying Logical Switches

Earlier in the chapter, we said that Logical Switches are similar to VLANs in the physical environment. You can think of them as Overlay Switches that live in the virtual environment or as switches that only carry one VLAN. Stick with the description that makes the most sense to you. Although Logical Switches can span multiple hosts, they are local to a single vCenter Server NSX deployment. If you want a Logical Switch to span all vCenters in a cross-vCenter deployment, you can create universal Logical Switches. Whether a newly created switch is a Logical Switch or a universal Logical Switch depends on the Transport Zone type you choose when creating it. In the field for Transport Zone, shown in Figure 4.27, when you click Change, you will see the available Transport Zones. Selecting a non-universal Transport Zone will create a regular Logical Switch.

You can also see from Figure 4.27 that in order to create a Logical Switch, you'll need to choose a replication mode and optionally enable IP discovery and MAC learning. By default, IP discovery will minimize traffic caused by ARP flooding when ARP is used to discover the MAC address information between two VMs on the same Logical Switch. MAC learning is an option that creates a table on each virtual NIC to learn what VLAN is associated with what MAC address. This is helpful when working with vMotion. When a virtual machine is moved to a different location, these tables are transported with the VM. The Logical Switch then would issue a Reverse ARP (RARP) for all the entries in the tables.

Creating a Logical Switch

To create a Logical Switch, perform the following steps:

1. Open your vSphere client and go to Home ➤ Networking & Security ➤ Logical Switches.
2. Select the NSX Manager that will be associated with the Logical Switch.

   Remember that the Logical Switch is local to a single vCenter NSX deployment. For a cross-vCenter deployment, create the Logical Switch on the primary NSX Manager.
3. Click the green plus sign: New Logical Switch.
4. Enter a name for the Logical Switch. The description is optional.
5. Select the Transport Zone.

   If you select a universal Transport Zone, you will create a universal Logical Switch.

   You can select a replication mode (Unicast, Multicast, or Hybrid), but by default the Logical Switch will simply inherit whichever replication mode was previously selected when the Transport Zone was configured.
6. To enable ARP suppression, click Enable IP Discovery.

   As mentioned previously, you also have the option here to Enable MAC Learning.

Once deployed, you are ready to connect VMs to the Logical Switch.

The Bottom Line

Address Resolution Protocol Address Resolution Protocol (ARP) is used to discover the MAC address of the next hop along the path.

Master It You are troubleshooting a connectivity issue (see Figure 4.28). In one of your tests, you ping the server on the right from the PC on the left. Using a packet sniffer, you examine the packet received on the server. If everything is working as it should, what source MAC address do you expect to see in the Layer 2 header?

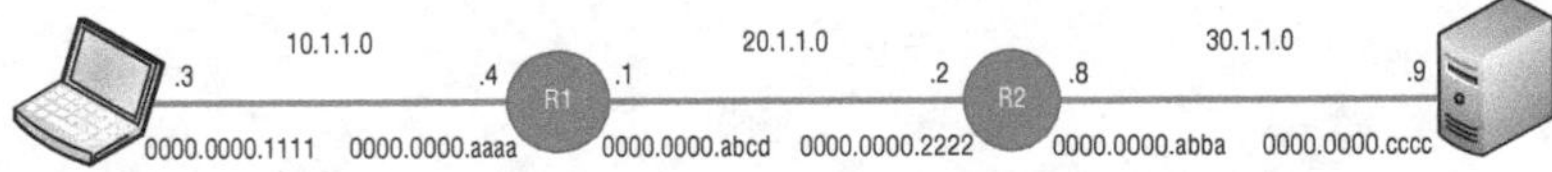

FIGURE 4.28 Troubleshooting connectivity

VTEP Table The Virtual Tunnel Endpoint can be thought of as a door or subway stop on the ESXi host to the VMs behind it. The VTEPs store the information for every VNI and VM that is local to the host. This information is then sent to the Controllers, which are responsible for distributing the information to all of the other ESXi hosts.

Master It You are troubleshooting an issue and need to verify that the mappings are correct. You issue the following command:

```
show logical-switch controller master vni 5001 vtep
```

What do you expect to see?

1. VNI 5001, the VTEP IP, and the VTEP MAC
2. VNI 5001, the VTEP IP, and the VM MAC
3. VNI 5001, the VM IP, and the VM MAC
4. VNI 5001, the VTEP IP, and the VM IP

VXLAN Encapsulation NSX is a virtual overlay that exists on top of your physical network, the underlay. Once implemented, it's possible to greatly simplify your data center L2 design and quickly deploy a VM to attach to any segment regardless of its location within the data center. This is possible due to VXLAN encapsulation, which allows the traffic from the NSX virtual environment to be tunneled through the physical environment. Doing so adds an additional 50 bytes to your Ethernet headers.

Master It In order to accommodate VXLAN encapsulation, what might you need to change in your physical environment?

1. Enable trunking on the physical switches
2. Install hardware VTEPs
3. Change the MTU size
4. Suppress ARP broadcasts

Chapter 5

Marrying VLANs and VXLANs

Up next, we will discuss Layer 2 bridging as a solution to allow virtual machines on a Logical Switch to extend their subnet beyond NSX and into the physical network.

This is commonly used in situations where you wish to have virtual machines (VMs) on the virtual side communicate directly with a firewall on the physical side. Normally, they would be in different subnets, but a Layer 2 Bridge allows them to share the same subnet, simplifying the design and your management of it.

IN THIS CHAPTER, YOU WILL LEARN ABOUT:

- Solving common challenges with a Layer 2 Bridge
- How Layer 2 bridging fits in the NSX Architecture
- Requirements to meet before deploying a Layer 2 Bridge
- The relationship between DLRs and L2 Bridges
- How to deploy a Layer 2 Bridge
- Comparing Layer 2 VPNs as an alternative solution
- Hardware VTEPs as a third solution
- Deploying Hardware VTEPs

Shotgun Wedding: Layer 2 Bridge

The X in VXLANs stands for eXtensible, allowing us to extend a Logical Switch, a Layer 2 domain, *across the entire virtual environment* regardless of any Layer 3 boundaries in the physical environment that must be traversed when traffic is sent from one ESXi host to another. The VXLAN allows members to communicate as if the physical environment were irrelevant or didn't exist by tunneling through the physical network. The same abstraction happens when you drive a car through a tunnel. From your perspective, you navigate as if the mountain weren't there. The tunnel provides a road to cut straight through.

But what if you want a VM connected to a Logical Switch in the virtual space to communicate with a device located *in* the physical network, instead of *through* it? How we get them to communicate depends on whether they belong to different subnets or the same subnet. If they are on two different subnets, we can route through an Edge Services Gateway (ESG). We'll look at routing in an upcoming chapter, but for now we'll continue exploring options to extend Layer 2 domains.

As an example of why you would want the ability to extend a Layer 2 segment into the physical environment, let's consider a common migration scenario. Say you are in the process of moving a workload from the physical environment to the NSX virtual environment. Four of the physical servers are members of VLAN 10 (10.1.1.2, 10.1.1.3, 10.1.1.4, and 10.1.1.5) and have been successfully migrated. They are now VMs attached to VXLAN 5002 on the 10.1.1.x subnet. However, the fifth physical server, 10.1.1.1, can't be moved or modified due to legacy issues.

The challenge is how to link NSX Logical Switch VXLAN 5002 with VLAN 10 in the physical network so that the 10.1.1.x subnet exists in both the virtual and physical environments.

To marry the virtual to the physical, Logical Switch to VLAN, and keep them in the same L2 domain, we need a Layer 2 Bridge. A Layer 2 Bridge allows communication between the Logical Switch and the physical network by going through a VLAN-backed distributed port group.

Having the ability to bridge a Layer 2 domain from logical to physical comes in handy for numerous use cases:

- When you are in the process of migrating a workload from the physical to the virtual and reducing or eliminating downtime is a priority, it's critical that the IP addressing doesn't change.
- When you are dealing with a legacy device, such as a database server, that can't be virtualized.
- You are migrating physical workloads to NSX but there is a security concern that requires that the server stay put within the physical environment where additional controls and security resources are in place.
- Very often, it's a matter of avoiding additional costs. A server you currently have a license for often requires a separate license to be virtualized. Perhaps you plan to move the server into NSX when the cost of the virtualization license can be factored into the budget for the next quarter, but for now, you need a temporary solution to keep things running.

A Layer 2 Bridge is frequently implemented as a solution for another use case: *service integration*. Although NSX can create virtual firewalls, load balancers, routers, and so forth, third-party vendors may offer network devices with services supporting capabilities that go beyond what NSX provides. Connecting the devices to a Layer 2 Bridge makes it possible for these features to be integrated transparently into NSX. Third-party service integration allows you to leverage your current infrastructure investments by incorporating network services from other vendors into NSX, augmenting its capabilities.

Architecture

The Layer 2 Bridge is a component of the NSX Logical Router (LR) Control VM. We will get into the routing functions in a later section, but for now, it's helpful to understand how it fits into the architecture. The LR Control VM (or just Control VM for short) provides a control plane, but not the data plane. This means that it is not responsible for forwarding traffic. The forwarding of traffic is handled in the data plane, in the kernel. The Control VM instead determines how the traffic should be forwarded and distributes those instructions to the kernel of each host. We will see later that it provides the same service for routing by distributing instructions (the routes to reach each destination) to each host. In the case of bridging, it provides the instructions for Logical Switch to VLAN connections.

Although the instructions are distributed, the virtual appliance itself is not. The LR Control *VM* is just that, a *virtual machine*, running on one of the ESXi hosts. Being that a Layer 2 Bridge is a component of a Control VM, it means that the L2 Bridge runs on the host where the Control VM is installed.

A mapping is provided by a Layer 2 Bridge. It will map a single Logical Switch VXLAN to a single VLAN port group. These mappings are distributed to the other hosts so that each is aware that the Logical Switch and the VLAN are the in the same L2 domain. For each pairing, you need to create a separate L2 Bridge. However, this does not mean that you need to configure multiple Control VMs. A single LR Control VM can support multiple L2 Bridges.

Challenges

When you're using a Layer 2 Bridge design, there are a few requirements to keep in mind. For one, devices connected to the L2 Bridge cannot use the Logical Router as their gateway. Another is that bridging is only possible when the VLAN port group and the VXLAN Logical Switch are both on the same vSphere Distributed Switch (vDS), and they both must share the same physical NICs. Another consideration is that a Layer 2 Bridge should only be used for its designed purpose: to extend a logical VXLAN to a physical VLAN. It can't be used to connect two Logical Switches together or connect two different VLANs together or connect different data centers.

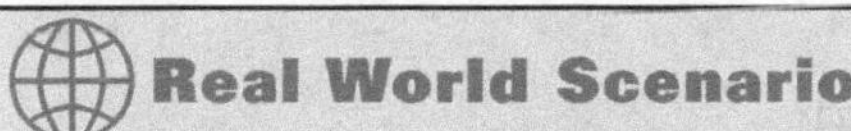

Bridging Logical and Physical to Minimize Costs

Now that your organization has implemented NSX, you have begun migrating workloads from the physical environment into the virtual. You were the architect who recommended NSX, and so far, the new director has been very pleased.

However, when you prepare to migrate the Oracle database, you realize a bit too late that a new license must be purchased for the virtualized version of Oracle. Rather than immediately reporting the bad news to your new boss, you focus on migrating everything else first, leaving the Oracle database where it is, on its physical server.

Adding to the complications, your original design had Oracle communicating with two other physical servers that were on the same subnet. These servers have been migrated and exist now as VMs.

Rather than having to modify your whole design, change IP addresses, and deal with routing to make this work, you implement a software Layer 2 Bridge. A Layer 2 Bridge can connect both sides: the Virtual Switch with its connected VMs and the VLAN port group that Oracle is a member of.

This solution allows every VM connected to the Virtual Switch and every device on the physical VLAN to remain in the same subnet, just like they were in the original physical design, without needing to spend more money to make it work.

Now instead of trying to dodge the director, you're looking forward to reporting how much money you just saved, avoiding the license fee.

Deployment

We'll start by creating an NSX VXLAN-based Logical Switch, allowing us to have a single L2 domain within the virtual environment as an overlay across our physical network infrastructure:

1. Within the vSphere Client, go to Menu ➢ Networking And Security ➢ Logical Switches and click the +Add button (see Figure 5.1).

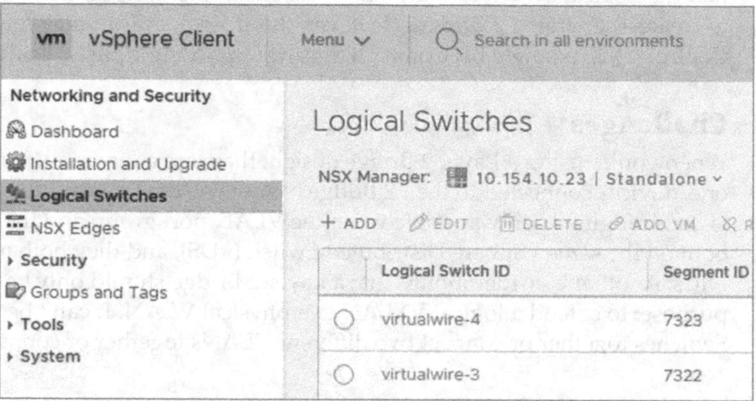

FIGURE 5.1 Adding a Logical Switch

2. For this example, name it **LogicalSwitch**.

   Here you can also select the Transport Zone, Replication Mode, and IP Discovery (see Figure 5.2).

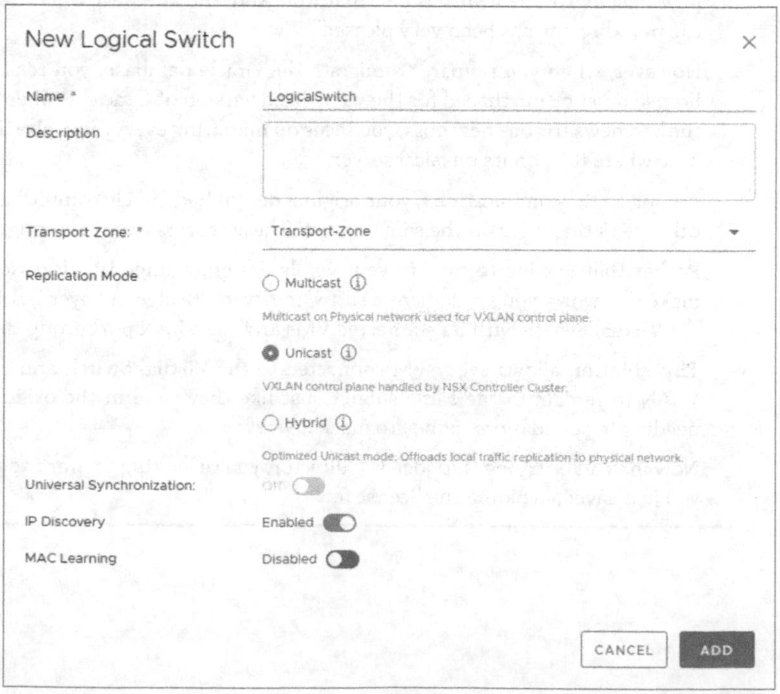

FIGURE 5.2 Configuring a Logical Switch

New Logical Switch

Name * LogicalSwitch

Description

Transport Zone: * Transport-Zone

Replication Mode
- Multicast — Multicast on Physical network used for VXLAN control plane.
- Unicast — VXLAN control plane handled by NSX Controller Cluster.
- Hybrid — Optimized Unicast mode. Offloads local traffic replication to physical network.

Universal Synchronization: Off

IP Discovery: Enabled

MAC Learning: Disabled

CANCEL ADD

Since a Layer 2 Bridge is a function that can be added to a Distributed Logical Router, we need to create that DLR before we can add the Layer 2 Bridge.

3. Within the vSphere Client, go to Menu ➤ NSX Edges (see Figure 5.3).

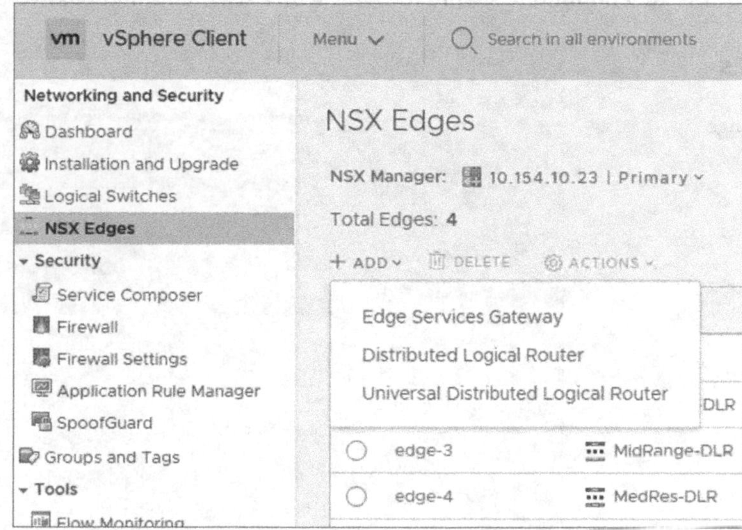

FIGURE 5.3
Adding a DLR

4. Click the + Add button and select Distributed Logical Router.

   The DLR setup wizard appears (see Figure 5.4). Step 1 of the configuration wizard asks for basic details.

FIGURE 5.4
Configuring DLR Basic Details

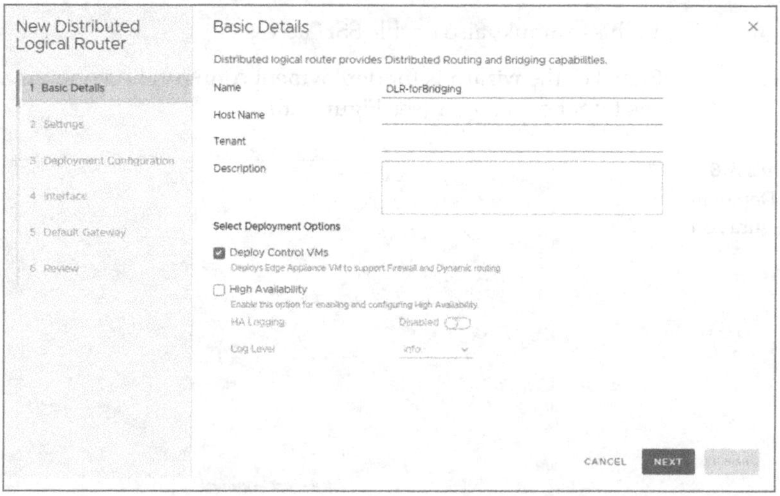

5. Enter DLR-forBridging in the name field and make sure that the Deploy Control VMs option is selected.

   Step 2 of the wizard is for Settings (see Figure 5.5).

6. At a minimum, supply the DLR with a username and password for CLI access.

FIGURE 5.5 Configuring DLR Settings

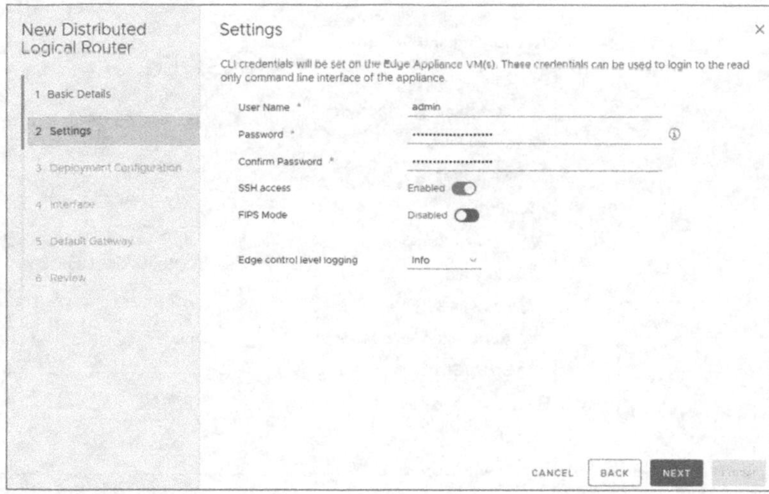

The password you enter must be at least 12 characters, with uppercase and lowercase letters, plus at least one special character. Additionally, no character can consecutively repeat three times. Also, not that it will constrict anyone . . . ever . . . but if you are especially fond of long passwords, the maximum is 255 characters.

7. In this example, also enable SSH access.

   Step 3 of the wizard is for deployment configuration options, adding the Control VM to the target data center (see Figure 5.6).

FIGURE 5.6 DLR Deployment Configuration

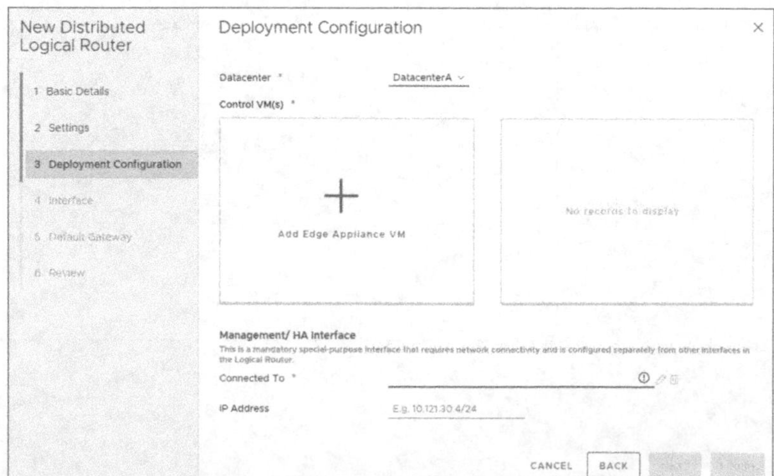

8. Select the data center from the drop-down and click the large + sign to add the Edge Appliance VM.

   A new window appears that allows you to configure the resources for the Control VM (see Figure 5.7). These include selecting which cluster of hosts to deploy it on, the datastore, the host, the folder, and how resource reservations are handled.

FIGURE 5.7 Configuration options for the Edge Appliance VM

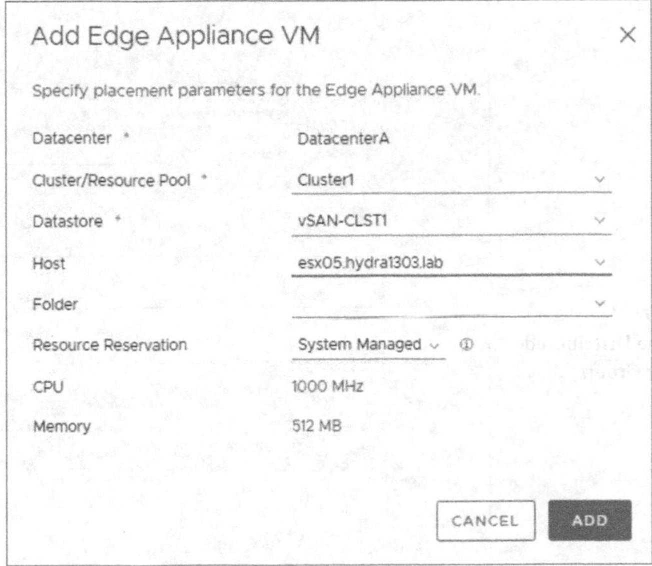

9. For this example, Cluster1 was selected using the vSAN-CLST1 datastore.
10. Also specify the ESXi host on which to deploy the VM (esx05.hydra1303.lab in our example), and keep the Resource Reservation option at its default, letting the system manage the resources.

    If you wish to manually configure CPU and memory settings, simply use the drop-down to choose Custom instead.
11. Click Add, and you will return to the previous window. Here we also need to configure the Management interface (see Figure 5.8).
12. To the right of the Connected To line, click the pencil icon.

    A new window appears (see Figure 5.9). At the top, there are two categories of networks to choose from: Logical Switch and Distributed Virtual Port Group.
13. For this example, select Distributed Virtual Port Group and choose to make it a part of the Host Management-CLST1 port group.
14. Click OK, and you will be taken back to the previous window where you can verify the deployment configuration options you have chosen (see Figure 5.10).

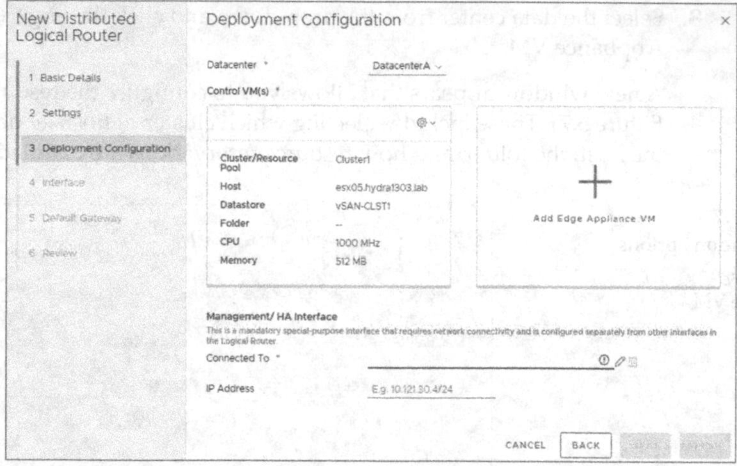

FIGURE 5.8
DLR Management Interface configuration

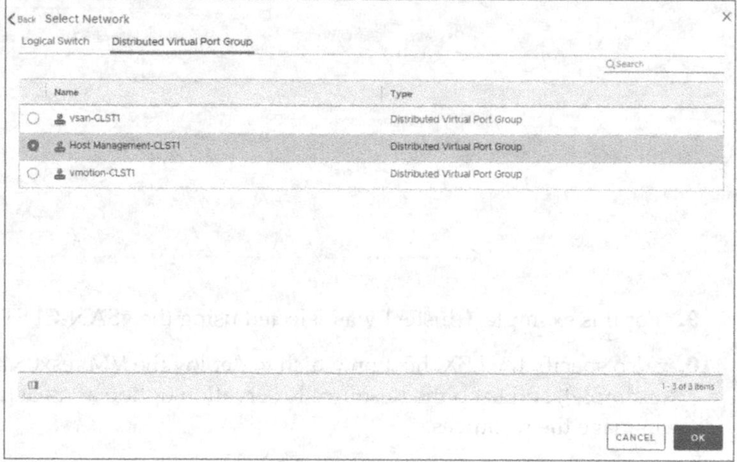

FIGURE 5.9
Selecting the Distributed Virtual Port Group

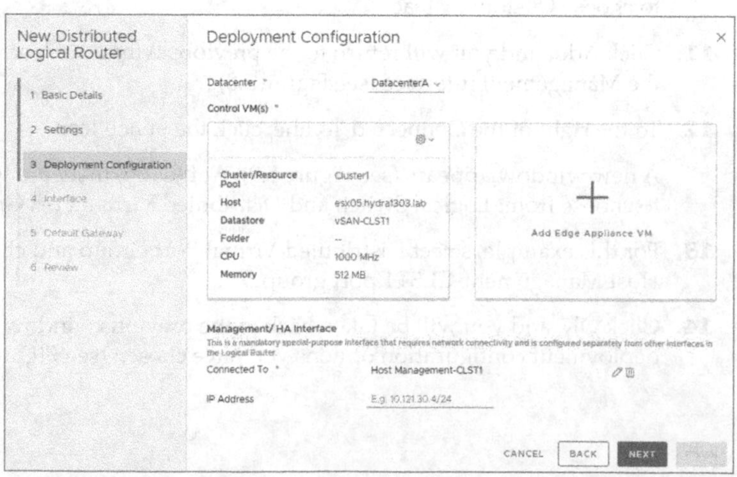

FIGURE 5.10
Verifying the DLR configured options

15. Click Next for steps 4 and 5 of the wizard where you have options to manually configure interfaces and choose a default gateway (see Figure 5.11 and Figure 5.12).

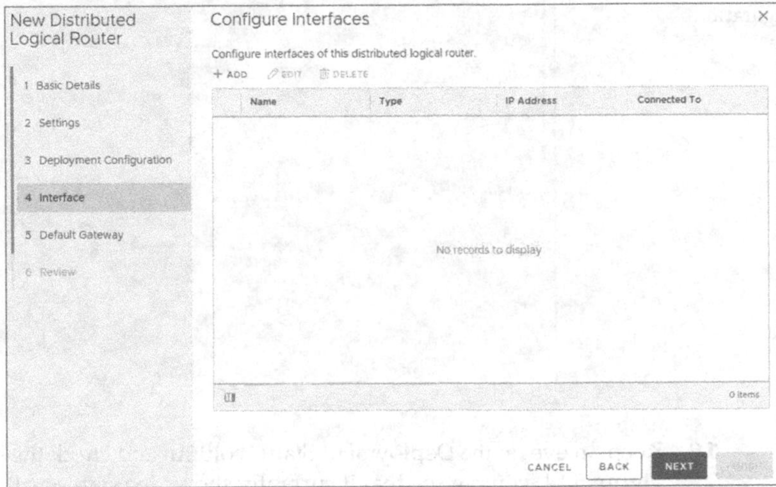

Figure 5.11 DLR option to Configure Interfaces

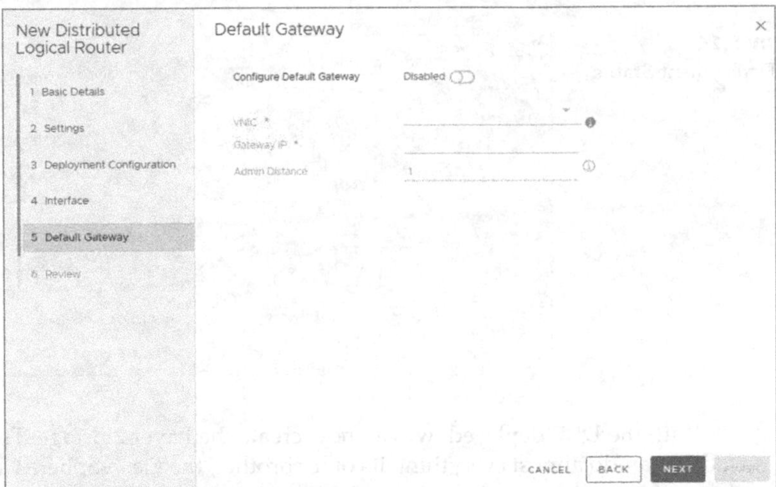

Figure 5.12 DLR option to specify Default Gateway

Since the DLR is only being implemented for its ability to provide Layer 2 Bridging functionality, leave both steps unconfigured.

16. Click Next until you see the final step, which is a Review window.

17. To deploy the DLR, click Finish (see Figure 5.13).

You will find that you are back at the NSX Edges screen.

FIGURE 5.13 DLR review of Deployment Configuration

18. Keep an eye on the Deployment Status column and check the status of your DLR. In Figure 5.14, you can see that it currently shows the status as Busy. Wait until the status changes to Deployed.

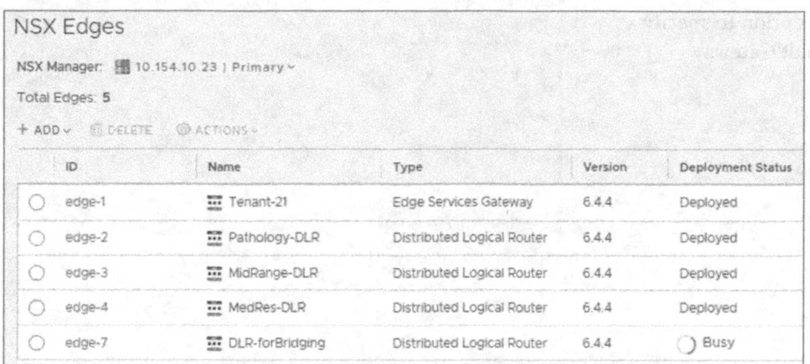

FIGURE 5.14 DLR Deployment Status

With the DLR deployed, we can now create the Layer 2 Bridge. The newer HTML5 vSphere Client can do almost everything its older brother, the Flex vSphere Client, does to manage NSX, but unfortunately creating a Layer 2 Bridge isn't one of them yet.

1. Exit out of the HTML5 client and reconnect to vSphere using the Flex client (see Figure 5.15).

FIGURE 5.15 vSphere Flex Web Client

2. Go to Home ➤ Networking & Security ➤ NSX Edges and double-click the newly created DLR (see Figure 5.16).

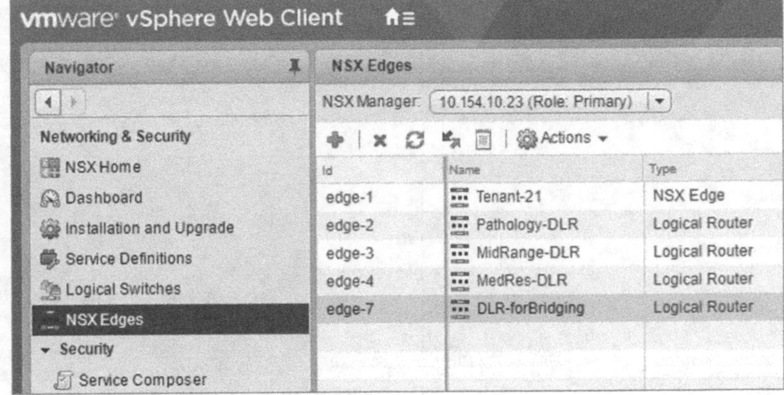

FIGURE 5.16 Selecting the new DLR

3. On the next screen, go to Manage ➤ Bridging and then click the green + sign to add a Bridge (see Figure 5.17).

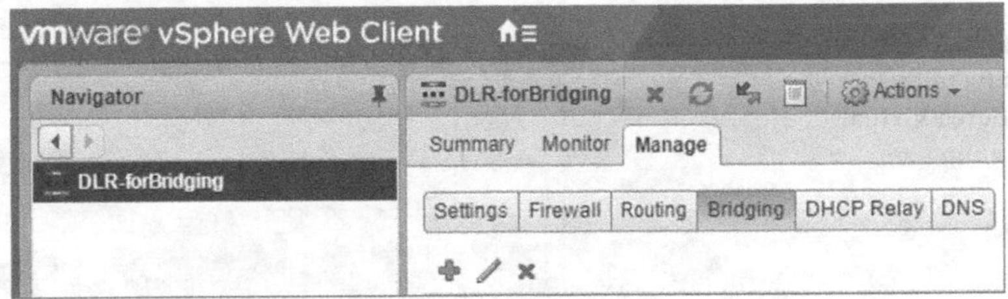

FIGURE 5.17 DLR Manage Bridging

4. Give a name to the bridge, such as **L2Bridge** (see Figure 5.18).

   This is where we finally marry the Logical Switch VXLAN (in the virtual NSX environment) with the VLAN-backed Distributed Virtual Port Group (connected to the physical network).

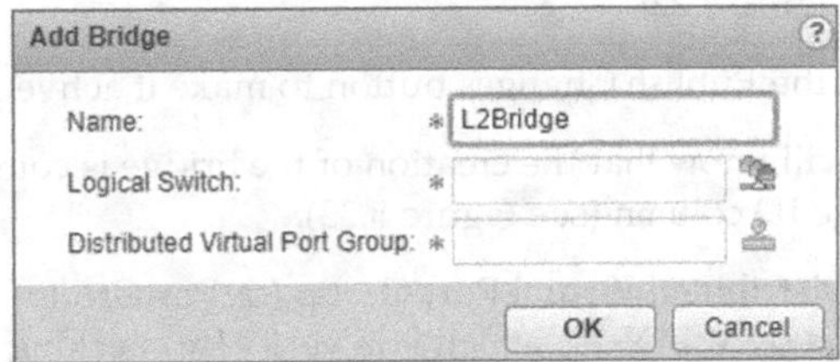

FIGURE 5.18 Naming the Bridge

5. To the right of the Logical Switch text box, click the icon.

6. This brings up a new window where you select the Logical Switch created earlier (see Figure 5.19).

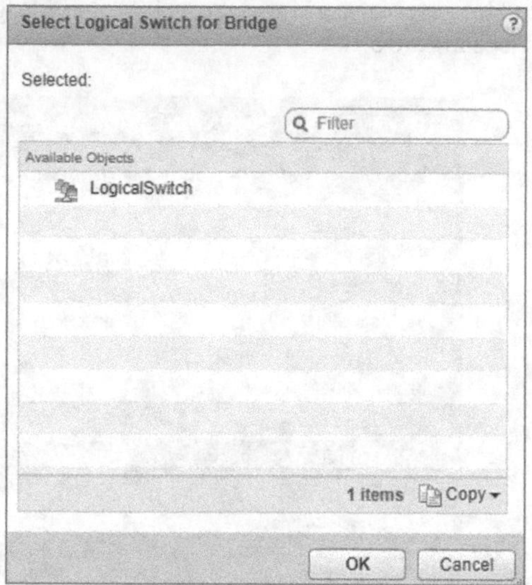

FIGURE 5.19 Selecting the Logical Switch

7. Click OK, and select the Distributed Virtual Port Group by clicking the icon to the right of the text box (see Figure 5.20).

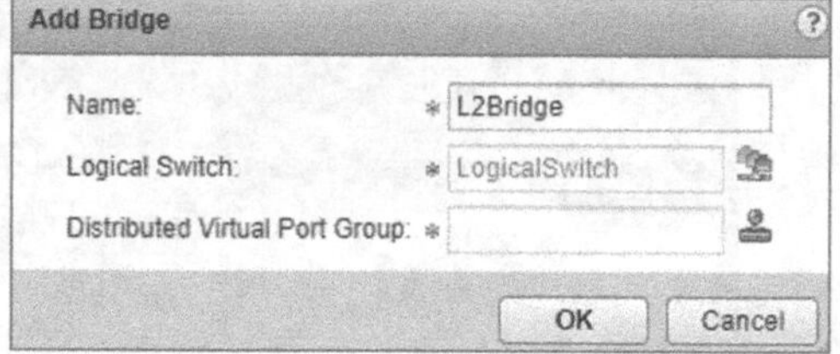

FIGURE 5.20 Browsing to the Distributed Virtual Port Group

   The port group must be on the same vSphere Distributed Switch as the one used for VTEPs.

8. In this example, select the port group named Host Management-CLST1 (see Figure 5.21).
9. Click OK twice. This will take you to a screen where it appears to have created L2Bridge (see Figure 5.22).
10. Click the Publish Changes button to make it active.

    You will know that the creation of the bridge is complete when a number appears in the Bridge ID column (see Figure 5.23).

11. The Distributed Virtual Port Group (dvPortGroup) we chose, Host Management-CLST1, is backed by VLAN 10, which you verify by checking its settings (see Figure 5.24).

The Layer 2 Bridge now allows VMs connected to the VXLAN-backed Logical Switch on the virtual side to directly communicate with servers and VMs that are VLAN-backed using VLAN 10 on the physical side.

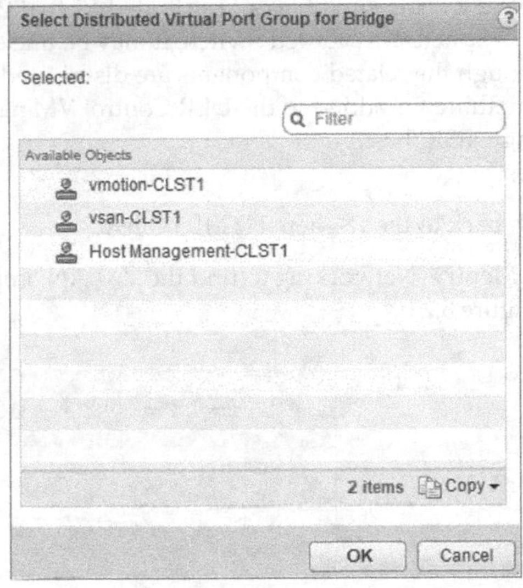

Figure 5.21 Selecting the Distributed Virtual Port Group

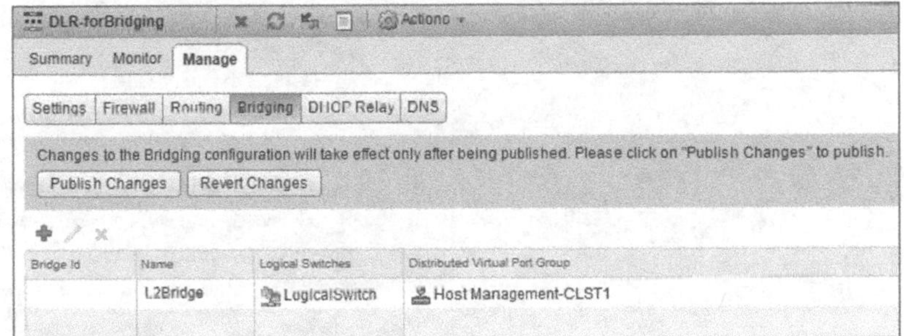

Figure 5.22 Publishing the changes

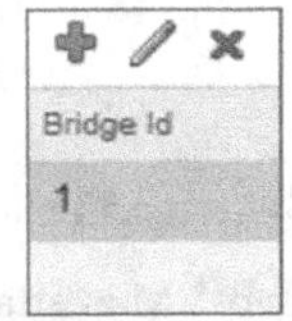

Figure 5.23 Verification that the bridge has been deployed

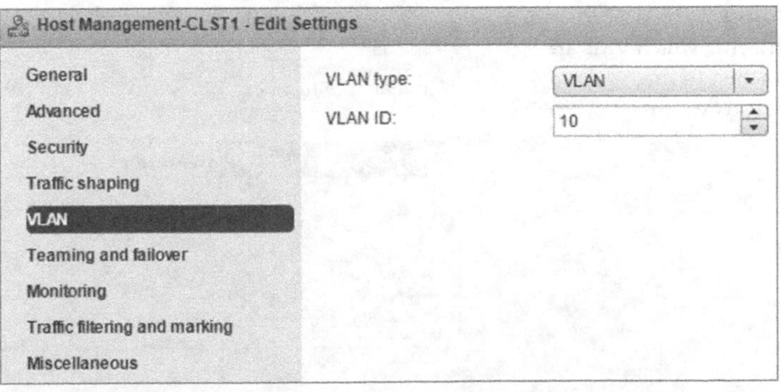

Figure 5.24 Verifying that the dvPortGroup is backed by VLAN 10

Since a Layer 2 Bridge involves a Distributed Virtual Port Group, a Distributed Logical Router, and a vSphere Distributed Switch, it may be unclear as to where the L2 Bridge itself is located. Although the related components are distributed across ESXi hosts, recall that the L2 Bridge is something we added to the DLR Control VM named DLR-forBridging. Being a VM, it lives on a single ESXi host.

Now to test:

1. Switch back to the vSphere HTML5 Client.
2. Go to Menu ➤ Networking to find the VXLAN, LogicalSwitch, we created previously (see Figure 5.25).

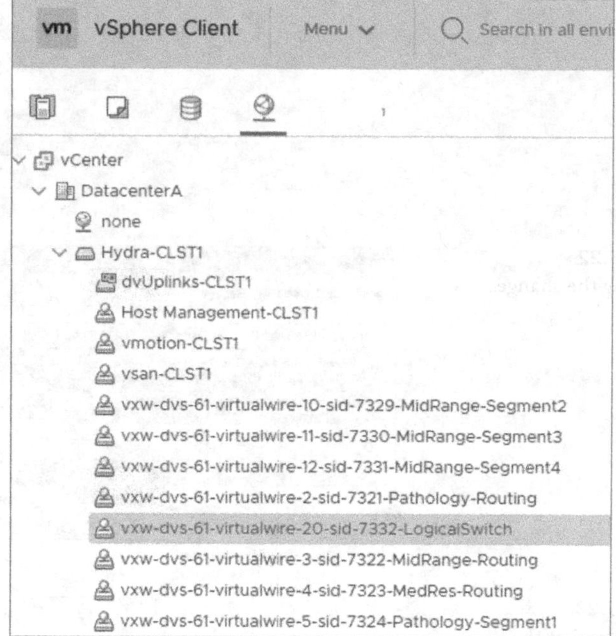

FIGURE 5.25 Selecting the Logical Switch created previously

3. Highlight LogicalSwitch and click the VMs menu to see the attached virtual machines.

   Here we see that App-VM is attached (see Figure 5.26).

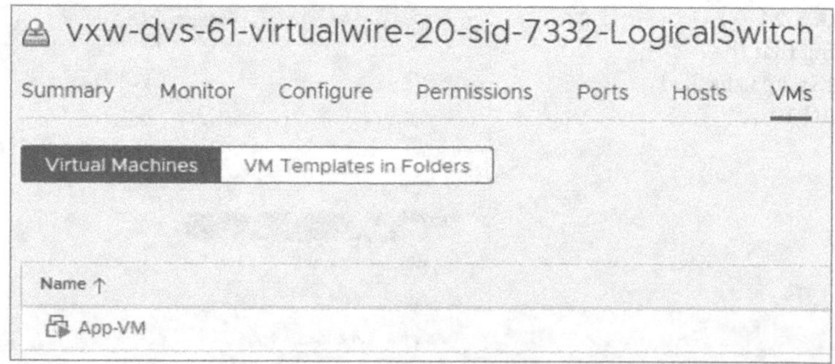

FIGURE 5.26 Verifying which VMs are attached to the Logical Switch

We're going to attempt to ping Server1, 10.1.1.100 on the VLAN 10–backed ExternalConnection network, from App-VM, 10.1.1.5. We know that Server1 is not on LogicalSwitch since App-VM is the only VM currently listed as being attached.

Server1 is on the ExternalConnection network, which is backed by VLAN 10 (see Figure 5.27).

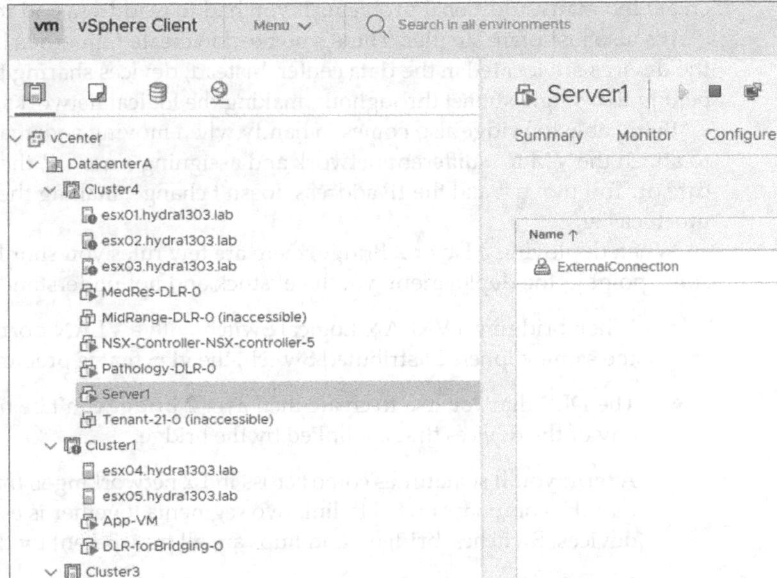

FIGURE 5.27 Confirming that Server1 is not connected to LogicalSwitch, but instead to VLAN 10 on the External-Connection network

4. To verify connectivity, log in to App-VM, 10.1.1.5/24, and ping Server1, 10.1.1.100/24 (see Figure 5.28).

FIGURE 5.28 Verifying that App-VM can ping Server1 via the L2 Bridge

```
centos login: root
Password:
Last login: Wed Oct  2 16:43:35 on tty1
[root@centos ~]#
[root@centos ~]# ping 10.1.1.100
PING 10.1.1.100 (10.1.1.100) 56(84) bytes of data.
64 bytes from 10.1.1.100: icmp_seq=1 ttl=64 time=6.55 ms
64 bytes from 10.1.1.100: icmp_seq=1 ttl=64 time=6.60 ms
64 bytes from 10.1.1.100: icmp_seq=1 ttl=64 time=7.19 ms
64 bytes from 10.1.1.100: icmp_seq=1 ttl=64 time=7.77 ms
64 bytes from 10.1.1.100: icmp_seq=2 ttl=64 time=3.27 ms
64 bytes from 10.1.1.100: icmp_seq=2 ttl=64 time=3.31 ms
64 bytes from 10.1.1.100: icmp_seq=2 ttl=64 time=3.31 ms
64 bytes from 10.1.1.100: icmp_seq=2 ttl=64 time=3.32 ms
```

Both IP addresses belong to the same 10.1.1.x Layer 2 domain. Now that we have the Layer 2 Bridge linking their networks, the ping should be successful.

Under the Hood

As you have seen, an NSX Layer 2 Bridge provides the ability to have a VXLAN-based subnet extended into the physical network with devices belonging to the same subnet using a VLAN-backed port group.

The ability to bridge logical and physical while maintaining the same IP scheme on both sides is both useful and flexible for situations where your IP addresses can't be changed or would create too many additional problems if you had to readdress and route.

It's also just plain simpler. There's no need to create numerous little subnets based on where the devices are located in the data center. Instead, devices sharing the same workloads can belong to a single subnet throughout, making the logical networks, well . . . more logical.

Being able to bridge also comes in handy when moving a virtual machine. Instead of having to attach the VM to a different network and assigning a new IP, the addressing is already taken care of. You move it and the IP address doesn't change, making the management of the VM much easier.

When deploying a Layer 2 Bridge, there are few rules you should be aware of; otherwise, at some point in the deployment, you'll get stuck and not understand why:

- When bridging a VXLAN Logical Switch with a VLAN port group, they both must be on the same vSphere Distributed Switch, the vDS that is prepared with the VXLAN VTEP.
- The DLR that you use to create the Layer 2 Bridge can't be used as the default gateway for any of the devices that are linked by the bridge.

  A term you'll sometimes come across in L2 networking is *transparent bridging*. It means that the component used to link two segments together is essentially invisible to end devices. Switches, bridges, and hubs are all transparent by this definition.

  Routers, on the other hand, are not invisible. Think about a trace route. The IP addresses that are returned list every router the packet traversed as well as the end device. If that same path contained dozens of switches or bridges, you wouldn't know. They're transparent to you.

- The Layer 2 Bridge has a specific purpose. You can only use it to bridge a VXLAN-based Logical Switch with a VLAN-based port group. It can't be used to bridge any other combinations.

Layer 2 VPN

Layer 2 Bridging isn't the only solution to connect segments that share IP space. The same can be accomplished using a proprietary VPN tunnel between Edge Service Gateways (ESGs). One benefit with a standalone Edge is that it doesn't need an NSX license.

A use case for this is cloud bursting. With this design, applications that begin to exhaust compute resources in the data center can burst to additional compute resources from a public cloud when demand spikes.

The drawback of this design is the impact on throughput and the CPU. Throughput is limited to 2 Gbps and there is an increased CPU load due to encapsulation, decapsulation, and encryption.

NSX Native L2 Bridging

As we have discussed, in order to have Layer 2 Bridge functionality, a Distributed Logical Router is required. The DLR itself is a Control VM; however, its job as it relates to bridging is to simply provide the Layer 2 Bridge configuration, the control plane for the Layer 2 Bridge.

The data plane, the Layer 2 Bridge itself, is separate. It is created in the ESXi VMkernel hypervisor from the instructions configured on the DLR VM. Being part of the VMkernel means that the L2 Bridge can take full advantage of line rate 10 Gbps throughput with negligible impact on the CPU. A Layer 2 VPN simply can't compete at the same level, not having the luxury of being embedded in the VMkernel.

Hardware Switches to the Rescue

As we have discussed, built into NSX is the ability to bridge a Logical Switch with a VLAN-backed distributed port group. This is software bridging, linking the two within the kernel of an ESXi host.

In order to prevent loops, only one ESXi host can bridge for a specific Logical Switch/VLAN pair. Because that job is performed by a single host, we need to have the means to continue bridging if the ESXi host fails. High Availability (HA) provides the mechanism for failover to another ESXi host in under 10 seconds.

Although only one host can provide bridging for an LS/VLAN pair, a single DLR can support multiple Layer 2 Bridges. As more L2 Bridges are added for a single host to handle, it can impact on the overall throughput. One solution is to spread the load by creating L2 Bridges for different LS/VLAN pairs on multiple hosts.

Hardware VTEPs

Starting in NSX 6.2, an alternative bridging solution was added: the ability to bridge from a VXLAN Logical Switch to a third-party vendor's hardware switch. The vendor's physical switch has been modified so that it can be used as a VXLAN Tunnel Endpoint (VTEP), creating a direct connection from virtual to physical. Vendors developing physical switches with hardware VTEPs have a special partnership with VMware to provide the solution .

The hardware VTEP enables the overlay to connect VMs on the NSX side with servers on the physical side. In function, this sounds just like the other two solutions we discussed: native NSX Layer 2 Bridge and the Layer 2 VPN.

So, what's the benefit of using hardware VTEPs and why would you buy one of these customized switches when the other two solutions are already included in NSX? Recall earlier that with the Layer 2 Bridge solution, the software bridge for a VXLAN/VLAN pair is essentially pinned to a single ESXi host. If that host fails, within 10 seconds the bridge will failover to another ESXi host. If 10 seconds is unacceptable, this is one case for upgrading to hardware VTEPs.

Other benefits include increased performance with lower latency and scalability. Software bridges take up resources on your hosts. Hardware VTEPs, on the other hand, don't. There's no need to create software bridges or drastically reduce throughput using a VPN when using a hardware VTEP.

Deployment

To bridge a Logical Switch to a physical switch with a hardware VTEP, the steps on the NSX side are straightforward. For the physical switch, you'll need to get those instructions from the vendor you purchased it from.

Before initiating the deployment, it's a good idea to have some information about the physical switch handy, including the name of the switch, the port you will be connecting to, and the VLAN you are ultimately bridging to. You'll need this information to complete the steps for the NSX portion of the setup:

1. Open the vSphere Client.
2. Go to Menu ➤ Networking & Security ➤ Logical Switches.
3. Select the Logical Switch that you want to bridge to the hardware VTEP (see Figure 5.29).

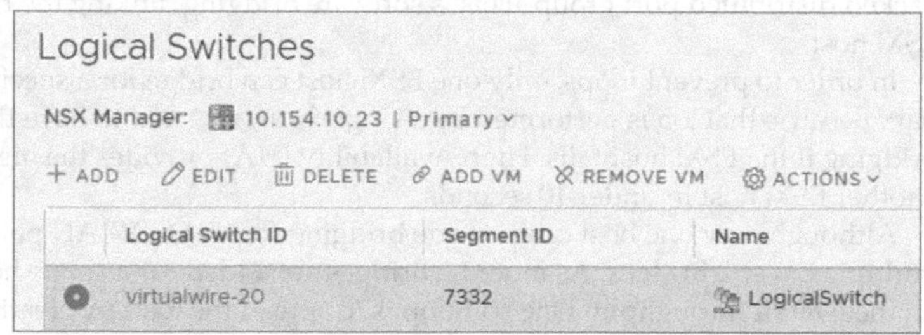

FIGURE 5.29 Selecting the Logical Switch

4. Click the Actions menu.
5. Select Manage Hardware Bindings (see Figure 5.30).

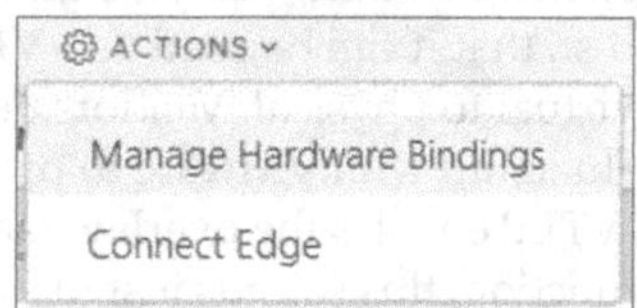

FIGURE 5.30 Choices in the Actions drop-down

6. Enter the information you gathered at the start about the physical switch, including the name, port, and VLAN ID.
7. Click OK, and you're all set on the NSX side.

Under the Hood

The hardware VTEP switches developed by third-party VMware partners use the OVSDB (Open vSwitch Database management protocol), which allows a server to have control over virtual switches. Vendors have partnered with VMware to create OVSDB servers running inside these hardware switches with VTEPs. This allows NSX to communicate with the OVSDB server, creating a direct tunnel to the hardware, hence hardware VTEP. To bring it under NSX's umbrella, the hardware VTEP is managed from NSX using the OVSDB protocol. This allows the control plane of the hardware VTEP to be managed by the NSX Controllers.

The Bottom Line

Creating a Layer 2 Bridge Getting VM 172.16.1.5 on ESXi Host1 to communicate with VM 172.16.1.7 on ESXi Host9 can be easily accomplished in NSX using a VXLAN. The X is for eXtensible. You can use it extend your Layer 2 domain across any of your hosts, regardless of where they are located in your data center. NSX provides the virtual overlay network, and it's easy to have virtual talk to virtual. But we often want to be able to just as easily have virtual talk to physical: VXLAN to VLAN.

Master It You are configuring a Layer 2 Bridge to connect the VMs on VXLAN 5005 to the physical servers on VLAN 20. You're logged in to vSphere and you go to Menu ➤ Networking & Security (see Figure 5.31).

FIGURE 5.31
Network And Security (NSX) menu options

To create a Layer 2 Bridge, what do you click next?

1. Dashboard
2. Installation and Upgrade
3. Logical Switches
4. NSX Edges

Hardware VTEP NSX provides several ways to bridge a VXLAN with a VLAN sharing the same IP subnet. You could create a Layer 2 Bridge (software bridge), use a hardware VTEP, or configure a Layer 2 VPN.

Master It You have been tasked with choosing a solution to bridge a workload on VXLAN 5005 with VLAN 15 on the physical network. Which of the following reasons might you give for implementing a hardware VTEP?

1. Least cost
2. Lowest latency
3. Single vendor solution
4. Services embedded in the VMkernel have a negligible impact

To Bridge or Not to Bridge Virtualization involves abstraction, and abstraction is all about hiding the underlying complexities. Moving workloads into the virtual environment provides options for simplification, including the ability to have single subnets that span the data center vs. lots of smaller individual domains to manage.

Some situations don't allow you to move workloads from the physical network to the virtual overlay in their entirety. When faced with this issue, knowing how to bridge the two can help to solve the problem with minimal effort.

Master It In which of the following situations would bridging *not* be considered?

1. Servers attached to a VLAN need to communicate at Layer 2 with VMs attached to a Logical Switch.
2. You are unable to virtualize an application due to licensing costs.
3. A VLAN port group on vDS-1 needs to communicate at Layer 2 with a VXLAN Logical Switch on vDS-2 in the same data center.
4. A legacy server can't be virtualized.

Chapter 6

Distributed Logical Router

In the previous chapter, we found that in order to create a Layer 2 Bridge, you first need a Distributed Logical Router (DLR). Providing bridging capabilities, however, is more of a side job for the DLR. Its primary purpose is to provide routing. Routers are needed to connect different subnets and to find the best path to remote subnets. Bridges connect different segments that are on the same subnet. For example, if two virtual machines (VMs) in the same data center have the IP addresses of 10.1.1.1 and 172.16.1.1, a router is needed to route from one to the other. But if the VMs have the IP addresses of 10.1.1.1 and 10.1.1.2, that segment is a single VXLAN and we don't need a bridge or a router. Even if these VMs are located on different hosts on opposite ends of the data center, the VXLAN extends the segment. The X is for eXtensible.

Remember that the Layer 2 Bridge was for a third scenario. If VM 10.1.1.1 wants to communicate with physical server 10.1.1.2, they are in the same subnet, but two different environments: virtual and physical. A Layer 2 Bridge provides that solution. Now, we will examine the primary use case for a DLR: routing East-West traffic across the data center.

IN THIS CHAPTER, YOU WILL LEARN ABOUT:

- The role of the LR Control VM deployed with the DLR
- DLR Uplink Logical Interfaces (LIFs) vs. Internal LIFs
- Comparing DLR pMACs and vMACs
- Edge Services Gateway (ESG) and LR Control VM differences in supported routing protocols
- Open Shortest Path First (OSPF) operations and architecture
- BGP routing between and within Autonomous Systems (eBGP versus iBGP)
- Implementing static routes in NSX
- Deploying a DLR
- DLR routing design benefits and limitations

Distributed Logical Router (DLR)

The main job of a Distributed Logical Router is to route. It's in the name. In terms of routing, when we compare a DLR to a physical router, they perform the same job. They both route traffic from one subnet to a different destination subnet, but the DLR has some extra tricks up its sleeve.

The DLR is logical, not physical. It lives in the logical environment, in NSX, whereas a physical router is an integral part of the physical network. However, the most distinguishing functional difference between the two is that a DLR is distributed. The physical router is a centralized device in a single location.

Upon the deployment of a DLR, the distributed routing function is added to the data plane in the ESXi kernel by installing kernel modules called vSphere Installation Bundles (VIBs). The DLR virtual instance within the kernel is distributed to every ESXi host in the same transport zone. Adding this routing function to the data plane allows the forwarding of traffic to different subnets. Because it is distributed, it means that if ESXi host-1 knows how to reach network 172.16.1.0, so does ESXi host-2, 3, 4 . . . all of them. Once the information needed to route packets for a destination is learned, all the hosts will have that same 172.16.1.0 route entry.

Control Plane Smarts

When you deploy a DLR, another component is also installed at the same time. It's not distributed, and it's not in the hypervisor. It's a virtual machine installed on a host. The job of this VM is to provide the control plane of the DLR. This is the Logical Router Control VM. One of its responsibilities is to peer with the NSX Edge via a dynamic routing protocol, such as BGP or OSPF so that it can dynamically learn routes. A static route, on the other hand, requires each route be manually configured per device. Since static routes are unidirectional, this means that if you were only relying on static entries, you would need to enter a static route to send traffic to a remote network and another static route for the return traffic.

A walkthrough of how a route is ultimately learned by every ESXi host would look something like Figure 6.1. A default route, 0.0.0.0/0, is configured on the NSX Edge, which basically says, "If a destination route is not in my routing table, rather than dropping the packets, send them to this next hop." In the example, the next hop would be a router in the external network. A single default route to reach all other external networks is a common configuration. Your home router has a default route, with the next hop being the service provider. If this were not the case, every home router would have to support over 800,000 routes to reach Internet destinations. Instead, it has a single route for everything outside your house (0.0.0.0/0) pointing to the provider. In the Figure 6.1 example, the NSX Edge has a default route, but to get this information to each of the individual hosts, there are a few intermediate steps.

Logical Router Control Virtual Machine

The LR Control VM learns the default route because it is communicating with the NSX Edge via the OSPF dynamic routing protocol, in the Figure 6.1 example.

The LR Control VM provides a control plane that is wholly separate from the data plane DLR functionality in the hypervisor. That separation is more than a matter of location. The LR Control VM isn't allowed to communicate directly with the hypervisors of each host. Anything that needs to be distributed to each host is sent to the NSX Controller cluster. Even the NSX Controller isn't allowed to communicate with the kernel directly. Instead, Controller-to-kernel communication must go through a User World Agent (UWA), which is the Network Control Plane Agent (netcpa) process on the hypervisor. It basically functions as an interface to the hypervisor.

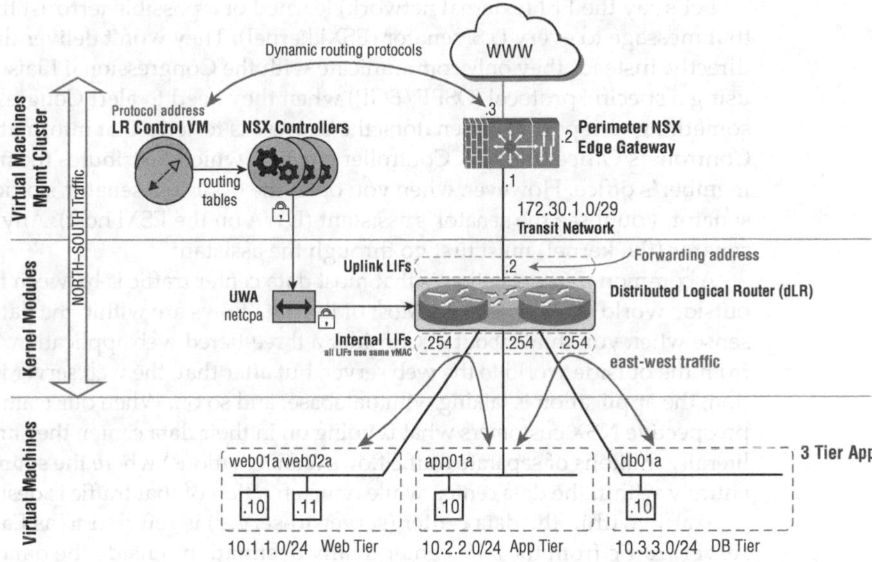

FIGURE 6.1 ESXi host learning routes

If all those intermediaries sound confusing, let's try to make things easier by showing how new routing information gets from an external router to the DLR using an analogy. The path for this route is 1. External network → 2. NSX Edge → 3. LR Control VM → 4. NSX Controller Cluster → 5. UWA → 6. DLR in the kernel (see Figure 6.2).

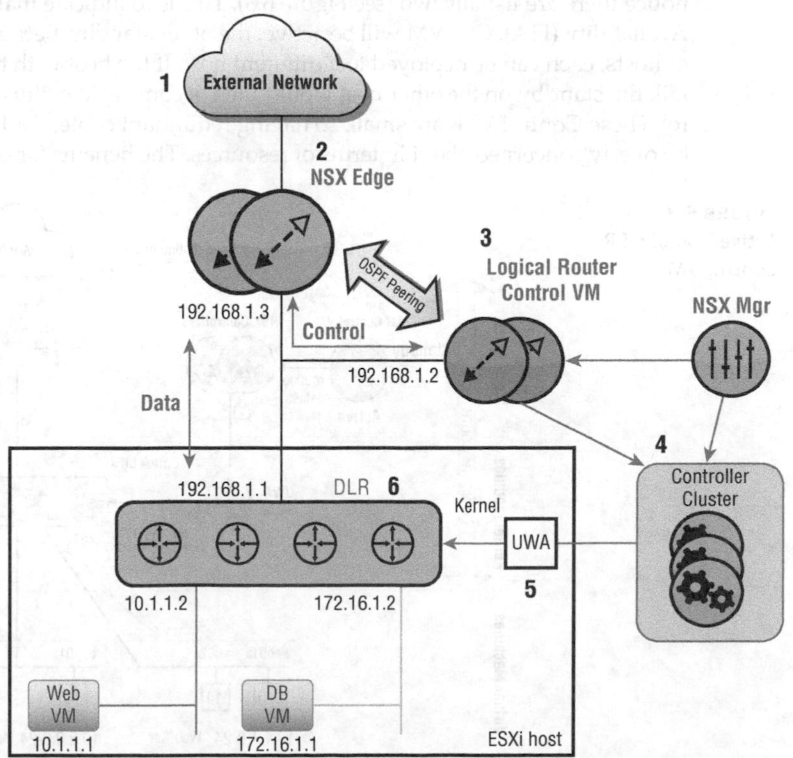

FIGURE 6.2 Following the routing path with an analogy

Let's say the FBI (external network) learned of a possible terrorist threat and they need to get that message to every U.S. senator (ESXi kernel). They won't deliver the message to each senator directly. Instead, they only communicate with the Congressional Liaison Office (the NSX Edge) using a specific protocol (OSPF/BGP) when they need to alert Congress. Any time there is something to report to all senators, the process is to send that information to the Congressional Controllers Office (the NSX Controller cluster), which distributes the messages to each Senate member's office. However, when you open the door to a senator's office, you won't see the senator, you'll see the senator's assistant (UWA on the ESXi host). Any message intended for the senator (the kernel) must first go through the assistant.

A common misconception is that most data center traffic is between the data center and the outside world. This is not true. Most of the data flows are within the data center itself. This makes sense when you think about it. Consider a three-tiered web application. There is the initial call from the outside world to the web server, but after that, the web server is talking with the application, the application is talking with database, and so on. When our team has run baselines to show prospective NSX customers what is going on in their data center, they are often shocked to see literally millions of separate traffic flows (conversations) where the source and destination are entirely within the data center, while only a fraction of that traffic is destined for the outside world.

Traffic within the data center (server-to-server) is referred to as East-West traffic. Client-server traffic from the data center to any destination outside the data center is called North-South traffic. The main job of a DLR is to provide a highly efficient routing for East-West traffic within the data center and to do so in a way that can scale easily. North-South traffic, on the other hand, is handled with the Edge Services Gateway (ESG).

When the DLR is deployed, that LR Control VM is placed within the Edge cluster. Why a cluster and not a single host? When you see the icon for the Control VM in most NSX diagrams, you'll notice there are usually two (see Figure 6.3). This is to indicate that the VMs are implementing High Availability (HA). One VM will be active, the other standby. Because they are deployed on a cluster of hosts, each can be deployed to a different host. If the host with the active Control VM were to fail, the standby on the other host would then become active, thus improving the overall availability. These Control VMs are small, so having redundant copies for HA failover is not something to be overly concerned about in terms of resources. The benefits far outweigh the costs.

FIGURE 6.3
Active/standby LR Control VMs

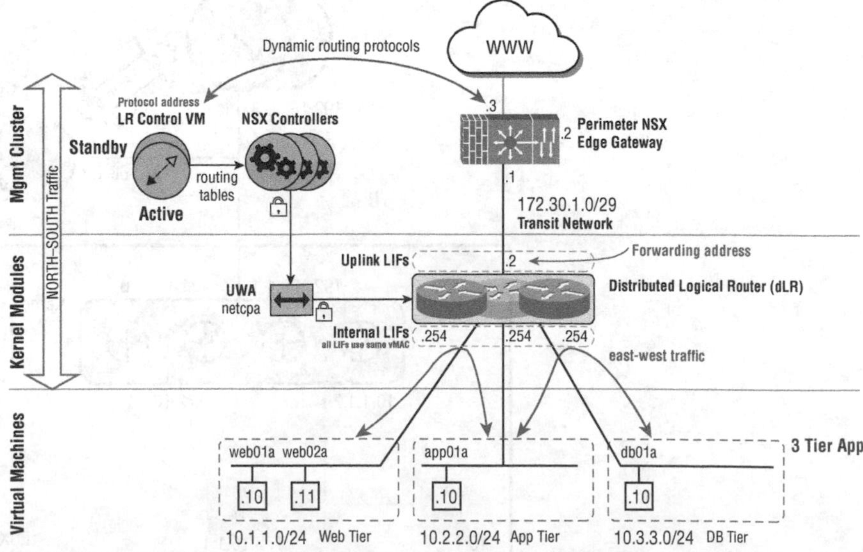

Although both the DLR and ESG are capable of routing, from a design perspective, VMware recommends that you try to have the ESG handle all North-South traffic have the DLR handle all East-West traffic. The reason for this is that the DLR, being distributed to every host, is then highly optimized to route traffic from one host to another, the East-West traffic. The ESG, in comparison, is not distributed.

Understanding DLR Efficiency

To understand why the DLR is so efficient, let's contrast it with an ESXi host prior to implementing NSX, and therefore, without distributed routing.

In the Before NSX diagram (see Figure 6.4), we see a single ESXi host with two VMs. One VM is on the 10.1.1.0 network, the other is on the 10.1.2.0 network. Because these are different subnets, we must route. A physical router is shown at the top left. This would be the default gateway for the VM. Even though the VMs are on the same ESXi host, in order to send packets from one to the other, the traffic must leave the ESXi host, go to the external router, the router then does a lookup, and then finally routes it to the second VM.

FIGURE 6.4 Two VMs on same ESXi host and an external router

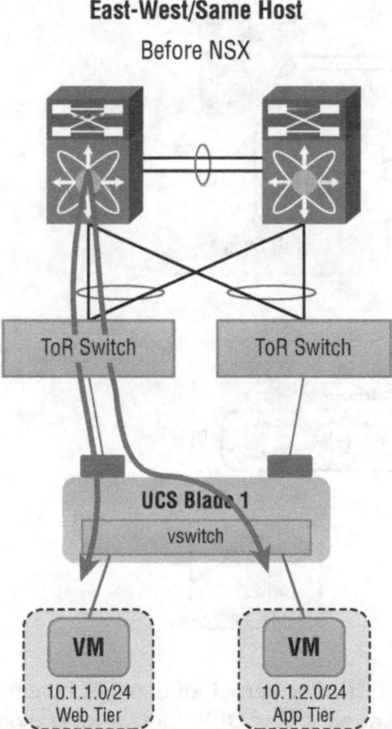

Imagine if you were teamed up with a coworker from a different department and your desks were adjacent, but being from different departments, you weren't allowed to talk directly; everything said had to go through a department manager. Your conversations would involve additional delay and would take more effort. Going from VM to VM in different subnets on a single host is the same. This is referred to as *hairpinning*. Your traffic must essentially leave and then come back to the same place to communicate. This adds latency, takes up more CPU, and involves additional bandwidth.

The reason that packets must travel to the router first is that the VM behaves like any PC. It doesn't have knowledge of remote networks. It simply asks itself, "Am I trying to talk to something local or remote?" Local being on the same subnet, and remote being a different subnet. If they are on the same subnet, then it's simple. Just send it. But if the destination is on a different subnet, they need to first forward it to a device that will have that information: a router. In our Before NSX example, the router doesn't live on the host, so the traffic must leave the host altogether, make it to the router, look up the route, and then go all the way back—all of that even though the destination was on the same host.

Now, let's look at the same situation, but this time, we have NSX and have deployed a DLR to handle East-West traffic within the data center (see Figure 6.5).

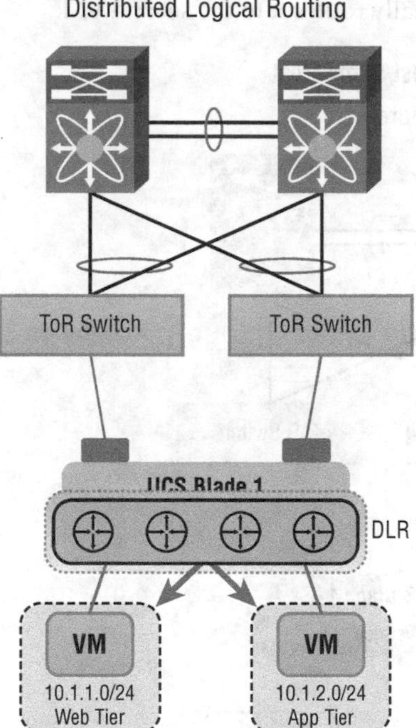

FIGURE 6.5 Two VMs on same ESXi host with NSX

The DLR lives in the hypervisor (in the kernel) of the ESXi host (see Figure 6.6). Since the routes, 10.1.1.0 and 10.1.2.0, are known to the DLR, there is no reason to leave the host at all. On the DLR are Logical Interfaces (LIFs) that can be configured with IP addresses. With the DLR in place, the external router no longer needs to be the default gateway. Instead, the VM's default gateway is an IP address on the DLR.

FIGURE 6.6
The DLR is distributed to the kernel of each ESXi host.

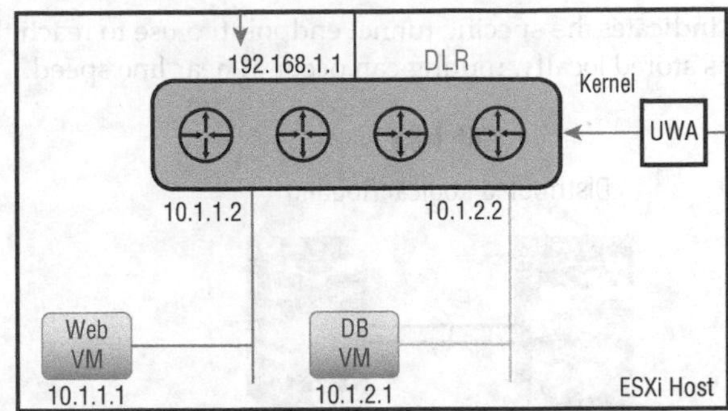

Let's see what happens when VMs located on separate ESXi hosts communicate (see Figure 6.7). Prior to having NSX, we still have hairpinning. In order to communicate, the traffic needs to leave one host, go to the external router, and then get routed to the second host to reach the other VM.

FIGURE 6.7
Two VMs on different ESXi hosts and an external router

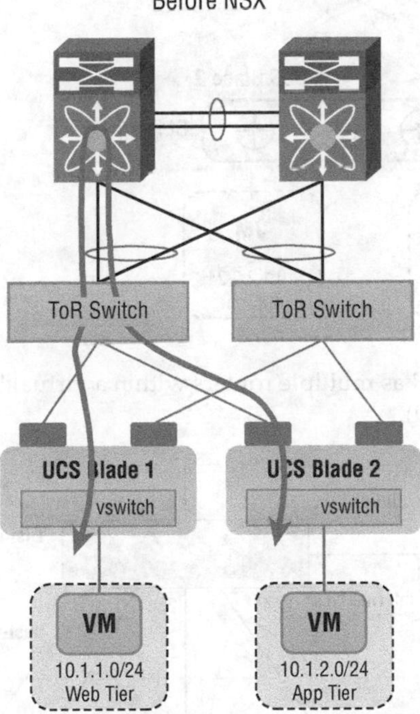

With NSX, we immediately see the benefit of the DLR being distributed among the ESXi hosts (see Figure 6.8). Although the VMs live on different hosts, there is still no need to involve the external router. Because the routing information has been distributed to every host, each host has all the information it needs to send traffic to the destination VM. That information, along with the VTEP table, indicates the specific tunnel endpoint to use to reach the ESXi host housing the VM. Because it is stored locally, routing can occur at near line speed.

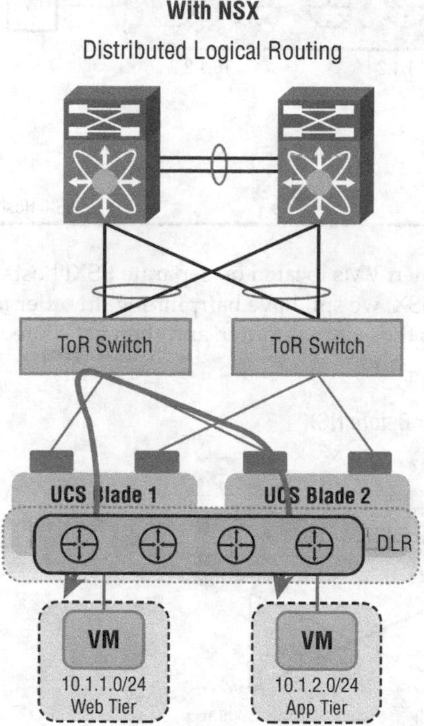

FIGURE 6.8 Two VMs on different ESXi hosts with NSX

Some diagrams depict a DLR as multiple routers within a virtual box to indicate it is distributed across hosts (see Figure 6.9).

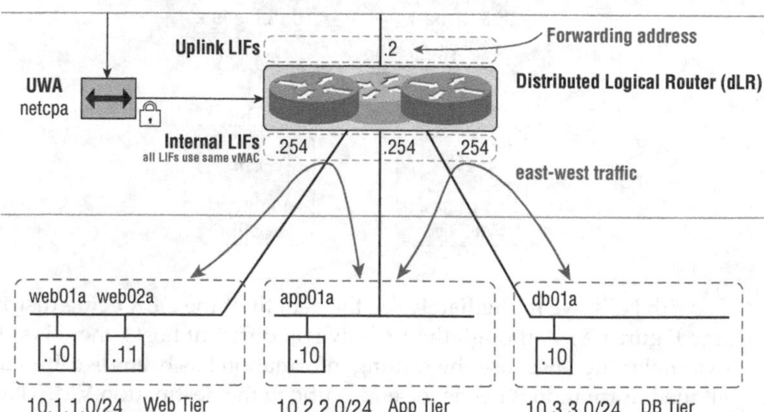

FIGURE 6.9 Representing a DLR in NSX diagrams

The Logical Interfaces on the DLR are given IP addresses, but come in two flavors. Internal LIFs connect to the Logical Switches. In this example, there are three Logical Switches for networks 10.1.1.0, 10.2.2.0, and 10.3.3.0. VMs connected to these Logical Switches use the Internal LIF IP addresses of the DLR as their respective default gateways. The other type of interface on the DLR is an Uplink LIF. This, too, has an IP address. The DLR uses the Uplink LIF address to forward North-South traffic from the VMs to the NSX Edge Gateway.

Keep in mind that unlike a physical router, which houses both its control and data planes together, the planes are separate for NSX. The DLR does not use the Uplink LIF to exchange dynamic routes with the ESG. The Uplink LIF is only used to forward traffic. This would be like having a phone system to receive customer orders (regular/data plane traffic through the Uplink LIF) and a separate intercom system to receive instructions from your manager (management/control plane traffic such as routing information). The routes are learned within the control plane. This dichotomy helps to make NSX more resilient, increasing availability, since if the control plane were to fail (the LR Control VM), the data plane remains intact. The control plane does not actually route any traffic. Instead, it is simply learning the routes and ultimately pushing that information to the hosts. Once the hosts have the information, they can use it to route (forward) the traffic appropriately.

Therefore, even with a control plane failure, it's business as usual for the data; traffic will still be routed within the NSX environment and routed to the outside world. The failure of the control plane only means that new routes cannot be learned and distributed to the ESXi hosts. A traditional physical router doesn't have this flexibility and resilience. If that router fails, the data plane is affected (it can no longer forward traffic) as well as the control plane (it can no longer learn routes).

Another Concept to Consider

LIFs on the DLR presented to one ESXi host will be identical for every other host. Therefore, if you were to add a VM to the 10.3.3.0 segment on any host, the default gateway would not change (in this example, 10.3.3.254). The benefit of the design may not be readily apparent until you consider the implications of moving a VM from one host to another. The default gateway does not change. The IP address of the VM doesn't change. As a comparison, if you've ever moved a PC from one department to another, the IP address and default gateway change: new segment = new subnet. Even with the help of DHCP, they still change; but moving a VM to a different host is even simpler because the addressing remains the same.

What about the virtual MAC address of the Internal LIF? If that were to change, that means we need to bring ARP into the mix again for the migrated VM to relearn the IP-to-MAC mapping of the Internal LIF's IP: 10.3.3.254. The good news is that the vMAC is the same on every host. ARPing is completely unnecessary after a move. To further make your design simpler, VMware decided to use the same vMAC of 02:50:56:56:44:52 for *every* Internal LIF. If you had three Internal LIFs and only a single host, they would still be identical for each subnet. At first, it may seem like there would be massive confusion with duplicate MAC addresses. However, if you step back and consider how MAC addresses are used, recall that a MAC address is for communication on a single Layer 2 link. If there aren't duplicate MAC addresses on that specific link, there isn't a problem.

As an analogy, let's say we have a colleague that is a renowned research scientist named Dr. E. Todd Weber, III (IP address). But around the office, we all refer to him as MadDog (MAC address). He's the only MadDog we work with, so there's never a point of confusion. On a different floor of our office building is another company who also happens to have a coworker they call MadDog. It doesn't matter. Since the name (MAC address) is only used locally within each office, it doesn't matter if it is also used in a different office, a different segment.

There would only be confusion if we hired someone else in the *same* office who also goes by MadDog. Then we would have duplicate MadDogs (duplicate MACs).

In terms of design, having the same MAC address assigned to every Internal LIF is far simpler. You automatically know that the vMAC address of any Internal LIF is going to be 02:50:56:56:44:52. The Uplink LIF is a little different. Whereas the MAC on the Internal LIF is referred to as a vMAC (virtual MAC), the MAC address on the Uplink LIF is called a pMAC (physical MAC). It will be different for each copy of the logical router on each host. Each ESXi host generates its own pMAC for the DLR, always starting with the first six characters of 00:50:56. The first six digits of any MAC address are used to identify the vendor (in this case, VMware) and is called the Organization Unique Identifier, or OUI for short. The pMAC is the MAC address of the ESXi host's physical NIC.

MAC addresses are made up of 12 hexadecimal digits, the first six being the OUI, and the last six are more like an individual serial number. Those last six digits of the pMAC assigned to the Uplink LIF are automatically generated by each ESXi host. The reason for each pMAC being unique is so that the Edge Gateway knows which host it is talking to, and therefore, which physical NIC it should forward traffic to.

Consider this example (see Figure 6.10). There is currently a conversation going between an outside user and a web server VM on Host8. The user has clicked a link that triggers a GET request for an image. The web server needs to send the image to a destination that it sees is not local. It therefore sends the packets to the DLR for routing. The DLR has a route to the end user that indicates it should forward the packets to the Edge Gateway, 172.30.1.1. Here is where the unique pMAC is important. If we were to look at the individual frames at the point when the DLR is forwarding the image to the ESG, the source MAC would be the pMAC of the Uplink LIF on Host8. The destination MAC would be that of the 172.30.1.1 interface on the ESG. Remember that source and destination MAC addresses are only used to traverse a single segment. The ESG uses that unique pMAC assigned to the DLR Uplink LIF to know which ESXi host is sending it traffic. Likewise, when the user sends the GET request, the Edge Gateway needs to know the specific host to send it to. From the Edge Gateway's perspective, each host is identified uniquely by its own pMAC. For that GET request, the ESG will use its own MAC address as the source and the pMAC of Host8's DLR as the destination to ensure that it is forwarded to the correct host.

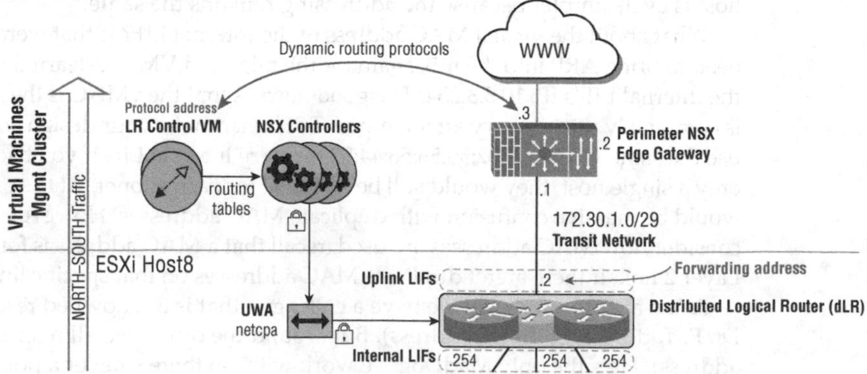

FIGURE 6.10 Packet walk from end user to web server VM on ESXi Host8

When comparing a DLR to a physical router, as we have seen, the DLR has far more flexible options and optimizations for routing traffic. However, one restriction to keep in mind in your design regarding DLRs is that a Logical Switch can only connect to a single DLR. With traditional physical routers and switches, there is no limitation for switch-to-router connections.

Let's Get Smart about Routing

Because the control and data plane functions for routing have been separated in NSX, there are distinct differences when comparing the operation of a DLR to a physical router. On a physical router configured with a dynamic routing protocol such as BGP or OSPF, the protocol is often running on all the router's interfaces. Recall that BGP and OSPF are protocols that live in the control plane. BGP and OSPF can't run on the DLR itself, because it is all data plane. Instead, the routing protocols exchange routes between the Edge Gateway and the LR Control VM over a shared segment. Referring to a diagram we looked at previously (see Figure 6.11), you see that not only are the Edge Gateway and the LR Control VM on the same 192.168.1.0 subnet, but the Uplink LIF of the host also connects to this same segment using the IP address, 192.168.1.1.

FIGURE 6.11
Transit segment shared by DLR, NSX Edge, and LR Control VM

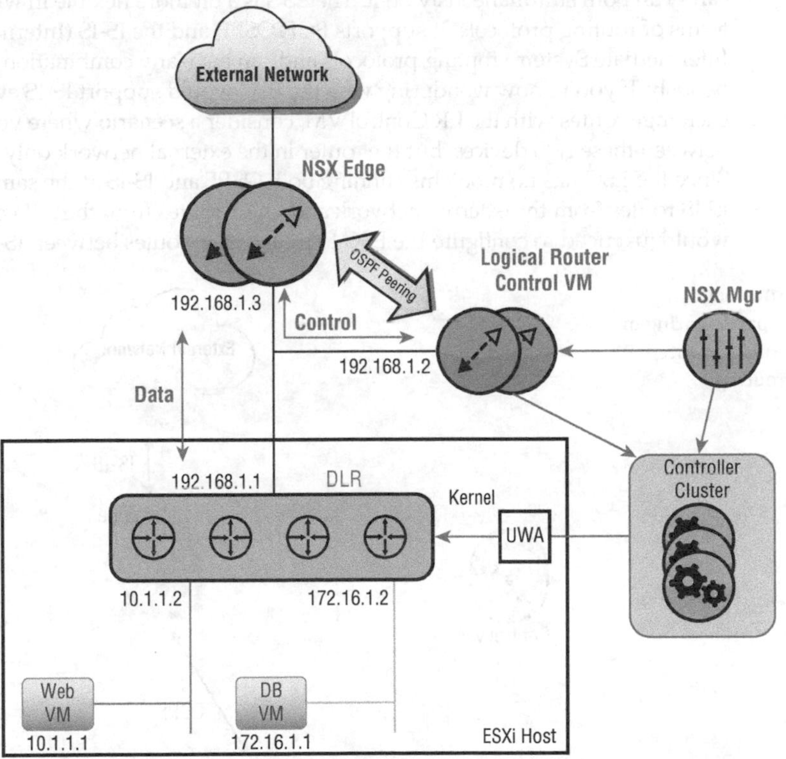

The Edge Gateway and LR Control VM communicate on this segment to form a neighbor adjacency and, once established, can exchange information regarding the subnets they are aware of. To summarize, all three are on the same 192.168.1.0 segment, but the shared segment is used for two different things. First, it is used by the NSX Edge to communicate with the LR Control VM. The LR Control VM (in this example, running OSPF) needs to form an adjacency with the NSX Edge in order to exchange routes. If you think about what adjacent means, it implies something is right next to it. For OSPF, you form adjacencies with other OSPF routers that are on the same segment, your neighboring OSPF routers. In this case, its OSPF neighbor is the NSX Edge.

The second use of this 192.168.1.0 segment is to allow the NSX Edge to directly communicate with the DLR. It is not to exchange routing information; it's used to forward your workload traffic.

You will later see when we configure OSPF that two different addresses are defined for communication with the ESG: a Forwarding Address and a Protocol Address. The Forwarding Address in this example is 192.168.1.1. It's used for *forwarding* traffic to the ESG. We also have the Protocol Address (in this case, it is 192.168.1.2). It is used to exchange routing *protocol* information with the ESG.

Let's say that you wanted to check the routing table on a physical router. You simply log in and enter **`show ip route`**. Where do we get this information in NSX? Recall that the component learning those routes in NSX is the LR Control VM. We can enable SSH access when the Control VM is created. Had we done that in this example, we would simply SSH into 192.168.1.2 and enter the **`show ip route`** command.

The LR Control VM can run BGP or OSPF as its dynamic routing protocol to learn routes, but you can't run both simultaneously on it. The ESG is a bit more flexible in what it's permitted to do in terms of routing protocols. It supports BGP, OSPF, and the IS-IS (Intermediate System to Intermediate System) routing protocols and can have any combination of the three running simultaneously. If you're now wondering why the ESG would support IS-IS even though it can't be used to exchange routes with the LR Control VM, consider a scenario where you were running OSPF between these two devices, but the router in the external network only runs IS-IS (see Figure 6.12). Since the ESG has no problems running both OSPF and IS-IS at the same time, it would have learned IS-IS routes from the external network and OSPF routes from the data center. At that point, we would just need to configure the ESG to redistribute routes between IS-IS and OSPF.

FIGURE 6.12 Edge participating in external and internal routing

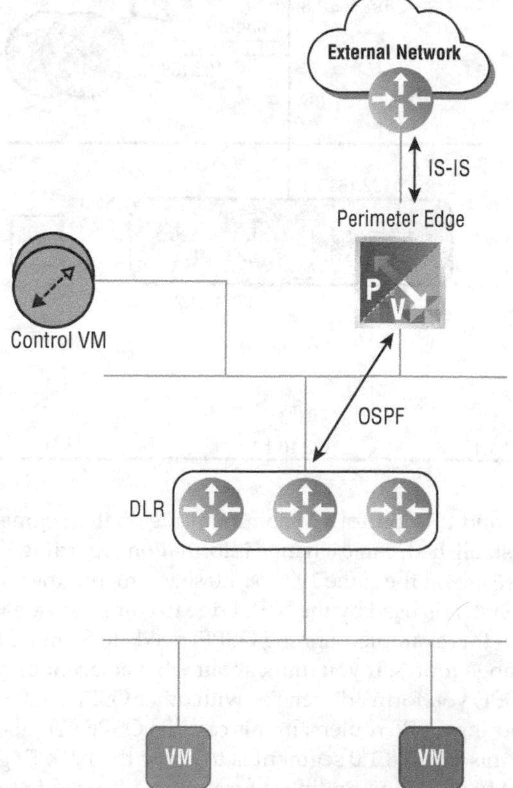

OSPF

OSPF stands for Open Shortest Path First. The first word in the title, *open*, isn't a verb. It's an adjective, describing that it is an open standard, not a proprietary protocol. I mention that because in working with a US Navy team a few years back, they had all been taught that the protocol allowed you to "open" a path to a given destination. Their assumption of what open means doesn't cause any harm, but the actual definition underscores that if you have routing between network devices from different vendors, OSPF is a good choice because it will be supported in a multi-vendor environment.

As far as the rest of the abbreviation goes, OSPF works by creating a map of the network and then choosing what it considers the lowest-cost path, or shortest path, to choose when forwarding traffic to a specific destination. When you drive using a GPS, its algorithm for choosing the best path is very similar. The GPS has a map. A value based on the speed limit is assigned to each road. The cost value of a road is an inverse: the higher the speed, the lower the cost. With this information assigned, when you punch in a destination on your GPS, it looks at all possible ways to get there. A 75-mile-per-hour highway might have a cost of 5, whereas a 15-mile-per-hour dirt road might have a cost of 100. The GPS figures out each total path cost for each possible path and then picks the one with the lowest cost as the preferred route to get there. We, of course, don't see all of that happening. We only see the result telling us where to turn next. OSPF keeps track of the state of each link: not only the up or down status, but the bandwidth. It does this by exchanging aptly named Link State Advertisements (LSAs) with neighboring OSPF routers.

OSPF is often optimized by dividing the routing domain into areas. One of OSPF's rules is that all routers in the same area must have the same database, the same map of the network. Again, we can use the analogy of a GPS. Two users with a Garmin GPS would have the same map, but the SPF algorithm is applied based on where they are located on the map and where they want to go. The algorithm discovers the path with the lowest cost. OSPF requires that all the routers within an area agree on a single shared map. They use the exchanged LSA messages to build the map. As the network grows, it can take longer and longer for them all to agree to the same database. Any time there is a change, that change is propagated throughout so that each OSPF router can update its database.

This is where areas can come into play. If you have over 75 routers within an area and begin to incur delays in convergence (routers coming to an agreement), it's time to split into multiple areas. In this way, a change in one area only requires agreement within that domain and does not cause a convergence ripple through other areas, thus making your network much more stable. There are other optimizations we can take advantage of in a multi-area OSPF design as well. We're giving some background on multi-area OSPF here to make it easier to understand why a specific area is chosen when configuring your LR Control VM to communicate with the ESG.

There are a few rules regarding OSPF areas that are helpful to troubleshoot issues such as an adjacency not being formed as it should between the ESG and LR Control VM.

First is the numbering of areas. If you only have one area, you can number it anything you like. If you think it's fun to have an Area 51, go ahead. However, if you have multiple OSPF areas, one of them must be numbered Area 0 to represent it as the Backbone Area (see Figure 6.13).

A second rule is that two routers on the same segment must belong to the same area. Looking again at the diagram, you see that both interfaces connecting R3 to R1 are in Area 0. You also see that both interfaces connecting R4 to R6 are in Area 2. The link between any router and its neighbor must always belong to the same area.

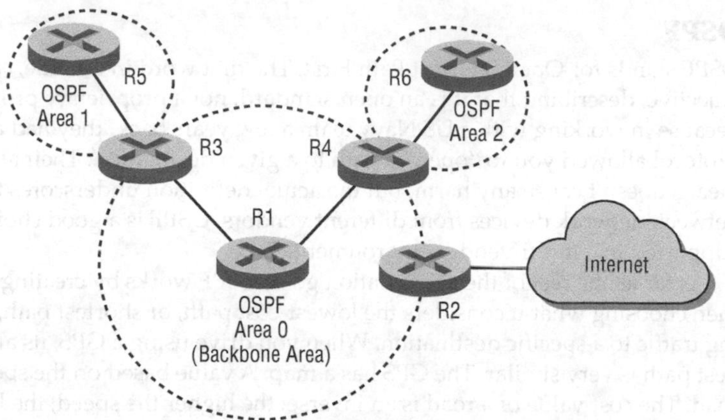

FIGURE 6.13 For scalability, Area 0 is designated as the Backbone with all other Areas attached to Area 0, not to each other.

Third, if you are trying to optimize OSPF by dividing the routers into areas, all areas must directly connect to Area 0. The diagram in Figure 6.13 shows Area 1 directly connecting to Area 0 through R3. Area 2 is directly connected to Area 0 through R4. What you can't do is daisy-chain the areas. You can't have Area 1 – Area 2 – Area 3 – Area 4 – Area 0. The reason for this rule is scalability. To make the example a bit exaggerated, let's say you had 100 areas, all connected sequentially. If you needed to get from Area 2 to Area 90, the route would mean traveling through 88 areas to get there, incurring a lot of latency.

However, by following the recommended design of OSPF that states that all areas should have a direct connection to the Backbone Area, Area 0, it means that to go from Area 2 to 90, you only have to go through one other area at most: Area 0. To get from Area 17 to Area 99, you would only have to go through one other Area: Area 0. This design requirement allows OSPF to be highly scalable.

Border Gateway Protocol (BGP)

Border Gateway Protocol (BGP) is another dynamic routing protocol supported in NSX. Overall, it does the same job as OSPF in that it allows routes to destination networks to be learned dynamically. However, the way it determines the *best* route is different. In some networking classes, the differences for when to use OSPF vs. BGP are oversimplified by saying, "OSPF should be used to exchange internal routes (routes within your organization) since it is an internal routing protocol, and BGP should be used to exchange external routes (routes from other organizations) when connecting your organization's router to an ISP, since it is an external routing protocol." But then, you learn that there are external and internal implementations of BGP (eBGP and iBGP), and confusion ensues. To make matters worse, you then learn about all the bells and whistles BGP offers in terms of controlling exactly how traffic enters and exits your network by manipulating path attributes. If you weren't already familiar with BGP prior to that networking class, learning this seemingly endless list of options and tie-breakers may make you consider a new line of work.

In terms of using BGP to exchange routes in NSX, the good news is that 95 percent of the details regarding path attributes, filtering, route maps, and the like are unnecessary. When we get into configuration later in the chapter, you'll see that on the contrary, it can be argued that BGP is easier to configure than OSPF for what we need it to do to support NSX.

Before we get into the overall design though, let's step back and consider why you would choose BGP as your routing protocol between the ESG and the LR Control VM. BGP has two major things going for it:

- It's ridiculously scalable.
- It's very stable.

BGP is the routing protocol of the Internet, the largest network on earth, spanning the entire globe. No other protocol is as scalable.

The second major benefit with BGP is stability. BGP is more concerned about being stable and being scalable than it is about getting your traffic to its destination as quickly as possible. It has built-in loop-prevention mechanisms and rules to keep it stable. A full-blown BGP Internet router will have over 800,000 IPv4 routes to get to any destination on the Internet. If you want to see a specific count, go to `http://tinyurl.com/bgproutes`. You'll see two different numbers for the IPv4 count. The reason for this is that it depends on where that BGP router is located. It may be that some routes have been summarized into a block for one BGP router for optimization, but an admin in a different part of the world may be summarizing differently or not at all. The site listed shows two examples. You can average the two together to get a fair idea of the number of routes a typical BGP router would have.

The point is, that's a lot of routes. Stability is a very high priority. Otherwise, issues would cause Internet access globally to go down daily. Thanks, BGP! This brings us to NSX. That LR Control VM can run either OSPF or BGP to dynamically learn and propagate its routes. If you had taken that network class and found BGP to be overwhelming, OSPF probably felt a lot more comfortable in comparison. However, to simply exchange your data center routes (not 800,000 routes) and not needing to manipulate all those path attributes, BGP is both stable and easy to manage. OSPF, in comparison, has several structural rules that we must be aware of and follow. We've already mentioned some of these rules regarding area design:

- Areas must match to form an adjacency.
- With multiple areas, there must be an Area 0.
- All other areas must directly attach to Area 0.

BGP, in contrast, doesn't use an area construct in its design. It does emphasize the concept of an Autonomous System (AS), though. In BGP, each organization is identified by an AS number. To be valid on the Internet, this number needs to be assigned to your organization. If you go back to `http://tinyurl.com/bgproutes`, you'll notice that the two IPv4 BGP routers have AS numbers assigned. Therefore, we know they are routers from different organizations.

One way to think about how BGP operates is that in some ways it treats an entire organization, each Autonomous System, as a giant router. One of the primary ways it chooses the best route to a destination is to count how many hops it needs to get there and pick the route with the lowest number. This sounds a lot like the legacy routing protocol, RIP. The difference here, though, is that it considers each AS to be a single hop. It may be that to go through the ISP, AS 6447, you are routed through 12 of the ISP's routers. But BGP considers the entire AS to be one hop.

Simplified, it means that a BGP router asks the question, "How many Autonomous Systems (how many organizations) do I need to go through to get to a particular destination network?" (see Figure 6.14).

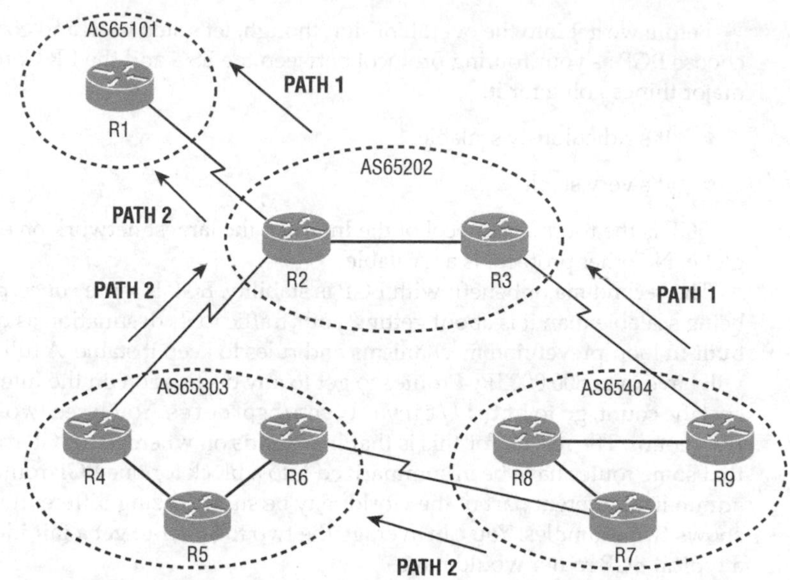

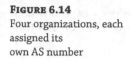

FIGURE 6.14 Four organizations, each assigned its own AS number

Let's say that your organization has been assigned AS 65404 and you need to get to a server attached to one of the networks in AS 65101. To understand the path it will prefer, forget about the individual routers and treat each Autonomous System as a single router. It has two paths. It can choose:

Path 1: 65404, 65202, 65101

or

Path 2: 65404, 65303, 65202, 65101

The first path involves three Autonomous Systems, the second involves four. Provided that we haven't made any configuration modifications, BGP would choose Path 1 because it involves fewer Autonomous Systems to hop through.

When configuring BGP, knowing a few things about how it operates under the hood can help you to avoid hours of troubleshooting:

Under the Hood 1 For stability reasons, BGP is never going to discover neighboring BGP routers just because you enabled it. You need to specifically enter the IP address of your neighbor, and the neighboring BGP router must do the same to peer with you. Virtually every other routing protocol, including OSPF, is different in terms of discovery. All we do with OSPF is turn it on, and it actively finds every OSPF router configured on the same link.

By requiring you to manually nail up the BGP router you are attempting to peer with, it prevents someone from accidentally causing BGP problems worldwide simply by enabling the protocol. If I enable BGP on a router connected to my ISP and I enter their BGP router's IP address, no adjacency is formed because they would also have had to enter my router's IP address as a BGP neighbor.

Under the Hood 2 Your BGP router can only belong to one Autonomous System. With OSPF, areas are configured per interface. One OSPF router could sit between two areas: Area

0 and Area 1. This would be accomplished by simply assigning one interface to Area 0, the other to Area 1. But with BGP, the entire router, including each one of its interfaces, belongs to a single AS.

Under the Hood 3 When configuring BGP, you must specify not only the IP address of your neighbor, but also the AS number they are a part of.

It's easier to see how these details come together with an example. We won't even bring NSX into this one. We'll keep it simple using a few physical Cisco routers (see Figure 6.15).

FIGURE 6.15 Simple Cisco router BGP example for R1 to peer with R2

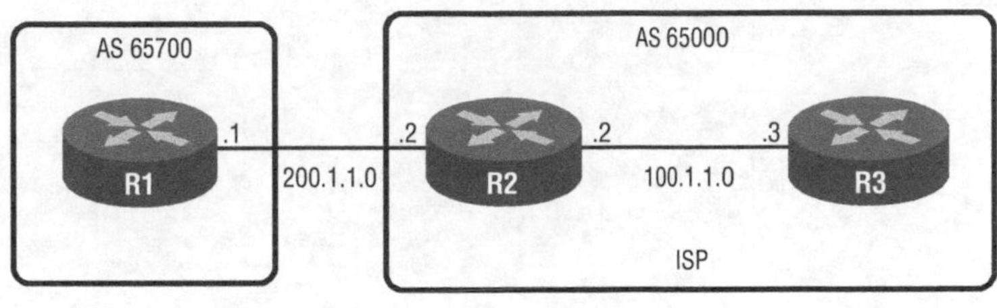


```
R1
    router bgp 65700
      neighbor 200.1.1.2 remote-as 65000
```

Router1 is in AS 65700. Let's say that is our organization and we are attempting to peer with our ISP, AS 65000. We define our AS in the first command: `router bgp 65700`.

Next, we must manually specify the BGP neighbor's IP address to peer with them. The second configuration line in the diagram says that we want to peer with neighbor 200.1.1.2, which is the directly connected IP address on Router2.

When we specify our neighbor's IP, we need to specify the AS it belongs to. This is specified in the latter portion of the command: `remote-as 65000`.

The ISP would have to do a mirror configuration on Router2. It would look like this:

```
router bgp 65000
  neighbor 200.1.1.1 remote-as 65700
```

That's it. We're peering. With just these few configuration lines, Router1 would begin to receive those 800,000+ routes. Don't worry about the syntax of those commands, that's Cisco. We're going to do the same using the vSphere Client GUI, but the concepts are the same. Furthermore, with NSX we're most likely not using BGP to learn every destination on the Internet. We are instead using it simply to allow the ESG and LR Control VM to dynamically exchange routes without having to enter them manually. What is more common in an NSX design is to use BGP to learn all of the subnets in the data center so that this information can be propagated to every host, and then to get to everything else on the Internet, we have a single default route, 0.0.0.0/0, which ultimately points us to the external network.

Oh Yeah, Statics Too

It's possible to not use a dynamic routing protocol at all and instead, configure every route statically. The downside is that each time a VXLAN or VLAN is added or removed, you must remember to do the extra step of configuring a corresponding static route. Not only would this need to be done on the LR Control VM, but also on the ESG. In comparison, enabling a dynamic routing protocol on these components would allow for routes to be added or removed based on the status of whether there are active VMs or servers on the VXLANs or VLANs.

Recall from the previous chapter where we discussed the creation of a Layer 2 Bridge. To do this, we created a DLR and only configured the Bridging tab. There was another option that was checked by default that you might have missed (see Figure 6.16).

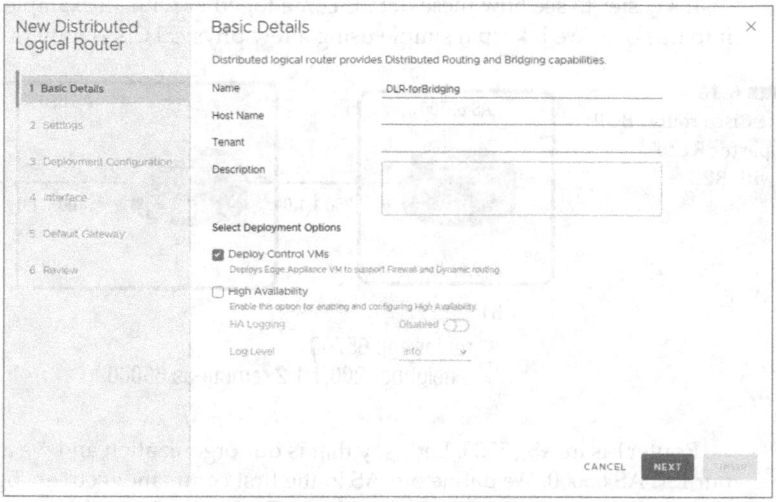

FIGURE 6.16 New DLR step 1: Basic Details

The first step, where basic details are configured, had the option to deploy a Control VM. Deploying a DLR creates a distributed router in the kernel and creates a separate Control VM to provide the control plane. But what would the impact be of deploying a DLR (not for bridging, but for routing) and unchecking this box?

The answer is the distributed routing function would still be injected into the kernel; however, with no LR Control VM, there's nothing for the ESG to form an adjacency with. BGP and OSPF would be unable to function without a control plane to exchange routing information.

The same is not true for static routes. Since static routes are directly and manually configured instructions describing where to route packets to reach each destination, there is no need for the control plane. This means that there is no need for the LR Control VM if you are only doing static routing.

Let's say that you decide to implement your NSX design in smaller steps. The first phase of your plan is to start with static routes only and verify that routing is working properly across all hosts. After confirming that the static routes work, your plan is to change to a dynamic routing protocol. When you create the DLR, you uncheck the box for deploying a Control VM, knowing the statics aren't going to use it. After verifying that the static routes have been learned by every ESXi host, you move onto phase two, where you add BGP as your dynamic routing protocol.

What you discover is that you can't go back into the DLR and simply add the LR Control VM. You only get to choose when initially deploying the DLR. Your only option now is to remove the DLR and create it again, this time with the Control VM box checked. Knowing that you only get one shot at deciding whether the Control VM will be deployed alongside the distributed routing function in the kernel, a better way to go would be to simply leave the box checked from the beginning and configure your static routes. Just because the VM exists, it's not attempting to do anything related to dynamic routing. It's only taking up a small amount of resources on the Edge cluster to house the VM. However, with it in place, you then have the option to add a dynamic routing protocol at any point in the future.

Deploying Distributed Logical Routers

To create a DLR, the initial steps are the same as the ones performed for the Layer 2 Bridge:

1. Within the vSphere Client, go to Menu ➢ Networking And Security ➢ NSX Edges (see Figure 6.17).

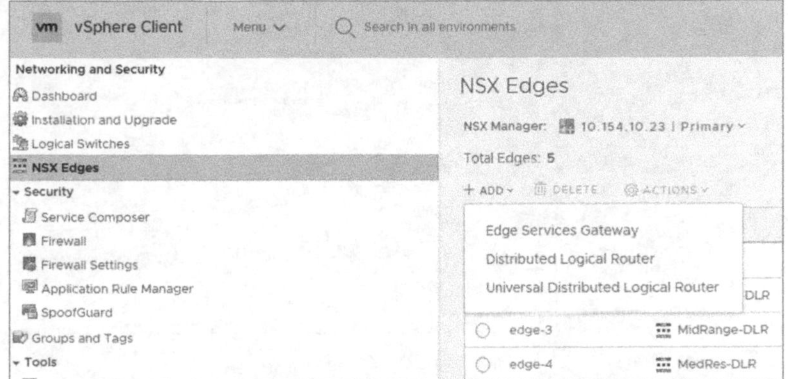

FIGURE 6.17 Within NSX, navigate to NSX Edges to create a DLR.

2. Click the + Add link and select Distributed Logical Router, and a new window appears (see Figure 6.18).

FIGURE 6.18 Providing basic details for the DLR

3. For step 1: Basic Details, enter **DLR** as the name.
4. Place check marks beside Deploy Control VMs and High Availability, and click the slider so that HA Logging is enabled.
5. In the step 2: Settings window (see Figure 6.19), enter a username and password for CLI access and enable SSH access as well.

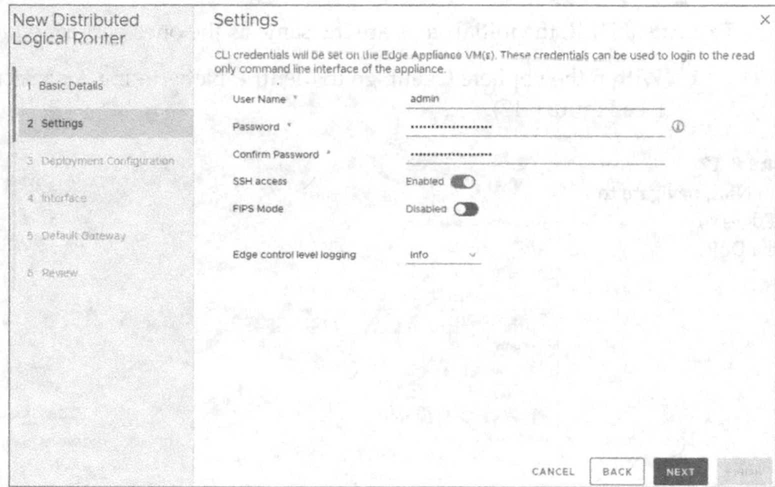

FIGURE 6.19 New DLR step 2: Settings

Recall from the deployment of the Layer 2 Bridge that the password has some special rules: 12 characters, uppercase and lowercase, one special character, and no character can consecutively repeat three times in a row.

6. For step 3: Deployment Configuration (see Figure 6.20), select the Datacenter using the drop-down menu and then click the large + sign to Add Edge Appliance VM.

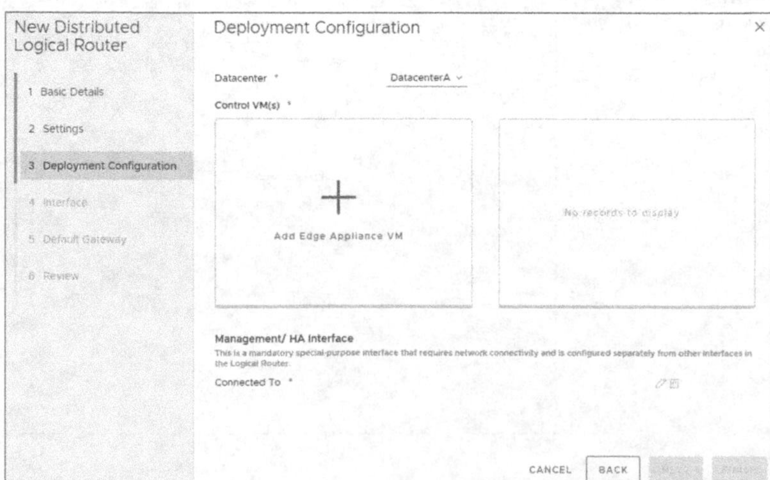

FIGURE 6.20 New DLR step 3: Deployment Configuration

7. The Add Edge Appliance VM window will appear (see Figure 6.21), giving you the opportunity to configure the resources for the control VM.

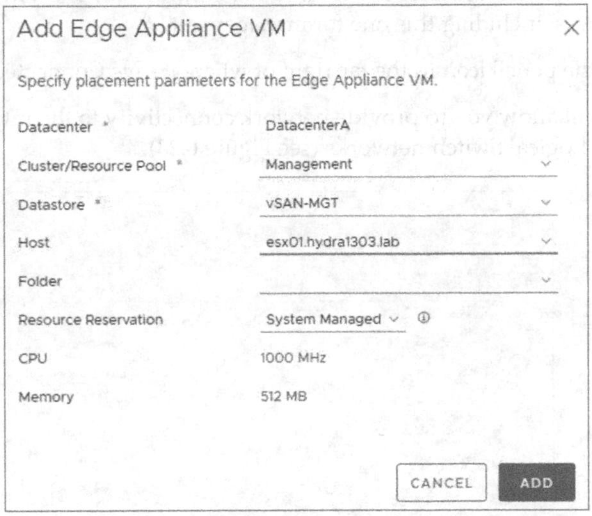

FIGURE 6.21
Assigning resources to the Control VM

8. Here, assign the Edge appliance VM to the Management cluster and select vSAN-MGT for the datastore.

9. Also specify the ESXi host on which to deploy the VM (esx01.hydra1303.lab in our example), and keep the default Resource Reservation option, letting the system manage the resources.

10. Click Add to return to the step 3: Deployment Configuration main window (see Figure 6.22).

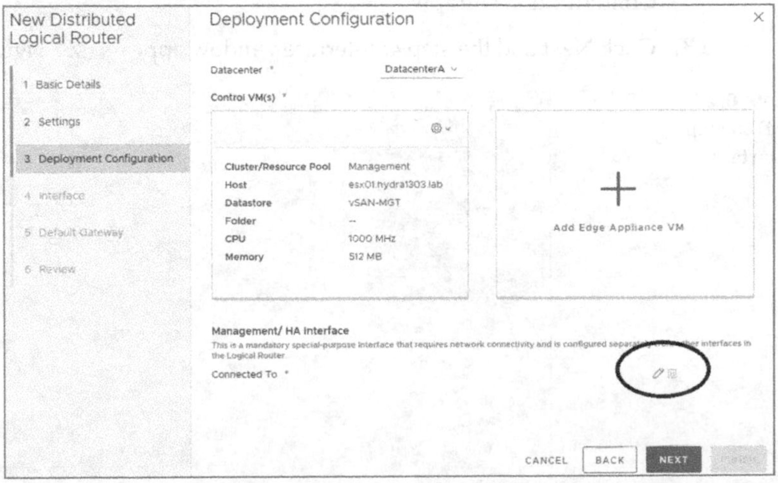

FIGURE 6.22
New DLR returning to step 3: Deployment Configuration

Notice that the resource details for the Control VM now show in the small window. Below that is the option to configure the Management/HA Interface. The Management Interface is what we will use later to SSH into the Control VM. The VM can have up to 10 virtual interfaces, including this one for management.

11. Click the pencil icon to the far right of where it says Connected To.

    This will allow you to provide network connectivity to the interface by assigning it to one of our Logical Switch networks (see Figure 6.23).

FIGURE 6.23 Selecting a network for LR Control VM connectivity

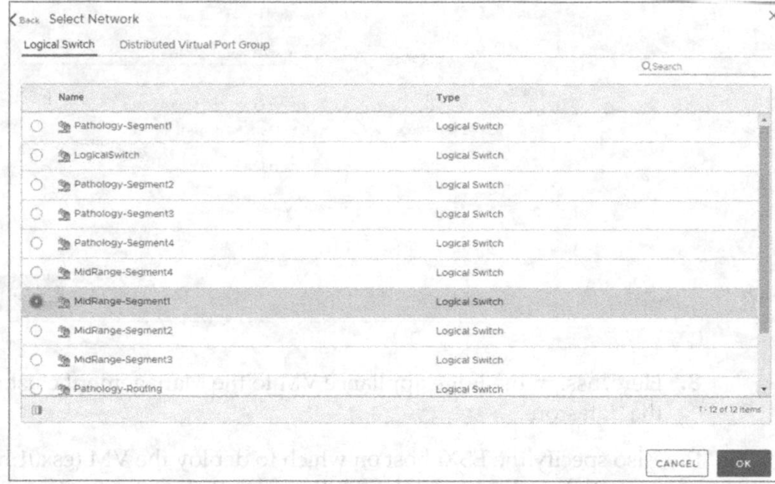

12. Here, you have Logical Switch selected at the top; choose the segment the VM will connect to.

    This will once more bring you back to the main step 3: Deployment Configuration window.

13. Click Next and the step 4: Interface window appears (see Figure 6.24).

FIGURE 6.24 New DLR step 4: Interface

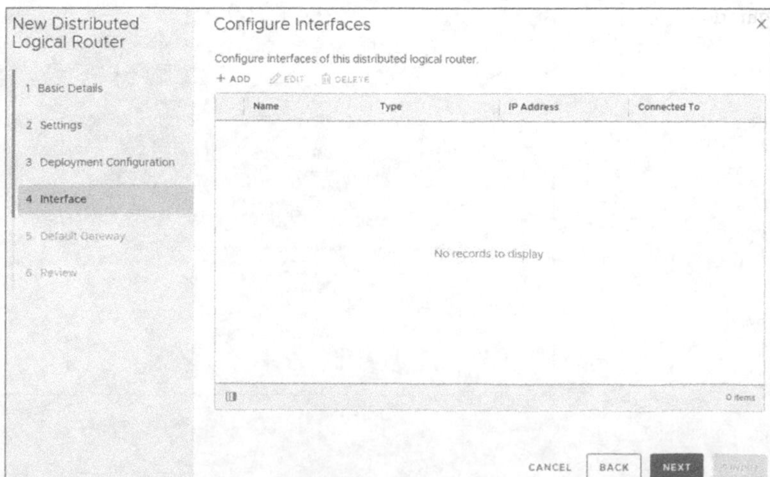

14. Click the + Add link to add an interface.

    The Configure Interfaces window appears (see Figure 6.25).

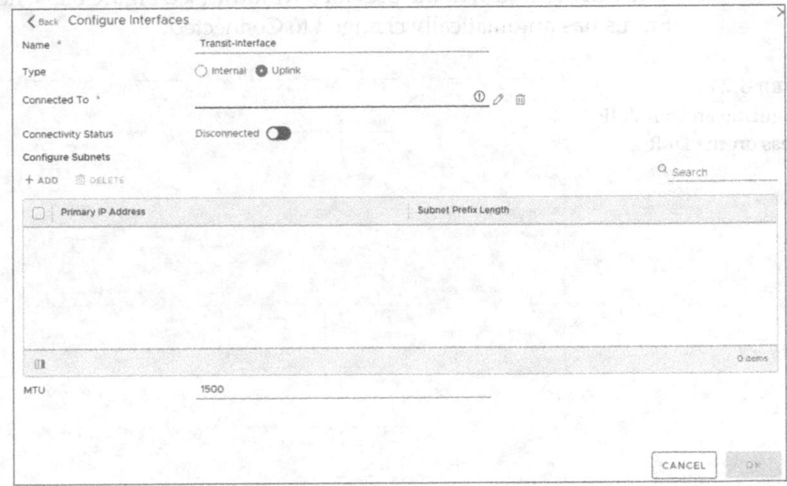

FIGURE 6.25 Adding an Uplink interface for the DLR to communicate with the ESG

15. Here, create the Uplink LIF on the DLR.

    This is the interface the DLR will use to forward traffic to the ESG.

16. Provide the name **Transit-interface** and make sure that Uplink is selected for the type.

17. Click the pencil icon to the far right of Connected To to bring up another window (see Figure 6.26).

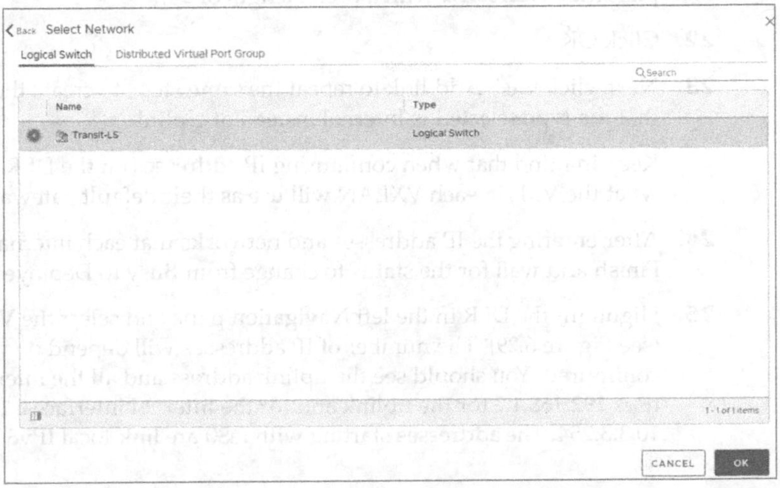

FIGURE 6.26 Selecting a network shared by the DLR, ESG, and Control VM

18. Select the Logical Switch network that the DLR will share with the ESG and the LR Control VM. In this example, choose the Transit-LS network.
19. Click OK to return to the previous window (see Figure 6.27); notice that the Connectivity Status has automatically changed to Connected.

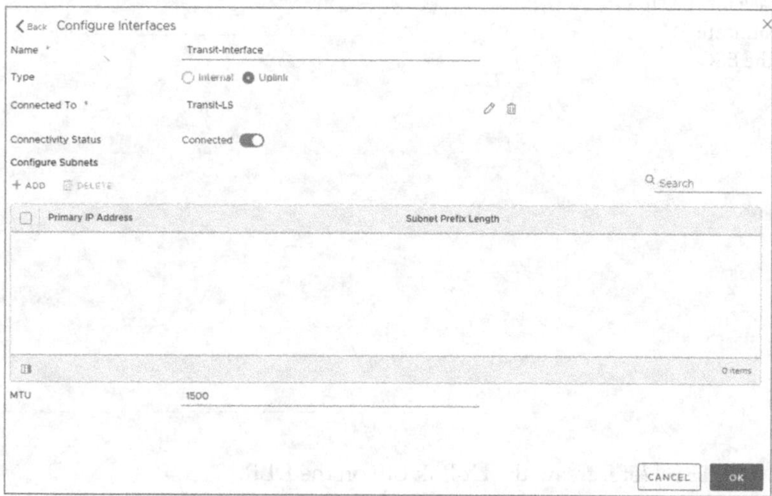

FIGURE 6.27 Configuring an Uplink IP address on the DLR

At this point, the DLR Uplink interface exists, but it has no IP address.

20. Click the + Add link to add the address.
21. A new line will appear. Enter the IP address and the subnet prefix length. For our example, enter **192.168.1.2** with a prefix length of **24**.
22. Click OK.
23. Next, click the + Add link to repeat the same steps to create the Internal LIFs, making sure that the type selected is Internal instead of Uplink.

    Keep in mind that when configuring IP addresses on the DLR internal interfaces, these are what the VMs in each VXLAN will use as their default gateway.
24. After entering the IP addresses and networks that each internal interface connects to, click Finish and wait for the status to change from Busy to Deployed (see Figure 6.28).
25. Highlight the DLR in the left Navigation pane and select the View all 9 IP addresses link (see Figure 6.29). The number of IP addresses will depend on what you have previously configured. You should see the uplink address and all the internal addresses. Our example uses 192.168.1.2 for the uplink and for the internal interfaces: 10.1.1.254, 10.2.2.254, and 10.3.3.254. The addresses starting with fe80 are link-local IPv6 addresses.

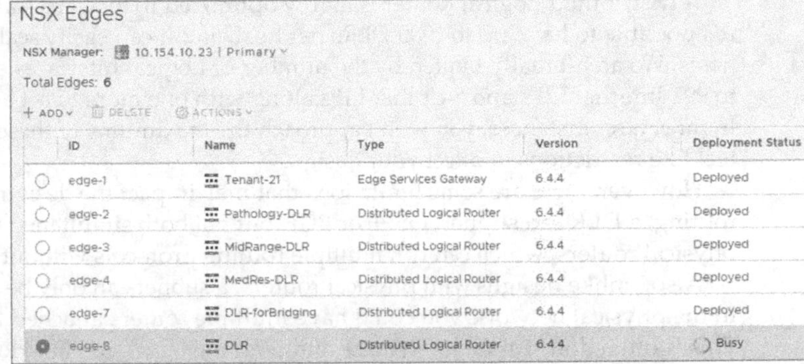

FIGURE 6.28 Checking the Deployment Status column for the DLR

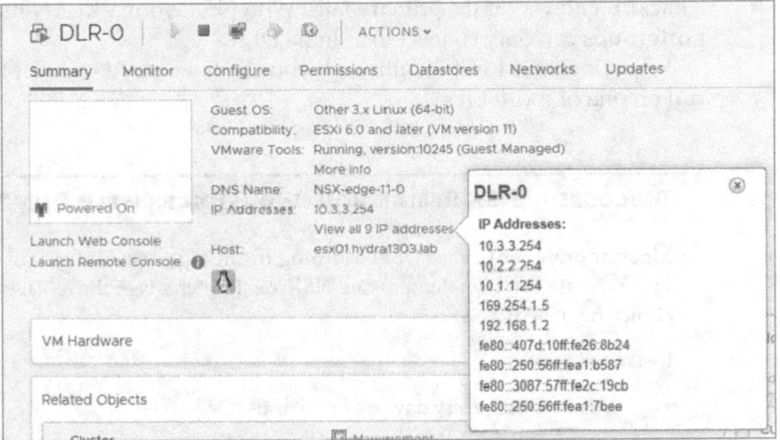

FIGURE 6.29 Viewing the IP addresses of the Uplink and Internal interfaces

26. To test connectivity, ping the DLR internal interface 10.1.1.254 from the web server, 10.1.1.100.

Both are connected to the same Logical Switch. In our example, the ping was successful (see Figure 6.30).

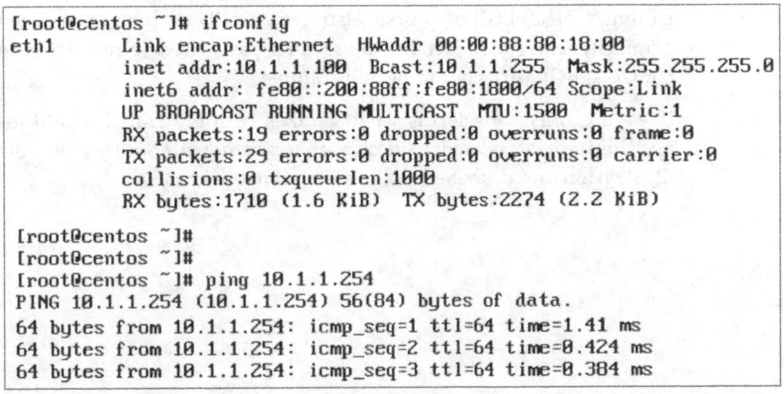

FIGURE 6.30 Verifying connectivity from a web server VM to its gateway, the DLR

```
[root@centos ~]# ifconfig
eth1      Link encap:Ethernet  HWaddr 00:00:88:80:18:00
          inet addr:10.1.1.100  Bcast:10.1.1.255  Mask:255.255.255.0
          inet6 addr: fe80::200:88ff:fe80:1800/64 Scope:Link
          UP BROADCAST RUNNING MULTICAST  MTU:1500  Metric:1
          RX packets:19 errors:0 dropped:0 overruns:0 frame:0
          TX packets:29 errors:0 dropped:0 overruns:0 carrier:0
          collisions:0 txqueuelen:1000
          RX bytes:1710 (1.6 KiB)  TX bytes:2274 (2.2 KiB)

[root@centos ~]#
[root@centos ~]#
[root@centos ~]# ping 10.1.1.254
PING 10.1.1.254 (10.1.1.254) 56(84) bytes of data.
64 bytes from 10.1.1.254: icmp_seq=1 ttl=64 time=1.41 ms
64 bytes from 10.1.1.254: icmp_seq=2 ttl=64 time=0.424 ms
64 bytes from 10.1.1.254: icmp_seq=3 ttl=64 time=0.384 ms
```

A Distributed Logical Router is highly optimized to forward traffic between VMs (East-West). It's possible to have up to 1000 DLRs per host, and it can easily scale by simply adding more hosts. We aren't really limited by the number of Logical Interfaces either. A DLR can support up to 991 Internal LIFs and 8 Uplink LIFs along with one more to act as the management interface. In most circumstances, you won't approach the maximums of these limits, so they don't really feel like restrictions or affect your design.

However, there are some limitations that may impact the design. For instance, with dynamic routing, a DLR can support OSPF or BGP, but not both simultaneously. This is different from physical routers, which can run multiple routing protocols without issue.

Also, unlike designs with physical routers, a subnet can only be associated with a single DLR. In the physical network, you could have multiple routers attached to say, network 172.16.1.0. This is often done for fault tolerance and with the help of a First Hop Redundancy Protocol (FHRP). FHRP routers in the physical network allow you to have a default gateway and a backup gateway if the primary fails. With NSX, your VXLAN-backed or VLAN-backed portgroups can only connect to a single DLR.

When it comes to OSPF, although you can have up to eight Uplink interfaces, it can only be run on one of those LIFs.

Discussing NSX Design Routing Choices with Our Customers

Most of our clients have OSPF running in their physical infrastructure. So, when we are brought in to create and implement an NSX design, many believe OSPF in NSX would be a better choice over BGP.

Reasons include:

- "We use OSPF every day. We know it better."
- "BGP is too complicated. No thank you."

It's true that BGP has the potential to be very complex when it is being used to provide control knobs for ingress and egress traffic. These controls (path attributes) are made for peering with other organizations that you need to route through, but you don't trust those organizations the same way you trust your own network. By manipulating BGP path attributes, you control exactly how traffic enters and exits your network from outside organizations like service providers. In addition to controlling traffic, BGP, of course, also dynamically exchanges routing information. With NSX, we're primarily using BGP just for the routing part. If we're not bothering with all of those additional controls, BGP turns out to be quite simple.

If we are only considering what it takes to route traffic, OSPF in comparison has several rules and limitations related to design that are not a concern with BGP, as shown in the following illustration and described in the bulleted list below that.

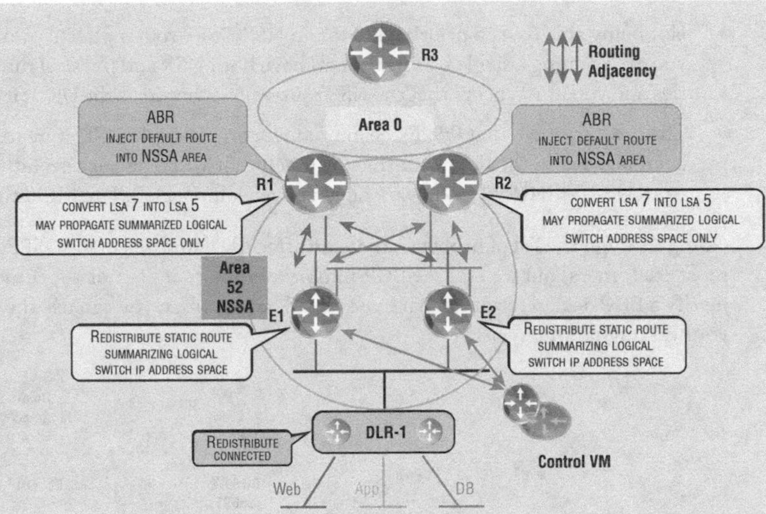

- OSPF natively supports different area types for optimization. With a physical Cisco router as an example, there can be standard areas, stub areas, not-so-stubby areas, totally stubby areas, and totally not-so-stubby areas. (If you're not familiar with Cisco, these types sound made up. They're not.) However, NSX only supports two types: standard and NSSA (not-so-stubby area).
- The problem with NSSAs is that they cause Type 7 NSSA Link State Advertisements (LSAs) to be flooded from NSX into the physical network. The LSAs get messy quickly. The DLR would receive all LSAs if it is configured with a standard area, but if it's connected to an NSSA area, all Type 5 External LSAs are filtered out (the key benefit in non-standard areas is the reduction of LSAs flooding through the area). Despite the DLR filtering out the Type 5s, the Edge will still see them and there is no special filtering at the Edge. The bottom line is that NSX ends up generating Type 7 LSAs into the physical network, which means there is an extra LSA for the infrastructure folks to deal with.
- OSPF has a way to optimize multi-access networks like Ethernet (vs. point-to-point). On a point-to-point link, neighbors directly exchange their LSAs. It's simple. But imagine in the physical network a switch with 10 OSPF routers attached. Each would try to form adjacencies with every other router, creating a full mesh (or full *mess* since it would create 45 connections all doing the same job). Instead, a Designated Router (DR) and a Backup Designated Router (BDR) are chosen to reduce the number of adjacencies and all the repeat chatter. Imagine having nine neighbors all telling you the same story. With a DR and BDR, only the DR is telling the story, so to speak. We can control which router is DR/BDR, or prevent a router from participating in the DR/BDR election by setting a priority. In the physical world, you can opt a router out of the election by setting the priority to 0. However, with NSX, setting a priority of 0 on a device running OSPF will prevent it from forming an adjacency with neighbors altogether. It gets stuck in a two-way state and can cause countless hours of troubleshooting if you don't know about that behavior.

- Not being able to set a priority of 0 for an NSX OSPF router affects your design in another way. If you are running a single OSPF area and have both NSX and physical routers, you must use priorities and you must ensure that the NSX router never becomes the DR. If it does, all hell breaks loose.
- The bottom line is that OSPF doesn't reduce complexity in NSX, it increases it. Hard lessons have been learned in the field with this, so much that with the next evolutionary step in NSX (going from NSX-V to NSX-T), VMware doesn't even support OSPF to avoid these potential issues.

Going through the list of problems that can affect design when using OSPF in NSX is enough to sway most customers, but we still see BGP-phobic admins that are not yet convinced. If you're trying to justify a BGP design to your department head or customer, you can use the following illustration for your talking points.

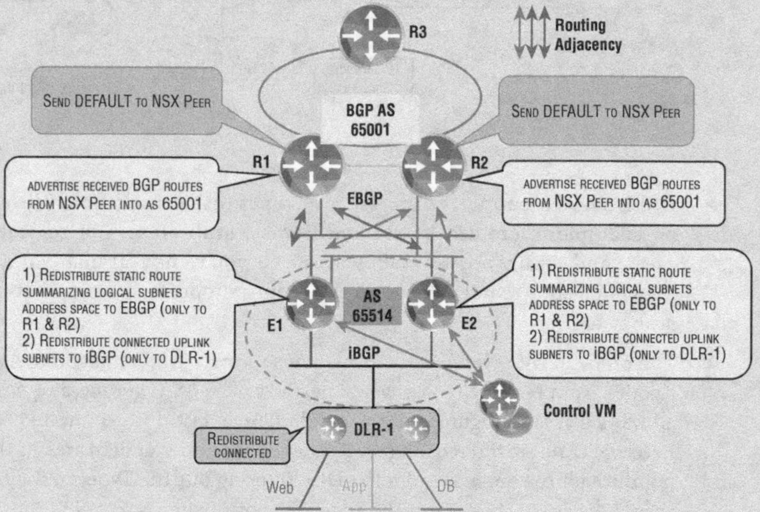

- BGP running in NSX is child's play. (We'll prove that when we get to configuration in the next chapter.)
- BGP is simple if you're only using it for routing. BGP in NSX has nothing too fancy regarding controls other than the ability to leverage prefix lists for filtering.
- Unless there is a technical reason that the boss or customer wants OSPF, we always go with BGP, and by the way, there is no technical reason.
- The proof is in VMware's decision to only support BGP as a dynamic routing protocol for NSX-T. Use it.

The Bottom Line

Forwarding Address vs. Protocol Address The control and data planes are separate in NSX. The separation allows for higher availability since it's possible for the control plane to fail, while the data plane continues to route traffic.

Master It Because of the dichotomy of routing functions, there is a Protocol Address and a Forwarding Address assigned to learn routes and to route traffic. Which component would be assigned the Forwarding Address?

1. DLR
2. ESG
3. LR Control VM
4. UWA

North-South East-West NSX handles VM-to-VM (East-West) traffic as well as NSX-to-physical (North-South) traffic. By a large margin, most traffic flows in a data center are made up of East-West traffic.

Master It What component specializes and is optimized for East-West traffic?

1. ESG
2. DLR
3. Layer 2 Bridge
4. Internal LIF

OSPF Design Rules OSPF is one option to use as a dynamic routing protocol for NSX. OSPF implementations require adhering to rules designed for scalability and stability. OSPF can operate in a single area, but convergence can be optimized by subdividing OSPF into multiple areas.

Master It If your OSPF design has multiple areas, which of the following is true?

1. All LSAs are Type 7 NSSA.
2. One area must be numbered 0.
3. No areas can be numbered 0.
4. Adding areas reduces scalability.

DLR Minus a LR Control VM When installing a DLR, a Logical Router Control VM is also deployed, by default. However, it's possible to deploy the DLR without the Control VM.

Master It Which could be a valid reason for purposefully choosing not to deploy the LR Control VM with the DLR?

1. You are only using the DLR to route North-South traffic.
2. You don't need the Control VM with OSPF.
3. You don't need the Control VM with static routes.
4. The LR Control VM is only necessary if the DLR is supporting multiple routing protocols simultaneously.

Chapter 7

NFV: Routing with NSX Edges

Network Function Virtualization (NFV) is not synonymous with Software-Defined Networking (SDN), although they are closely related and have some overlap. NSX is VMware's SDN solution for network virtualization and security. A key concept that we continue to emphasize is how NSX decouples the control and data planes. This is SDN's primary focus and is a paradigm shift from traditional network devices with network control functions and network forwarding functions combined. SDN is all about pulling these two apart, abstracting control from the physical network. If you break down the word *abstract* into its Latin roots, that's exactly what it means. "Tract" translates to pull or remove, and "Abs" means from.

NFV also deals with abstraction but with a different emphasis. Service providers typically go beyond simply providing customers with an Internet connection. Services also include network functions such as NAT, DNS, firewall, encryption, and load balancing. Traditionally, each function was deployed at the customer's site using proprietary hardware, making upgrades difficult and costly. NFV decouples network functions from physical hardware and moves them to virtual machines. So, although SDN and NFV are both contributing to the overall solution and performing abstraction, they are different.

To underscore the difference, it's possible to have NFV without SDN. For example, you could add a virtualized firewall (which is Network Function Virtualization) to your environment without separating the control and data planes (SDN) at all.

IN THIS CHAPTER, YOU WILL LEARN ABOUT:

- Edge High Availability
- Comparing Edge cousins: DLR vs. ESG
- Uplink and Internal LIFs
- Configuring BGP or OSPF between the DLR and ESG
- Static routing
- Troubleshooting routing with CLI commands
- Improving scalability and availability with ECMP

Network Function Virtualization: NSX Has It Too

The NSX Edge incorporates both Software-Defined Networking (SDN) and Network Function Virtualization (NFV) concepts. The NSX Edge is a component of NSX, VMware's SDN network virtualization and security platform, and it provides network services that include the examples we have already listed for NFV: Network Address Translation (NAT), Domain Name System (DNS), firewall, etc. (see Figure 7.1). In the previous chapter, our focus on routing was with the Distributed Logical Router (DLR). We saw how NSX pulls the actual routing of traffic, the packet forwarding, into the kernel and moves control plane functions, like dynamic routing with Open Shortest Path First (OSPF) and Border Gateway Protocol (BGP), into a VM. That VM exchanges routes with the Edge Services Gateway (ESG). The ESG provides all the network functions mentioned as well as routing.

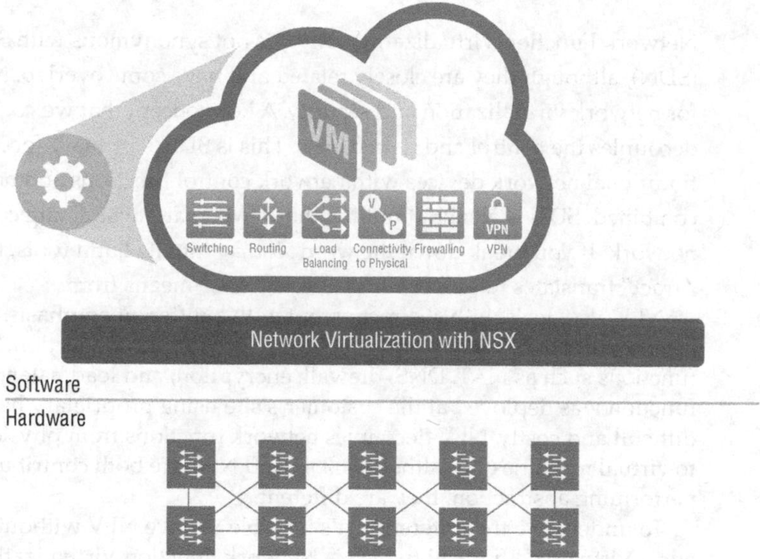

FIGURE 7.1 Network functions virtualized and offered by an NSX Edge

Since we have been discussing dynamic and static routing for the LR Control VM, we'll build on that with the ESG and look at how to configure routing for both the Control VM and the ESG. The steps are similar. The chapter following this one will center around the other virtualized network functions the ESG can provide.

This Is Nice: Edge HA

When an ESG is deployed with High Availability (HA) enabled, it creates a second VM (see Figure 7.2). The main idea with HA is to have an active unit and a standby unit, each deployed on different ESXi hosts, which you can ensure by configuring an anti-affinity rule. The primary ESG will be active, doing all the work and providing the services, while the secondary ESG has the same configuration, but acts as backup in case the primary fails.

For this to work, there must be a way for the standby ESG to know when the primary is alive and when it isn't. This is accomplished with heartbeat messages sent every 3 seconds. When we enable HA on the Edge device, we also specify an HA interface. This interface is used, in part, for the HA heartbeat.

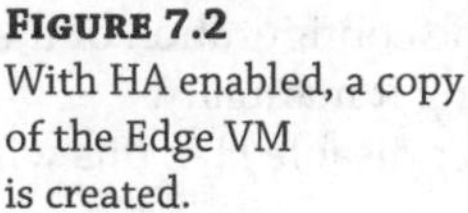

FIGURE 7.2
With HA enabled, a copy of the Edge VM is created.

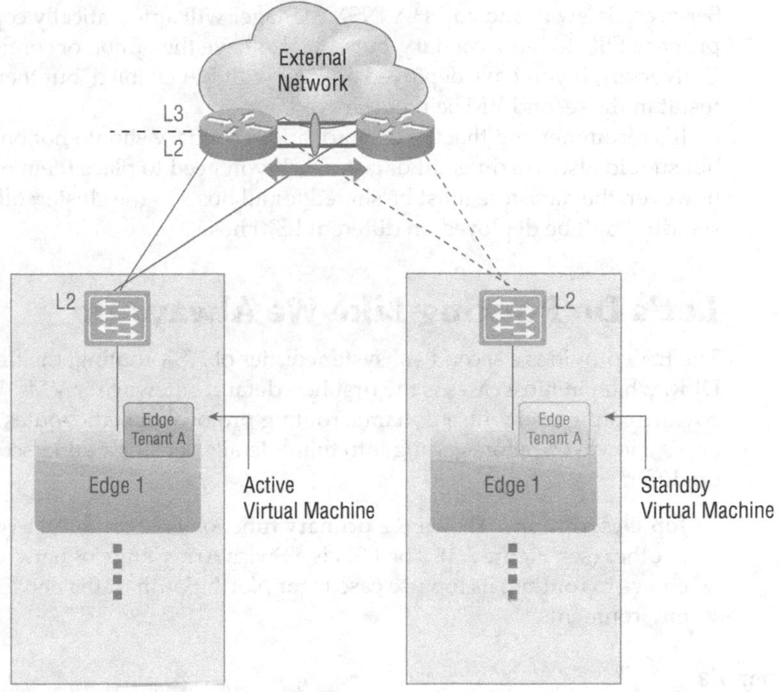

By default, the standby has a Dead Timer set to 15 seconds. If the heartbeat from the active Edge VM is not received for 15 seconds, the standby Edge takes over takes over as active. Since it has the same configuration, the newly active ESG will take over the responsibility for providing those same network functions. Although 15 seconds is the default, this can be tuned to 6 seconds for faster failover.

Something common to active/standby designs is that the standby makes its decision to become active based on the lack of heartbeat messages. Therefore, if anything prevents the communication of those messages, you can end up with a situation where both are in the active state.

Once the communication between the two is reinstated and they become aware of each other, a negotiation should occur, with one remaining active and the other, standby. However, certain conditions sometimes interfere with the negotiation. These conditions are usually related to the reason why they lost communication in the first place. The result is that both continue to operate as active, resulting in what is called a *split-brain condition*. The negotiation failure can be due to a lack of resources (CPU, memory, or storage), connectivity issues, and/or network congestion. Until a split-brain condition is resolved, network services will be unavailable for the most part. Also keep in mind that heartbeats use the IANA standard UDP port, 694. If this port is blocked, heartbeats will not be received.

Adding HA

If you did not enable HA when deploying the ESG, you can add it after the fact. You do not need to delete the VM and redeploy it. Using your vSphere Client, you can select the existing Edge

Services Gateway and add HA. NSX Manager will automatically copy the configuration of the primary ESG to the secondary, but you also have the option of configuring it manually. Conversely, if you have deployed an ESG with HA enabled, but then later disable HA, this will result in the second VM being destroyed.

It's recommended that the primary and secondary should not only be on different ESXi hosts, but should also use different datastores. If you need to place them on the same datastore, however, the datastore must be shared for all hosts in the cluster; otherwise, the active and standby can't be deployed on different ESXi hosts.

Let's Do Routing Like We Always Do

The ESG provides a second subsystem or tier of NSX routing, the first being provided by the DLR, which in most cases is the first hop default gateway for VMs. When it comes to how these two are configured with a dynamic routing protocol or static routes, there aren't many differences. However, before getting into those details, let's first underscore how the DLR and ESG do differ:

Job Description The DLR's primary function is to route East-West traffic from one VM to another (see Figure 7.3). The ESG is a Swiss Army knife of network functions, but when it comes to routing, its top use case is for North-South traffic between the virtual and physical environments.

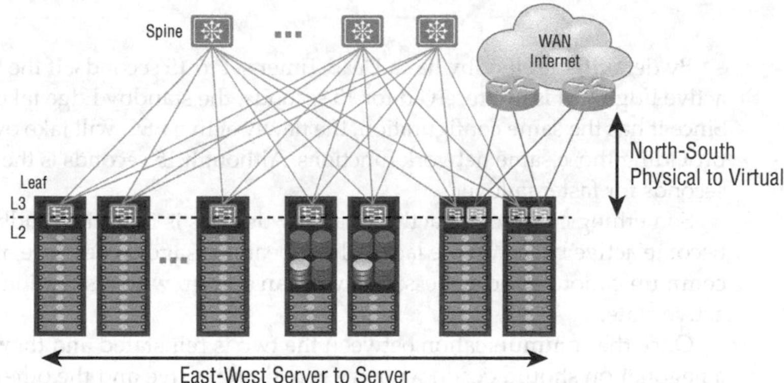

FIGURE 7.3 The DLR routes E-W traffic, and the ESG routes N-S.

VM vs. Kernel The ESG is a virtual machine. The DLR is a kernel module, but in order to support dynamic routing, it creates a Logical Router Control VM. Routing protocols such as BGP and OSPF expect to communicate with another router also running the same protocol. The Control VM provides a peer that can run a routing protocol and exchange routes with the ESG. However, unlike the ESG, which can both learn dynamic routes and forward traffic, the LR Control VM doesn't forward the traffic. It leaves that responsibility to the kernel module.

Distributed vs. Centralized The routing information that determines which next hop will be chosen to reach specific networks is distributed across all ESXi hosts within a transport zone for the DLR (see Figure 7.4). It behaves as if identical routers were installed on each host, but is supercharged compared to a VM because it is part of the kernel itself. There's no need to go to an external router or VM to get the information it needs. Since most traffic flows are from East to West across the data center, this design eliminates hairpinning and greatly improves routing performance. The ESG's routing is centralized within a VM, not distributed to every ESXi host.

FIGURE 7.4 Distributed vs. centralized routing

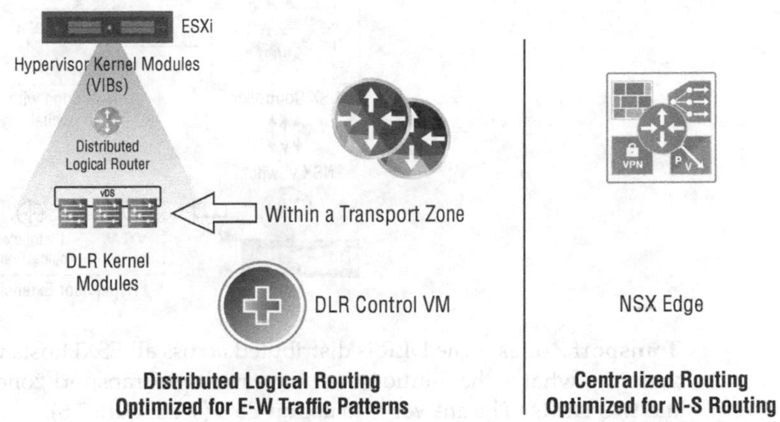

Impact of Host Failure Consider the impact of routed traffic if an ESXi host were to fail. The DLR is distributed across hosts and therefore, the duplicated routing information would still be present on the remaining hosts. But what happens when the host that fails is where the LR Control VM is deployed? This failure only has a minor effect on the remaining hosts, but not in terms of forwarding traffic. Traffic continues to be routed to the correct destination networks even with the LR Control VM no longer functioning. The reason is due to the forwarding of traffic being handled in the kernel, completely separate from the control plane functions provided by the Control VM. The other hosts will behave as if their routing tables have been frozen in time. They can't learn new information regarding new networks, new paths, or networks that are no longer available. They simply route based on the latest information that originated from the Control VM before it died. The failure of the host with the Control VM does not bring down the network. Instead, the data plane forwarding continues to be available due to the separation of the control and data planes.

Fault tolerance must be handled in a completely different way for the ESG. Being that it is entirely a VM housed on an ESXi host, we must have a mechanism to fail over to a different host. That solution is to configure High Availability (HA). With HA enabled, a copy of the ESG is created on another host, but it remains in a standby state until it detects that the primary ESG is no longer available (see Figure 7.5). The time that it takes to fail over can affect some network functions provided by the ESG. For example, the Load Balancer and VPN services both rely on TCP for their connections. TCP is a connection-oriented protocol, which basically means that no data will be sent until the connection is first established using a three-way handshake to 1) request the connection, 2) acknowledge the request, and then 3) acknowledge that the first acknowledgment was received and that it's OK to proceed in sending the data. TCP connections with the ESG would be lost in the event of a host failure and would need to be re-established with the secondary ESG.

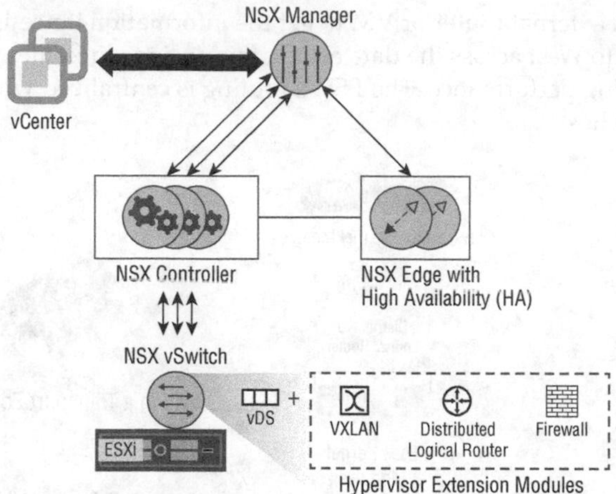

Figure 7.5 Distributed and centralized routing approach host failure differently.

Transport Zones The DLR is distributed across all ESXi hosts within the *same* transport zone. So, what is the solution if we have multiple transport zones and need to route between the two DLRs? The answer is to use an ESG (see Figure 7.6).

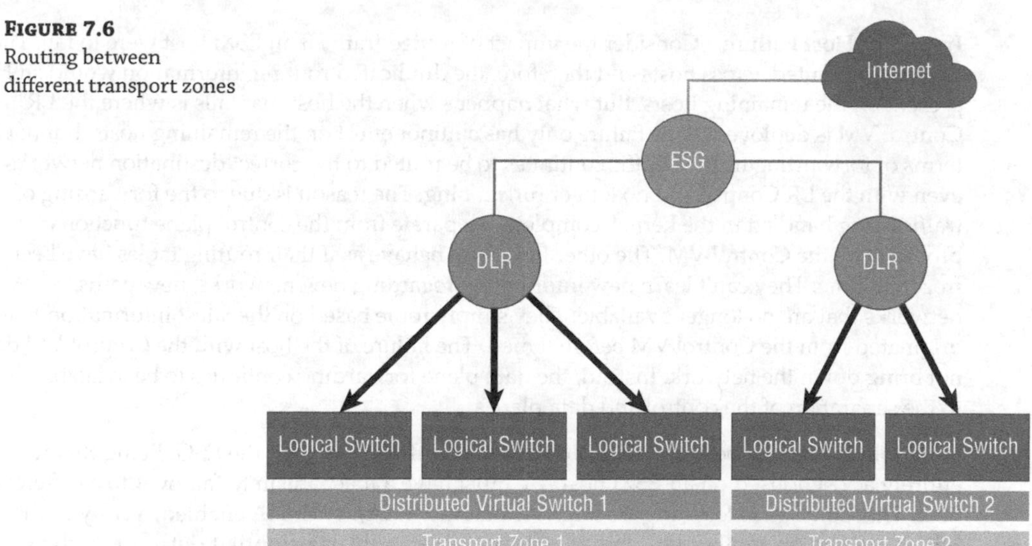

Figure 7.6 Routing between different transport zones

Routing Protocols For dynamic routing, the DLR supports BGP and OSPF, but both can't be run simultaneously (see Figure 7.7). Keep in mind that the DLR is only exchanging routes with entities within NSX. The ESG, on the other hand, exchanges routes within the NSX environment and the outside world. Because of this, the ESG supports BGP, OSPF, and Intermediate System to Intermediate System (IS-IS) routing protocols. Therefore, if the provider router is running IS-IS, the ESG can be configured to exchange routing information with it, while still communicating internally within NSX using BGP or OSPF.

FIGURE 7.7
Routing options available for the DLR and the NSX Edge

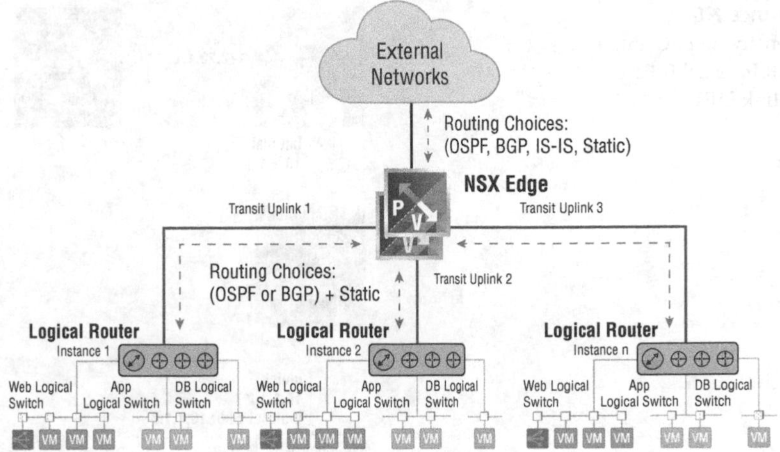

Although the ESG is aware of these IS-IS routes, it doesn't mean that the routing information will automatically be passed to the LR Control VMs running OSPF or BGP. Each routing protocol maintains its own separate tables of information. To allow the external IS-IS routes to be learned in the NSX environment, we configure redistribution on the ESG: redistributing the IS-IS information into OSPF or BGP and vice versa. However, a more common design is to have the ESG announce a single default route for the DLRs to reach external networks. To advertise NSX routes to the outside world, redistribute them into the routing protocol used by the provider and filter out any routes that you do not wish to be externally advertised. Unlike the DLR, the ESG can run multiple routing protocols simultaneously. Not to forget static routes, both the DLR and the ESG support statics. Also, the DLR only has an issue running multiple dynamic routing protocols simultaneously. It has no problem supporting a single dynamic routing protocol and multiple static routes at the same time.

Logical Interfaces (LIFs) Both the DLR and ESG have two categories of logical interfaces: Internal and Uplink (see Figure 7.8).

The DLR's internal interfaces connect to Logical Switches. VMs are attached to the Logical Switches, enabling them to connect to the network. The VMs will use the DLR's Internal LIF IP addresses as their respective default gateways. For example, VM 10.8.8.5 connected to the Application Logical Switch uses the DLR Internal LIF address 10.8.8.1 as its gateway to reach other networks.

The Uplink LIF on the DLR is used to forward VM traffic North to the ESG. The DLR and ESG share this common segment and belong to the same subnet. The interface used by the ESG to accomplish this is one of the ESG's Internal LIFs.

The ESG's Uplink LIF is used to connect to the external network, with its next hop address being that of a physical router. The internal interfaces are used to send traffic South to the DLRs.

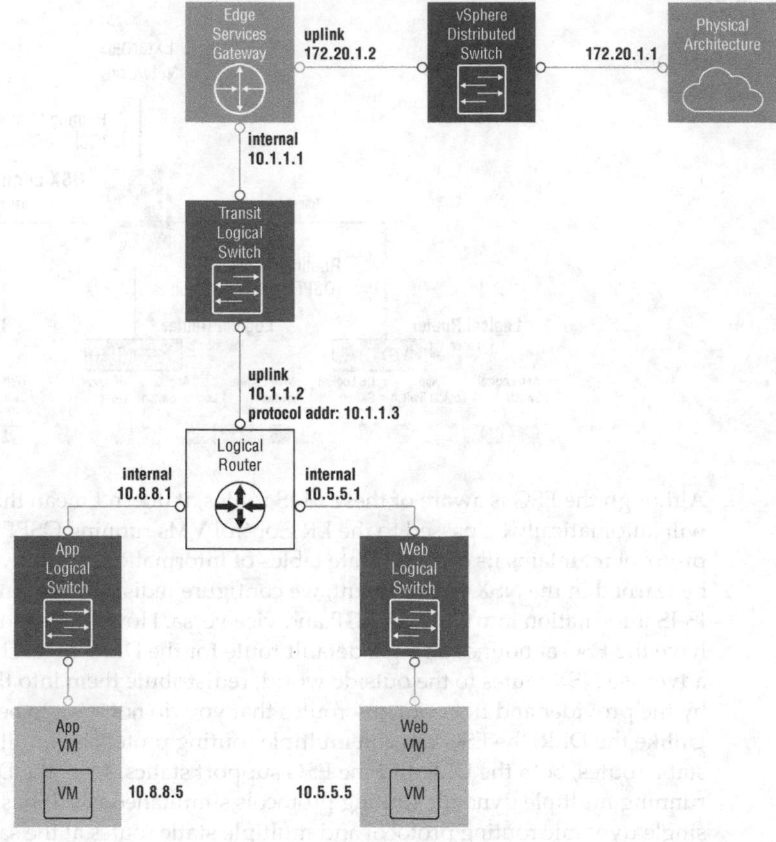

FIGURE 7.8 Identifying ESG and DLR Internal LIFs and Uplink LIFs

In total, the DLR supports 1000 LIFs. One is an uplink used for management, with 8 more uplink interfaces available. The other 991 virtual interfaces that can be created are Internal LIFs. Furthermore, a single ESXi host can support up to 250 DLRs.

The ESG can have up to 10 internal, uplink, or trunk interfaces, a limitation imposed by the NSX Manager. Additionally, each trunk interface can support 200 subinterfaces.

Deploying the Edge Services Gateway

You can install multiple NSX Edge Services Gateways and can configure multiple external IP addresses for load balancing, site-to-site VPNs, and NAT. Each NSX Edge supports two VMs for High Availability. Here, we will go through the steps to configure an ESG with HA:

1. First, open the vSphere FLEX Web Client and navigate to Home ➢ Networking And Security ➢ NSX Edges and click the green + sign to create a new Edge.

   A new window appears (see Figure 7.9).

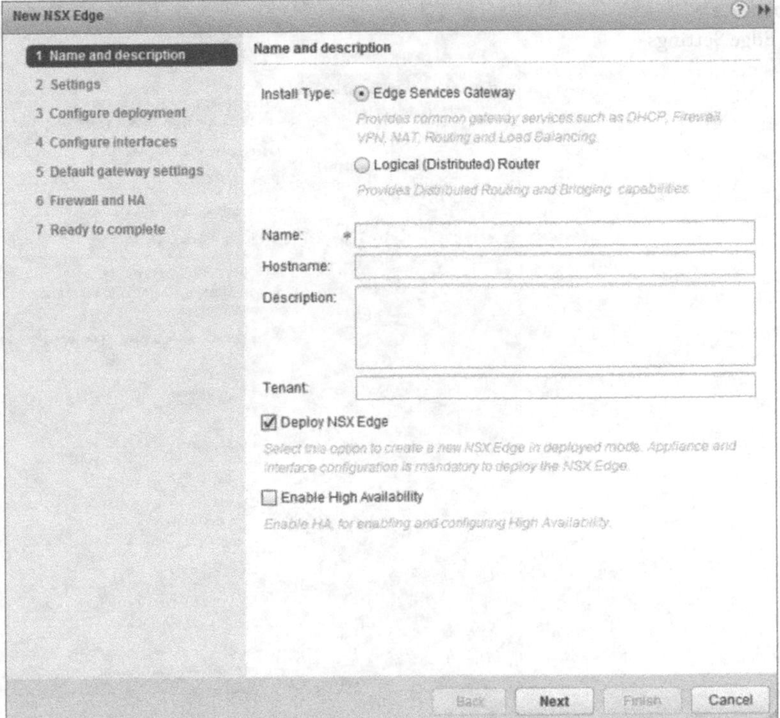

FIGURE 7.9 NSX Edge name and description

2. Select Edge Services Gateway and give it a name. Make sure there is a checkmark beside Deploy NSX Edge.

   You also have the option to place a check mark to Enable High Availability, which will create a second ESG placed in standby mode, backing up the primary ESG should it fail.

3. In the next window, which relates to general settings for the ESG, configure the admin password (see Figure 7.10).

   Just like we saw previously with the DLR and Layer 2 Bridge configurations, this password has to be at least 12 characters, contain uppercase and lowercase letters, and have one special character, with no character consecutively repeating three times in a row.

4. Click Next; the Configure Deployment window appears (see Figure 7.11).

5. Select the data center from the drop-down and choose the appliance size.

   The larger the size, the more resources that are required to support it.

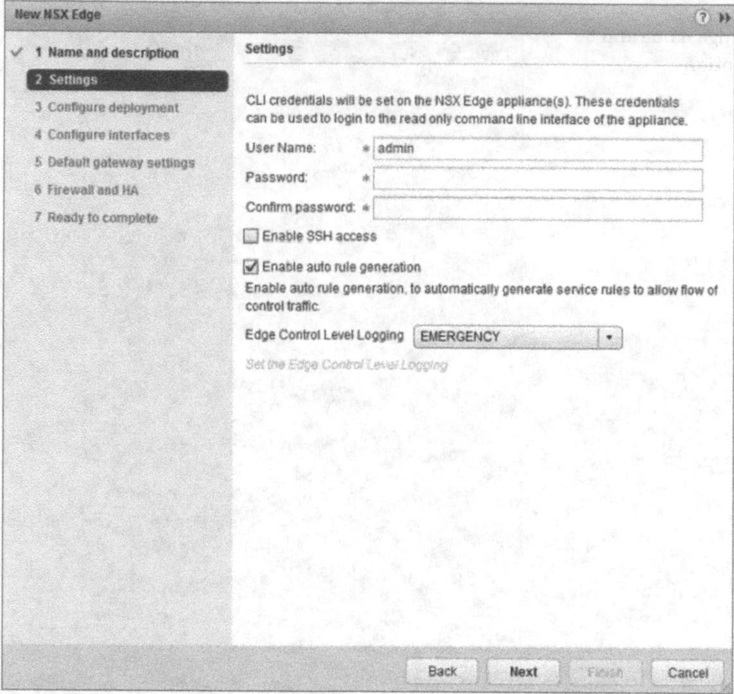

FIGURE 7.10
NSX Edge Settings

FIGURE 7.11
NSX Edge Configure Deployment

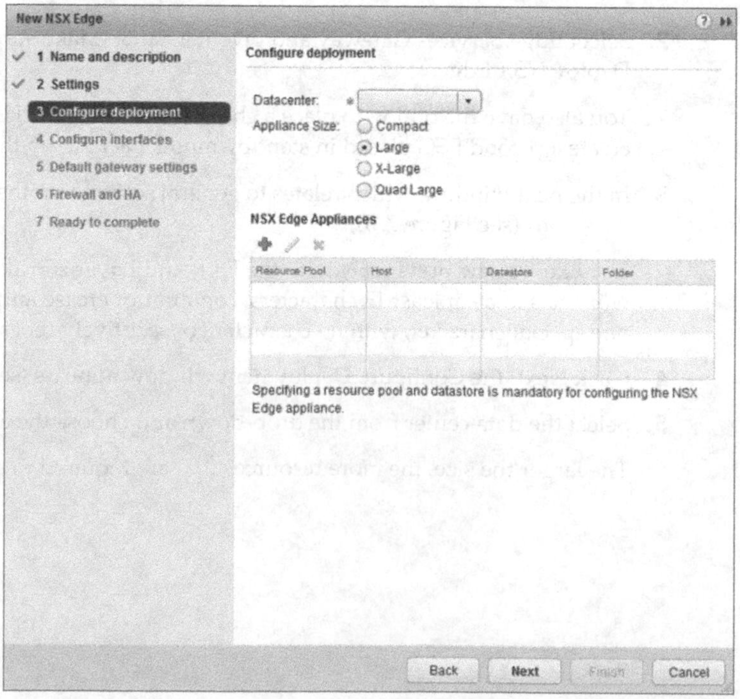

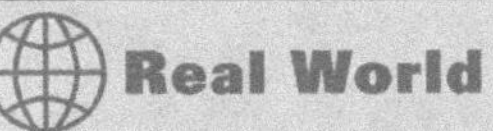

CHOOSING NSX EDGE APPLIANCE SIZE

The Compact form-factor (Figure 7.11) is rarely used in production. However, it comes in handy in test lab environments since it only requires a single vCPU and 512 MB of memory.

Typically, customers will start out with the Large form factor for their ESG. It is ideal for supporting a single service, such as routing North-South traffic. In the next chapter, we will dig into additional services the ESG can provide, including firewall, NAT, DHCP, site-to-site VPN, SSL VPN, load balancing, HA, Syslog, and L2 VPN, along with what we have been focusing on in this chapter, dynamic routing.

As you tack on these additional services, you may find that Large does not have enough resources to maintain the same level of performance. Some services are more resource-intensive than others, such as the firewall service and ECMP. The Quad Large form factor can provide better performance to handle these services since it has twice the number of vCPUs compared to Large. In terms of memory, both Large and Quad Large use 1 GB.

You may find that even the Quad Large is not enough to maintain the same high-performance levels if your design includes load balancing with a Layer 7 engine, for example. The X-Large form factor can help in this regard. It has three times the number of vCPUs compared to Large and eight times the memory.

6. In the same Configure Deployment window, click the green + sign to specify the cluster where the ESG will be deployed and select the datastore (see Figure 7.12).

FIGURE 7.12 NSX Edge Cluster and Datastore selection

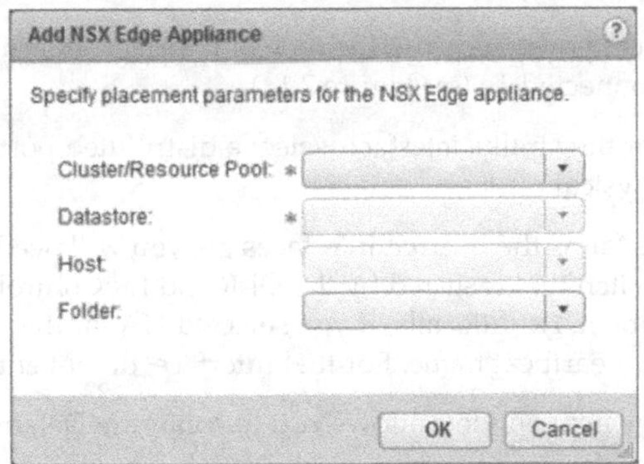

If you had previously selected HA, it's recommended that the second appliance be assigned to a different datastore.

It may seem a bit odd that specifying the cluster and datastore is optional. What if you didn't include these details and simply clicked Next? Essentially, the ESG would be created but not deployed. It would remain in offline mode until you added those details.

7. Click OK and then Next. The Configure Interface window appears (see Figure 7.13).

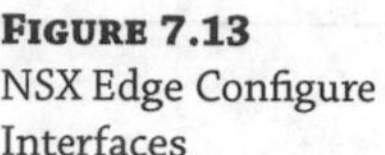

FIGURE 7.13
NSX Edge Configure Interfaces

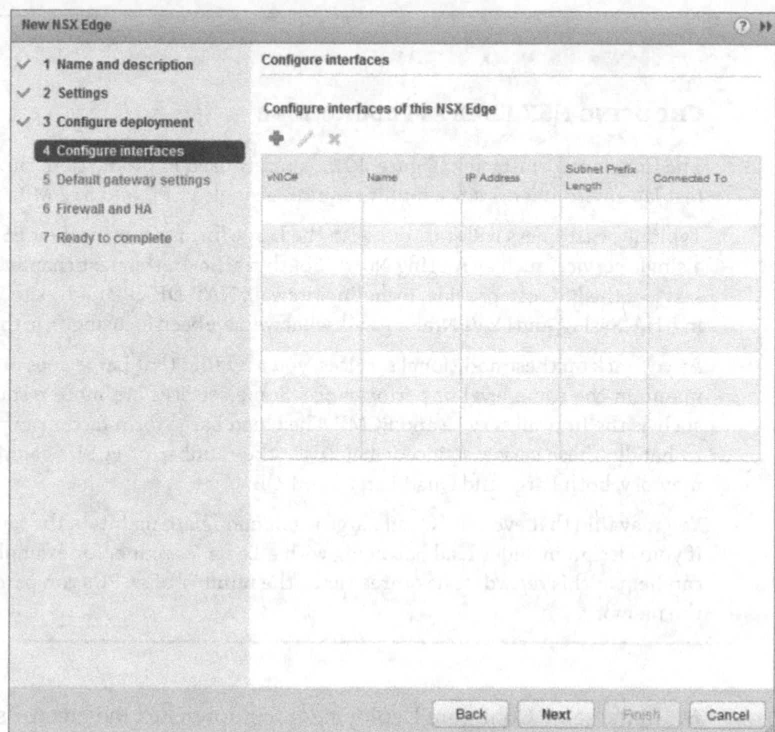

8. Click the green + sign.

   Here you can choose the type of interface, Internal or Uplink, and choose the network it is Connected To (see Figure 7.14).

9. For the Uplink interface, select a distributed port group that connects to the external physical router.

   As far as the Internal interfaces go, you will need one to attach to the same transit Logical Switch that is shared by the DLR and LR Control VM. All three need to be on the same subnet. Additionally, if you selected HA for the ESG, you'll need another Internal interface for heartbeat traffic. For that interface, do not enter an IP address.

   The next window allows you to configure Default Gateway settings (see Figure 7.15).

   Depending on your routing design and the specific routing information that is exchanged, you may not need to manually configure a default gateway. If it is necessary, the gateway will typically be the next hop physical router reachable by the ESG uplink interface.

   The next window is to configure Firewall and HA (see Figure 7.16).

FIGURE 7.14
Adding an NSX Edge interface

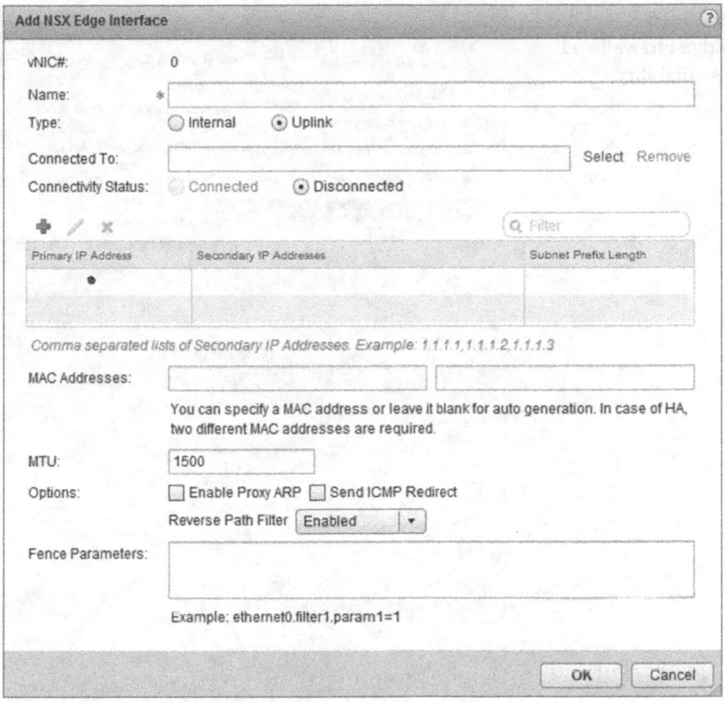

FIGURE 7.15
NSX Edge Default Gateway Settings

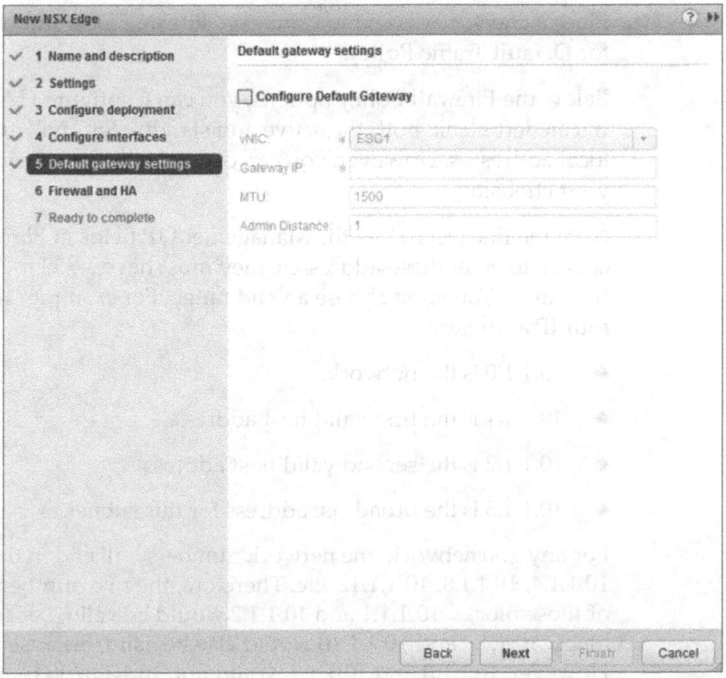

FIGURE 7.16
NSX Edge Firewall and High Availability

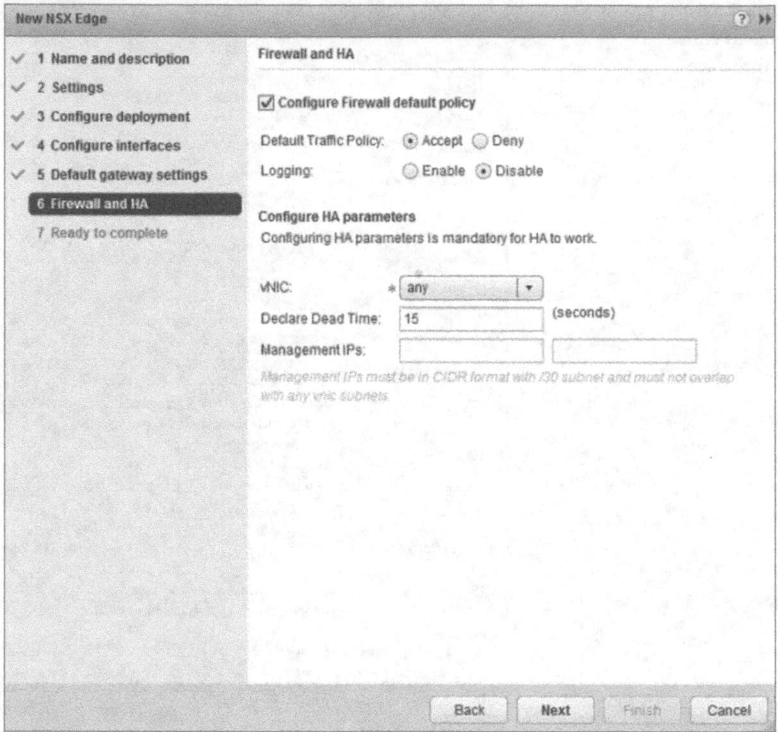

10. Place a check mark next to Configure Firewall Default Policy, and select Accept on the line for Default Traffic Policy.

    Below the Firewall Policy options, you can Configure HA Parameters. If the Management IPs are left blank, both the active and standby ESG will automatically be assigned link local addresses. However, you can override this by entering management IP addresses of your choosing.

    Note the line just below the Management IP fields in Figure 7.16. It specifies that if you choose to enter these addresses, they must have a /30 mask. A /30 network only supports two hosts. You must choose a valid range. For example, 10.1.1.0/30 will contain a total of four IP addresses:

    - 10.1.1.0 is the network.
    - 10.1.1.1 is the first valid host address.
    - 10.1.1.2 is the second valid host address.
    - 10.1.1.3 is the broadcast address for this subnet.

    For any /30 network, the network numbers will end in 0 or a multiple of four, such as 10.1.1.4, 10.1.1.8, 10.1.1.12, etc. Therefore, the two numbers you enter must fall *within* one of those blocks. 10.1.1.1 and 10.1.1.2 would be valid, because they belong to the 10.1.1.0 block. 10.1.1.9 and 10.1.1.10 would also be valid, because they belong to the 10.1.1.8 block. However, 10.1.1.8 and 10.1.1.9 would not. 10.1.1.8/30 represents the network, not a host address.

11. Click Finish to deploy the ESG.

If you previously chose to enable HA, you will see that two ESGs are deployed, both sharing the same name with the exception that one has a -0 suffix added and the other, -1. Starting out, the ESG with the -0 suffix will be active and -1 will be standby.

Now that the Edge Services Gateway has been deployed, we can access it and configure routing. Since the ESG and DLR share nearly identical configuration steps for routing, we will focus on just the DLR next for brevity.

Configuring BGP

Before configuring BGP as the dynamic routing protocol running between the ESG and the DLR, let's plan out what our design will look like so that we know what values to plug in when they are needed in the configuration. We will be using Autonomous System (AS) number 65501. This has already been configured on our ESG. Anytime two neighboring BGP routers belong to the same AS, it is referred to as internal BGP (iBGP). When the neighbors are from different organizations and therefore have different AS numbers, it is called external BGP (eBGP):

- The DLR's uplink interface has been assigned 192.168.1.1.
- The ESG's interface is 192.168.1.2. This will be the DLR's gateway.
- The LR Control VM interface will be 192.168.1.3, used for routing protocol messages.

1. Begin by opening the vSphere FLEX Web Client and going to Home ➤ Networking And Security ➤ NSX Edges and double-click the DLR.

2. Under the Manage tab, make sure Routing is selected, and then click Global Configuration (see Figure 7.17).

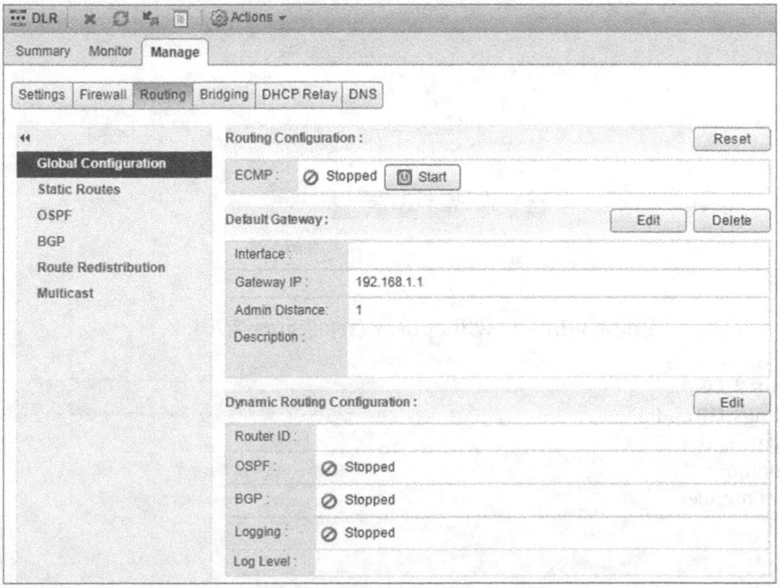

FIGURE 7.17 DLR Routing Global Configuration

3. The bottom panel is titled Dynamic Routing Configuration. All the way to the right on that line, click the Edit button.

   You may have to scroll right to see the button (see Figure 7.18).

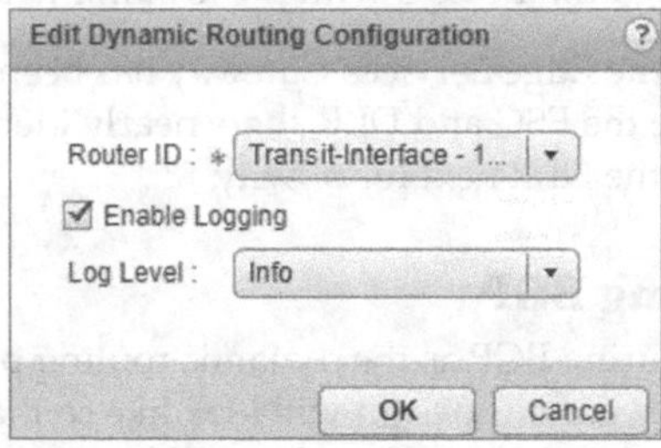

FIGURE 7.18 A Router ID is required when configuring OSPF or BGP.

4. Choose your transit Logical Switch as the Router ID.

   BGP and OSPF both require a Router ID to uniquely identify the router within the routing domain. In this case, it must be unique within AS 65501.

5. Additionally, check Enable Logging with the Log Level set to Info.
6. Click OK.
7. Select Publish Changes so that the routing configuration can take effect.
8. Select BGP from the menu, and click Edit to the far right of the BGP Configuration line (see Figure 7.19).

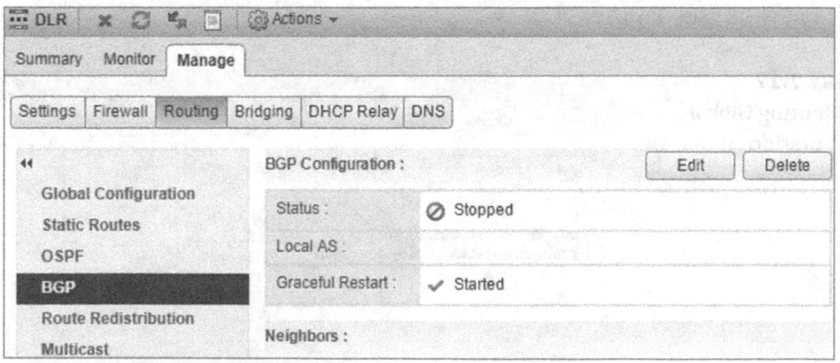

FIGURE 7.19 Configuring BGP

A new window will appear (see Figure 7.20).

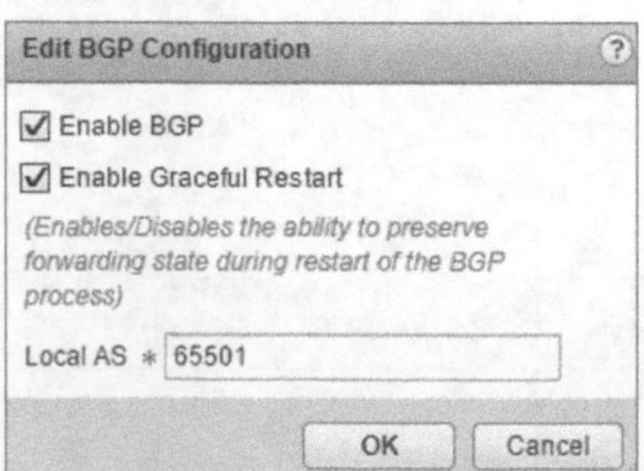

FIGURE 7.20 Enabling BGP and configuring the Autonomous System number

9. Place check marks next to Enable BGP and Enable Graceful Restart.

10. Enter **65501** for the Local AS number and click OK.

11. Click the Publish Changes button again for the configuration to be applied.

12. After the changes have been published, click the green + sign in the Neighbors pane.

    A new window will appear (see Figure 7.21).

FIGURE 7.21
Adding the ESG as the DLR's BGP neighbor

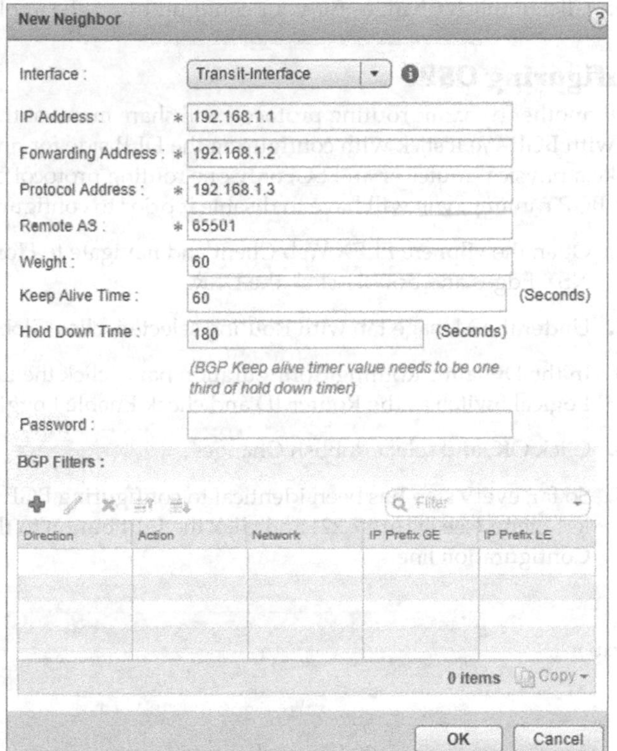

USING THE DROP-DOWN MENU

When selecting the interface from the drop-down, the forwarding address will automatically be populated for you. The forwarding address belongs to this DLR and is used to forward traffic to the ESG.

13. Enter the following information:

    - IP Address (the ESG neighbor): **192.168.1.1**
    - Forwarding Address (the DLR uplink address): **192.168.1.2**

- Protocol Address (the LR Control VM address for peering): **192.168.1.3**
- Remote AS (the AS number of the ESG): **65501**

Both the ESG and the DLR are using the same AS number, 65501. AS numbers between 64512 and 65534 are valid for internal use and therefore do not require an assignment from IANA, the Internet Assigned Numbers Authority.

14. For the remaining options, accept their default settings, and click OK.
15. Click Publish Changes for your configuration to be applied.

Configuring OSPF

OSPF, another dynamic routing protocol, will share many of the same configuration steps as we saw with BGP. We'll stick with configuring the DLR side for now before moving on to the ESG. Unlike a physical router or an ESG, only one routing protocol can be chosen for a DLR. If you have BGP running, you will have to disable it prior to configuring OSPF:

1. Open the vSphere FLEX Web Client and navigate to Home ➢ Networking And Security ➢ NSX Edges and double-click the DLR.
2. Under the Manage tab with Routing selected, click Global Configuration.
3. In the Dynamic Routing Configuration pane, click the Edit button. Choose your transit Logical Switch as the Router ID and check Enable Logging with the Log Level set to Info.
4. Click OK, and select Publish Changes.
5. So far, every step has been identical to configuring BGP. This time, select OSPF from the left menu (see Figure 7.22) and click the Edit button to the far right of the OSPF Configuration line.

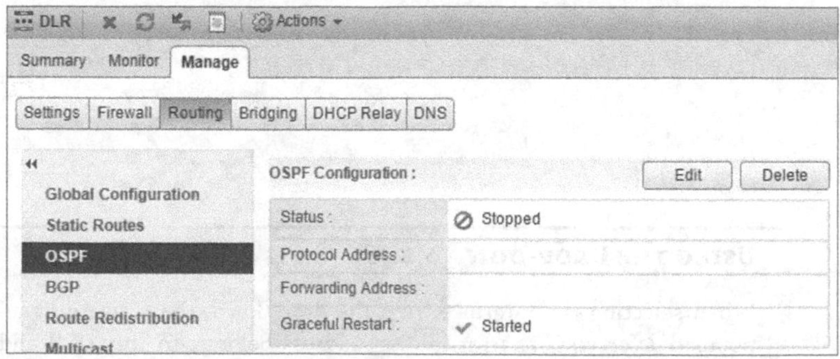

FIGURE 7.22 OSPF Configuration

6. When the new window appears, select the transit interface to automatically fill in the Forwarding Address, as it did before.
7. Be sure to place a check mark to Enable OSPF, enter **192.168.1.3** as the Protocol Address, and leave the box next to Enable Graceful Restart checked.

8. Click OK and then click Publish Changes to apply the configuration.
9. Click the green + sign in the middle pane labeled Area Definitions (see Figure 7.23).

FIGURE 7.23
Configuring the Protocol and Forwarding Addresses

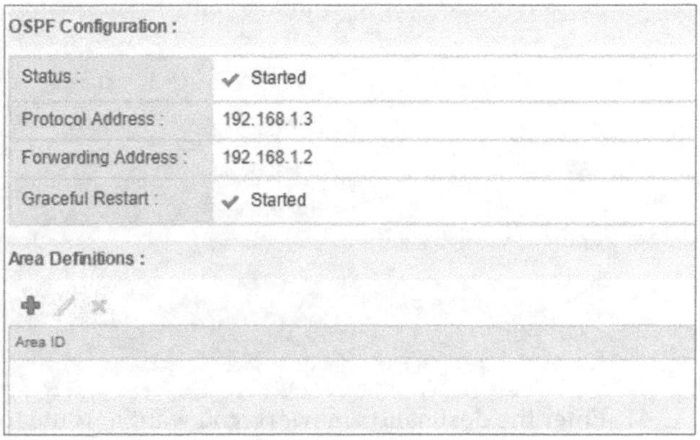

OSPF Configuration :

Status :	✔ Started
Protocol Address :	192.168.1.3
Forwarding Address :	192.168.1.2
Graceful Restart :	✔ Started

Area Definitions :

Area ID

10. Enter the Area ID.

    In this example, we are using only one OSPF Area and therefore aren't restricted (you can choose any number from 0 to ~4 billion). However, the neighboring ESG will also need to share the same OSPF Area ID.

11. Click OK.

Notice that unlike BGP, we are not explicitly configuring the OSPF neighbor's address. We only configure the forwarding address (the address on the DLR uplink) and the protocol address (the LR Control VM address). Once these are entered, OSPF discovers its neighbors. BGP, in contrast, only works if both sides explicitly point to one another as being a neighbor to peer with.

Configuring Static Routes

Instead of using a dynamic routing protocol like OSPF or BGP, we also have the option to manually configure static routes. Some administrators prefer the use of static routes in smaller environments due to their simplicity (referring to the routes, not the admins). However, as more networks are added, the number of static routes to maintain can become difficult to manage and the likelihood of configuration mistakes increases.

To configure a static route on a DLR, perform the following steps:

1. Open the vSphere FLEX Web Client and navigate to Home ➢ Networking And Security ➢ NSX Edges and double-click the DLR.
2. Under the Manage tab with Routing selected, click Static Routes.
3. Click the green + sign (see Figure 7.24) to add a static route.

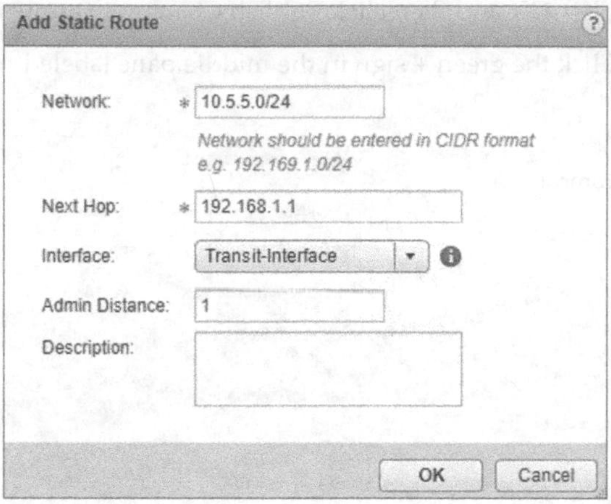

FIGURE 7.24
Adding a Static Route

Add Static Route	
Network:	* 10.5.5.0/24
	Network should be entered in CIDR format e.g. 192.169.1.0/24
Next Hop:	* 192.168.1.1
Interface:	Transit-Interface
Admin Distance:	1
Description:	
OK	Cancel

4. Enter the destination network you want to route to. In our example, we have network 10.5.5.0/24, a subnet located on the other side of the ESG:
   - Network: **10.5.5.0/24**
   - Next Hop: **192.168.1.1**
   - Interface: Transit-Interface
5. After adding the routing information, click OK, and then click Publish Changes to apply the configuration.

Routing with the DLR and ESG

The primary difference in the routing configuration windows for DLRs and ESGs is that the DLR will require both a forwarding address and a protocol address. As we have discussed, this is due to the DLR being split into two components: one is a kernel module doing the forwarding, the other is a Control VM exchanging routing information with a routing protocol. The ESG is centralized and therefore doesn't prompt for a separate IP to handle the routing communication.

To troubleshoot routing issues, there are several CLI commands to clarify routing operations.

Using CLI Commands

In the previous chapter, we did a walkthrough of how a route learned from the external network eventually made its way to the ESXi host kernel. You can verify the ESXi-1's routing table by entering the following command:

```
net-vdr -l --route ESXi-1
```

The last word in the command is the host name. If you're not sure about the name given to the host, you can find it by entering the following CLI command on the NSX Controller:

```
show control-cluster logical-routers instance all
```

If routes you are expecting to see aren't showing up, it could be that the ESG and LR Control VM aren't forming the necessary neighbor adjacency required before routes can be exchanged. You can SSH into the ESG and enter any of the following commands:

- `show ip route`: View the learned routes that have been selected as the best path.
- `show ip route ospf`: Show only OSPF routes.
- `show ip route bgp`: Show only BGP routes.
- `show ip ospf neighbor`: Verify that the adjacency has been formed and with which neighbor.
- `show ip bgp neighbor`: Verify the neighbor adjacency.
- `show ip ospf database`: Verify the specific LSAs that collectively form a map of the OSPF network.
- `show ip bgp`: Verify the BGP table (this is more comprehensive since it includes alternate routes that were not installed in the routing table).

Default Behaviors to Be Aware Of

Related to troubleshooting, it's important to understand some of the underlying default behaviors. If you are using a combination of static and dynamic routes, be aware that a static route, by default, will be preferred over a dynamic route. However, this behavior can be overridden by changing the Administrative Distance.

With Administrative Distance, lower numbers are preferred. Static routes have an Administrative Distance of 1. OSPF is 110. eBGP is 20, and iBGP is 200. If both a static route entry (Administrative Distance 1) and a dynamic OSPF entry (Administrative Distance 110) for the same destination exist, the static route wins. To override the default behavior, simply change the Administrative Distance.

For example, let's say we have an OSPF route to network 10.3.3.0/24 but wanted to also have a static route to 10.3.3.0/24 using a different path as a backup. By default, only the static route would be used since it has a lower Administrative Distance. By manipulating the Administrative Distance of the static route to make it less attractive than the dynamic route, we can turn the routing behavior upside down, having the dynamic route selected over the static. This trick is referred to as a *floating static route*.

Knowing that OSPF is 110, We could make our static route's Administrative Distance equal to 115. Your routing table only stores what it considers to be the best route. Therefore, only the OSPF route to the 10.3.3.0/24 network would be used since its Administrative Distance (110) is preferred over the static route (115). If the next hop router that OSPF specifies went down and the neighbor adjacency was lost, the OSPF route would drop out of the table and the floating static would be used instead.

Equal Cost Multi-Path Routing

Both the DLR and the ESG support Equal Cost Multi-Path (ECMP) routing in NSX. ECMP is a protocol that increases bandwidth for North-South traffic by adding multiple paths and essentially bundling them together (see Figure 7.25). Traffic is load balanced across the paths, dividing the load. This design also provides fault tolerance. If one path fails, the traffic continues to be forwarded on the remaining paths.

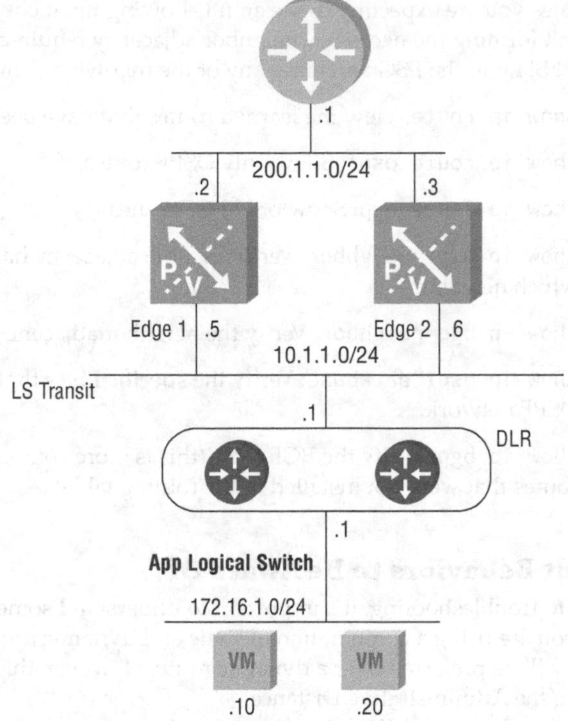

FIGURE 7.25 DLR with pathways to the physical router via two ESGs

If you were running BGP between the DLR and ESG and were to configure another ESG to provide a secondary path for northbound traffic, you would still get fault tolerance without enabling ECMP. However, there's a catch. BGP, by default, is no fan of load balancing. It wants to select a single best route path, even when other equal paths are available. This is different from other routing protocols like OSPF and IS-IS. When multiple equal-cost paths exist for them, they install both routes in their routing tables and automatically load balance across them. Since one of BGP's prime directives is stability, its default behavior is to avoid load balancing; the idea being that it lessens the chance of a routing loop.

For this example, without ECMP enabled, if we are running BGP between the DLR and the ESGs, even though both paths through the ESGs to the external network are equal, BGP will choose only one of them, with no load balancing. If the ESG in the primary path were to fail, the DLR and remaining ESG will figure this out through BGP messages and North-South routing will resume through the other ESG.

The point is, routing will continue without ECMP after a delay while BGP figures things out. However, if we enable ECMP on the DLR, because the two paths are then seen as being part of the same bundle, the traffic will be load balanced despite learning the routes through BGP. In addition, if one ESG fails, there is no delay in forwarding traffic. Traffic continues to be sent through the remaining ESG; it's just no longer load balancing.

Therefore, by deploying multiple ESG appliances and enabling ECMP, you increase scalability (more bandwidth) and availability (fault tolerance) for your North-South traffic.

ECMP can be configured as a solution for the DLRs sending traffic North to the ESGs, but can also be configured on the ESGs, to send their traffic North to an external network (see Figure 7.26).

FIGURE 7.26
ECMP routing between the ESGs and the physical network

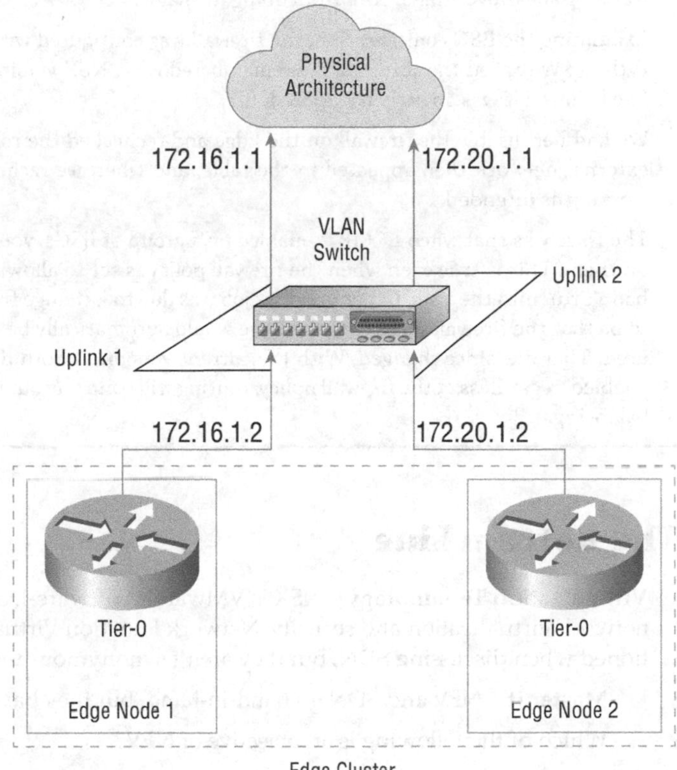

Furthermore, as the size of your data center expands and your design requires having a dedicated Edge cluster, you can continue to increase the amount of bandwidth by using ECMP to load balance across a maximum of eight ESG appliances.

TROUBLESHOOTING AN ECMP BANDWIDTH PROBLEM

One of our clients was in the process of configuring ECMP routing on their ESGs to increase available North-South bandwidth. She mentioned having some experience configuring ECMP routing in a previous job. In this design, the ESGs were connected to four physical routers. However, instead of quadrupling the bandwidth, testing indicated that the amount of available bandwidth remained unchanged.

Continues

Continued

Verifying the routing tables, instead of showing four equal-cost paths into the physical network, there was only a single entry. This explained in part why there was no increase in bandwidth. There was an issue preventing ECMP from doing its magic.

Examining the ESG configuration, the firewall was configured with the default policy to allow everything. We asked the admin if she remembered what NSX version they were using at her old job. She believed it was an early iteration of 6.1.

We had her disable the firewall on the Edge and rechecked the routing table. All four paths to the external network then appeared in the table, and when we rechecked the bandwidth, ECMP was working as intended.

The issue was that when ECMP is enabled on a group of ESGs, you must disable the firewall service on them. This is true even when the firewall policy is set to allow all traffic. The reason this admin hadn't run into the issue in her previous job was due to a change from early versions of NSX. It used to be that the firewall service on the Edge would automatically be disabled when ECMP was configured. That has since changed. With the current version, if both ECMP and the firewall service are enabled, regardless of the firewall policy, routing will continue but without the benefit of ECMP load balancing.

The Bottom Line

Virtualization Terminology NSX is VMware's Software-Defined Network solution for network virtualization and security. Network Function Virtualization (NVF) is often mentioned when discussing SDN, but they aren't synonymous terms.

Master It NFV and SDN go hand-in-hand, but they have different objectives.

Which of the following is an objective of NFV?

1. Abstracting network functions from physical to virtual
2. Abstracting the control plane from the data plane
3. Abstracting routing functions from the kernel
4. Abstracting routing protocols

DLR Routing Restrictions Physical routers can easily run multiple routing protocols simultaneously and often support proprietary routing protocols like Cisco's EIGRP as well. They take a "ships in the night" approach with each protocol keeping track of its own information independently. With an NSX DLR, the supported routing options are different.

Master It Which of the following can a DLR support?

1. Only one routing method: BGP, OSPF, or static routes
2. BGP and OSPF simultaneously
3. BGP and static routes simultaneously
4. BGP, OSPF, IS-IS, and static routes

Configuring BGP on a DLR or ESG BGP comes in two flavors: internal BGP (iBGP) and external BGP (eBGP). Both are supported by the DLR and the ESG.

Master It The ESG is using BGP to exchange routes with the DLR. Examining the configuration, you find that the DLR uses AS number 65000 and the ESG is configured with AS 65001. Which statement is true?

1. iBGP is configured.
2. eBGP is configured.
3. 65000 is not a valid AS number.
4. The AS number must match to exchange routes.

Justifications for Enabling ECMP Equal Cost Multi-Path (ECMP) routing is a mechanism for routing packets over parallel links all having the same cost. Because they are both parallel and equivalent in terms of routing characteristics, the protocol allows the links to act as if they were bundled together.

Master It Which of the following would *not* be a valid reason for enabling ECMP for connections between NSX and the external network?

1. To increase scalability
2. To increase availability
3. BGP does not load balance by default
4. OSPF does not load balance by default

More NVF: NSX Edge Services Gateway

Breaking down the name, Edge Services Gateway (ESG), you get a few clues about what it does and how it fits in your NSX design. The word *edge* implies location, the boundary of our network. The ESG sits on that edge between the virtual NSX network and the physical network. The term *gateway* is an older word for router. In the preceding chapter, we focused on the routing function provided by the ESG. The ESG routes traffic in and out of the NSX environment. It is the *gateway* that NSX uses to forward traffic to a physical router.

The focus here will be on *services*: the network services provided by the ESG. In addition to routing, the ESG provides several L3-L7 services including NAT, load balancer, firewall, VPNs, DHCP, DHCP relay, and DNS forwarding. You'll recall that the ESG is an appliance and not part of the distributed topology. This means that to use these ESG services, the data is going through a virtual machine (VM).

IN THIS CHAPTER, YOU WILL LEARN ABOUT:

- ESG clustering
- Source NAT and Destination NAT
- ESG load balancer
- ESG VPNs: Layer 2, SSL, and IPsec
- ESG DHCP server
- DHCP Relay services
- ESG DNS Relay

ESG Network Placement

Services can be used in combination or an ESG can be dedicated to provide a single service, such as load balancer, and do nothing else.

In terms of network placement and design, you can create as many ESGs as you need, up to 250 per host and up to 2,000 per NSX Manager. The flexibility in having a VM form factor means that you can create dedicated ESGs to provide services for specific applications. Once the application is no longer necessary, the ESG can be removed with it as well. VMware's recommendation is to place all ESGs in an edge cluster so that all North-South (N-S) traffic goes through one cluster (see Figure 8.1).

FIGURE 8.1
Separating edge services from compute

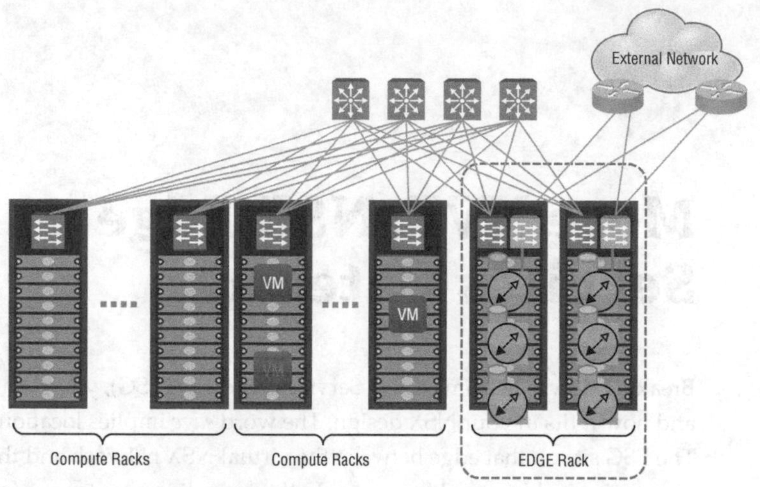

Network Address Translation

The first ESG service we will examine is Network Address Translation (NAT). NAT is most commonly used to map private and public IP addresses. For example, a VM with the address 10.20.6.21 needs to send traffic to the Internet server 8.8.8.8 (see Figure 8.2). Without NAT, the packet isn't routable outside the organization because the source address, 10.20.6.21, falls within the private address range outlined in RFC 1918. With NAT, we can translate the source address, 10.20.6.21, to one that's publicly routable. When the external server responds, NAT will translate the public address within that packet back to 10.20.6.21 so that it can be routed to the correct VM.

FIGURE 8.2
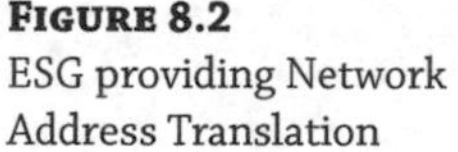
ESG providing Network Address Translation

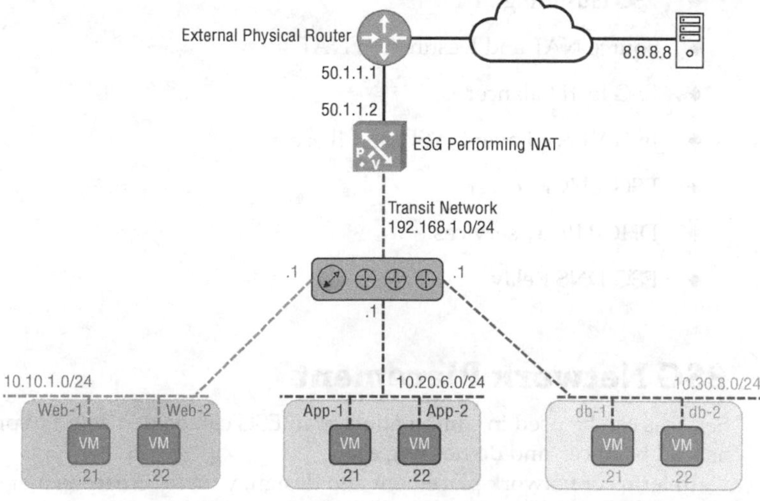

Real World Scenario

NAT Isn't Only for Private to Public Address Translation

NAT is also often used as a solution for overlapping private IP addresses. A prominent health care network based in Pittsburgh has been rapidly absorbing smaller hospitals. With each acquisition, the network team has two goals. The long-term goal is to re-IP the smaller acquired network. This design choice is to make the network overall easier to manage and troubleshoot.

For example, IP addresses for every device in the newly acquired Bessemer hospital will be changed to start with 10.17.X.X. Beyond making the network site easier to identify and troubleshoot, their IP scheme also contributes to improved scalability and optimization. The network team has designed it so that the IP addresses of every hospital in western Pennsylvania starts with 10 and has a second octet ranging from 1 to 31. This grouping allows for route summarization, which increases stability and consumes fewer routing resources.

However, the short-term goal is simply to get connectivity. There are often overlapping IP addresses between the acquired hospital and corporate, causing routing issues. For example, imagine corporate PC 10.1.1.6/24 needs to access file server 10.1.1.7/24 located in the smaller hospital's network. Even with a site-to-site VPN between corporate and the hospital, the packets will not be routed properly. From the corporate PC's perspective, 10.1.1.7 appears to be local. Both the PC and the file server belong to the same Layer 2 broadcast domain.

When a destination does not appear to be remote, packets will not be sent to the default gateway at all. Remember, the router acts as the gateway to *leave* the local network. Because both corporate and the smaller hospital have their own 10.1.1.0/24 subnet, this overlap prevents the packet from being routed. However, NAT can translate so that the source and destination addresses no longer appear to share the same subnet. This will cause the user's traffic to be forwarded to its default gateway as intended. You can think of it as telling a white lie to the PC. Instead of the user, 10.1.1.6, attempting to reach 10.1.1.7, NAT has translated 10.1.1.7 to 172.16.1.7, for example. When the user attempts to send traffic to 172.6.1.7 (which appears to be a remote network), it sends the packet to the router as intended. Once the packet is received by the router, NAT steps in and translates our white lie (that the destination is 172.16.1.7) back to its actual address, 10.1.1.7. The same would occur in the opposite direction, going from the smaller hospital to corporate. Configuring NAT allows the team to quickly provide connectivity, buying them time to later change the IP scheme to conform with the rest of the network.

Some organizations use NAT as a permanent solution for overlapping address ranges. Consider a service provider with multiple tenants. Rather than the provider dictating a separate IP scheme for each customer to avoid overlapping, NAT is an option often implemented.

Overlapping IP addresses are sometimes purposefully implemented for application life cycle or development. For example, you could have two VMs that both have the IP 172.16.8.1, but each is behind a different ESG. Using NAT, it's possible to have them communicate with each other.

The ESG supports two types of NAT. Your choice depends on what you are trying to change: the source or destination address. If you're somewhat familiar with NAT, Source NAT (SNAT) is probably what first comes to mind. As we go through the steps to configure SNAT next, focus on what happens to the source address.

Configuring Source NAT

In an earlier example, the source, 10.20.6.21, was trying to initiate a conversation with the destination, 8.8.8.8:

1. When the packet leaves the VM, we would see exactly that:

   ```
   S=10.20.6.21 D=8.8.8.8
   ```

2. The packet goes through the ESG, which is performing Source NAT.

   Let's say it is configured to translate 10.20.6.21 to 50.1.8.21. The readdressed packet leaving the ESG and bound for the physical router would look like this:

   ```
   S=50.1.1.21 D=8.8.8.8
   ```

3. The packet is routed to the 8.8.8.8 server.
4. When the server responds, the packet's source and destination are now flipped, since the server would now be the one sending (the source) and the VM would be the one receiving (the destination):

   ```
   S=8.8.8.8 D=50.1.1.21
   ```

5. The packet is eventually routed to the ESG.
6. The ESG would then translate the destination address back to its original (the address of the VM):

   ```
   S=8.8.8.8 D=10.20.6.21
   ```

Note that in every step, the address 8.8.8.8 was never translated. It was only the original source address, 10.20.6.21, that was translated to 50.1.1.21 and then back again to 10.20.6.21. With Source NAT, it translates the original source address.

Configuring Destination NAT

The second type of NAT we can implement on the ESG is Destination NAT (DNAT). It is used to translate the destination address. Before getting into the details, let's clear something up that's often confused. In the previous example, two translations took place: when the packet was going outbound, it translated the original source address (from 10.20.6.21 to 50.1.1.21), and on the return response, it translated the destination address (from 50.1.1.21 to 10.20.6.21). Even through a destination address was translated here, this is not an example of DNAT; it's entirely Source NAT. So, how is DNAT different? It's all about which side initiates the conversation.

Let's look at the previous SNAT example again. It allows the device on the inside (in our example, the VM) to initiate a connection to a device on the outside (server 8.8.8.8). The VM's address is the only one that gets changed going out and coming back. Notice in the previous walkthrough detailing the changes that 8.8.8.8 never changed, regardless of direction. The key takeaways here are that it was *initiated by the VM, a device on the inside of our network,* and it is the *source address* (the VM's) that is changed.

Now, let's compare this with DNAT. We will use the same diagram but focus on different devices (see Figure 8.2). For this example, imagine a user on the Internet with the IP 200.1.1.1 wants to connect to our web server, 10.10.1.21. The problem for the user is that the destination is a private address, so without NAT, there's no way for the user to connect to it. The solution is to configure DNAT on the ESG. In the ESG configuration we configure DNAT mapping 10.10.1.21 (the web server's actual address) to 50.1.1.100 (what the user believes the address to be).

This is what the conversation would look like:

1. The Internet user (200.1.1.1) sends a packet to 50.1.1.100:

   ```
   S=200.1.1.1 D=50.1.1.100
   ```

2. The packet is eventually routed to the ESG. The ESG then translates the destination 50.1.1.1 to the web server's real address, 10.10.1.21:

   ```
   S=200.1.1.1 D=10.10.1.21
   ```

3. The web server receives the packet and responds by flipping the source and destination, since the web server is now the source sending the response:

   ```
   S=10.10.1.21 D=200.1.1.1
   ```

4. The ESG receives the response, changes the web server's address to 50.1.1.100, and then routes the packet to the user:

   ```
   S=50.1.1.100 D=200.1.1.1
   ```

The key takeaways for this DNAT example are that it was *initiated by the user's PC, on a device outside our network*, and it is the *destination address* (the web server's) that is changed.

When deciding which type of NAT to use, ask yourself who is initiating the traffic. If it is being initiated within your network, use SNAT. If it is initiated from outside your network, use DNAT.

In addition to modifying IP addresses, TCP and UDP port numbers can be changed as well. For example, we developed some remote labs for the US Army. The Army was not *at all* amenable to modifying their outbound firewall to connect to our lab TCP port 23 , and suggested we bring the lab gear to the base and re-rack it there. The whole point of our developing a remotely accessible lab environment was to save the time and cost involved in shipping. Instead of following the Army's suggestion, we solved it with DNAT. Users on base were able to connect remotely over port TCP 80, a port that was allowed by their firewall. We simply added a NAT rule on our side that did two things. It translated our rack private IP address to a public one the Army could route to and translated our actual port, TCP 23, to TCP 80, a port already open on their firewall.

Configuring SNAT on the ESG

Traffic initiated from the NSX environment with a private address needs to be translated using SNAT:

1. Within the vSphere Client, go to Menu ➤ Networking And Security ➤ NSX Edges (see Figure 8.3).
2. Double-click the ESG you want to configure, and then select the NAT tab.
3. Click + Add and select Add SNAT Rule (see Figure 8.4).

   A new panel appears: Add SNAT Rule (see Figure 8.5).

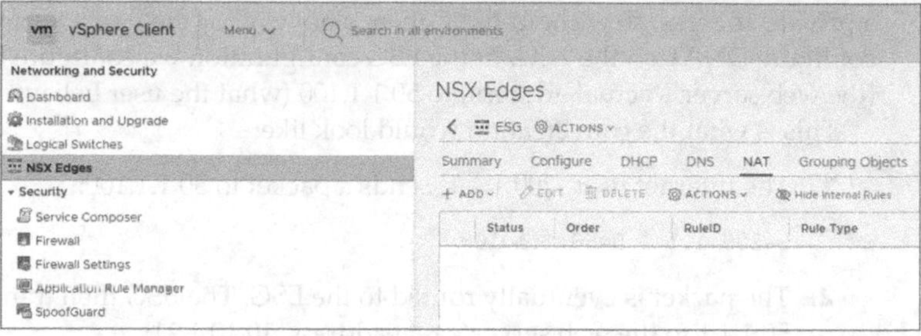

FIGURE 8.3 Configuring NAT on the NSX ESG

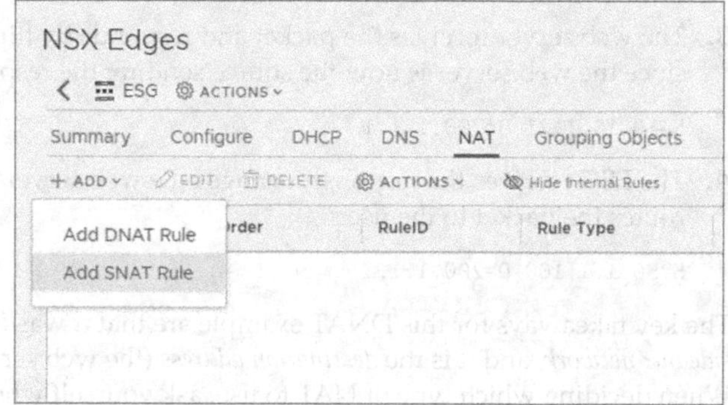

FIGURE 8.4 Adding a Source NAT rule

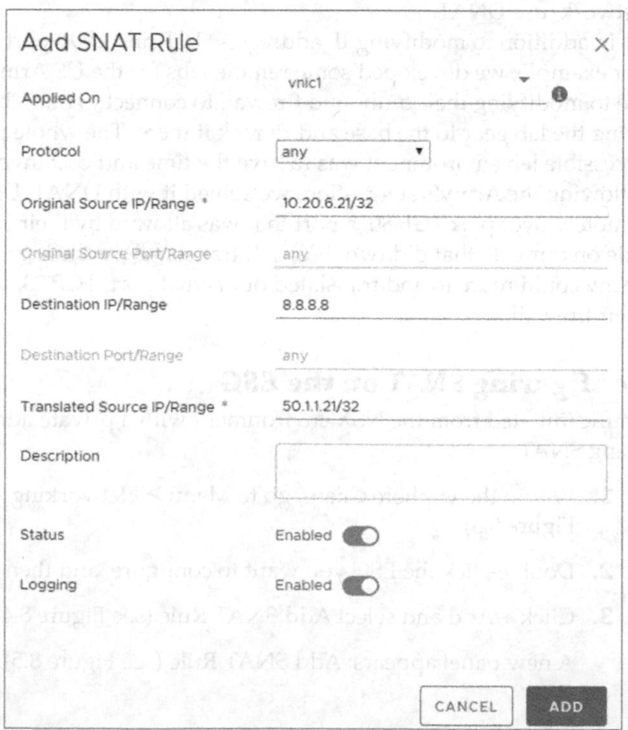

FIGURE 8.5 Configuring the translated address

The following are explanations of the presented options:

Applied On We want the rule applied to the uplink interface of the ESG.

Protocol By selecting Any, the fields below for source and destination ports will be grayed out. This is because Any implies matching any port for that IP address. If you wanted to get more granular and selected UDP, for example, the fields would no longer be grayed out and you could enter a port number or a range of ports. Since 8.8.8.8 is a DNS server, we could have alternatively specified UDP 53, which is the port DNS listens on for name resolution requests.

Original Source IP/Range Here we have chosen to translate the single address, 10.20.6.21. Notice the prefix /32. This essentially says to match on all 32 bits of the IP address. It is not the subnet mask configured on the device. By adding /32, it says that you want to translate this *exact* address. In contrast, we could have entered 10.20.6.0/24 to translate all of the addresses on the 10.20.6.X subnet.

Destination IP/Range This specifies that we only want to perform NAT when 10.20.6.21 is sending traffic destined for 8.8.8.8. If 10.20.6.21 attempted to send traffic to 176.32.98.166, no translation would occur.

Translated Source IP/Range 50.1.1.21 is the exact address (/32) we are translating 10.20.6.21 into.

4. Click the Add button.

   The NAT configuration is not applied until the rule is published.

5. Click the Publish button on the far right (see Figure 8.6).

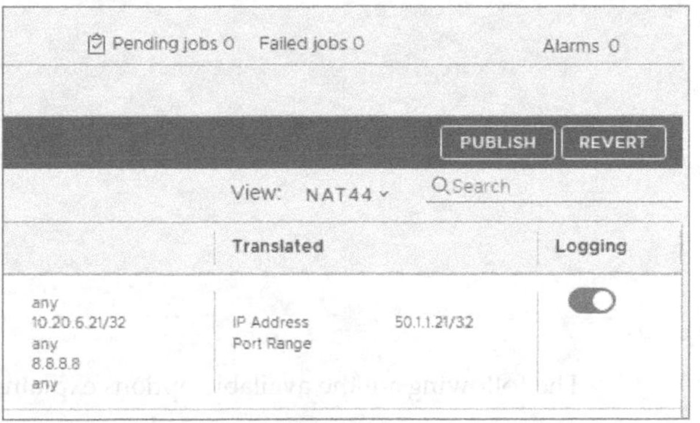

FIGURE 8.6 Publishing the changes

Configuring DNAT on the ESG

When traffic is initiated from outside our network attempting to access a resource like a company web server, for example, we need to configure DNAT. Within the vSphere Client:

1. Go to Menu ➤ Networking And Security ➤ NSX Edges.
2. Double-click the ESG you want to configure, and then select the NAT tab.
3. Click + Add and select Add DNAT Rule (see Figure 8.7).

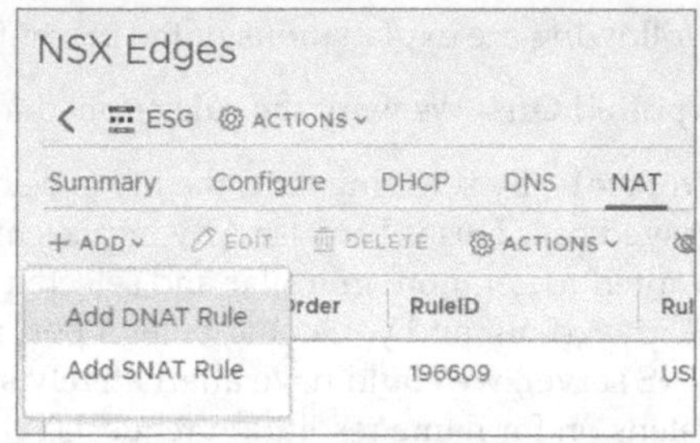

FIGURE 8.7 Adding a Destination NAT rule

A new panel appears: Add DNAT Rule (see Figure 8.8).

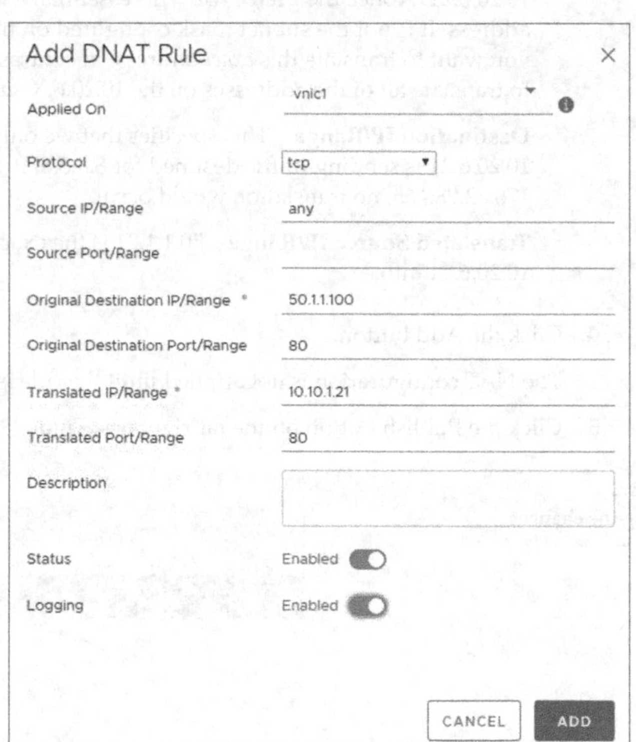

FIGURE 8.8 Configuring the translated address

The following are the available options explained:

Applied On Again, we want this to be configured on the ESG uplink interface.

Protocol For this example, let's say that the scenario is to allow anyone from outside our network to be able to reach our web server. According to DNS, the address associated with www.hydra1303.com is 50.1.1.100. However, the actual address configured on the web VM is 10.10.1.21. Since web traffic is TCP based, select TCP for the protocol.

Source IP/Range Remember, with DNAT, this applies to traffic initiated from outside our network. Instead of entering a single address here, if we want any device on the Internet to be able to access our web server, enter **any** here.

Original Destination IP/Range Again, thinking from the perspective of the outside user trying to reach the web server, the destination IP is what they believe it to be, the public address 50.1.1.100.

Original Destination Port/Range The TCP port the server is listening on is 80. From the user's perspective, the connection is to 50.1.1.100 TCP port 80.

Translated IP/Range When the packet from the outside user reaches the ESG, we want NAT to translate 50.1.1.100 to 10.10.1.21, the actual address configured on the web server.

Translated Port/Range We're not doing anything fancy here in translating the ports. They stay the same. We're only translating the destination IP address, so the port remains unchanged at 80.

4. Click the Add button, and then click Publish to apply the new rule.

ESG Load Balancer

The ESG load balancer takes incoming traffic and distributes it among multiple servers in a way that is completely transparent to end users. By distributing the traffic load, throughput is maximized, latency is reduced, and overall resource utilization is optimized.

In a nutshell, the way it works is by presenting an external IP address that users from the outside can access. An example might be the public IP used to access a company web server. The load balancer maps this address to a set of internal servers and distributes the load among them. As an admin, you can choose the algorithm that dictates how the traffic will be load balanced. The load can be split based on weighted round-robin, IP hash, least used connection, and others.

The ESG load balancer is no slouch compared to physical load balancers when it comes to options and features. These include:

- Load balancing up to Layer 7
- High throughput and high connections per second
- IPv6 support
- Health checks (checking connections to hosts, the stability of the host, and any issues overall with the load balancing)
- One-arm mode (also known as proxy mode)
- Inline mode (also known as transparent mode)
- Connection throttling
- SSL termination and certificate management

- Ability to place individual servers from the load balancing pool in maintenance mode
- HA support for L7 proxy load balancing
- URL rewrite and redirection
- Ability to accept TCP, UDP, FTP, HTTP, and HTTPS requests sent to the external IP address and choose which internal server to forward it to
- Stateful HA

We previously discussed the choices for the size of the ESG, going from Small to X-Large. If your ESG is performing load balancing, VMware recommends that you use the X-Large form factor. The size doesn't change what the load balancer is capable of in terms of function, but the extra resources are necessary for high performance throughput and high connections per second.

Comparing the ESG load balancer and a physical load balancer, you'll find them equal in terms of performance. However, when it comes to creating complex context rules, an F5 load balancer will have more granular control options compared to the virtual ESG load balancer.

More than 75 percent of load balancing that companies perform is basic. They require an L3-L7 high-performance load balancer that's capable of handling things like SSL terminations and certificate management, but they are not creating complicated context rules. If this is the case for your company, the NSX ESG load balancer is an easy choice.

That's not to say that you can't have a proprietary load balancer in NSX. Rather than trying to beat F5 at its own game, VMware has chosen to partner with them, allowing a virtualized F5 load balancer to be added to the IOChain. If your organization needs the additional functionality that the F5 provides for advanced scripting, it can be easily integrated into NSX. Rather than limiting your options, NSX extends them.

If the ESG load balancer is set to proxy mode, it's deployed on the same subnet as the VMs (see Figure 8.9) and is separate from the router (another ESG). It receives traffic on a virtual IP and then uses NAT to forward the traffic to one of the internal VMs. In this design, the backend servers are not able to see the original client IP address due to NAT.

FIGURE 8.9
One-armed load-balancing design

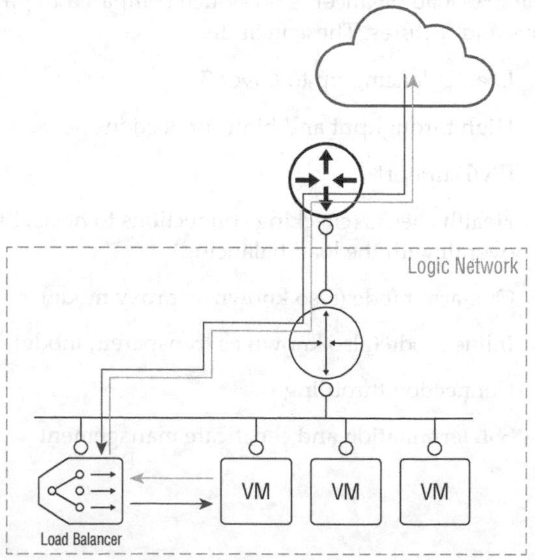

If this is an issue and your backend servers require the ability to view the original client addresses, you can use inline mode instead (see Figure 8.10). With inline load balancing, the ESG load balancer is not separate from the ESG router handling North-South traffic. Instead, both services are provided by the same appliance.

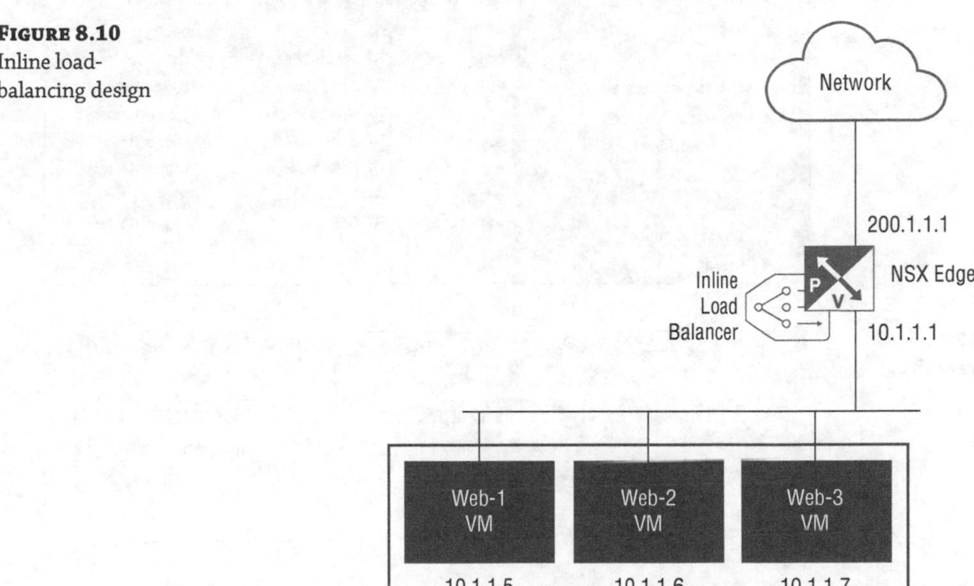

FIGURE 8.10
Inline load-balancing design

With this design, the virtual IP address receiving user traffic is the one on the ESG's uplink interface (200.1.1.1). The internal interface (10.1.1.1) is what the VMs will use as their default gateway.

Although the ESG load balancer can be configured to load balance based on Layer 4 or Layer 7 information, Layer 4 should be your choice if higher performance is desired. Keep this in mind when configuring the ESG. You select the parameters that will be examined for the load-balancing decisions. If you happen to choose any of the L7 options, it will load balance at Layer 7.

Configuring an ESG Load Balancer

For this, we will use the standard vSphere Web Client and perform the following steps:

1. Go to Home ➤ Networking & Security ➤ NSX Edges (see Figure 8.11).
2. Double-click the ESG you want to configure, and then select the Load Balancer tab (see Figure 8.12).
3. With Global Configuration selected on the left, click the Edit button on the far right.

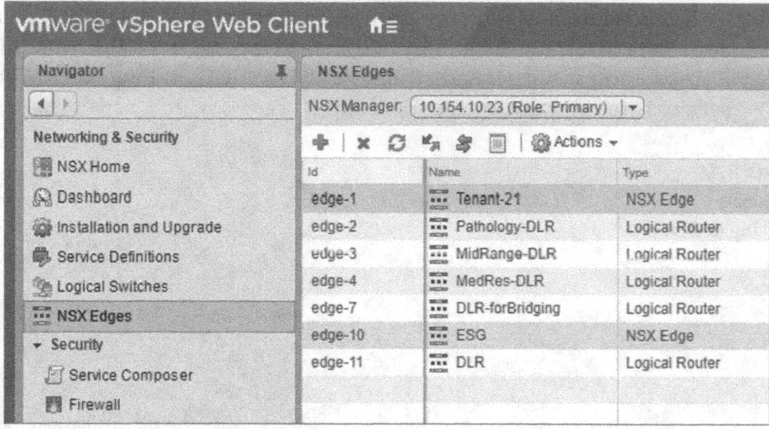

FIGURE 8.11 Selecting the ESG

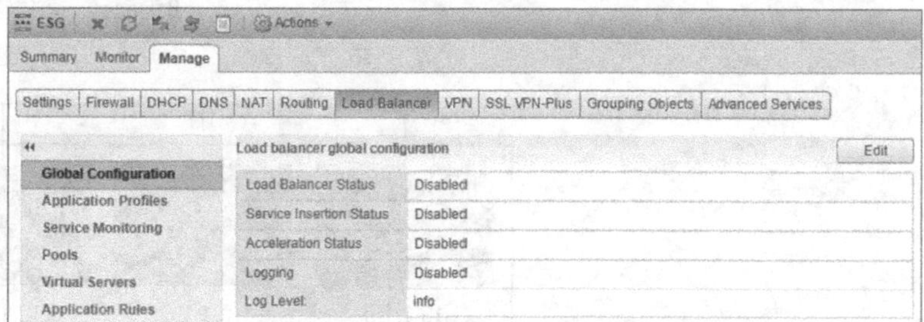

FIGURE 8.12 Load Balancer tab

4. Place check marks next to Enable Load Balancer and Enable Acceleration (see Figure 8.13). Then click OK.

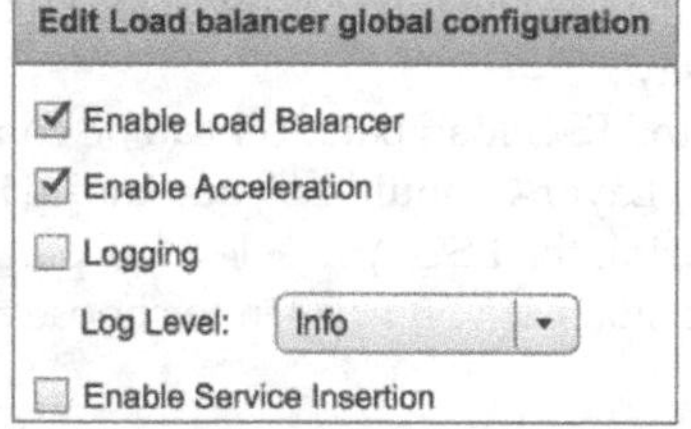

FIGURE 8.13 Enabling the load-balancer service

5. In the left menu, select Pools (see Figure 8.14) and then click the green + sign.

   A new panel appears. In the top half of this pane, we will define the load-balancing method to use for a pool of web servers (see Figure 8.15).

6. Give the pool a name and a description.

   Here, we are choosing a simple round-robin method to split the traffic load across the web servers.

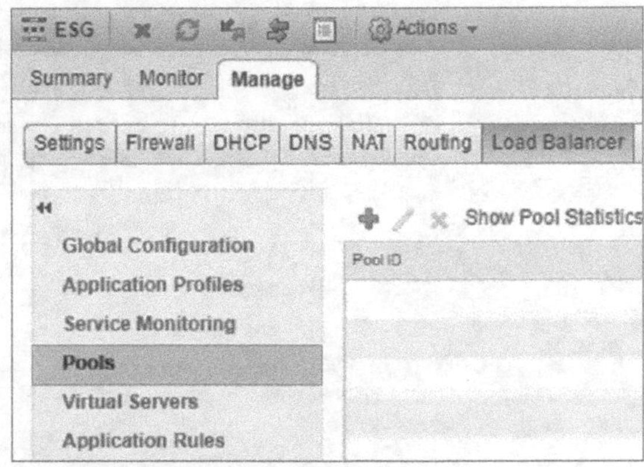

FIGURE 8.14 Creating a pool of servers to load balance across

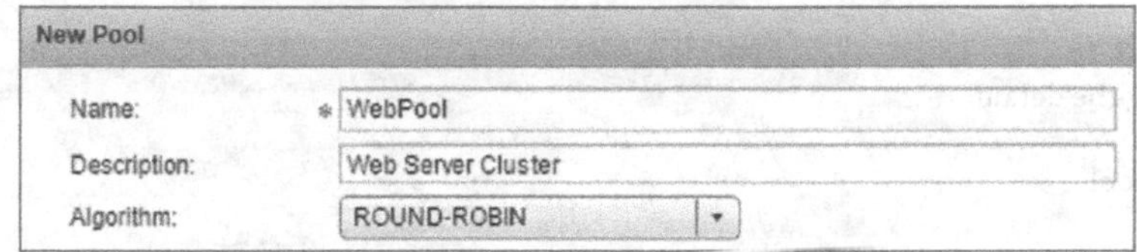

FIGURE 8.15 Selecting the load-balancing algorithm

In the lower half of the pane, we can define the web servers that will be members of the pool.

7. Click the green + sign (see Figure 8.16).

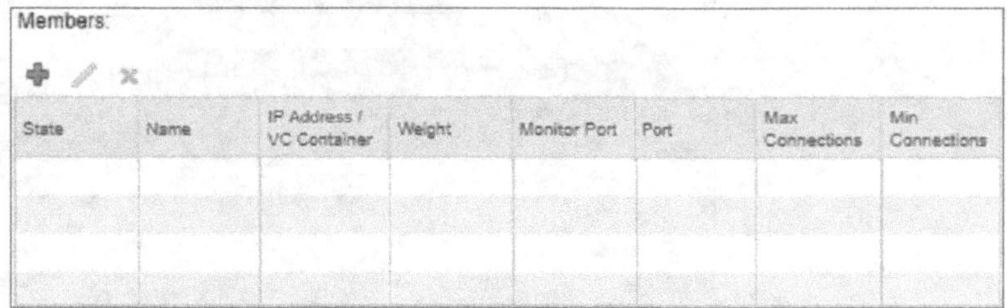

FIGURE 8.16 Adding members to the server pool

Web-1 10.10.1.21 and Web-2 10.10.1.22 are the members we wish to add.

8. Starting with Web-1 (see Figure 8.17), enter the name, the IP address, and the web port, 80.
9. Click OK and then repeat for Web-2 10.10.1.22.
10. After adding the server members to the pool, change the Monitors drop-down from NONE to default_http_monitor (see Figure 8.18) and click OK.
11. To verify the status of the pool, click the Show Pool Statistics link on the same line as the green + sign (see Figure 8.19).

    NSX comes with a preconfigured application profile for web servers. A profile is essentially just a set of parameters indicating how the application should be handled.

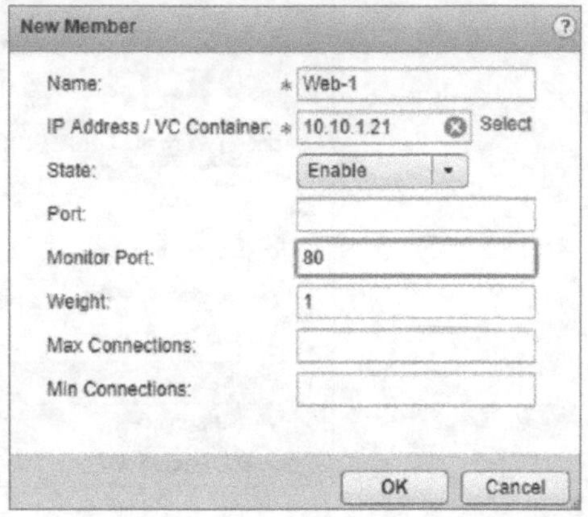

FIGURE 8.17 Configuring each member of the pool

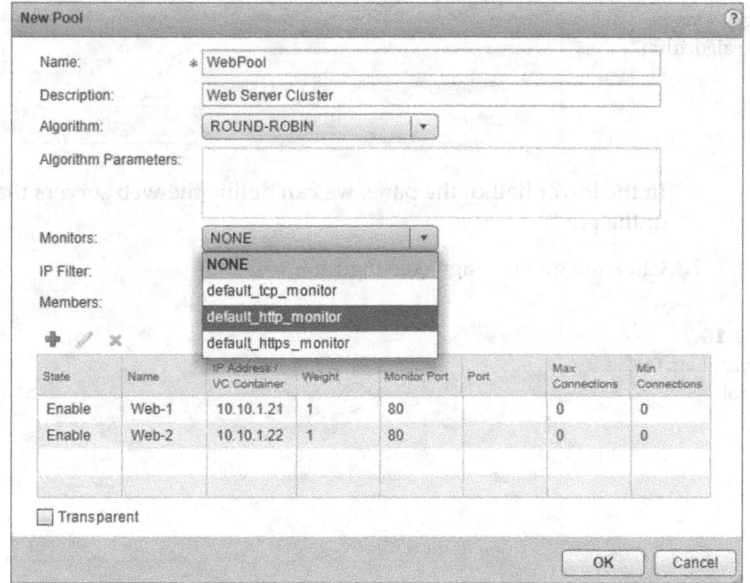

FIGURE 8.18 Selecting the default http monitor for the pool

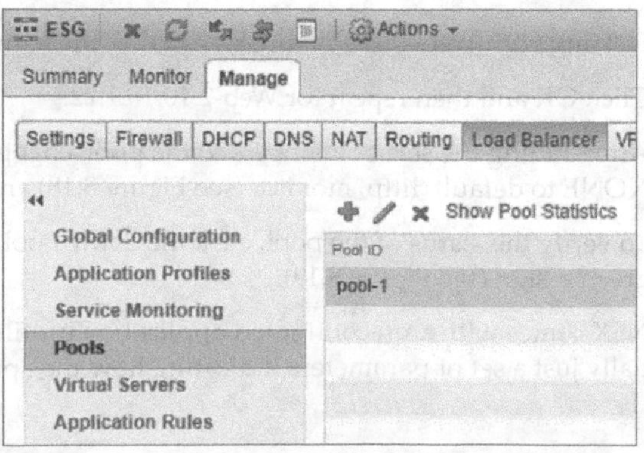

FIGURE 8.19 Verifying the status of the pool

12. Select Application Profiles in the menu on the left (see Figure 8.20) and click the green + sign.

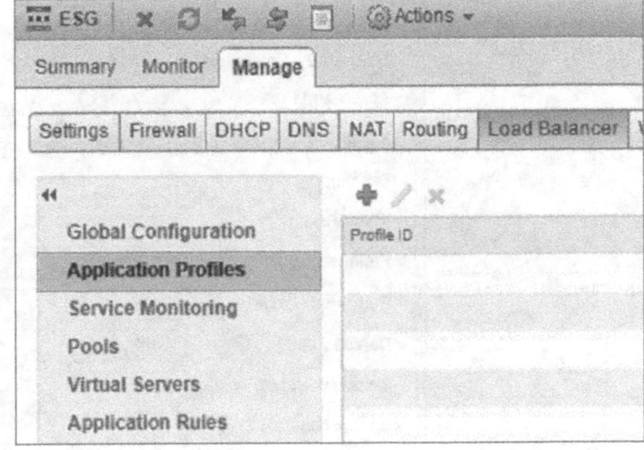

FIGURE 8.20 Load balancer application profiles

A new panel appears: New Profile (see Figure 8.21).

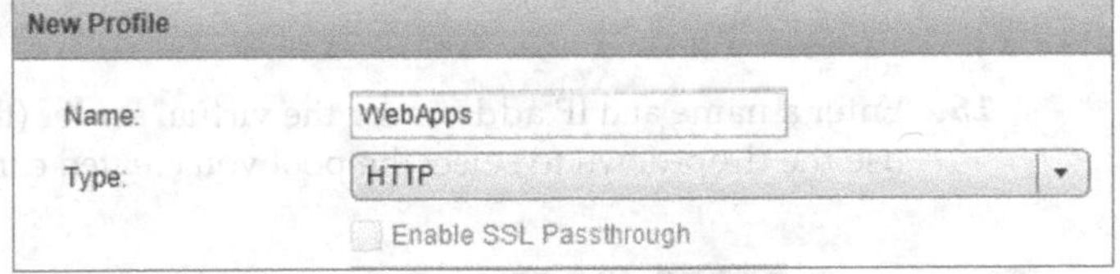

FIGURE 8.21 Selecting a preconfigured application profile

13. Enter a name for the profile and select HTTP from the drop-down. Click OK.

    The last step is to create a virtual server. This is where we enter a single IP address that will be used to access the entire pool of web servers.

14. Click Virtual Servers in the menu on the left (see Figure 8.22) and then click the green + sign.

    A new panel appears: New Virtual Server (see Figure 8.23).

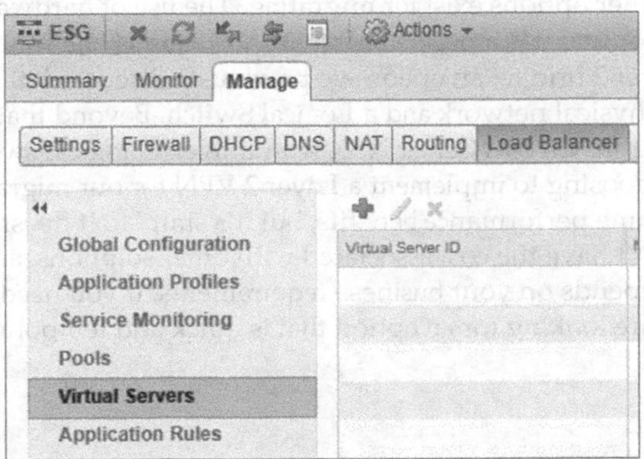

FIGURE 8.22 Creating a virtual server to be the front end

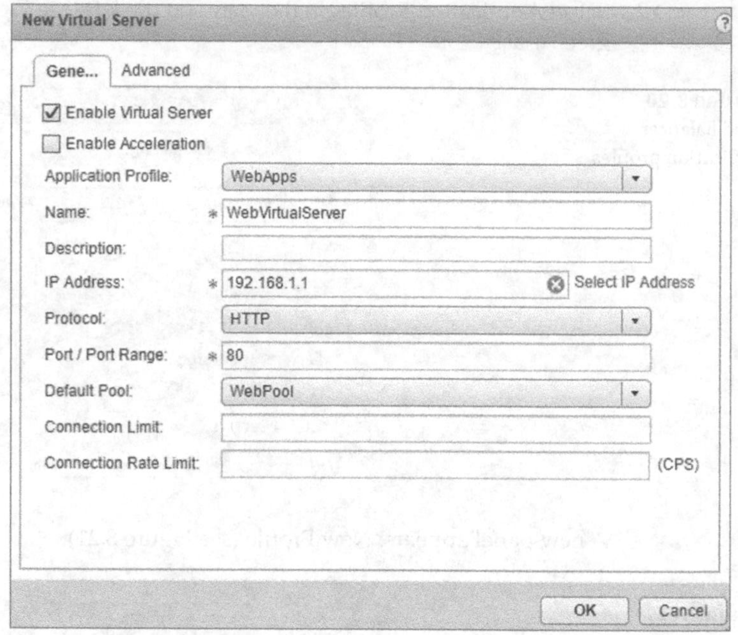

FIGURE 8.23 Selecting an IP address and port number for the virtual server

15. Enter a name and IP address for the virtual server (this is an IP address on the ESG) and use the drop-down to select the pool you created earlier.

Layer 2 VPN (If You Must)

The ESG provides several VPN solutions to fit different use cases. The SSL VPN is a user VPN that allows remote contractors and road warriors to securely connect to network. The site-to-site VPN is used to connect multiple data centers or remote sites. There's also the option to create a Layer 2 VPN (L2VPN), which allows you to extend your data center's subnets across geographical boundaries. This provides a simple solution, for example, when trying to migrate a legacy data center to a virtualized NSX data center because it means that IP addresses don't have to change for the migration from A to B. The same broadcast domain (subnet) exists on both sides. The Layer 2 VPN simply ties them together with a tunnel.

Other options exist for migrating. The use of hardware VTEPs on a physical device made by a vendor that has a partnership with VMware is one solution. Another solution would be to create a Layer 2 bridge, an option we previously discussed, that creates a bridge between a VLAN on the physical network and a Logical Switch. Beyond that, we could deploy NSX on both sides and configure Cross-vCenter NSX with universal logical switching.

Choosing to implement a Layer 2 VPN for our migration strategy over the others won't have the same performance benefits, but it's simpler. It doesn't require changing IP addresses, it doesn't have the cost associated with other solutions, and overall, there's minimal downtime. It all depends on your business requirements. If you need a long-term solution, this isn't it. But if you are looking for an option that is quick and temporary, consider the L2VPN.

The diagram in Figure 8.24 shows an L2VPN that forms a tunnel connecting the L2 domain 10.1.1.X on the right, the legacy site, with the same L2 domain 10.1.1.X on the left, the NSX domain.

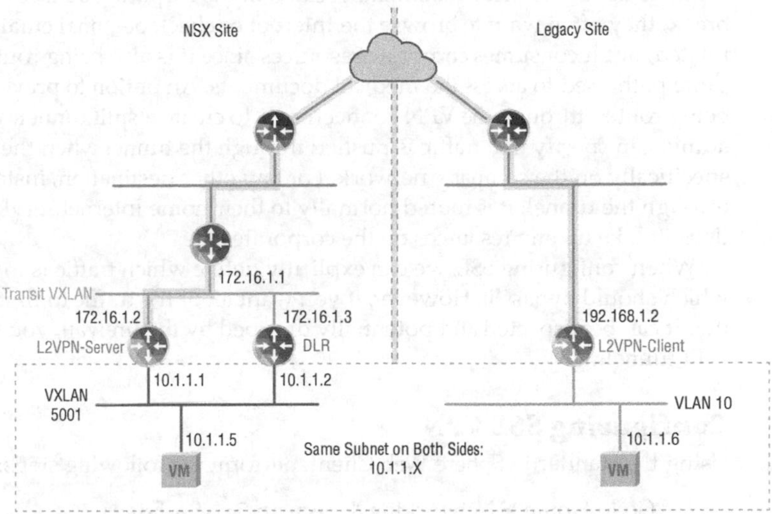

FIGURE 8.24 Implementing an L2VPN as a temporary solution to connect two sites

Secure Sockets Layer Virtual Private Network

Outside users can securely connect to NSX networks that sit behind the ESG using Secure Sockets Layer Virtual Private Network (SSL VPN) (see Figure 8.25). The user can initiate a connection to the ESG and dynamically establish an encrypted tunnel. An SSL tunnel doesn't always require the installation of a VPN client on the user machine. SSL capabilities are built into all modern web browsers; however, using a web browser in place of a standalone VPN client only provides web access mode. If the network resource can be accessed with a web browser interface, there's no need to install a separate VPN client. If full network access is desired, a VPN client must be installed on the user machine.

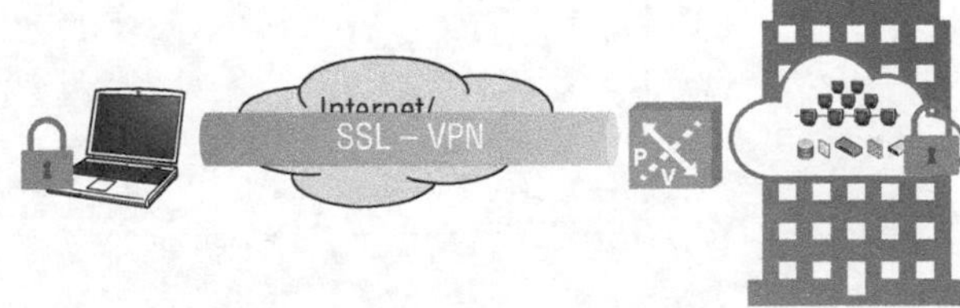

FIGURE 8.25 SSL VPNs allowing remote mobile users to connect

When the initial connection is made to the ESG, the ESG hands the user an IP address from a configured pool of addresses. In addition to the IP pool, the ESG will have a list of networks the user is permitted to access.

Split Tunneling

Let's say that the user is Susan, a nurse working for a health insurance company, who triages patients over the phone when they call the nurse line for advice. The SSL secure tunnel allows Susan to access medical documents located in the corporate data center. When the nurses are on break, they often want to browse the Internet or check personal email. This traffic is not business related, but it consumes corporate resources since it is also being routed through the VPN, the same path used to access the medical documents. An option to prevent non-business traffic from being routed through the VPN connection is to create a split tunnel. With a split tunnel, the admin can specify that traffic is pushed through the tunnel when the user is accessing resources specifically on the company network. For any other destination, instead of sending that traffic through the tunnel, it is routed normally to their home Internet service provider (ISP) and doesn't take up any resources on the corporate side.

When configuring SSL, we can explicitly define which traffic is to be sent over the tunnel and which should bypass it. However, if you want all of the traffic to first go through the tunnel so that it can be inspected and potentially dropped by the firewall, you have the option to not use split tunneling.

Configuring SSL VPN

Using the standard vSphere Web Client, perform the following steps:

1. Go to Home ➤ Networking & Security ➤ NSX Edges.
2. Double-click the ESG you want to configure and select the SSL VPN-Plus tab (see Figure 8.26).

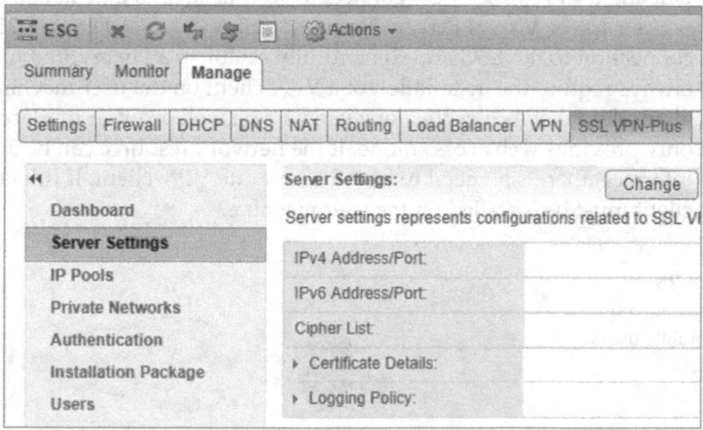

FIGURE 8.26 Configuring the SSL VPN service on the ESG

3. Click the Change button to the right of Server Settings.

   The Change Server Settings window appears (see Figure 8.27).
4. Select an IP address on the ESG that your end users will use to VPN in. The standard port number for SSL is 443. This should already be populated in the Port field.
5. Choose an encryption algorithm, and then click OK.

Change Server Settings
IPv4 Address: 2.2.2.2 (Primary)
IPv6 Address: None
Port: * 443
Cipher List: AES128-SHA
AES256-SHA
AES128-GCM-SHA256
Server Certificate: Use Default Certificate
Common Name
Issued To
Valid Dates
OK
Cancel

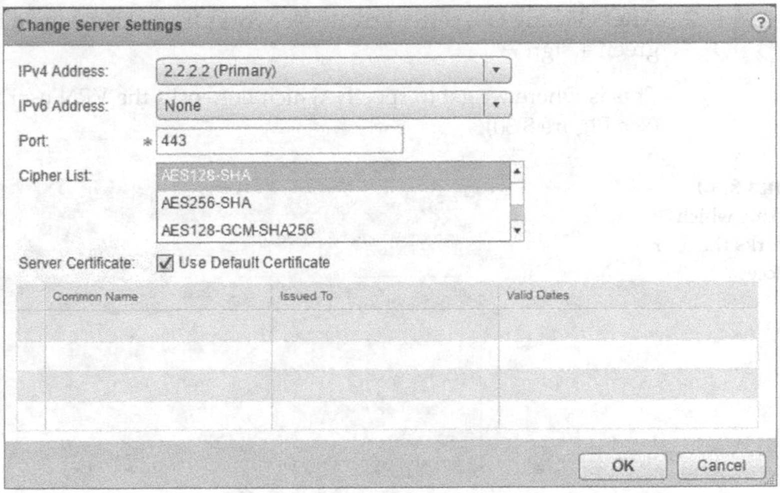

FIGURE 8.27
Choosing the IP address and port users will VPN to

6. From the menu on the left, select IP Pools, and then click the green + sign (see Figure 8.28).

ESG
Actions
Summary
Monitor
Manage
Settings
Firewall
DHCP
DNS
NAT
Routing
Load Balancer
VPN
SSL VPN-Plus
Dashboard
Server Settings
IP Pools
Private Networks
Authentication
Installation Package
Order
IP Range

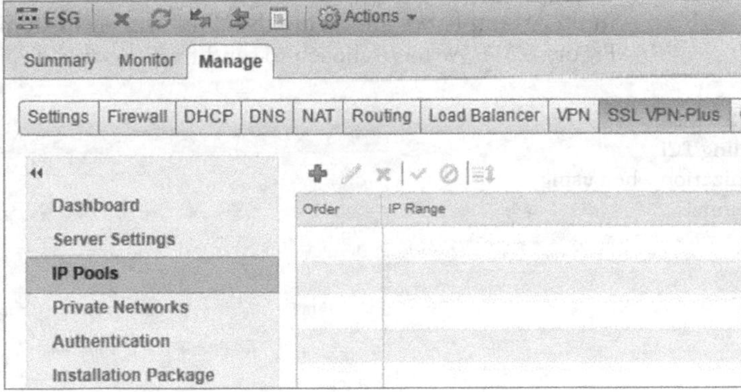

FIGURE 8.28
Creating an IP pool

When a VPN end user connects, they will be assigned an IP address, subnet mask, and default gateway for their end of the VPN tunnel. In this window, we configure a range of addresses so that multiple users can simultaneously connect, each with their own IP address assigned from the pool (see Figure 8.29).

Add Static IP Pool
IP Range: * 10.8.8.2
To 10.8.8.30
Netmask: * 255.255.255.0
Gateway: * 10.8.8.1
This will add an IP address in na0 interface.

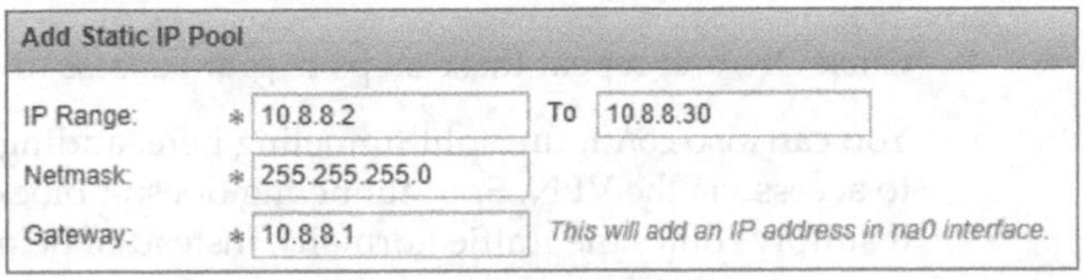

FIGURE 8.29
Configuring a range of addresses to assign to VPN users

7. After clicking OK, select Private Networks from the menu on the left and click the green + sign.

   This is where we get to specify which networks the VPN user will have access to (see Figure 8.30).

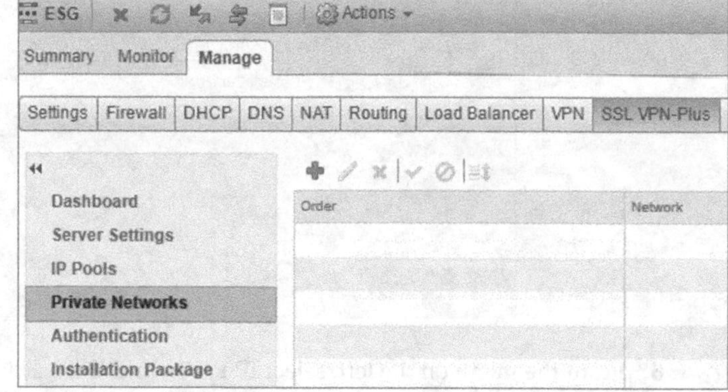

FIGURE 8.30 Selecting which networks the user can access

In this example, we are giving the VPN user access to network 10.30.8.0/24 (see Figure 8.31). We have chosen to send traffic to this destination over the tunnel.

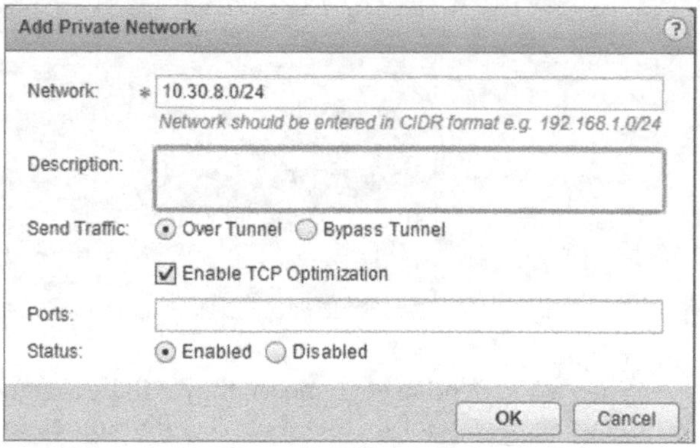

FIGURE 8.31 Enabling TCP optimization when using the tunnel

8. To optimize the speed over the tunnel, make sure there is a check mark next to Enable TCP Optimization.

9. Click OK, and repeat these steps to grant access to additional private networks.

   You can also configure split tunneling here, adding networks that you don't want the user to access via the VPN. Split tunneling doesn't block users from accessing these networks; it simply routes the traffic normally, instead of being routed through the VPN tunnel.

10. Select Authentication from the menu on the left, and click the green + sign (see Figure 8.32).

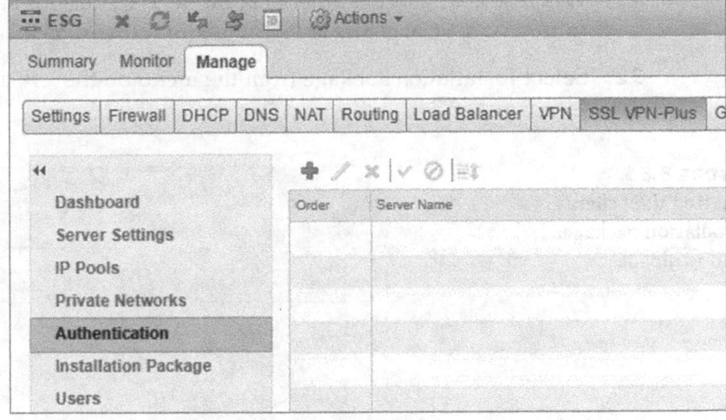

FIGURE 8.32 Authenticating VPN users

To authenticate users, you can point to an authentication server using Active Directory, LDAP, RADIUS, or RSA-ACE. Selecting one of these will allow you to enter the IP address of the server. Another option is to simply use local authentication, which we're using in this example (see Figure 8.33).

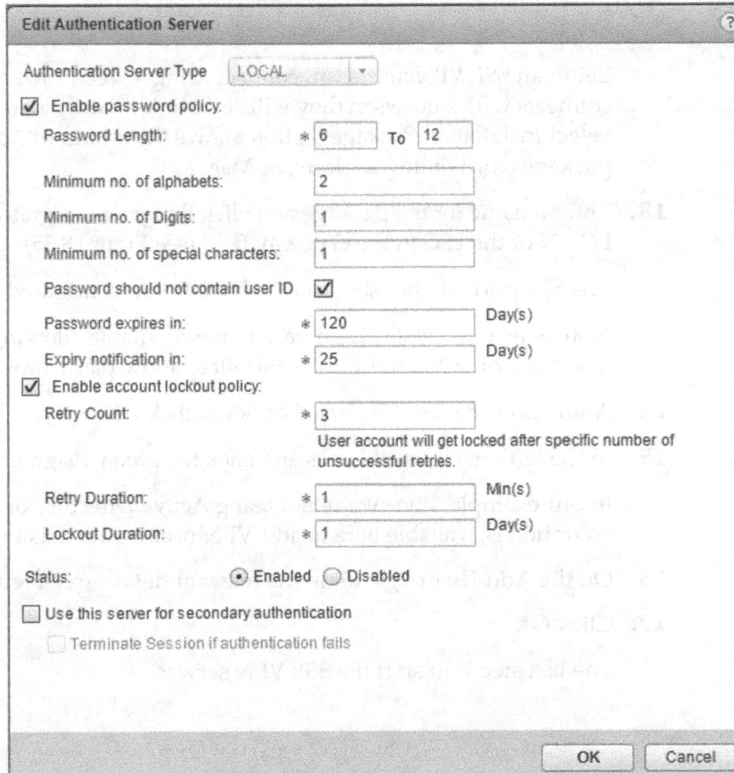

FIGURE 8.33 Configuring password rules for VPN access

11. When selecting local authentication, set the rules for passwords, including length, numbers, special characters, number of retries, etc. After making your choices, click OK.
12. Select Installation Package from the menu on the left, and click the green + sign (see Figure 8.34).

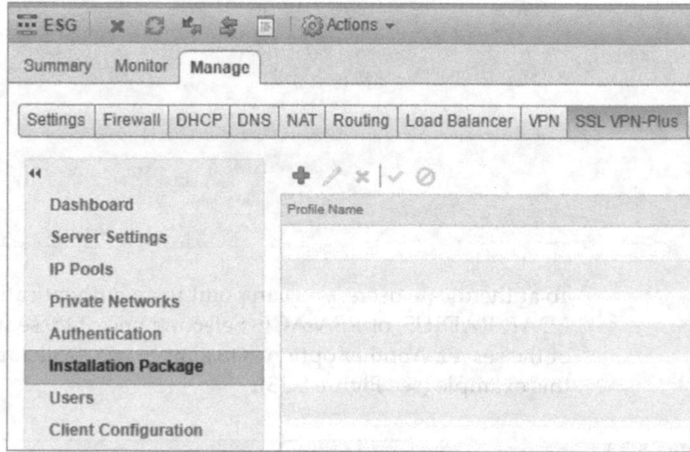

FIGURE 8.34 Creating VPN client installation packages for download

Being an SSL VPN, users can connect using a web browser or a VPN client. When the user connects with a browser, they will see a link to download a client installation package. The Select Installation Package section allows the admin to create VPN client installation packages for Windows, Linux, or Mac.

13. Enter a name for the package and click the green + sign to add the public IP address or FQDN of the ESG in the Gateway field (see Figure 8.35).

    The SSL port number should match what you configured previously.

    Notice the other installation parameters available allowing you to automatically create a desktop icon when the VPN is installed, allow passwords to be remembered, etc.

14. After choosing your preferred options, click OK.
15. In the left menu, select Users and click the green + sign (see Figure 8.36).

    In our example, since we're not using Active Directory or any other authentication server, an option is available here to add VPN user credentials to the local database.

16. On the Add User page, fill in the relevant details (see Figure 8.37).
17. Click OK.

    The last step is to start the SSL VPN service.

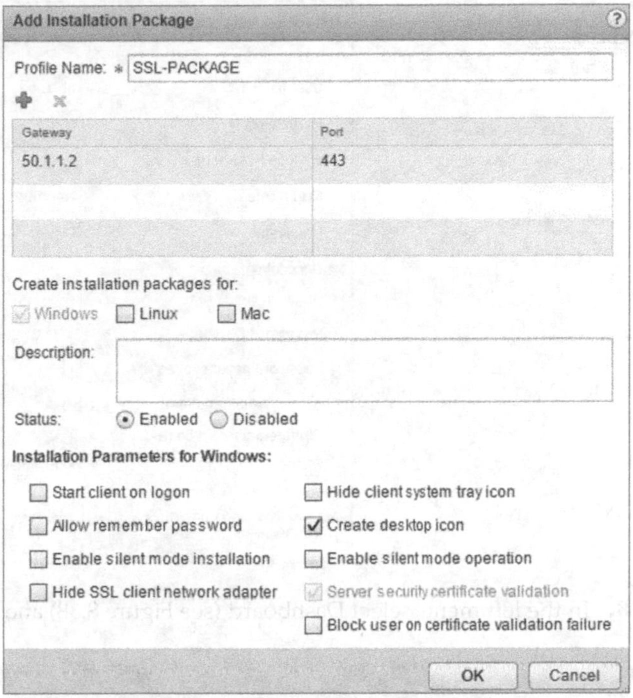

FIGURE 8.35 Creating and customizing packages for different platforms

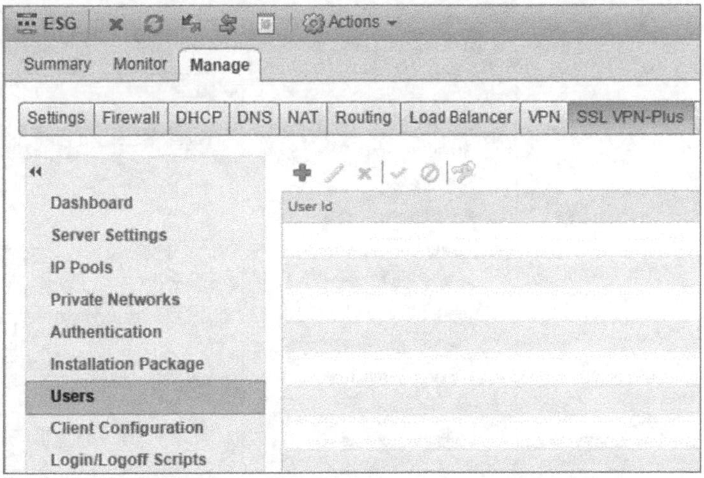

FIGURE 8.36 Creating credentials for VPN users

FIGURE 8.37
Adding a VPN user

18. In the left menu, select Dashboard (see Figure 8.38) and click the Start button.

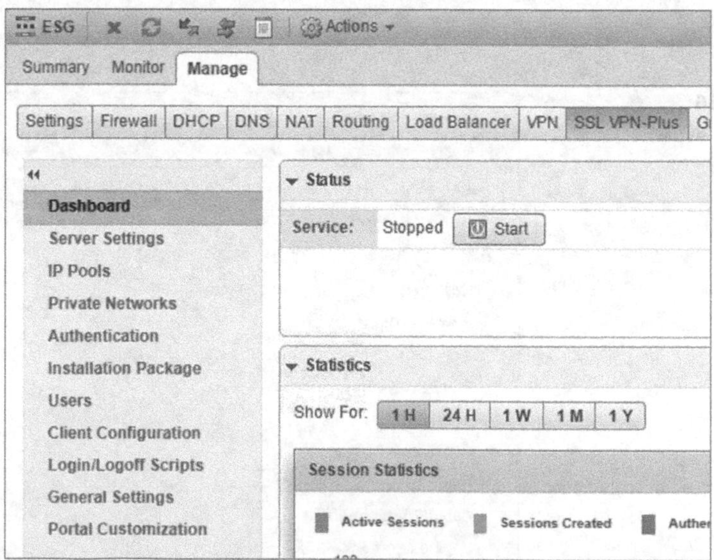

FIGURE 8.38
Starting the SSL VPN service

You will be prompted, "Do you want to start the service?"

19. Click Yes, and you're all set.

Internet Protocol Security VPN

To connect an ESG to a remote site, instead of a per-user SSL VPN, a site-to-site, Internet Protocol Security (IPsec) VPN can be created. With a site-to-site VPN, there is no need for users to have a VPN client installed to access resources at the remote site. Any traffic bound for the remote site is simply routed into the tunnel (see Figure 8.39).

FIGURE 8.39
Site-to-site IPsec VPN

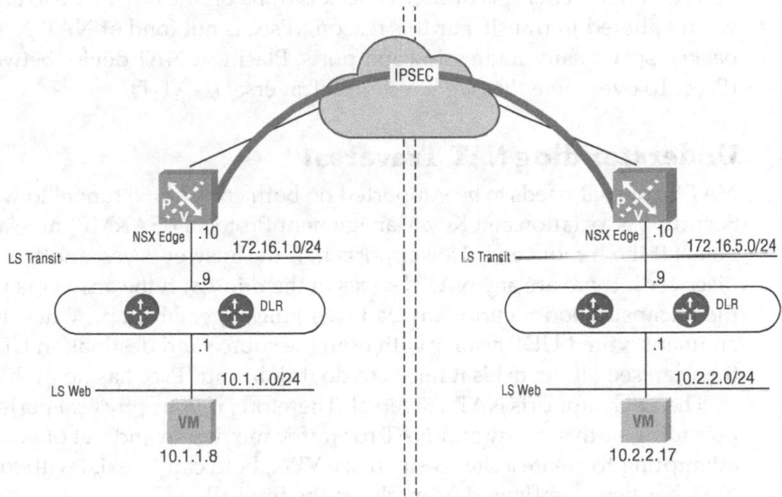

A standard IPsec VPN doesn't support multicasting, something dynamic routing protocols typically rely on to exchange information, and it only carries IP traffic. Years ago, Cisco developed a workaround with a new type of tunnel called Generic Routing Encapsulation, or GRE, which eventually became a standard. At the time, multiple Layer 3 protocol stacks were competing, such as IP, IPX, and AppleTalk. The limitations of an IPsec tunnel posed two problems at the time: no IPX or AppleTalk support. and no dynamic routing. Being generic, GRE didn't care what Layer 3 protocol it was carrying, so it supported protocols beyond IP. These days, that's not a concern because IP eventually won out and the other protocols are no longer used.

Despite this, GRE is still very much in use today, not for the multiprotocol support, but for the support of multicasts (and by extension, dynamic routing protocols). GRE by itself provides no encryption, whereas with IPsec, encryption is one of its best features. Most GRE tunnels you see today will be in combination with IPsec, running GRE over IPsec. However, the combination adds overhead.

NSX allows for Route-Based IPsec VPNs. This is very similar to GRE over IPsec, but with less overhead. For it to work, each tunnel requires a virtual IPsec tunnel interface (VTI). The ESG supports up to 32 VTIs, which means that a single ESG can have a maximum of 32 remote Route-Based IPsec VPN peers. The trick is that each VTI is mapped to a separate IPsec tunnel. The routing table contains its known destination networks and the next hop to reach each of them. For destinations on the other side of these tunnels, instead of the next hop address, it simply points to the VTI interface. All IPsec processing occurs on the VTI interface. Based on the mapping, the traffic is then forwarded out the appropriate IPsec tunnel.

The main takeaway here is that Route-Based IPsec VPNs allow for dynamic routing protocols, whereas regular IPsec VPNs do not. The catch with NSX is that as of version 6.4.2, only BGP is supported for this solution. However, as we discussed in Chapter 6, "Distributed Logical Router," BGP is a better choice for your design regardless. Remember, that with NSX-T, OSPF isn't supported at all. So, if you're looking to eventually upgrade from NSX-V to NSX-T, you're going to be using BGP either way.

When IPsec encrypts traffic, a check is done on the other side to ensure that that the packet wasn't altered in transit. For this reason, IPsec is not fond of NAT. NAT's job is to modify the packet; specifically, addressing and ports. Placing a NAT device between two IPsec peers breaks IPsec. To overcome this, we have NAT Traversal (NAT-T).

Understanding NAT Traversal

NAT Traversal needs to be supported on both ends of the tunnel to work, so it sends an Internet Security Association and Key Management Protocol (ISAKMP) message to the other side to detect if the remote end also supports it. If the answer is yes, another ISAKMP message is sent to discover if there are any NAT devices in the middle. If the answer is yes, NAT-T will encapsulate the Encapsulation Security Payload (ESP) message, which provides the security services, inside an unencrypted UDP header with both the source and destination UDP ports set to 4500. NAT then can see all the fields it needs to do its job, and IPsec has no problem with it either.

The ESG supports NAT Traversal. Therefore, if your physical perimeter firewall is currently providing both security and NAT for traffic moving in and out of your network and your ESG is attempting to create a site-to-site IPsec VPN, both can co-exist without problems provided that NAT has been configured properly on the firewall.

Configuring IPsec Site-to-Site VPN with the ESG

Using the standard vSphere Web Client, perform the following steps:

1. Go to Home ➢ Networking & Security ➢ NSX Edges.
2. Double-click the ESG you want to configure, and select the VPN tab (see Figure 8.40).

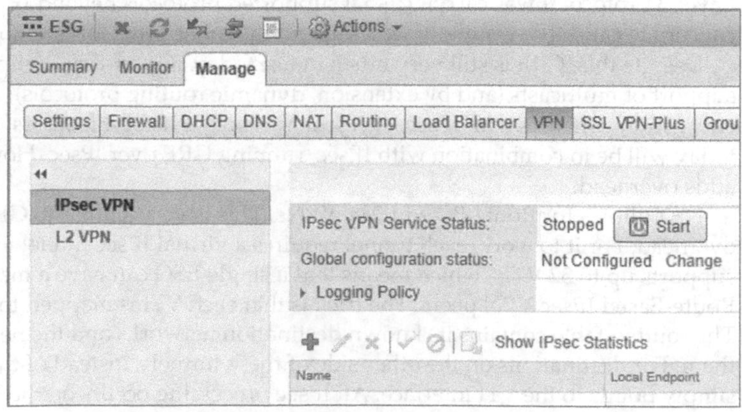

FIGURE 8.40 Deploying a site-to-site IPsec VPN

3. Make sure that IPsec VPN is highlighted on the left, and then click the green + sign. A new panel will appear (see Figure 8.41).

FIGURE 8.41 Configuring tunnel endpoints and peer subnets

Add IPsec VPN

☑ Enabled
☑ Enable perfect forward secrecy (PFS)
☐ Responder Only

Name: Site2Site
Local Id: * SiteA
Local Endpoint: * 50.1.1.2
Local Subnets: * 10.30.8.0/24
Peer Id: * SiteB
Peer Endpoint: * 200.1.1.1
Peer Subnets: * 10.2.2.0/24

IKE Version: IKEv1
Digest Algorithm: SHA1
Encryption Algorithm: AES
Authentication: ⦿ PSK ○ Certificate
Pre-Shared Key: *********
☐ Display shared key
Diffie-Hellman Group: DH14
Extension:

OK Cancel

In our example, the IP address on the ESG's uplink interface, which is used to connect to the perimeter router, is 50.1.1.2. This is the local endpoint of the tunnel. The other end of the tunnel is at SiteB. It's address, 200.1.1.1, is the peer endpoint of the tunnel.

Our goal is to give SiteB access to network 10.30.8.0/24. We see this listed in the Local Subnets field.

4. To allow additional networks, simply add them to the same line but separate the addresses with commas.

   SiteA requires access to network 10.2.2.0/24 on SiteB. We see that listed next to Peer Subnets.

In this example, beyond assigning the name Site2Site and entering the local IDs SiteA and SiteB, the rest are default options with the exception of the pre-shared key, which needs to be entered on both sides and must match.

5. After making your preferred configuration choices, click OK.

   You must publish your configuration for it to be applied (see Figure 8.42).

6. Click the Publish Changes button.

FIGURE 8.42 Publishing the changes

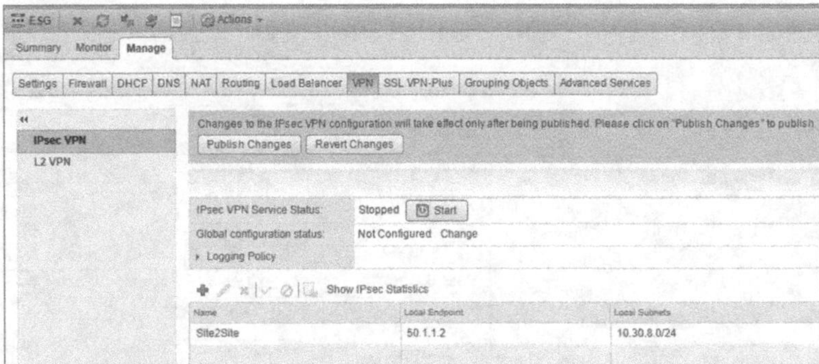

7. Once publishing is complete, click the Start button (see Figure 8.43).

FIGURE 8.43 Starting the IPsec tunnel service

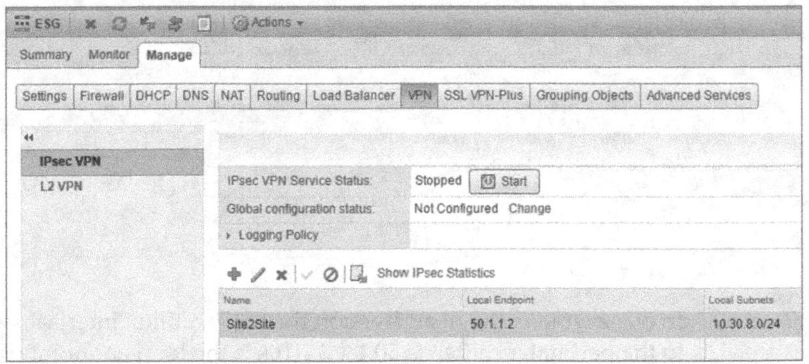

With the VPN similarly configured at the remote site, the tunnel will be established.

Round Up of Other Services

So far, we've looked at the primary services provided by an Edge Services Gateway: SNAT, DNAT, SSL VPNs, IPsec site-to-site VPNs, Route-Based IPsec VPNs, Layer 2 VPNs (if you must), NAT, NAT-T, one-armed load balancer, inline load balancer, and let's not forget routing. With routing there was so much information, we had to give it its own chapter, especially since it was important to contrast the centralized routing provided by the ESG with the distributed routing provided by the DLR.

We still have another major ESG service to cover, that being the firewall. There is a lot of detail to cover there, so we're going to give it its own chapter as well. And just like we did with routing, we'll compare and contrast the centralized firewall service provided by the ESG to the Distributed Firewall (DFW).

But even putting that aside, there are still additional secondary services we have yet to discuss. These include the Dynamic Host Configuration Protocol (DHCP) service, DHCP Relay, and forwarding Domain Name System (DNS) requests to DNS servers.

DHCP Service

DHCP allows devices powering up to request an IP address from a pool of addresses configured on a DHCP server. The conversation between the device and the server goes like this (see Figure 8.44):

1. Discover message from the client:

   "Is there a DHCP server on this segment that can give me an IP address?"

2. Offer message from the server:

   "Yes, I'm a DHCP server. Here's my offer. Sign this lease and you'll get the IP 10.1.1.45, the subnet mask 255.255.255.0, the default gateway 10.1.1.1, the DNS server 8.8.8.8, and the domain name of Hydra1303.com. If you take it, you'll have the lease for 1 day."

3. Request message from the client:

   "Perfect. I'll take it."

4. Acknowledgment message from the server:

   "It's all yours. I'm going to jot down your MAC address so I remember who I gave this IP address to and put it in my binding table."

FIGURE 8.44 The exchange of DHCP messages

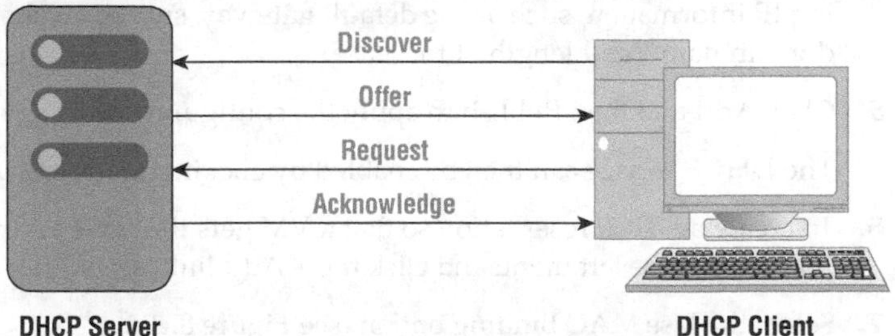

Since the IP address is pulled from a pool of addresses, it's possible to be assigned a different IP once the lease expires. If you want a VM to always be assigned the same IP address through DHCP, you can create a static reservation on the DHCP server. When the VM comes online and sends out the initial discover message, the DCHP server always hands it the same reserved address.

The NSX ESG can be configured to provide those DHCP services. Let's say that you have 20 Logical Switches. Each is a different subnet: 10.1.1.0/24, 10.1.2.0/24, 10.1.3.0/24, and so on. If you are using ESG to provide DHCP services, you do not need to deploy separate ESGs to support address pools for each subnet. Instead, a single ESG can support multiple pools of addresses. Physical DHCP servers can do the same.

Configuring the ESG as a DHCP Server

Using the standard vSphere Web Client, perform these steps:

1. Go to Home ➤ Networking & Security ➤ NSX Edges.
2. Double-click the ESG you want to configure, and select the DHCP tab (see Figure 8.45).

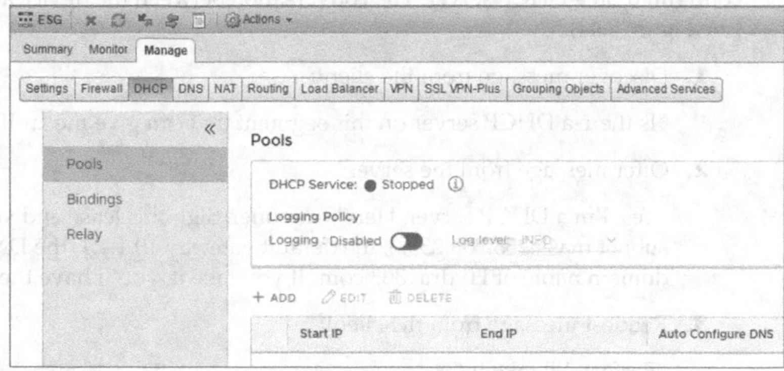

FIGURE 8.45 Adding a DCHP pool of addresses

3. Select Pools from the left menu and click the + Add link.

   A new panel appears (see Figure 8.46).
4. Define the start and end range of IP addresses to hand out along with additional supporting IP information, such as the default gateway, subnet mask, DNS server addresses, domain name, and length of the lease.
5. Click Add and then Publish to apply the configuration.

   The DHCP service can then be enabled by clicking the Start button (see Figure 8.47).
6. To create a DHCP reservation so that a VM gets the same address every time, select Bindings in the left menu and click the + Add link (see Figure 8.48).
7. Select the Use MAC Binding option (see Figure 8.49).

   Once this is active, anytime the ESG receives a DHCP request from this specific MAC address, it will be assigned the IP address 10.30.8.22 with the default gateway of 10.30.8.1.

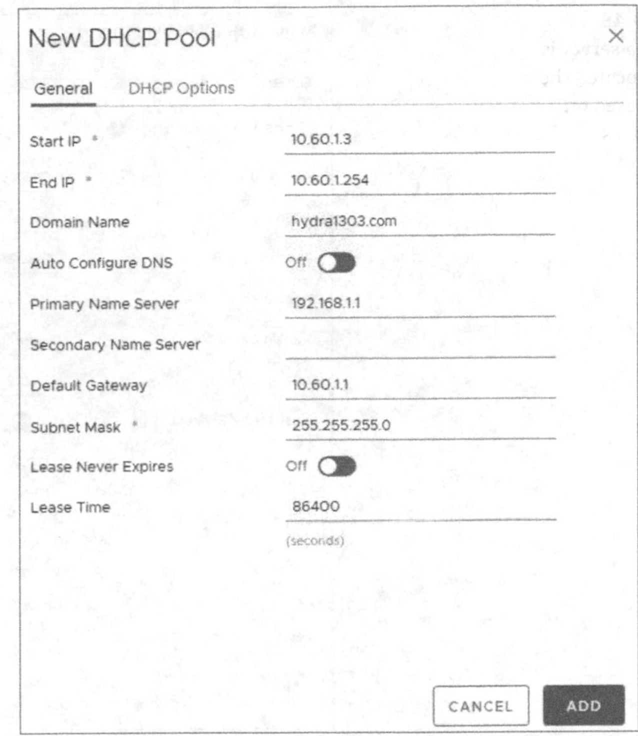

FIGURE 8.46 Defining the address range of the DHCP pool

FIGURE 8.47 Starting the DHCP server service

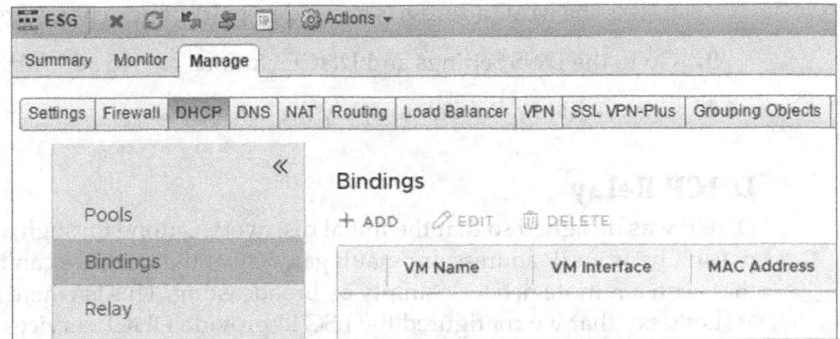

FIGURE 8.48 Configuring a DHCP reservation

FIGURE 8.49 Ensuring a server is always allocated the same IP based on MAC address

8. Be sure to set the Lease Never Expires option to On since we want the device to be assigned the same IP every time.

   The field for the MAC address is a bit picky. A MAC address contains 12 hexadecimal characters and is sometimes expressed in pairs separated by colons or dashes (like 00:01:A6:5C:92:F1 or 00-01-A6-5C-92-F1). Other times, it is shown in blocks of four numbers separated by dots (0001.A65C.92F1). You'll find that you can't complete this step unless the MAC address is entered as pairs of hex characters separated by colons.

9. Go to the DNS Settings and DHCP Options tabs to add further supporting IP information.
10. Click Add and Publish to apply the configuration.

DHCP Relay

DHCP was designed so that the initial discovery is done through a broadcast. Since the client doesn't have an IP address or default gateway at the start, we can't expect it find a DHCP server that is on a remote network simply by broadcasting. This is where DHCP relay comes in.

Let's say that we configured the ESG to provide DHCP services for every VXLAN. In the bottom-left corner of Figure 8.50, we have VM-A. It is configured as a DHCP client but has not yet been assigned an IP address.

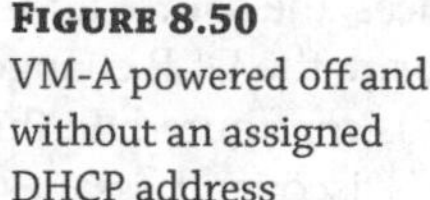

FIGURE 8.50
VM-A powered off and without an assigned DHCP address

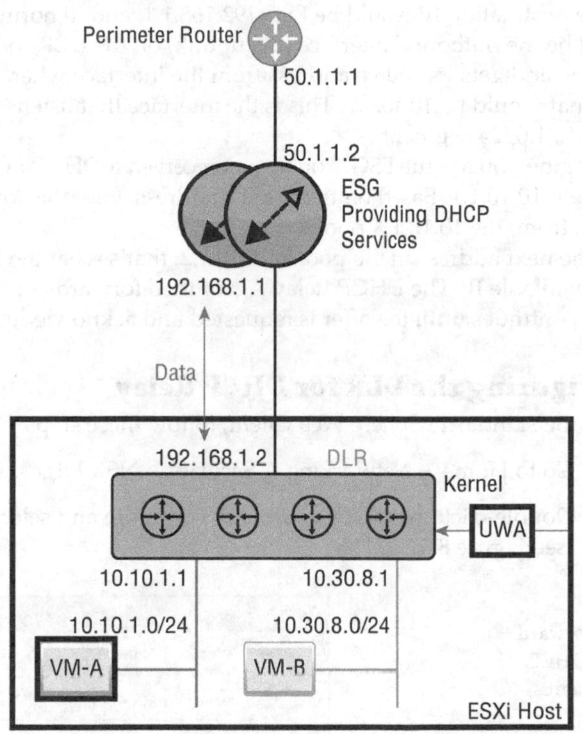

We power on VM-A. It sends the broadcast Discover message: "Is there a DHCP server on this segment that can give me an IP address?"

The answer is no. The VM is on the 10.10.1.X subnet. The DLR, being a router, forms the boundary for that broadcast domain. Therefore, the broadcast is only heard on that local segment between VM-A and the DLR. The broadcast can't reach the DHCP server.

The fix here is to configure the DLR interface 10.10.1.1 as a DHCP Relay Agent. Once configured, it listens on that interface for any DHCP Discover messages. When VM-A is powered on and broadcasts that it's looking for a DHCP server, the DLR steps in: "I'm not a DHCP server, but I know where it lives. Let me help you out." It then takes the broadcast Discover message, converts it to a unicast, and relays it to the ESG, the DHCP server.

The same back-and-forth DHCP conversation still takes place with Discover, Offer, Request, and Acknowledgment, but now with the DLR acting as the middleman. If the DHCP Relay Agent option didn't exist, we would need to have a separate DHCP server located on every segment. Managing all those servers would be a nightmare. Instead, we can centralize our DHCP pools and simply have the DHCP Relay Agents forward the requests they hear for IP addresses to the ESG.

It seems like the ESG might get confused. How does it know which pool to use when it gets a request for an IP address, especially since the devices requesting the IPs don't have addresses to begin with? The answer is simple. When the DLR changes the broadcast into a unicast, think what that packet (between DLR and ESG) would look like in terms of addressing.

The destination IP would be ESG 192.168.1.1, and in normal circumstances, the source address would be the outbound interface (the uplink) on the DLR, 192.168.1.2. Instead, the DLR changes its game and gets its source address from the interface where DHCP Relay is configured. In this case, that would be 10.10.1.1. This is the interface that listens for the DHCP Discover messages on the 10.10.1.0/24 segment.

Imagine you are the ESG. You've just received a DHCP message asking for an IP address from the agent 10.10.1.1. Based on the agent's address, you now know exactly which pool of addresses to pick from, the 10.10.1.X pool.

If the next address in the pool is 10.10.1.2, that's what the ESG sends to the DHCP Relay Agent as an available IP. The DHCP Relay Agent then forwards the message to VM-A, and the conversation continues until the offer is requested and acknowledged.

Configuring the DLR for DHCP Relay

Using the standard vSphere Web Client, follow these steps:

1. Go to Home ➤ Networking & Security ➤ NSX Edges.
2. Double-click the DLR you want to configure and select the DHCP Relay tab (see Figure 8.51).

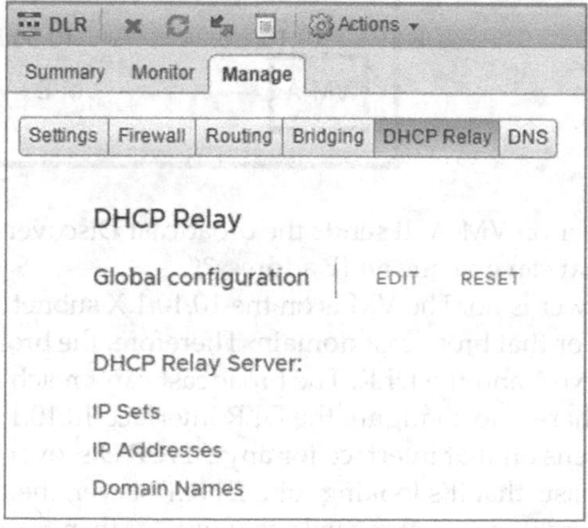

FIGURE 8.51 DHCP Relay to forward IP requests to a DHCP server on a different segment

3. Click the Edit link next to Global Configuration.

   There are several options to accomplish this, but the simplest is to add an IP address and domain name (see Figure 8.52). The IP address is the address of the DHCP server.

4. Since the ESG is the DHCP server in this example, enter **192.168.1.1**, and click Save and then Publish.

   The lower half of the panel is for configuring the DHCP Relay Agent (see Figure 8.53).

5. Click the + Add link.

   A new panel appears: Add DHCP Relay Agent (see Figure 8.54).

6. Select the vNIC on the DLR that the attached VMs use as their default gateway.

   When you do, the Gateway IP Address should be populated automatically. In this example, the segment with the database servers is 10.30.8.0/24.

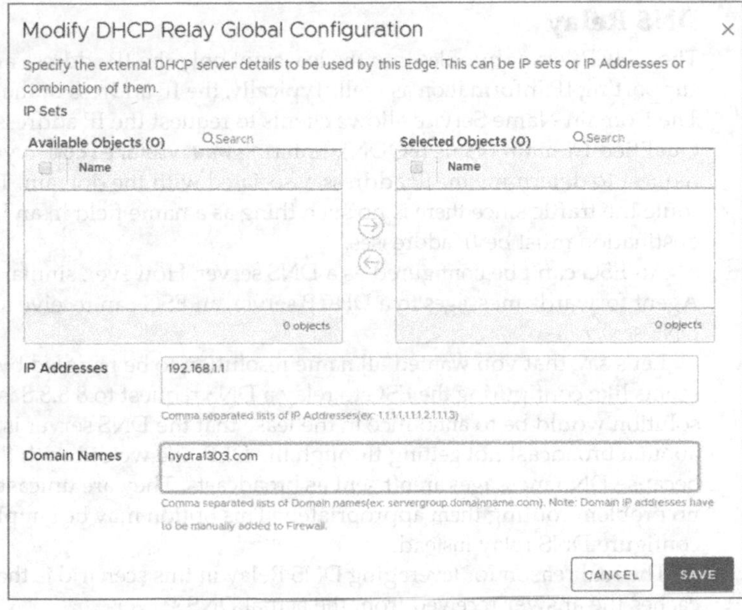

FIGURE 8.52 Pointing the DHCP Relay Agent to the DHCP server

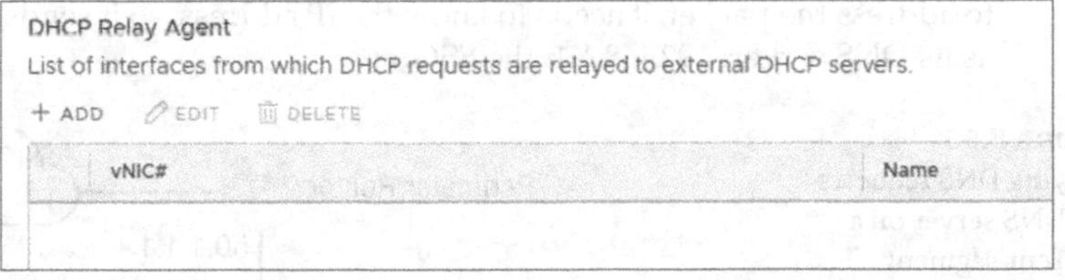

FIGURE 8.53 Adding the DHCP Relay Agent

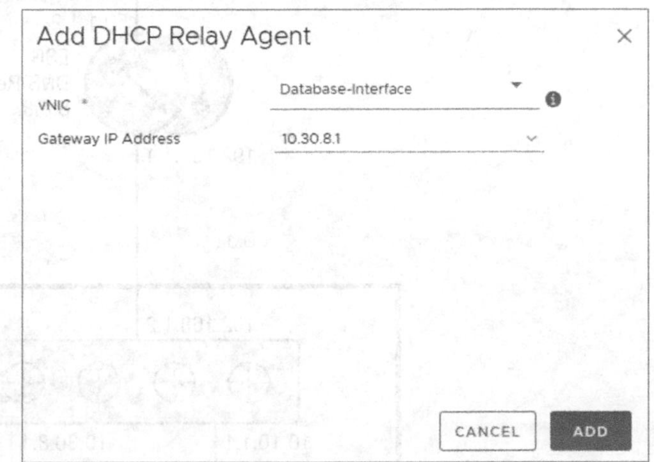

FIGURE 8.54 Selecting which interface will be the DHCP Relay Agent

Once configured, the interface listens for any DCHP messages heard on that connected segment.

7. Click Add and Publish.

DNS Relay

The DHCP server bundles into the lease not only the IP address and subnet mask, but other supporting IP information as well. Typically, the IP address of the DNS server is included. The Domain Name Service allows clients to request the IP address associated with a Fully Qualified Domain Name (FQDN). Entering **`www.vmware.com`** in your browser triggers a DNS request to determine the IP address associated with the domain. The destination IP is required to route the traffic since there is no such thing as a name field in an IP packet. The source and destination must be IP addresses.

An ESG can't be configured as a DNS server. However, similar to the way a DHCP Relay Agent forwards messages to a DHCP server, an ESG can receive a *DNS* request and relay it to a *DNS server*.

Let's say that you wanted all name resolution to be handled by Google's DNS server, 8.8.8.8. It seems like configuring the ESG to relay a DNS request to 8.8.8.8 is unnecessary. A simpler solution would be to announce in the lease that the DNS server is 8.8.8.8. We don't have to worry about a broadcast not getting through the DLR like we did with the DHCP Relay Agent example because DNS messages aren't sent as broadcasts. They are unicast messages. The DLR will have no problem routing them appropriately. This option may be simpler, but you'll still want to configure DNS relay instead.

The real reason for leveraging DNS Relay in this scenario is that when the request comes in, it caches the answer received from the actual DNS server.

In the diagram in Figure 8.55, VM-B needs to access a file on ftp.hydra1303.com, but in order to address the packet, it needs to know the IP address, so it sends the request to what it has listed as its DNS server: 192.168.1.1, the ESG.

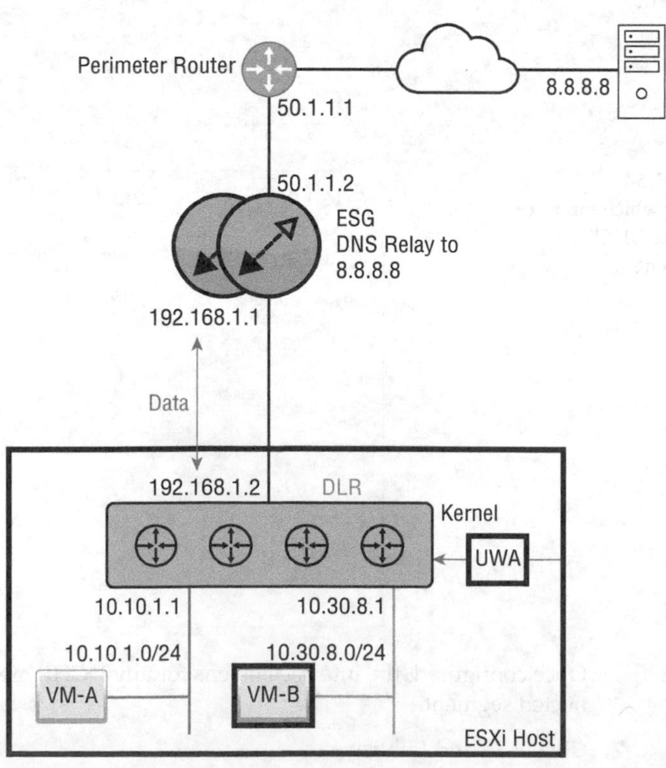

FIGURE 8.55 Relaying DNS requests to a DNS server on a different segment

The DNS request is received by the ESG, which isn't a DNS server, but it has been configured to relay any DNS requests to 8.8.8.8. The Google DNS server receives the request and answers the ESG, saying that the IP mapped to that domain name is 45.60.11.183.

At this point, the ESG caches the mapping ftp.hydra1303.com = 45.60.11.183 and sends the answer to VM-B. From this point on, if anyone from our organization needs to reach ftp.hydra1303 .com, the request will be answered immediately by the ESG without having to leave the NSX environment since the requested information is stored in cache.

Configuring DNS Relay on the ESG

Using the standard vSphere Web Client, perform the following steps:

1. Go to Home ➤ Networking & Security ➤ NSX Edges.
2. Double-click the ESG you want to configure, and select the DNS tab (see Figure 8.56).

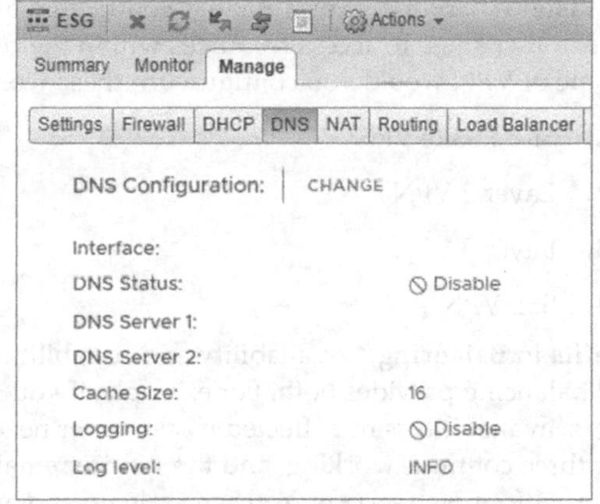

FIGURE 8.56 Configuring DNS forwarding on the ESG

3. Click the Change link.

   A new panel appears: Change DNS Configuration (see Figure 8.57).

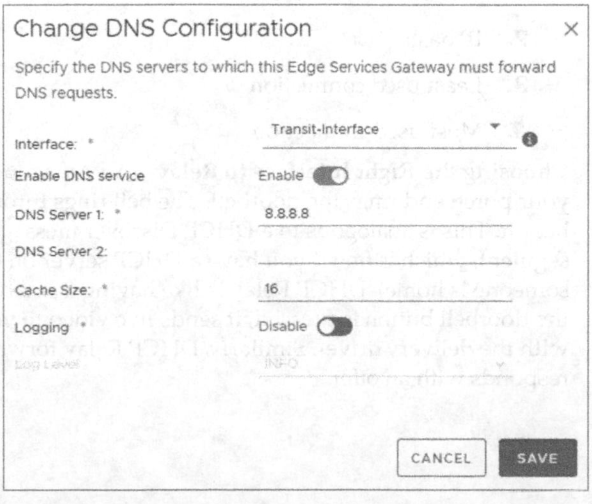

Change DNS Configuration
Specify the DNS servers to which this Edge Services Gateway must forward DNS requests.
Interface: * Transit-Interface
Enable DNS service Enable
DNS Server 1: * 8.8.8.8
DNS Server 2:
Cache Size: * 16
Logging * Disable
CANCEL SAVE

FIGURE 8.57 Directing the ESG to forward DNS requests to 8.8.8.8

4. Use the drop-down to select the interface that should be listening for DNS requests.
5. Click the slider to enable the DNS forwarding service. Then add the address of the DNS server.
   The DNS server doesn't have to be external to your NSX environment. You can also point to a local DNS server using the same steps.
6. Click Save.

The Bottom Line

Matching VPN Solution to Use Case The NSX Edge Services Gateway supports several types of VPNs to support different use cases. When choosing a VPN solution, factors to consider include temporary vs. permanent and mobile vs. fixed locations.

Master It Your organization has contractors based in different countries who travel to customer sites. To access resources within the corporate data center in New York, which type of VPN would you configure for these workers?

1. Site-to-site VPN
2. Layer 2 VPN
3. Layer 3 VPN
4. SSL VPN

Benefits in Balancing Availability and scalability are always a concern in any network. Load balancing provides both. For example, if you are load balancing traffic across four servers, availability is not affected if one server needs to be taken down for maintenance. The other three continue working, and the service remains available. Or say you are load balancing across four web servers. You can scale up and add more servers to improve performance when needed or scale down by removing servers when overall utilization decreases.

Master It Which of the following is *not* a valid load balancer configuration choice when specifying how the ESG will split the incoming traffic to connected servers?

1. Weighted round-robin
2. IP hash
3. Least used connection
4. Most used connection

Choosing the Right Interface to Relay An Amazon delivery driver places a package on your porch and rings the doorbell. The bell rings throughout the house but no one is home to hear it. This is analogous to a DHCP Discover message. It's a broadcast intended for the local segment, which is fine if you have a DHCP server on that segment (or for the analogy, that someone is home). DHCP Relay is like having a smart doorbell connected to the cloud. When the doorbell button is pressed, it sends live video to your phone allowing you to communicate with the delivery driver. Similarly, DHCP Relay forwards the message to the ESG, which responds with an offer.

Master It In Figure 8.50, the admin configured a DHCP Relay Agent so that VM-B could successfully receive an IP address from the ESG. On which interface did the admin configure DHCP Relay to get this to work?

1. 192.168.1.1
2. 192.168.1.2
3. 10.30.8.1
4. 10.10.1.1

Chapter 9

NSX Security, the Money Maker

Within NSX, there are two kinds of firewalls available. The Edge Firewall is centralized. Its primary function is to filter North-South traffic in and out of the NSX environment. In many ways, it behaves like a traditional firewall. The real game changer, though, is the NSX Distributed Firewall (DFW), which is the main focus of this chapter. Instead of sending all traffic to be inspected through a centralized point, the firewall rules are distributed to all hosts and applied to the vNICs of the individual VMs. As we will see, applying security this close to the VM not only improves performance, but it allows for much tighter security through microsegmentation.

IN THIS CHAPTER, YOU WILL LEARN ABOUT:

- Distributed Firewall placement in the IOChain
- Guest introspection to extend functionality
- Adding Distributed Firewall rules
- DHCP snooping, ARP snooping, and SpoofGuard
- Gratuitous ARP
- Identity Firewall
- RabbitMQ and AMQP Messaging

Traditional Router ACL Firewall

Network security designs have traditionally been built around the idea of protection at the network perimeter: keeping the bad guys out. We have described this as North-South traffic, packets that enter and leave your network. Your physical perimeter firewall is highly optimized for this. It protects both the physical and NSX environments. The NSX Edge has a similar complementary function filtering ingress and egress traffic from the NSX environment but isn't a complete replacement for your perimeter firewall.

Consider security at a sports stadium. With one main entrance and exit it makes sense to put security there, verify attendees' tickets, and check for anything that is not allowed. For the security guard, there is an order to these rules:

First rule: Does the attendee have authorization?

They could be authorized as a ticket holder or someone who works at the stadium. Their credentials are checked. If authorized, go to the next rule. If not, they are not permitted to attend the event and there's no reason to examine the next rule at all.

Second rule: Are they attempting to bring any prohibited items into the stadium?

If they don't have weapons or their own food and drink, they pass through. Otherwise, they are blocked from access. It's easy to see that this design is excellent for verifying people that must pass through a single main gate at the perimeter of the stadium.

Traditional firewalls operate in much the same way as gate security at a sporting event: inspect at the perimeter and go through a list of access rules, starting at the top and working down. To apply security policy to the traffic *within* the data center from one virtual machine (VM) to another, the traditional strategy has been to perform routing on an edge firewall device and then shepherd the traffic from the VMs to the data center edge, since that is primary security checkpoint.

The VM-to-VM traffic is East-West. The hardware perimeter firewall *can* handle this as well; but, it's not really a matter of can it be done; it's more of an issue of not being optimal. There is a performance hit and an increase in latency since the East-West traffic must travel to the firewall and then be routed back to its destination.

The perimeter firewall strategy is often exploited by modern attacks. When an attacker succeeds in getting through those perimeter filters, the result can be devastating to the business, allowing the attacker to move unnoticed from server to server internally with little resistance.

Access Control List (ACL) rule maintenance is another common issue. With the traditional perimeter security design, consider what must be done when a VM with a separate workload is added. A rule must be manually entered on the firewall. This rule may need to be modified later or even deleted when VMs are decommissioned. Not only does this increase the likelihood of configuration mistakes and the possibility of rules remaining when they should have been removed long before, but it also means more work for the admins, ultimately contributing to longer delays in getting networks provisioned.

One solution to combat performance issues in handling East-West traffic is to pour even more money into the already expensive physical firewall: adding more CPU, more interfaces, more bandwidth. Even if you have the budget, your underlying issue is not addressed: building on a design that no longer matches your current architecture. Traditional router ACL firewall solutions were built around the idea that most of your traffic is what enters and exits the network (North-South), while server-to-server traffic (East-West) is secondary in volume. Modern data centers have turned that ratio upside down. Most traffic is not North-South, not by a long shot. It's East-West, which means that the traditional firewall design in modern data centers is analogous to a square-peg in a round hole (see Figure 9.1).

With most traffic being East-West or server-to-server, it doesn't make a lot of sense to lean on a solution that isn't designed to optimally handle it. The NSX Distributed Firewall (DFW), on the other hand, is primarily focused on providing a highly optimized solution for East-West traffic.

I Told You about the IOChain

NSX uses a set of IOChain slots that handle how packets are processed at the kernel level. The first four, slots 0–3, and the last three, slots 13–15, are reserved by VMware. That leaves slots 4–12 for integrating third-party services from VMware partners (see Figure 9.2).

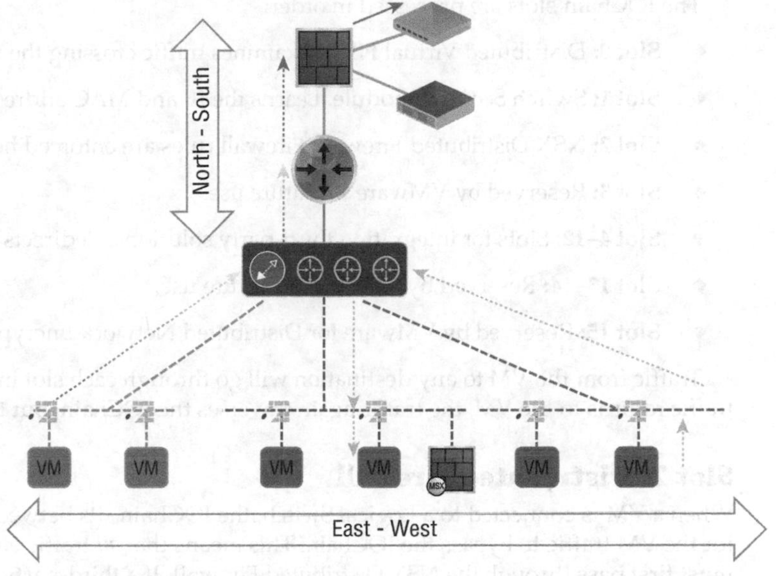

FIGURE 9.1
Traditional firewall design is best suited for N-S traffic.

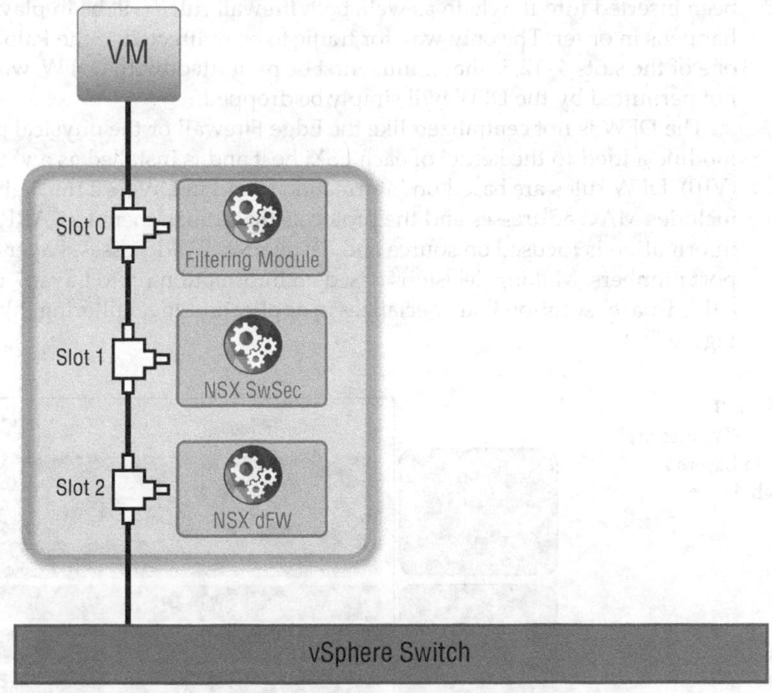

FIGURE 9.2
NSX IOChain slots 0–2

The IOChain slots are processed in order:

- **Slot 0:** Distributed Virtual Filter. Examines traffic crossing the vNIC.
- **Slot 1:** Switch Security module. Learns the IP and MAC address of the VMs.
- **Slot 2:** NSX Distributed Firewall. Firewall rules are enforced here.
- **Slot 3:** Reserved by VMware for future use.
- **Slot 4–12:** Slots for integrating third-party solutions. Redirects to a third-party VM.
- **Slot 13–14:** Reserved by VMware for future use.
- **Slot 15:** Reserved by VMware for Distributed Network Encryption future use.

Traffic from the VM to any destination will go through each slot in order, from 0 to 15. When traffic returns to the VM, the traffic again traverses the IOChain, but this time in reverse order.

Slot 2: Distributed Firewall

When a VM is connected to a Logical Switch, the IOChain sits between them and there is no way for the VM traffic to bypass the IOChain. This means that *all* traffic entering and exiting the VM must first pass through the NSX Distributed Firewall. If a third-party firewall, like Palo Alto, has been inserted into the chain as well, both firewall rules will be in play. However, the processing happens in order. The only way for traffic to be redirected to the Palo Alto firewall, which sits in one of the slots 4–12, is that it must first be permitted by the DFW, which it hits at slot 2. Traffic not permitted by the DFW will simply be dropped.

The DFW is not centralized like the Edge Firewall or the physical perimeter firewall. It is a module added to the kernel of each ESXi host and is installed as a vSphere Installation Bundle (VIB). DFW rules are based on information found in Layers 2 through 4. Layer 2 information includes MAC addresses and the protocols that utilize them like ARP, RARP, and LLDP. Layer 3 information is focused on source and destination IP addresses. Layer 4 deals with TCP and UDP port numbers. Making decisions based on information up to Layer 7 is a use case for integrating a third-party solution that specializes in application-level filtering, like the Palo Alto firewall (see Figure 9.3).

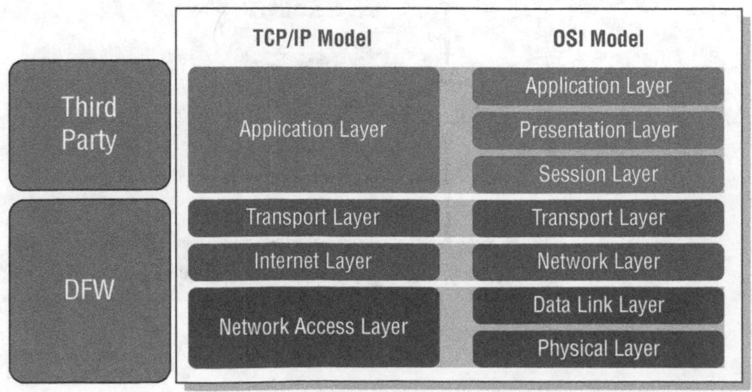

FIGURE 9.3 Native DFW rules are based on Layers 2 through 4.

Under the Hood

The DFW is distributed to the kernel of every ESXi host and is automatically activated when a host is prepared for NSX. The firewall rules are enforced at the vNIC of each VM by default. If you wish to exclude a VM from DFW inspection, you can manually add it to a DFW exclusion list. However, there is no need to add the NSX Controller cluster, the ESGs, or the NSX Manager to the exclusion list to ensure internal communication. These NSX objects are excluded by default. A key component you do need to add to the DFW exclusion list, though, is the vCenter Server. Since it exists outside of NSX, it's not automatically excluded. VMware recommends that you manually add vCenter Server to the list.

Because of the distributed nature of the DFW, scaling is accomplished automatically as you add ESXi hosts to the clusters. Therefore, as your business grows, you will need to add more servers. More servers mean more hosts. More hosts mean more DFW capacity (see Figure 9.4).

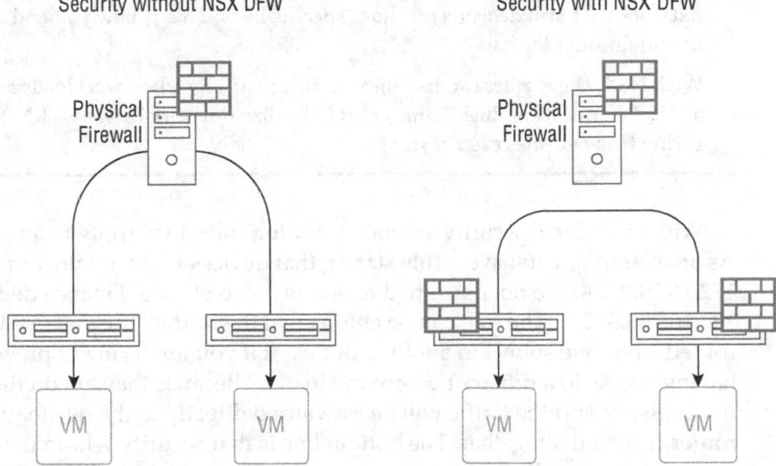

FIGURE 9.4 Firewall services distributed to the kernel of every ESXi host

We configure rules for the DFW using the vSphere client. Once created, they are stored in the NSX Manager database and are ultimately distributed to every host. Because they are distributed, it means all ESXi hosts have the same policies stored locally. Not only is this simpler to maintain, but it also means that when we move a VM, the rules table associated with the VM goes with it, which again, simplifies maintenance by the admin. Furthermore, if you delete a VM, the associated rules are removed with it. This prevents firewall rule sprawl, which is common with centralized firewalls.

NSX Makes Firewall Rule Maintenance Easy

Let's say your organization currently does not have NSX deployed but is considering it for next quarter's budget. In the meantime, your director has asked you to optimize the perimeter firewall's access list by removing any rules that are no longer needed.

Continues

Continued

This task terrifies you. You know how to build an access list. You know how to read an access list. But you aren't the only admin to have ever configured the firewall. There's a whole team of admins; plus, some of the administrators who've worked on the firewall no longer work for the company. The list of rules has built up over the years and it's doubtful that the rationale behind every line has been documented. Optimizing the list means that some lines will be combined, deleted, or moved. Making changes could very well have a negative impact on the network, not to mention your job. You're not alone with your fear. Adding firewall rules is common practice for any network team. Equally common is the fear of affecting network availability by removing rules. The result is a firewall with bloated and ever-expanding access lists.

Your organization's firewall may have numerous access rules that are unnecessary. They may relate to a previous design or workloads that no longer exist. Yet, none of your colleagues are stepping up to the plate to clean up the configuration just in case there is something somewhere in the network that still depends on those specific lines. This is how you end up with firewall rule sprawl. Sound familiar?

With NSX, these rules can be removed automatically when workloads are removed. Plus, tools such as NSX Application Rule Manager and vRealize Network Insight (vRNI) make managing and monitoring firewall rules even easier.

With traditional security solutions, adding rules that apply to an entire segment is common. As an example, you have a rule stating that devices in the Engineering department (on subnet 172.16.20.0/24) are not permitted to access devices in the Finance department (on subnet 192.168.50.0/24). The rule can be enforced at the router/firewall used to check traffic being routed from one subnet to another. But what if you are trying to prevent a device in Finance from having access to a different device in Finance? Because they are on the same subnet, routing is unnecessary and the traffic will be forwarded directly to the destination device, avoiding the router/firewall altogether. The bottom line is that security within the same Layer 2 domain (same subnet) has been difficult to enforce.

The DFW solves this issue easily. Because traffic must pass through the DFW filter within the IOChain both when exiting and entering the VM, it doesn't matter if the destination is on the same subnet or otherwise. There's also no added latency caused by traffic *hairpinning* to an external physical firewall and then back into the logical environment. The security is local, but enforced just outside the VM. This means that if a VM is compromised, the attacker can't simply turn off firewall services within the OS. The firewall services are embedded in the ESXi hypervisor. The result is that latency due to hairpinning is eliminated altogether and the rules can be checked at near line speed due to being placed within the kernel itself.

The traditional firewall router is made to handle segment-to-segment traffic when going from one subnet to another, but is not so good at providing security at a micro level within the same segment as the DFW can. Wrapping security around these smaller groups of virtual resources is known as *microsegmentation*. With microsegmentation, the VM is isolated from the moment it is powered on, and if compromised, it prevents the attacker from taking down the rest of the network from the inside.

Consider a three-tier application with a subnet for web servers, a subnet for application servers, and a subnet for database servers in a traditional design (see Figure 9.5).

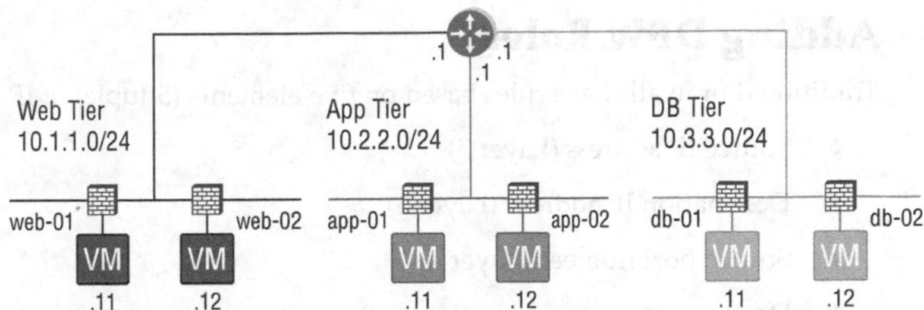

FIGURE 9.5
Three-tier application separated by a traditional router ACL firewall

The router provides a way to route traffic from one segment/subnet to another. Creating a router firewall access rule that specifies what type of traffic can be exchanged between segments is simple because the traffic has no choice. In order to go from one segment to another, it must go through the router, making it the ideal location to check the traffic against the rules. But what if you wanted to limit communication between two web servers? There is no reason for them to talk to each other. Since they are on the same subnet, they have direct communication and don't use the router. Therefore, no security is applied between them, and if even one web server is compromised in an attack, the other web servers are vulnerable.

This problem only worsens if web, app, and database VMs for an application are all placed together on the same subnet. But with NSX microsegmentation, these issues disappear. Traffic between VMs (even on the same subnet) is easily controlled (see Figure 9.6).

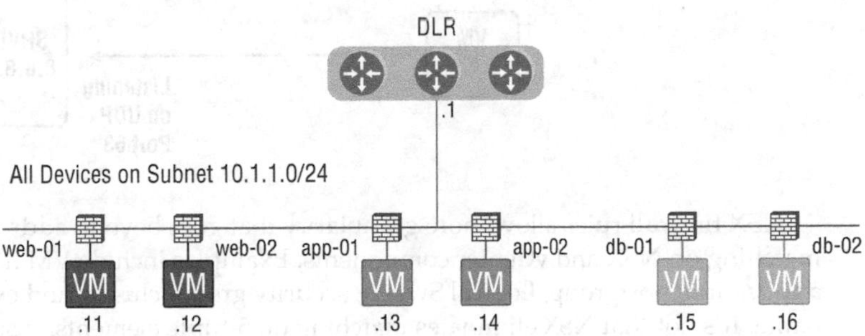

FIGURE 9.6
Single Layer 2 domain microsegmented by the DFW

The example in the diagram is not to recommend collapsing a three-tier application into a single tier. It's merely showing that even when *multiple* rules need to be applied to control traffic on the same subnet, microsegmentation provides an easy solution.

With traditional firewall policy, when you want to permit or deny traffic, you're dependent on the network topology. NSX microsegmentation is topology agnostic. Instead of a security strategy that primarily relies on a single castle drawbridge, security is embedded throughout. The underlying network topology doesn't matter. The vendor of the hardware doesn't matter. A Layer 2 or Layer 3 topology doesn't matter. Securing VXLANs or VLANs? It doesn't matter. Microsegmentation locks it all down and cannot be bypassed.

Adding DFW Rules

Traditional firewalls have rules based on five elements (5-tuple) of IP traffic:

- Source IP address (Layer 3)
- Destination IP address (Layer 3)
- Source port number (Layer 4)
- Destination port number (Layer 4)
- Protocol (Layer 4, will be TCP or UDP)

For example, you could have a rule specifying that source IP 10.1.1.5 with any UDP source port can access the destination IP 8.8.8.8, on destination UDP port 53 (see Figure 9.7). Or you could simply have a rule that says any device accessing 8.8.8.8 is permitted. The 5-tuple elements can be used to identify traffic in any combination.

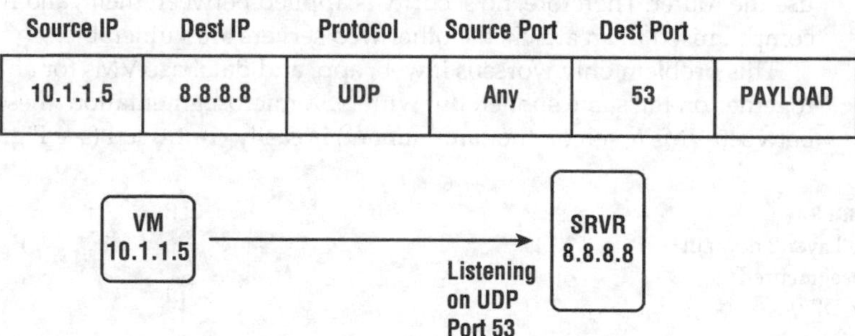

FIGURE 9.7 Matching ACL rules based on datagram header fields

NSX firewall rules allow more granularity that goes beyond addresses, ports, and protocols, matching on NSX and vCenter components. Examples include VM name, vNIC on a VM, application, portgroup, Logical Switch, security group, cluster, and even an entire data center by name. It's not that NSX eliminates matching on 5-tuple elements. It simply adds more options for what can be matched (like names.) For example, an NSX firewall rule can still match on IP addresses like you would normally do with a traditional firewall. You simply create an object called an IP set and specify the addresses.

To create a firewall rule, use your vSphere client and go to Menu ➢ Networking And Security ➢ Firewall. Then click the + Add Rule link (see Figure 9.8).

Note that there are three default rules already in play, numbered 2 through 4. (The rule in the number 1 slot is the new rule we are adding.) Within the same row for each rule, you would see that the action is set to Allow. The first default rule says to allow all Neighbor Discovery Protocol (NDP) traffic. This is needed for IPv6 to function. If your network isn't currently implementing IPv6, this rule won't affect anything. The second default rule says to explicitly allow DHCP traffic, and the third default rule allows everything else. We want that last default rule to be initially present to make sure we aren't blocking any communication channels required for NSX (see Figure 9.9).

FIGURE 9.8
Adding a new rule to the DFW

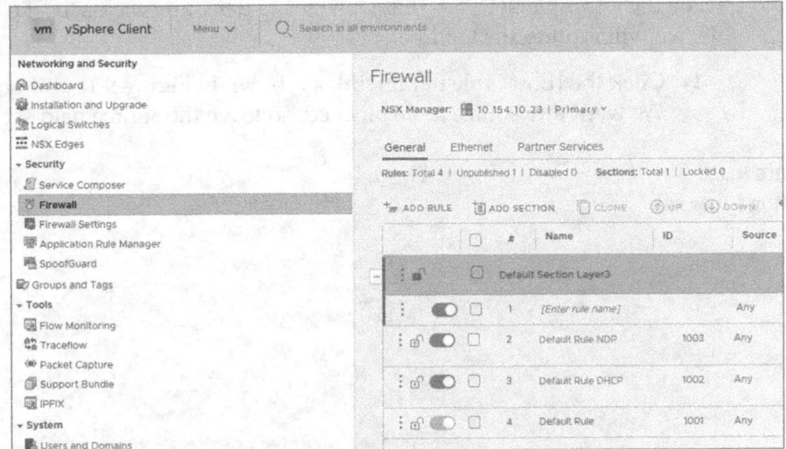

FIGURE 9.9
Three rules present by default

NAME	SOURCE	DESTINATION	SERVICE	ACTION
Default Rule NDP	Any	Any	IPv6 NDP	Allow
Default Rule DHCP	Any	Any	DHCP	Allow
Default Rule	Any	Any	Any	Allow

The rules are processed in order from the top down. Traffic is checked against each line until there is a match. For example, let's say we were attempting to access a web server in our NSX environment and have yet to add any rules (and therefore would only have rules 1 through 3, with Default Rule NDP being rule 1). The default permit statements are the only ones listed:

1. The first rule would be checked, which says, "Allow any NDP traffic."

   Since we are sending a web request (to TCP port 80), this has nothing to do with NDP. Therefore, there is no match on the first rule.

2. The second rule says, "Allow any DHCP traffic." Again, we are sending web traffic, which has nothing to do with this rule for DHCP, so there is not a match.

3. It then checks the third rule, which states, "Allow any other traffic."

   This last one is a match. Even though TCP port 80 was not specified, our traffic falls under the category of any other traffic. Once matched, we do whatever it says. In this example, it says to allow it through.

This final default rule is grayed out, unlike the other two default rules. It means that it can't be deleted. Although it can't be removed, the action can be changed from allow everything else to block everything else (see Figure 9.10).

FIGURE 9.10
Final default rule action can be modified, not deleted.

For this example, let's say that we want to deny any access to FTP services on Server1. To do this, we will modify the top line:

1. Click the [Enter rule name] link as shown in Figure 9.11 and type **Block FTP to Server1**. We want any source to be blocked, so leave the source field set to Any.

FIGURE 9.11
Creating a new rule

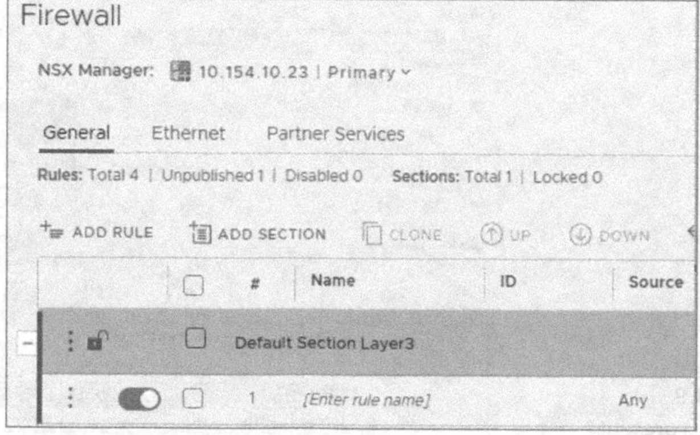

2. The destination is specifically Server1. Click this field to make a pencil icon appear.
3. Click the pencil icon and a new window opens (see Figure 9.12).

FIGURE 9.12
Choosing the destination object to match on

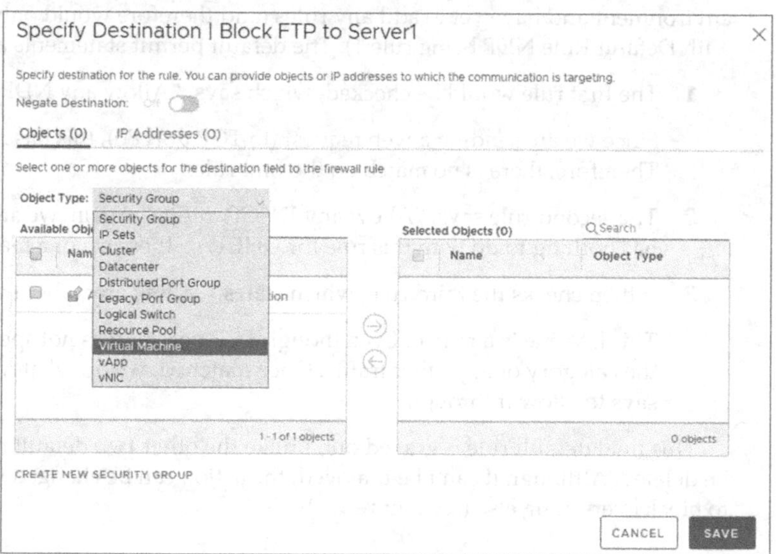

4. For the Object Type, click the drop-down and select Virtual Machine.

   By selecting Virtual Machine, only VMs will be listed.

5. Place a check mark next to Server1 from the list (see Figure 9.13) and then click the arrow in the middle to push it from the Available Objects pane to the Selected Objects pane.

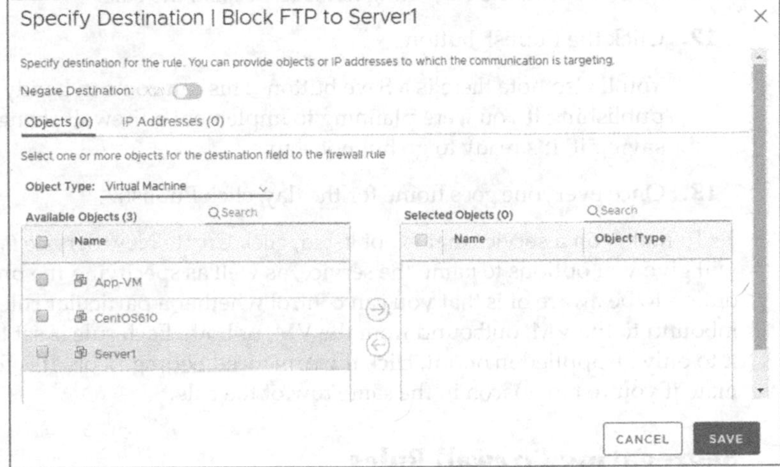

FIGURE 9.13 Selecting a specific server from the list of VMs

6. Click Save.
7. Click in the field under the Service column, and a pencil icon will appear.
8. Click the pencil icon and place a check mark next to FTP from the available services in the left pane (see Figure 9.14).

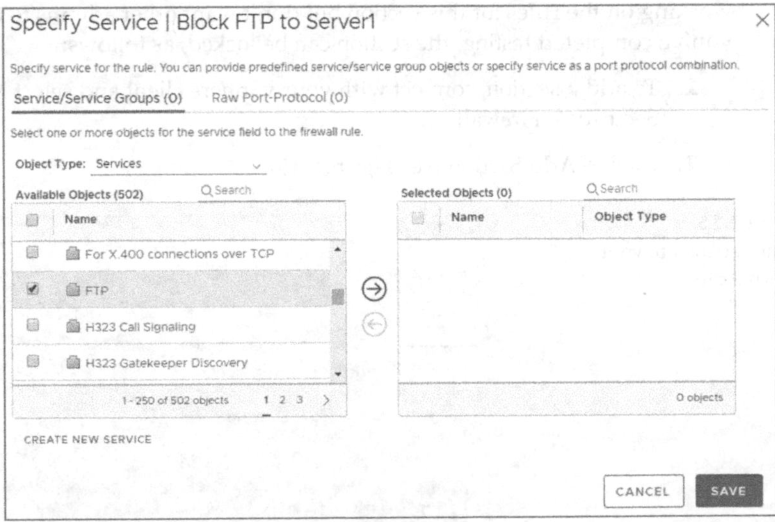

FIGURE 9.14 Selecting the specific service to match on

9. Click the center arrow to move the service to the Selected Objects pane and click Save.
10. Under the Action column, use the drop-down to change it to Block.

11. To create a log entry every time there is a match for this rule, click the slider button to enable logging.

    At this point, the only thing left is to publish the rule.

12. Click the Publish button.

    You'll also note there is a Save button. This can come in handy as an alternative to directly publishing if you were planning to implement a firewall change after business hours. By saving it, it's ready to go but not active.

13. Once everyone goes home for the day, click Publish.

To match on a service that is not listed, click Create New Service (see Figure 9.14 again). This will give you options to name the service, as well as specifying the protocol and ports. Another option to be aware of is that you can control whether a particular rule is only applied to traffic inbound to the VM, outbound from the VM, or both. Each rule is set to *both* by default. To change it to only be applied in or out, click the Advanced Settings icon. It is the next to last (or penultimate if you're fancy) icon in the same row of the rule.

Segregating Firewall Rules

Firewall rules over time tend to make a long list. You can make the list easier to manage by segregating your firewall rules into sections. For instance, all rules specific to the sales department can be listed under the Sales section. Not only does this make the rules easier to read and understand, but it also allows multiple admins to update the firewall rules without stepping on each other's toes.

For instance, you are working on a set of rules for a new app called Lesauce, developed by your dev team in France. You can create an AppLesauce section and add rules to it. If you're still working on the rules for this section but don't want other admins to be able to change them until you've completed testing, the section can be locked, as follows:

1. To add a section, connect with your vSphere client and select Menu ➤ Networking And Security ➤ Firewall.
2. Click + Add Section (see Figure 9.15).

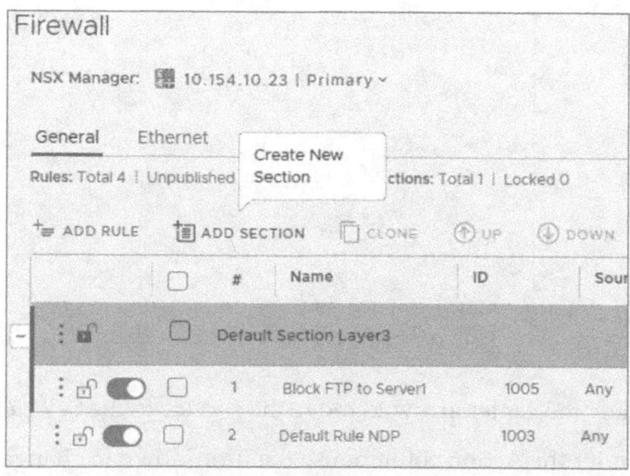

FIGURE 9.15 Adding sections to your DFW rule set

3. Enter **AppLesauce** for the name and click the Add button.
4. To move the rule we created previously under the new section, place a check mark next to the rule Block FTP to Server1 (see Figure 9.16).

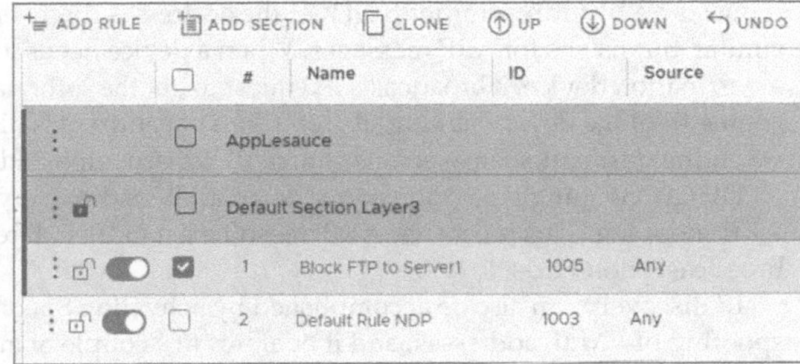

FIGURE 9.16 Adding a previous rule to the new section

When you add the check mark, the icons for arrow up and arrow down will no longer be grayed out.

5. Click the arrow up icon, and the rule now appears under the new AppLesauce section (see Figure 9.17).

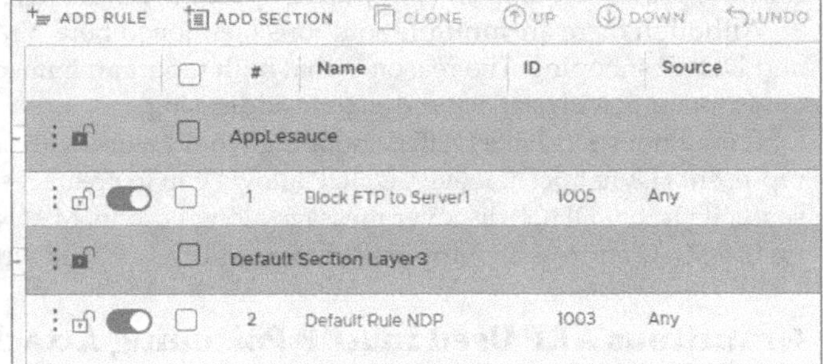

FIGURE 9.17 After publishing the change, the section is now lockable.

6. Click Publish.

When you do, you'll see a lock button appear for the AppLesauce section.

IP Discovery

If a vCenter object is specified in your DFW rule, like a VM name, NSX needs a way to discover the IP address of that VM before the rule can be enforced, or the mapping must be done statically. The default method to discover the IP address is to leverage VMware Tools. VMware Tools learns the IP address. That information is collected on the vCenter Server database. vCenter then relays it to NSX Manager for distribution.

For VMs that don't have VMware Tools installed, DFW will apply whatever has been configured as the default rule. For instance, if there are several specific firewall rules added by the admin allowing services to any VM with the prefix Sales_ and the last rule is to deny everything else, traffic would be denied for that VM, even with the name Sales_VM007, without the proper mapping.

However, if you do not want to install VMware Tools, there are other methods for IP discovery. Enabling DHCP snooping or enabling ARP snooping are two alternatives for NSX 6.2.1 and above. DHCP snooping works by being nosey when it comes to DHCP messages. When a VM requests an IP address through DHCP, the address is discovered and recorded. ARP snooping is similar, but listens for ARP messages. When a device needs to know the Layer 2 MAC address of a destination device, it broadcasts a request to get the information. Within that request is the source IP of the device making the request. That address is discovered and recorded. Likewise, when the destination answers, its source IP is discovered and recorded as well.

DHCP snooping is also supported as an address discovery method in IPv6 networks, but not ARP snooping. This is because ARP doesn't exist in IPv6. It relies on broadcasts to function, and broadcasts don't exist in IPv6.

IP discovery can also be accomplished by activating SpoofGuard. SpoofGuard prevents the spoofing of VM IP addresses, and it operates in a couple of modes. It can do either of the following:

- Automatically trust the first IP that it sees from a VM and record it as the legitimate address, otherwise known as Trust on First Use (TOFU).
- Be set to only allow the IP assignment if approved manually by the administrator.

If the IP address 10.3.3.15 was learned, but then someone changes the address to 10.3.3.100, traffic is prevented until an NSX admin approves the change.

Although there are multiple solutions mentioned here, VMware recommends VMware Tools and DHCP snooping. The reason is that both report an immediate change and both work in environments with static and dynamic addressing.

It may not sound like DHCP snooping would work with static IPs since the first letter literally represents Dynamic; however, DHCP allows you to create reservations so that when a device sends its initial DHCP discover message along with its MAC address, the DCHP server can look up the MAC address and apply the reserved IP associated with it.

Gratuitous ARP Used in ARP Poisoning Attacks

If ARP snooping is chosen as the discovery method, it's recommended that SpoofGuard also be implemented. Combined, they can prevent ARP poisoning. ARP poisoning is an attack that leverages gratuitous ARP, a function used to prevent duplicate IP addresses. The idea behind a gratuitous ARP is that you send out an ARP message essentially to yourself. Since it's not using ARP in the normal way (to discover a remote machine's MAC address on the same segment), it's gratuitous. For example, your IP address is 10.1.1.1 and you send out a request for 10.1.1.1's MAC address (see Figure 9.18). On the face of it, it seems ridiculous. Why would you ARP for your own address?

The key is, if no one answers, you know that IP is safe to use. If another machine replies, then you know 10.1.1.1 is already in use.

GRATUITOUS ARP
• NORMALLY, ARP REPLY SENT IF A NEIGHBOR REQUESTS YOUR MAC.

PC1
SW1
PC2
10.1.1.1
1111
10.1.1.2
?
L2 DEST
FFFF
L2 SOURCE
1111
L3 SOURCE
10.1.1.1
L3 DEST
10.1.1.2
• REPLIES SOMETIMES SENT EVEN WHEN NOT REQUESTED (GRATUITOUSLY SENT).
EXAMPLE : NEW PC TO SWITCH
GRATUITOUS ARP SENT TO DETECT IF THERE IS A DUPLICATE IP.

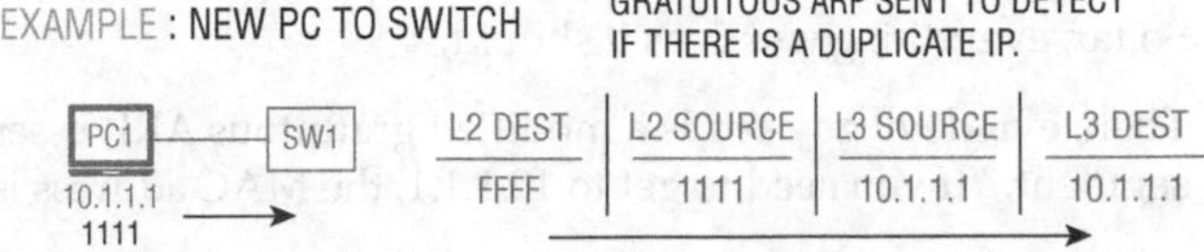
PC1
SW1
10.1.1.1
1111
L2 DEST
FFFF
L2 SOURCE
1111
L3 SOURCE
10.1.1.1
L3 DEST
10.1.1.1
• IF NO ONE ELSE REPLIES TO THIS MESSAGE, IT MEANS NO DUPLICATE IP DETECTED.
• ALSO ALL NEIGHBORING DEVICES UPDATE THEIR ARP CACHE 10.1.1.1 = 1111.

FIGURE 9.18 Comparison of a regular ARP and a gratuitous ARP

The initial ARP message goes out as a Layer 2 broadcast with your MAC address as the source. This means that every other device on the segment received the message (a broadcast) from your MAC address and your IP address. For efficiency, the other devices update their ARP cache with this information. That's the way it's supposed to work and what it was designed for. However, using Figure 9.19 as an example, an attacker can manipulate the gratuitous ARP packet and enter another device's IP address (10.1.1.1), while keeping the attacker's MAC address (BADD). Once the other devices update their ARP cache with the new information, it causes all traffic destined for 10.1.1.1 to be redirected to the attacker's device (10.1.1.66). So, by enabling SpoofGuard alongside ARP snooping, you prevent the attack. Also, just to note: An actual MAC address is 12 hex characters; so, written out, the attacker's MAC address in this example would have been 0000.0000.BADD.

GRATUITOUS ARP FEATURE USED FOR ARP POISONING

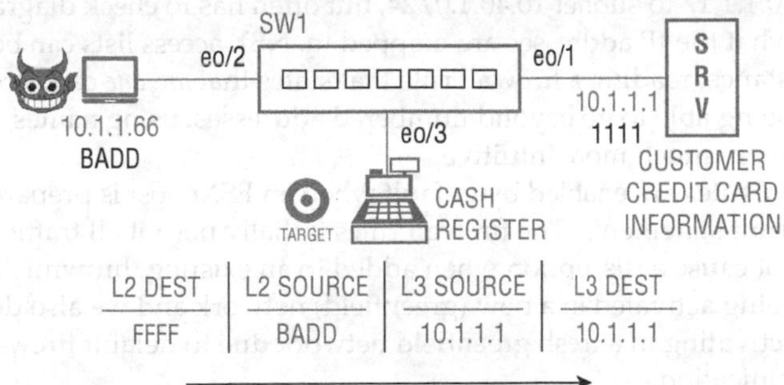
SW1
eo/2
eo/1
eo/3
10.1.1.66
BADD
S
R
V
10.1.1.1
1111
CUSTOMER
CREDIT CARD
INFORMATION
CASH
REGISTER
TARGET
L2 DEST
FFFF
L2 SOURCE
BADD
L3 SOURCE
10.1.1.1
L3 DEST
10.1.1.1
ATTACKER SENDS GRATUITOUS ARP, BUT INSTEAD OF HIS IP, HE ENTERS 10.1.1.1.
ALL NEIGHBORS (INCLUDING THE CASH REGISTER) UPDATE THEIR ARP CACHE:
10.1.1.1 = BADD
RESULT : CREDIT CARD INFO SENT TO 10.1.1.1 IS NOW GOING TO BADD.

FIGURE 9.19 ARP poisoning example

The way ARP poisoning works in this particular scenario would be something like this:

1. Prior to the attacker getting involved, when customers at Target swipe their credit cards at the cash register, the information goes to the Credit Card Information Server, 10.1.1.1.
2. Before the cash register sends this information initially, it will ARP for 10.1.1.1 to find out the server's MAC address, 1111. Being on the same subnet, it will use the destination MAC of 1111 to get the credit card numbers to the correct server.

   So far, everything works as it should.
3. Then, evil devil guy sends a modified gratuitous ARP, essentially announcing to the segment, "If you need to get to 10.1.1.1, the MAC address is now BADD."
4. Every cash register updates its ARP cache with the new mapping.

   From that point on, anytime a credit card is used at a register, the information is sent to evil devil guy.

Why Is My Traffic Getting Blocked?

Keep in mind that within the IOChain, the DFW rules are executed when it gets to slot 2. If a third-party service has been inserted into the chain (also known as guest introspection), traffic will not be forwarded to the third-party VM unless it has first been permitted by the DFW in slot 2. DFW rules can also be based on user credentials. This is also done through service insertion using one of the 4–12 slots to trigger a query to the NSX Identity Firewall service. We will take a deeper dive into guest introspection and service insertion in Chapter 10, "Service Composer and Third-Party Appliances."

Reading and understanding a traditional access list can be challenging due to being entirely based on numbers. For instance, an admin can look at an access list and see that traffic is denied from 10.1.1.17 to subnet 10.40.1.0/24, but often has to check diagrams or spreadsheets to determine what the IP addresses are mapped to. NSX access lists can be more user-friendly to read. For instance, reading a firewall rule that states that *anyone* can access *WebServer-1* is clear on its own. Being able to go beyond numbered addresses, using names, tags, and groups in access lists make them much more intuitive.

DFW rules are enabled by default when an ESXi host is prepared for NSX. The default rules are permit statements. The firewall rules initially permit all traffic to ensure that the deployment does not cause a disruption when added to an existing (brownfield) network or prevent NSX from being activated in a new (greenfield) network and we also don't want NSX to be prevented from activating in a fresh greenfield network due to default firewall rules blocking communication.

When NSX Manager deploys a VIB to a host cluster, any ESXi host added in the future will automatically be prepared for NSX. Being that the DFW is distributed, it means that the new host is also automatically protected by the same firewall rules. When adding third-party services to the IOChain, it's recommended that you add these services to the DFW exclusion list as well. This is done not only to ensure communication between the Guest Introspection services and NSX, but also to ensure that security tools with management servers can communicate with their virtual appliances in order to provide patches, security updates, and scans. Since these are all integral to security, excluding them from the DFW avoids network disruptions.

Great, Now It's Being Allowed

Being that the DFW is a stateful firewall, it keeps track of conversations. It's analogous to going to Disney World and once inside, you realize you left your phone in the car. When you exit to the parking lot, they give you a stamp. This is the stateful part. It's a way of keeping track of those who leave the park but want to get back in. You grab your phone and return to the park. They check for the stateful stamp and you're in. Hello, Mickey.

With stateful firewalls, there is a default timeout value for TCP and UDP sessions. Going back to the Disney analogy, their timeout value for letting you back in expires when the park closes for the night. You can't get a stamp as you leave and return with your unwashed hand two months later expecting entry. Plus, that's gross. Similarly, the stateful sessions have their limits regarding how long they will remain open on the firewall without activity before being removed from the table altogether. The default values typically suffice, but if you have an application that repeatedly times out, you can increase the timer values. If you increase the value, do so in moderation. When an application times out, it may be indicating that something failed. Therefore, setting the value too high could result in taking much longer for the failure to be recognized.

To change the timers:

1. Open your vSphere client, and go to Menu ➢ Networking & Security ➢ Firewall Settings.
2. Select the Timeout Settings tab (see Figure 9.20).

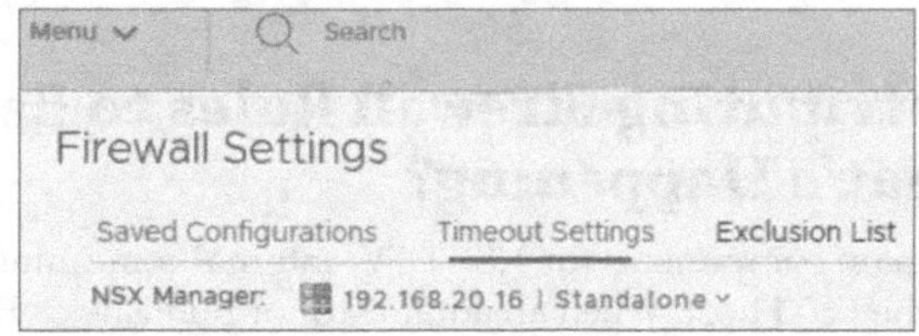

FIGURE 9.20 DFW firewall timeout settings

To troubleshoot an access list that is allowing or blocking traffic contrary to the rules you have configured for the DFW, you'll want to check the logs to see how the packets were processed. Specifically, you're checking to see if that specific rule had a match. You want to be able to effectively search through the output to find the rule in question. Each DFW rule is assigned a unique rule ID. This ID is so unique that even if you delete a rule, that ID will not be used in the future.

Logs are stored on the ESXi host in the `/var/log/dfwpktlogs.log` file. Any rule that has been configured for logging will be sent to the log file and will indicate the rule ID associated with each line. Although the rule IDs appear in the logs, they do not appear by default in the vSphere client in earlier NSX versions. To have the Rule ID column appear:

1. Go to Home ➢ Networking And Security ➢ Firewall and select the Configuration tab.

   Above the last column in the General section is an icon that looks like a mini spreadsheet (see Figure 9.21). It's actually representing columns.

2. Click that icon, and you'll see check marks next to the headings for each column.
3. Place a check next to Rule ID to have the column appear.

   With this information, you'll know what to search for within the log.

FIGURE 9.21
Icon to add or remove columns

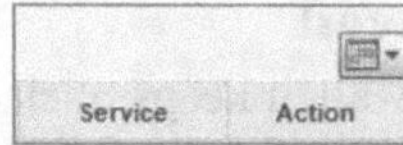

Identity Firewall: Rules Based on Who Logs In

The NSX Identity Distributed Firewall (IDFW) allows distributed firewall rules to be based on Active Directory user credentials. If Active Directory synchronization has been configured on the ESXi hosts, the IDFW needs to detect which desktop the user is logging in to so that the DFW rules can be applied. This can be accomplished either through Guest Introspection or via the Active Directory Event Log Scraper and the rules can be applied to both virtual and physical desktops.

With Guest Introspection, a guest agent on the user's desktop alerts the NSX Manager. The other option is to configure the AD Event Log Scraper in NSX Manager with the IP of the AD domain controller so that NSX Manager can retrieve events from Active Directory's security event log.

Once a method has been set up, the administrator creates an NSX security group. We will see how to do this in Chapter 10. Next, the Active Directory groups are added to the security group. Firewall rules can then be applied to the security group. When a user logs in, the login is detected along with the IP address of the desktop. The firewall policy for that user is then looked up and applied.

Distributing Firewall Rules to Each ESXi Host: What's Happening?

The main components for NSX DFW internal communications are vCenter, the NSX Manager, and the ESXi host. When an administrator publishes a DFW rule either through the vSphere client or by way of the REST API entry point, the rule is sent to the NSX Manager. In order to communicate with the vShield firewall daemon (vsfwd) process within the ESXi host, a client/server relationship is formed between the NSX Manager and the firewall service, with the NSX Manager acting as the server.

To accomplish this, the NSX Manager uses an open source message broker. But for this to work, we need a couple of things. We need a common language (protocol) so that both sides have a way of exchanging the messages. This is just a way of saying that the messages need to be in a certain format that both sides understand and that they follow the same rules to exchange the information so that messages aren't lost.

Advanced Messaging Queuing Protocol (AMQP) is an open standard that is very good at brokering message exchange between two entities. It receives messages from publishers (applications that send messages) and routes them to consumers (applications that process messages). AMQP provides the message bus (the protocol, the language) between client and server (see Figure 9.22).

But we need another piece as well. Think about another client/server example, FTP. We use File Transfer Protocol to exchange files. On the client side, we need more than just a protocol, we need software: the FTP client. On the server side, we install the necessary FTP server software, which the client connects to.

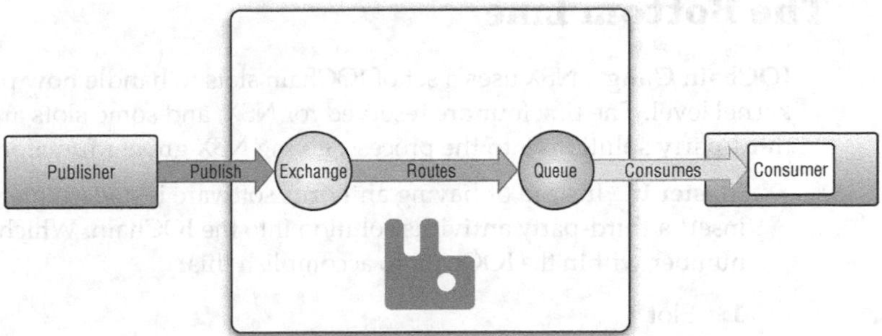

FIGURE 9.22
AMQP protocol is built for exchanging messages reliably.

RabbitMQ is the client/server software we use to exchange messages here. The language used between client and server is the AMQP protocol. Together, these create the message bus, a channel, between NSX Manager and the firewall service, vsfwd, on the ESXi host (see Figure 9.23).

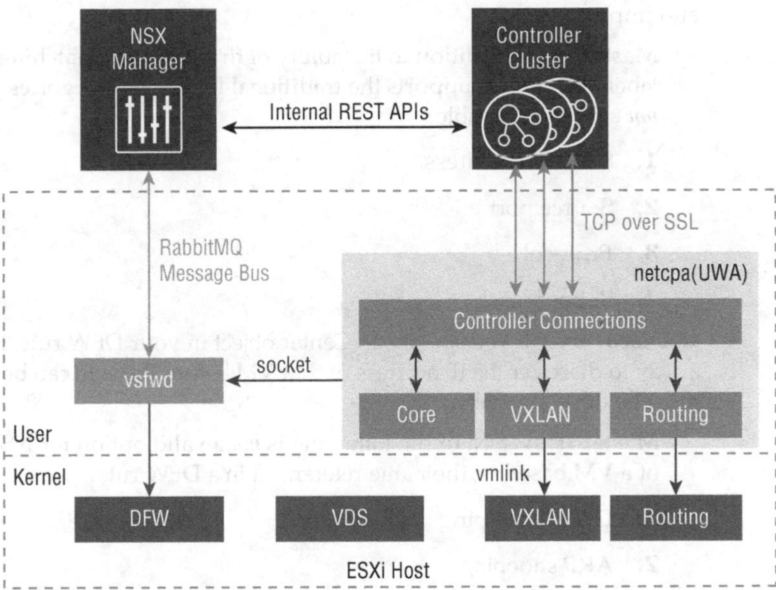

FIGURE 9.23
NSX Distributed Firewall architecture

The admin publishes a firewall rule. It is sent to NSX Manager. When NSX Manager pushes the rule to the firewall service on an ESXi host, it sends it over the established channel, which is encrypted with SSL. The firewall service is the client side of the connection. When powered on, each ESXi host establishes and maintains this secure connection to NSX Manager, allowing the same firewall policies to be propagated to every host.

The Bottom Line

IOChain Gang NSX uses a set of IOChain slots to handle how packets are processed at the kernel level. The first four are reserved for NSX, and some slots are available to integrate third-party solutions into the process, giving NSX greater functionality.

Master It Instead of having antivirus software installed internally on a VM, you want to insert a third-party antivirus solution into the IOChain. Which would be a valid slot number within the IOChain to accomplish this?

1. Slot 1
2. Slot 2
3. Slot 4
4. Slot 16

Matching on Access Lists NSX firewall rules can match on things like partial VM names, operating systems, security tags, data center, and so forth, making rules easy to understand and implement.

Master It In addition to the ability of firewall rules matching on various object types and labels, NSX also supports the traditional IP 5-tuple categories. Which of the following is *not* a 5-tuple variable?

1. Source IP address
2. Source port
3. Protocol
4. Subnet mask

IP Discovery If you specify a vCenter object in your DFW rule, like a VM name, NSX needs a way to discover the IP address of that VM before the rule can be enforced, or the mapping must be done statically.

Master It Which of the following is *not* a valid option for NSX to discover the IP address of a VM based on the name referenced in a DFW rule?

1. DHCP snooping
2. ARP snooping
3. Gratuitous snooping
4. SpoofGuard

Chapter 10

Service Composer and Third-Party Appliances

We've discussed key benefits of a distributed firewall service compared to legacy firewalls. Microsegmentation is easily achieved. Hairpinning, which adds latency, is eliminated since packets no longer need to travel to an external firewall appliance to be inspected. Rules are applied close to the virtual machine (VM) without taking up additional VM resources as is the case with software firewall solutions running within the operating system of the VM. The overall effect is a reduction in complexity, which is especially important in a virtual environment with virtual assets constantly being provisioned, removed, and moved on demand.

In the previous chapter, we discussed how to add DFW rules directly to the firewall table, an option well suited for primarily static environments. When provisioning network security services that not only include your firewall rules, but also involve contingencies based on what is discovered by Intrusion Prevention Systems (IPS), antivirus, malware protection, and the like, the management of these individual security services separately could easily become overwhelming.

This is where Service Composer comes in. It's a tool that's built into NSX providing an organized way of managing security services. It separates protected assets into groups and uses policies to define how you want to protect them. This modularity allows different policies to be linked with if/then functionality. *If* a VM belongs to group A, *then* apply these baseline scans. *If* a security issue is detected in the scan, *then* assign the VM to group B, triggering a different policy, possibly involving a redirect to a third-party security appliance, to be applied in real time.

IN THIS CHAPTER, YOU WILL LEARN ABOUT:

- Managing security services with Service Composer
- Defining security group membership with static and dynamic inclusion
- Using security tags for dynamic inclusion
- Leveraging Service Composer security groups in DFW rules
- Guest introspection service insertion
- Network introspection service insertion
- Applying security policies to security groups

Security Groups

Service Composer allows you to provision and assign security services to applications within the virtual environment. The security services can be native to NSX, such as distributed firewall rules, third-party guest introspection like Kaspersky Security for Virtualization to combat malware and McAfee MOVE for antivirus, or can include third-party network introspection such as Trend Micro's Intrusion Detection and Prevention Systems (IDS/IPS).

Service Composer has two main elements: security groups and security policy. You begin by determining what you want to protect and creating a group for it. Members of the group can be assigned statically or dynamically:

- Static assignments are appropriate when you are sure that there will be little to no change to the group membership.
- Dynamic groups are more powerful in that when a new asset is added that meets the defined criteria, it is automatically added to the group.

For example, say the naming convention used in the data center for web servers always includes the word WEB in them (WEB_01, CORPWEB, INTERNALWEB_02). You want to create a policy for every web server. The first step would be to create a group and assign the servers as members. Instead of manually adding each server to the group, a dynamic group matching on the word WEB would place every existing web server in the group automatically. Once a policy is mapped to the group, this means that any server provisioned in the future with WEB in its name would automatically belong to the same group and would share the same policy.

Examples of how VMs or users can be identified and then assigned dynamically to a security group are shown in Figure 10.1.

FIGURE 10.1 Defining group membership dynamically

Regular Expression	Example: VM name or partial name
Security Tags	Example: **ANTI_VIRUS.VirusFound.threat=high** label attached to a VM after a scan
IPset	Example: 10.1.1.1, 10.1.1.2
MACset	Example: 0000.01af.4578, 0033.6654.0412
Directory Group	Example: Active Directory

Dynamic membership is beneficial to Service Composer functionality since there are often multiple and frequent changes to group memberships.

Before getting into the details, let's examine a common example showing how Service Composer uses security groups and security policies to handle a virus discovered by a third-party guest introspection service.

SERVICE COMPOSER IN ACTION

1. The administrator defines a group called WEB.GROUP and a policy called WEB.POLICY, and then maps the policy to the group.

   WEB.GROUP The group contains every web server in the corporate data center.

WEB.POLICY A security policy that runs a virus scan on all members; if a virus is found, the label ANTI_VIRUS.VirusFound.threat=high is attached.

2. A newly created VM, Web_01, is automatically assigned to WEB.GROUP based on its name. Immediately upon joining the group, a virus scan is run. If a virus is found, the ANTI_VIRUS .VirusFound.threat=high label is attached.
3. The administrator creates another group/policy pair.

   QUARANTINE.GROUP The group contains any VM that has been assigned the label ANTI_VIRUS.VirusFound.threat=high.

   QUARANTINE.POLICY A security policy that blocks all outbound traffic to isolate the virus and removes any reported viruses; when complete, the policy removes the attached ANTI_VIRUS.VirusFound.threat=high label.
4. Immediately upon receiving the ANTI_VIRUS.VirusFound.threat=high label, the VM is assigned to QUARANTINE.GROUP. At this point, the VM belongs to two groups: QUARANTINE.GROUP and WEB.GROUP. They have conflicting rules. One is blocking traffic exiting the VM, the other is not. So, how does it know which to follow?

   When a new security policy is added, a weight value is assigned that is 1000 higher than the highest existing security policy, with the higher weight being preferred. To remember that higher weight is better, think of the idiom, "put your thumb on the scale"; the idea being that by making it heavier, it's more in your favor. Here, we are creating QUARANTINE.POLICY after WEB.POLICY, so in terms of rank, QUARANTINE.POLICY is preferred. The weight value can be manually changed if needed.
5. Look again at the description of QUARANTINE.POLICY. It says that after viruses are removed, the ANTI_VIRUS.VirusFound.threat=high label is to be removed. Since membership to QUARANTINE.GROUP is contingent on the presence of the label, it means that the VM no longer belongs to the QUARANTINE.GROUP and is immediately removed. At this point, it only belongs to WEB.GROUP. The weight doesn't matter now because the VM only belongs to one group, but the result is that the exiting traffic is no longer blocked.
6. The end result is that VM has been cleaned; it has been added and removed from groups with different policies applied and is now back in business with its original policy, all without any manual administrator intervention. Plus, anytime a new Web VM is added to network, the same policies are instantly applied, creating a consistent, end-to-end security framework throughout your data center. Your policies can be exported for backup, which means that when changes are made down the road, the earlier policy can be imported to easily roll back those changes if necessary.

This is the power of Service Composer. In addition to all of that, it provides a centralized interface to create those security groups and policies for your virtual assets, allowing you to consume both native NSX security services and third-party security services with mad efficiency.

Dynamic Inclusion

A security group can be defined through dynamic inclusion, static inclusion, and static exclusion: separately or in combination. When creating a new security group, you will see these listed as steps:

1. Name and description
2. Define dynamic membership

3. Select objects to include
4. Select objects to exclude
5. Ready to complete

Step 2 allows us to match on:

- Computer OS name
- VM name
- Computer name
- Security tag
- Entity

In the example we just discussed involving a virus quarantine and clean, we dynamically matched on the VM name, specifying any VM with the word WEB in its name.

Static Inclusion

If we had another web server that we wanted to include in the scan but for some reason, it didn't have WEB in its name, it could be added by static inclusion in step 3. However, another more powerful use of static inclusion is the ability to create nested security groups, allowing you to reference other security groups within that group. For example, if we have three separate security groups that match on VM names containing WEB, APP, and DB, and we wanted to add an umbrella policy to all three, these security groups could be selected in step 3. Each are independent, dynamically defined groups, but they are being selected statically to be included in the umbrella group.

Static Exclusion

Static exclusion gives the admin the ability to make exceptions to a security group defined by dynamic inclusion. Step 4 allows us to statically exclude objects* from the list based on the following:

- Virtual Machine
- vNIC
- Security Group
- Security Tag
- Cluster
- Logical Switch
- vApp
- IP Sets and MAC Sets
- Data center
- Resource Pool

* Static exclusion and static inclusion use the same object categories.

- Directory Group
- Distributed and Legacy Port Groups

The ability to combine dynamic inclusion, static inclusion, and static exclusion gives you full control to easily customize your security groups.

Defining a Security Group through Static Inclusion

To begin with a simple example, let's see how to create a security group with statically assigned members:

1. Open your vSphere client and go to Menu ➤ Networking And Security ➤ Service Composer.
2. Click the + Add link under the Security Groups menu (see Figure 10.2).

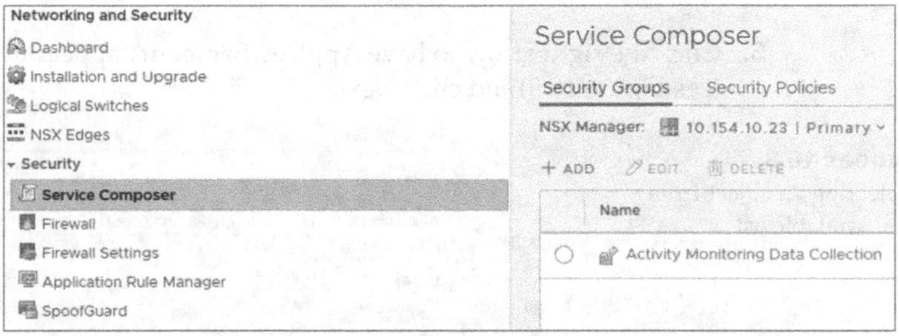

FIGURE 10.2 Adding a new security group with Service Composer

In this example, we want to create a security group for the network segment, AppDev, where applications are developed and tested.

3. Enter the name **Application Development Group**, noting steps 1–5 listed on the left (see Figure 10.3).

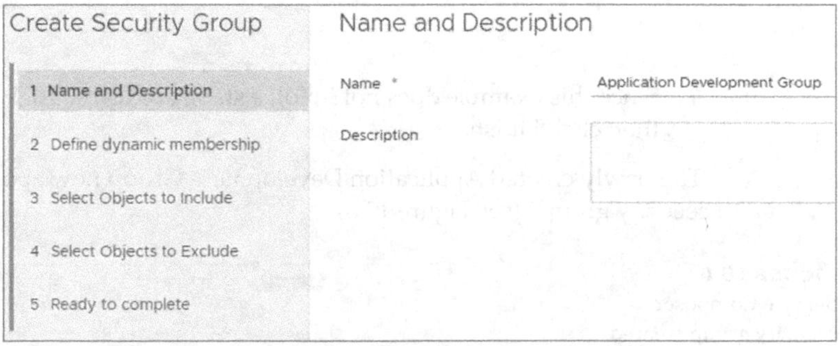

FIGURE 10.3 Naming the security group

4. Because this example will use static inclusion only, simply click Next to skip step 2, which is for dynamic inclusion.
5. In step 3, choose Logical Switch from the drop-down menu (see Figure 10.4) and place a check mark next to AppDev-Segment1 from the list of Available Objects.

FIGURE 10.4
Listing Available Objects by type

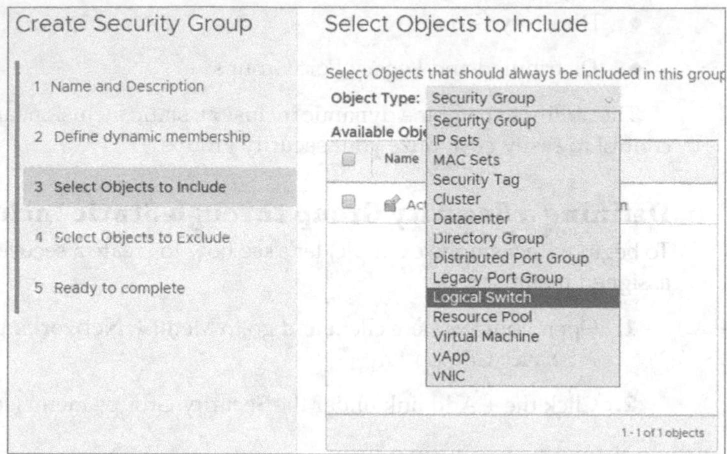

6. Click the right arrow to have AppDev-Segment1 appear in the Selected Objects pane (see Figure 10.5) and click Next.

FIGURE 10.5
Selecting an object from the available list

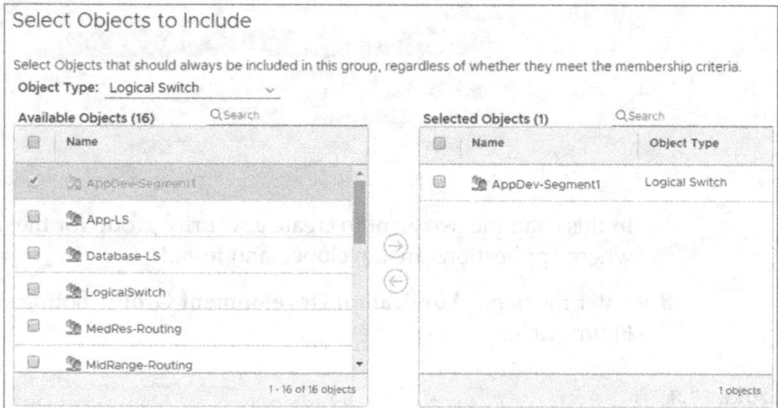

7. Since this example does not involve static exclusion, click Next again to skip step 4, and then click Finish.

The newly created Application Development Group now appears in Service Composer's list of security groups (see Figure 10.6).

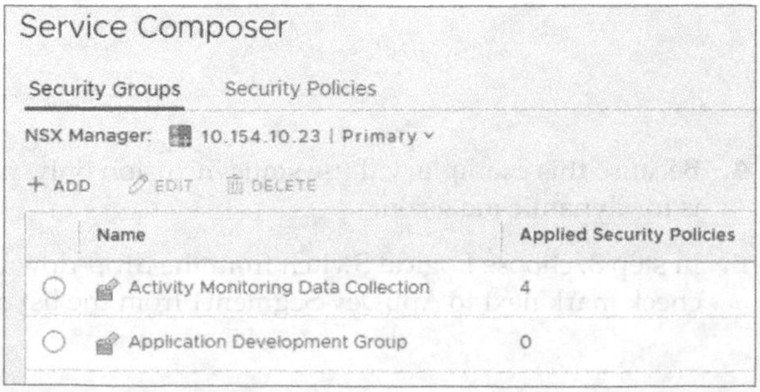

FIGURE 10.6
Service Composer security group created

Defining a Security Group through Dynamic Inclusion

To define group membership dynamically:

1. Open your vSphere client and go to Menu ➤ Networking and Security ➤ Service Composer.
2. Click the + Add link.
3. Enter **WEB VMs** for the name and click Next.
4. Select VM Name from the drop-down.
5. Select Contains in the middle column and enter **WEB** in the third column (see Figure 10.7).

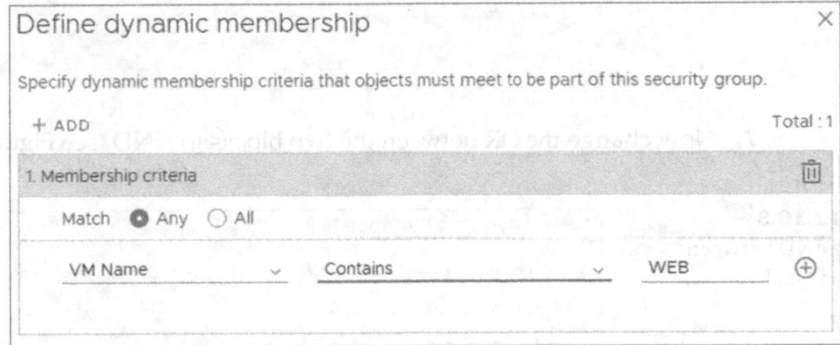

FIGURE 10.7 Dynamic membership criteria

Notice that there is an option to match Any or All.

6. Add additional criteria by clicking the plus circle to the right.

For example, let's say you wanted to add another line matching on the Computer OS Name containing the word Linux in the title. With these two criteria, if you select All, it would match any Linux VM with WEB as part of the VM name. However, if you selected Any, then it would match on all VMs running Linux *and* all VMs with WEB contained in the name.

Both lines make up membership criteria 1. Note the + Add link. This allows you to create membership criteria 2. You will then get the option of *both* sets required to make a match or *either* set required to make a match.

For example, see if you can determine what would be matched in Figure 10.8 and then read the next paragraph to see the answer.

Notice that between the first criteria block and the second, there is an OR selected. You would read the combination of membership criteria 1 and 2 as, "Match any Linux VM with WEB in its name, but also match any VM that starts with Dev_ regardless of whether or not it also has WEB in its name." It will match either/or.

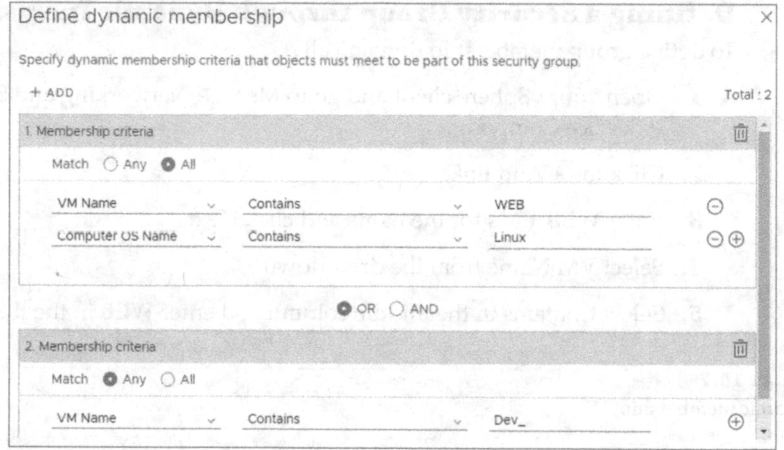

FIGURE 10.8 Customizing and combining multiple criteria groups

7. Now change the OR between the two blocks to AND (see Figure 10.9).

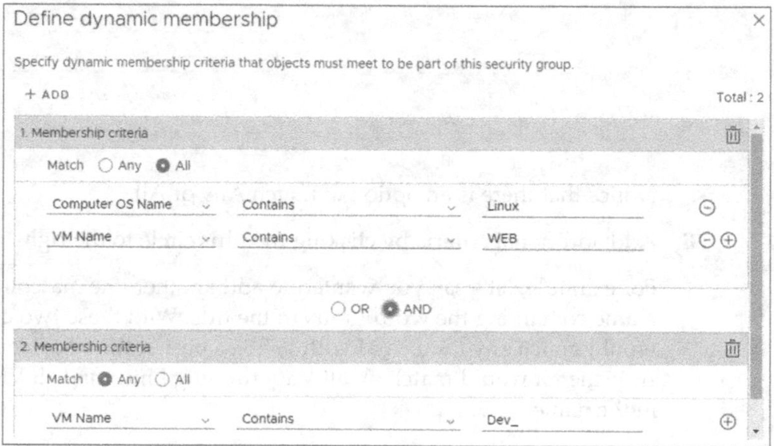

FIGURE 10.9 Using AND between criteria blocks

8. Try to determine what would be matched, and then check your answer in the following paragraph.

   If we were to select AND between the two blocks, the result would be to "Match any Linux VM with a name starting with Dev_ and also includes the word WEB." For example, *Dev_WEB06 with an OS named Linux7.4.1708* meets all the criteria. By selecting AND, both blocks must match for an object to be dynamically added to the security group.

Being able to use Any/All within each block combined with the OR/AND option between blocks gives you a lot of flexibility when defining dynamic membership.

Customizing a Security Group with Static Exclusion

Sticking with the previous security group definition, let's say there are two VMs that match all the criteria:

- Dev_WEB04 with an OS named Linux7.4.1708
- Dev_WEB05 with an OS named Linux7.3.1025

Despite both matching the group membership criteria, in this example, we do not want these to be automatically added to the group. This is where step 4, Select Objects to Exclude, comes in (see Figure 10.10). Here you could simply specify that Dev_WEB04 and Dev_WEB05 are exceptions to be excluded.

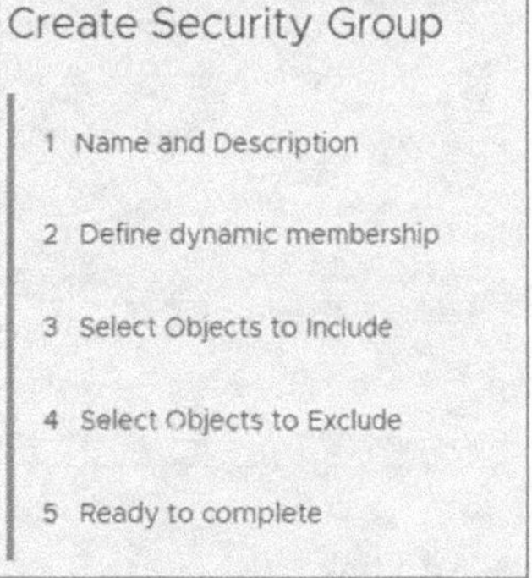

Figure 10.10
Creating exceptions by excluding objects

Defining a Security Group Using Security Tags

Another method used to add members to a security group is to use security tags. The Service Composer scenario in the beginning of this chapter that quarantined VMs infected with a virus was an example using security tags. When the virus was discovered, the security tag ANTI_VIRUS.VirusFound.threat=high was added to the VM.

Create the Security Group

For this example, we want to create a security group called DB-VM. Any VM that we manually add the SecTag.DBMaint to will dynamically be added as a member of the group:

1. Begin by opening your vSphere client and go to Menu ➢ Networking And Security ➢ Service Composer.
2. Click the + Add link.
3. In the Name field, enter **DB-VM** and click Next.
4. Change the fields within the three columns to read: Security Tag, Contains, SecTag.DBMaint.
5. Click Finish (see Figure 10.11).

Figure 10.11 Applying the created security group

Create the Security Tag

To create a security tag:

1. Open your vSphere client and go to Menu ➤ Networking And Security ➤ Groups And Tags and select the Security Tags menu (see Figure 10.12).

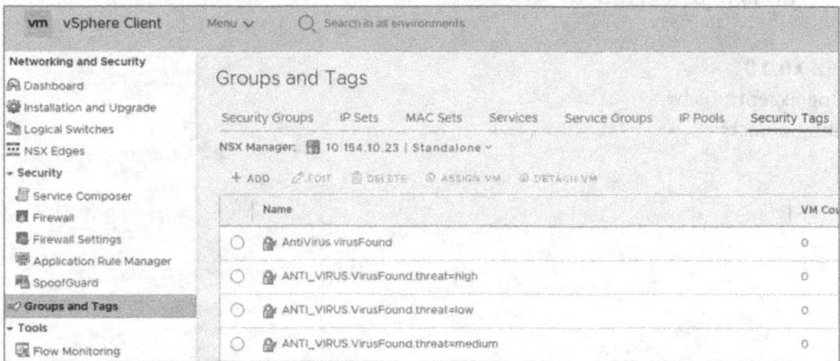

Figure 10.12 Navigating to the Security Tags menu

2. Click the + Add link.
3. In the Name field, enter **SecTag.DBMaint**.
4. In the Description field, enter **Databases tagged for system maintenance**.
5. Click the Add button.

Assign the Security Tag to VMs

To assign a security tag to VMs:

1. Select the SecTag.DBMaint security tag and click the Assign VM link.
2. From the list of Available Objects in the left pane, select DB_01-VM and DB_02-VM.
3. Place check marks next to each, and click the right arrow to move the objects to the Selected Objects pane (see Figure 10.13).
4. Click OK.

If you were to return to Service Composer and view the DB-VM security group, you would see that the two tagged VMs have been added to it (see Figure 10.14).

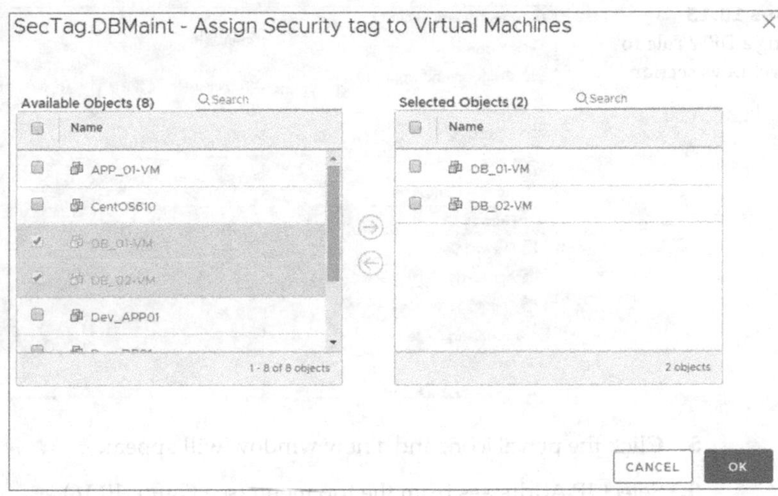

FIGURE 10.13 Moving VMs to the Selected Objects pane

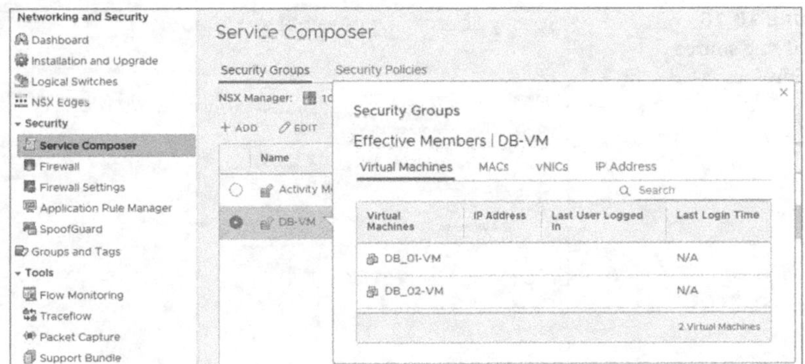

FIGURE 10.14 Verifying group membership

Adding to DFW Rules

Once these security group objects are created, we can use them not only within Service Composer, but they can be leveraged within your DFW rules as well. Using your vSphere Client:

1. Go to Menu ➤ Networking And Security ➤ Firewall and click the + Add Section link.
2. When prompted for Section Name, enter **WebDevs** and click the Add button.
3. Next, click the +Add Rule link (see Figure 10.15).
4. For the rule name, enter **DevTeam1 Linux Web**.

   Hovering your mouse over Any under the Source column will reveal a pencil icon to edit the field.

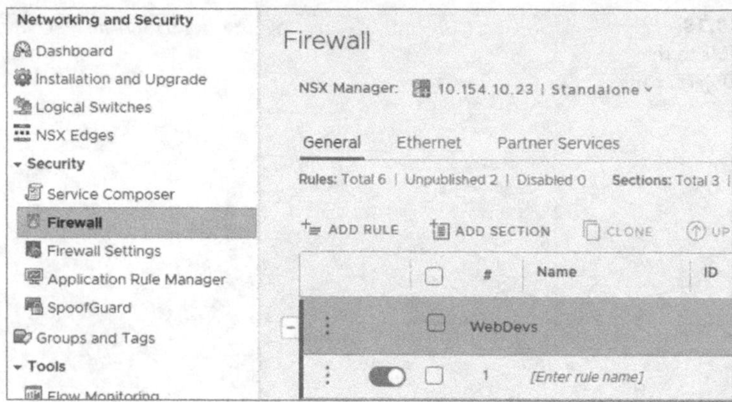

FIGURE 10.15 Adding a DFW rule to the WebDevs section

5. Click the pencil icon, and a new window will appear.
6. Select IP Addresses from the top menu (see Figure 10.16).

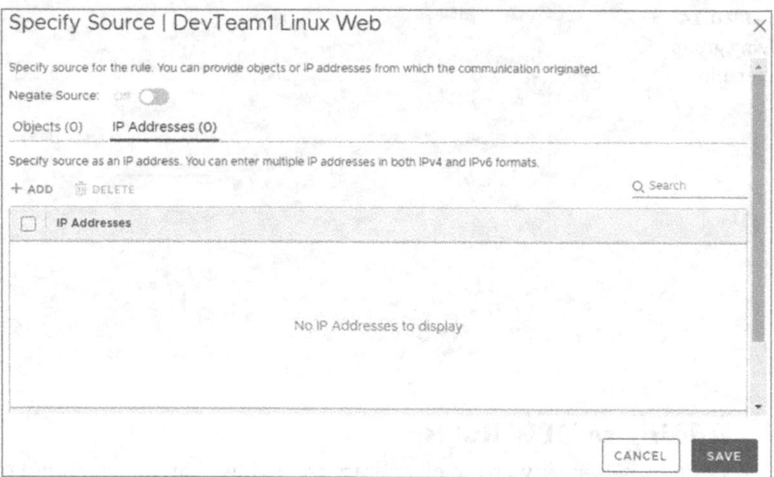

FIGURE 10.16 Specifying source IP addresses

In this example, we want to provide access to our DevTeam1 users. Their IP addresses all fall between 10.9.9.7 and 10.9.9.15.

7. Click the + Add link and enter the range **10.9.9.7-10.9.9.15**. Then click Save.
8. Next, edit the Destination field (see Figure 10.17).

   Before making a selection from Available Objects, let's take a closer look at the objects shown.

   Despite our not being within Service Composer, notice that the security group object we created using Service Composer, WEB VMs, is now an available option for the DFW to leverage.

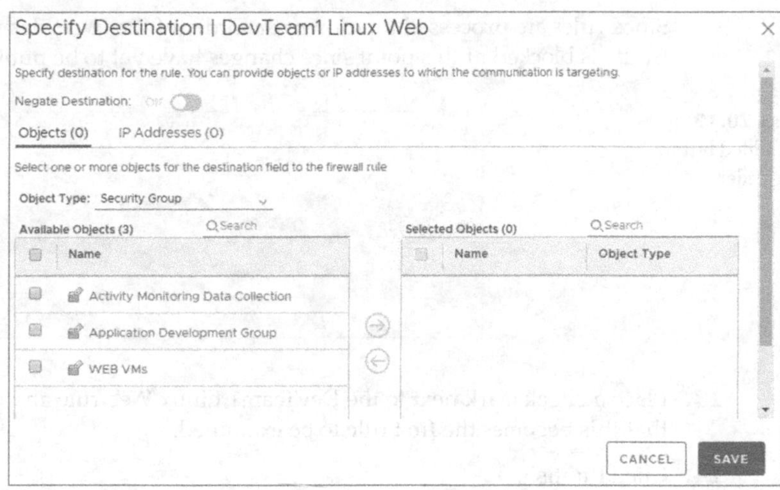

FIGURE 10.17 Security group object available for DFW rule

Recall that the WEB VMs rule said to "Match any Linux VM with a name starting with Dev_ and also includes the word WEB." We want to make a DFW rule here that specifies only DevTeam1 can access these Linux web servers set aside for development.

9. Place a check mark next to WEB VMs from Available Objects and click the right arrow to move it to the Selected Objects pane.

10. Click Save.

11. Click the +Add Rule link again.

    We've explicitly permitted DevTeam1 to access these VMs, but now let's add another rule denying access to everyone else. (Don't worry about the order of the rules at this point; we'll fix that next.)

12. Use the following information to create the rule (see Figure 10.18):

    Name: Block Dev Linux Web

    Source: Any

    Destination: WEB VMs

    Action: Block

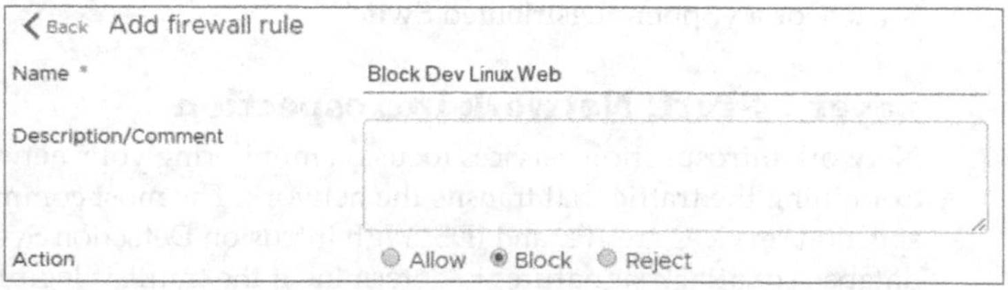

FIGURE 10.18 Adding a new firewall rule

Since rules are processed top-down, the order of the two rules needs to be reversed, but no traffic is blocked at this point since changes have yet to be published (see Figure 10.19).

FIGURE 10.19
Rules added but in wrong order

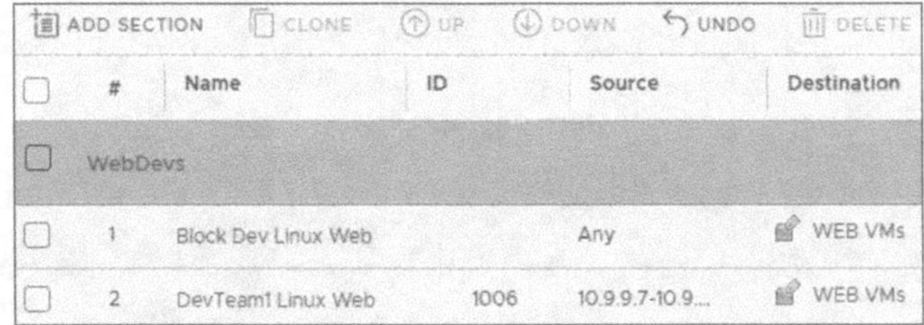

13. Place a check mark next to the DevTeam1 Linux Web rule and click the up-arrow icon so that this becomes the first rule to be examined.
14. Click Publish.

Service Insertion

Traditionally, for traffic within the data center to be properly serviced, it would need to be steered through various services such as Intrusion Detection and Prevention Systems (IDS/IPS), firewalls, and load balancers. With NSX, virtualization allows these services to be chained and inserted directly into the traffic path.

There are two types of services that can be inserted: guest introspection services and network introspection services. Guest refers to the VM and network refers to, well, the network. When you think of a VM, it's an endpoint. The network, on the other hand, is a through-point. Guest introspection is all about the endpoint, the data at rest. Network introspection deals with data in transit.

IOChain, the Gift that Keeps on Giving

Before packets from VMs can be forwarded to a connected Logical Switch, they pass through the IOChain, which determines how packets are processed in the kernel. Some of the slots in the chain are reserved by VMware and can't be modified, but as we mentioned previously, additional slots are available. It's here where service insertion takes place, allowing us to extend the capabilities of NSX for both data at rest and data in transit (see Figure 10.20).

Having the ability to insert functions directly into the data path means that the capabilities are present regardless of whether the VM is connected to a vSphere Standard Switch, an NSX Logical Switch, or a vSphere Distributed Switch.

Layer 7 Stuff: Network Introspection

Network introspection services focus on monitoring your network for malicious activity, examining the traffic that transits the network. The most common examples of network introspection services are IPS and IDS. With Intrusion Detection Systems, traffic is compared against a database of attack signatures to determine if the traffic is legitimate or illegitimate. Whereas most firewalls focus on the lower layers up to Layer 4, matching on IP addresses and port numbers found in the packet headers, an IDS provides a deeper inspection of packets through Layer 7 (the application layer). The inspection includes examining the payload itself, not merely header information. Information is collected and assimilated in its database, where intelligent algorithms build a predictive model to determine whether traffic is normal or part of an attack. Examples of attacks include Denial of Service (DoS), someone attempting to gain root access, and probing. Think of IDS as a highly trained analyst and whistleblower. It sounds the alarm of the attack but doesn't take any steps to mitigate it. Whereas IDS is all about monitoring and analysis, Intrusion Prevention Systems (IPS) actively kill traffic that threatens security before it has a chance to reach its target. If IDS is the whistleblower, IPS is a bounty hunter carrying out the response. Combined, they are key to network integrity (see Figure 10.21).

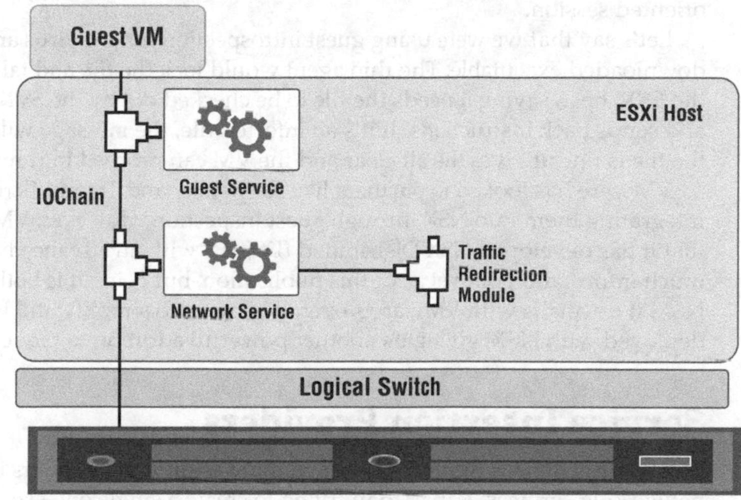

FIGURE 10.20 IOChain service insertion within the kernel

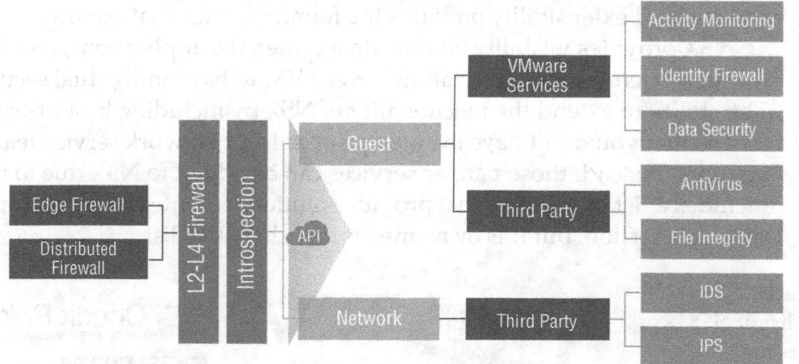

FIGURE 10.21 IDS and IPS are examples of third-party network introspection services.

Guest Introspection

Guest introspection is all about protecting the virtual appliance, the guest that lives in the ESXi host. When you want to protect your laptop from attacks, you install antivirus software and vulnerability management software. Antivirus and anti-malware agents are examples of guest introspection services, but the key difference is that as guest introspection services, they aren't consuming the VM's resources. Instead, the processing is offloaded to a Service VM (SVM), which is deployed when guest introspection is enabled, and it handles the brunt of the processing needed to address what needs to be done inside the VM's operating system.

The VM requires a thin agent to be installed for this to work, that being VMTools with guest introspection. When guest introspection is enabled on a cluster, a new VIB called *epsec*-mux is installed on each ESXi host. EPsec is short for Endpoint Security. Recall that network introspection deals with data in transit. In contrast, guest introspection is concerned with data at rest. The data *rests* at the endpoint, the VM. This MUX module is a multiplexer that receives information from the thin agent installed on the VM and forwards it to the SVM over a connection-oriented session.

Let's say that we were using guest introspection for antivirus and attempted to open a downloaded executable. The thin agent would lock the file and talk to the epsec-mux driver on the ESXi host, saying it needs the file to be checked out by the SVM. The SVM performs a scan and sends back instructions. If it's an infected file, the message will be to delete or quarantine. If the file is fine, it gives the all clear and the VM can proceed in running the executable.

VMware has looked to partners like Kaspersky and Trend Micro to provide IPS/IDS services, integrating them into NSX through guest inspection. However, VMware has recently announced that it has developed NSX Distributed IDS/IPS with an advanced Layer 7 firewall. There is not much information out yet as of this publication, but being it is both distributed and native to NSX, it dovetails with VMware's overall strategy to simplify and improve how security is deployed with NSX, giving us another powerful addition to the security toolbox.

Service Insertion Providers

Most data centers typically rely on a number of different vendors in their environment for networking services. Rather than trying to create a single one-size-fits-all forklift replacement for these solutions, NSX aims to look at the bigger picture. What is needed to create a secure Software-Defined Data Center? VMware believes that NSX's three-pronged strategy for visibility, control, and extensibility provides the foundation for that security.

NSX provides visibility into the data center, the applications, and the hosts. Granular control through microsegmentation allows every VM to have individual security policies and firewalls. The ability to extend the functionality of NSX by including best-of-breed partner integration means that you don't have to give up specialized network service features provided by other vendors. Instead, those partner services can be added to NSX due to its extensibility. Figure 10.22 includes a list of partners that provide solutions for integrating their products into NSX through service insertion, but it is by no means an exhaustive list.

FIGURE 10.22 Partial list of NSX partners for best-of-breed integration

When a partner's infrastructure service is instantiated in software as a virtual appliance, we can immediately reap new benefits that boost performance and simplify the process of managing network operations:

- The virtual appliance can be deployed, deleted, or moved anywhere across the SDDC.
- The amount of time to deploy is drastically reduced.
- These services can be dynamically added or removed without causing outages for other services in the IOChain.
- The inspection of packets can be done at a faster rate.
- Traffic can be filtered with application-based rules.
- Additional security services can be seamlessly inserted into NSX.

Partner companies customize their virtualized products to interoperate with NSX. Their third-party services are then easily added to the service chain. Here's an example of how a vendor customizes its product to integrate with NSX. A partner providing antivirus guest introspection will automatically apply a security tag when a virus is discovered. As administrators, we can then create the necessary security groups and security policies to isolate and protect the rest of the network based on the tag provided by the antivirus software. The partnership with the vendor creates a comprehensive solution.

Security Policies

We started the chapter stating that Service Composer has two main elements: security groups and security policy. We've discussed security groups: how to create them; how to assign objects to them statically; and how to add objects dynamically by defining criteria based on labels, addresses, security tags, and so forth. Once the security groups are created and members are added, the next step is to apply security policies to these groups.

Security policies are a collection of rules and services that can be applied to a security group. As you will see, they can include:

- Guest introspection services
- Distributed firewall rules
- Network introspection services

As we mentioned earlier in the overview, when multiple policies are applied to a group, their order is determined by a weight value assigned to each policy. The higher the weight, the higher it is placed in the table. When a new rule is added, it is automatically assigned the highest weight and therefore is placed at the top of the list. However, this value can be easily modified to adjust the order to your preference.

Creating Policies

Recall that earlier we created a security group called WEB VMs and using dynamic membership said to "match any Linux VM with a name starting with Dev_ and also includes the word WEB."

We're now going to create a simple security policy that blocks pings and then apply that policy to the WEB VMs security group:

1. Open your vSphere client and go to Menu ➢ Networking And Security ➢ Service Composer.
2. Select the Security Policies menu (see Figure 10.23).

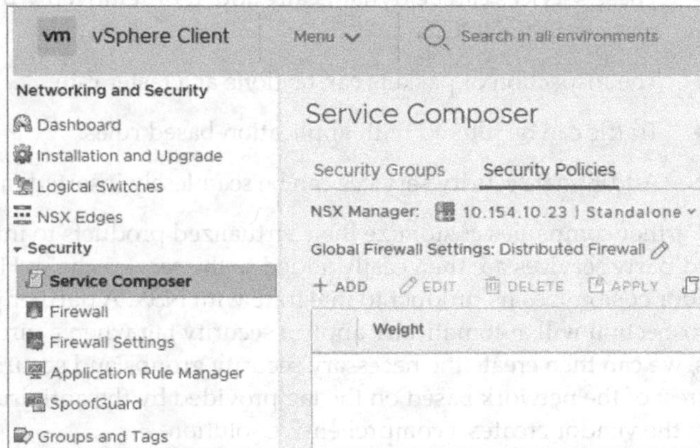

FIGURE 10.23 Creating a security policy in Service Composer

3. Click the + Add link.

   Note the steps shown in Service Composer for creating a security policy. A security policy is a collection of guest inspection services, firewall rules, and network inspection services, as indicated by steps 2 through 4, allowing us to secure VMs at the vNIC level (see Figure 10.24).

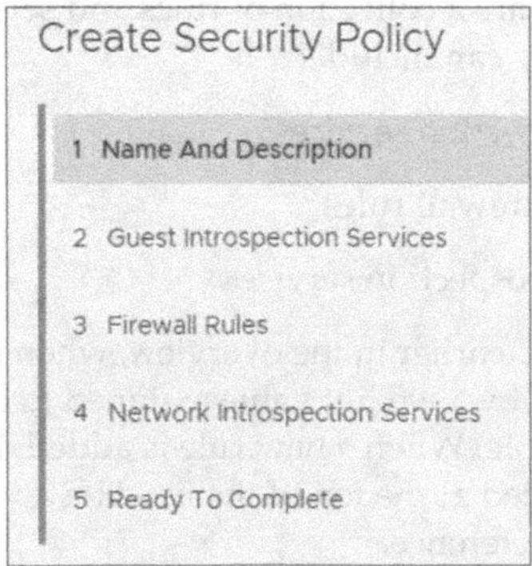

FIGURE 10.24 Steps within Service Composer to create a security policy

4. In the Name field, enter **block pings to security group** (see Figure 10.25).

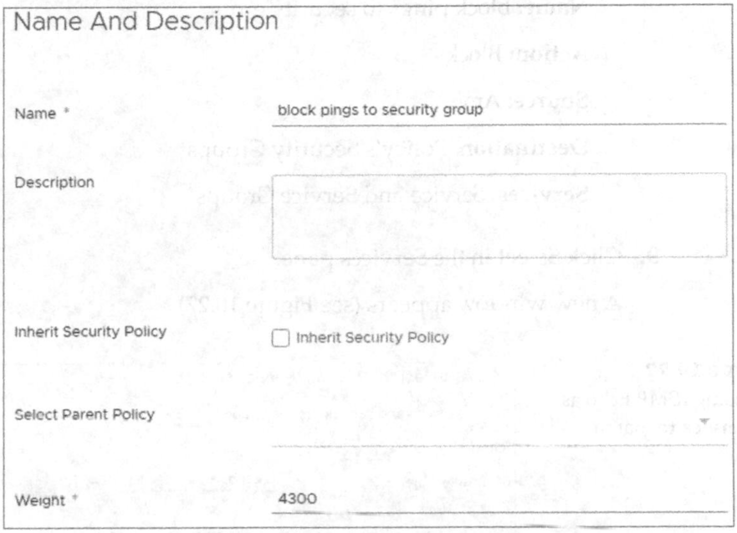

FIGURE 10.25 Options to change weight and inheritance when naming policy

Name And Description

Name * block pings to security group

Description

Inherit Security Policy ☐ Inherit Security Policy

Select Parent Policy

Weight * 4300

Notice the weight field has a value already filled in. NSX will assign a default weight. If other policies exist, this value will be 1000 more than the current highest weight. You can modify the value here or edit it after the policy is created. Also listed is an option to Inherit Security Policy. If this is checked, an option will appear to choose a parent policy.

5. For this example, leave weight and inherit at their defaults and click Next.
6. In this example, since we are not specifying guest introspection or network introspection services, skip steps 2 and 4 by clicking Next.
7. In step 3, to create this firewall rule, click the + Add link.

   A new window appears (see Figure 10.26).

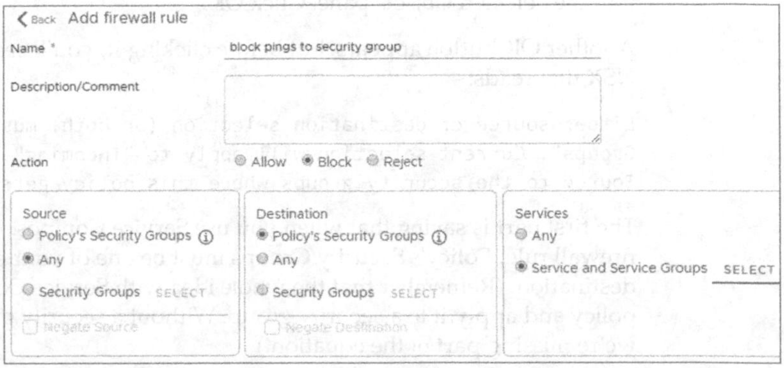

FIGURE 10.26 Adding a firewall rule to the security policy

Back Add firewall rule

Name * block pings to security group

Description/Comment

Action ◯ Allow ◉ Block ◯ Reject

Source: ◯ Policy's Security Groups ◉ Any ◯ Security Groups SELECT ☐ Negate Source

Destination: ◉ Policy's Security Groups ◯ Any ◯ Security Groups SELECT ☐ Negate Destination

Services: ◯ Any ◉ Service and Service Groups SELECT

8. Use the following information to create the rule:

   Name: block pings to security group

   Action: Block

   Source: Any

   Destination: Policy's Security Groups

   Services: Service and Service Groups

9. Click Select in the Services pane.

   A new window appears (see Figure 10.27).

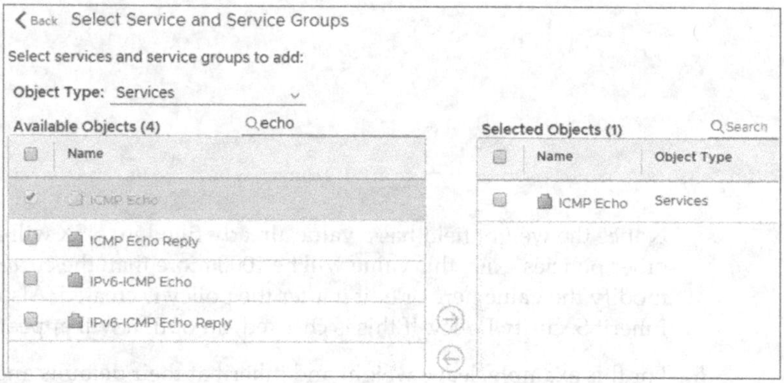

FIGURE 10.27
Choosing ICMP Echo as the service to match

10. Next to the Available Objects' magnifying glass icon, enter the word **echo**.

    A ping has two parts: the initial message that goes out (the echo) and the answer that comes back (the echo reply).

11. For this example, place a check mark next to ICMP Echo and click the right arrow to move it to the Selected Objects pane. Click OK.

    Another OK button appears, but before clicking it, you'll see an informational note from NSX that reads:

```
Either source or destination selection (or both) must be "Policies Security
Groups". Current selection will apply to "Incoming" traffic from the specified
Source to the security groups where this policy gets applied.
```

    The first part is saying that when you use Service Composer to create a policy with a firewall rule, Policy's Security Groups must be one of your choices for either source or destination. (Remember that the whole idea with Service Composer is to create a security policy and apply it to a security group. Without a security group to hang the policy on, we're missing part of the equation.)

In our example, what we've entered for the source and destination complies with the NSX note. Our choice is legitimate since Policy's Security Groups is selected for destination. The second part of the note might sound a bit confusing, so let's back up a bit. We are creating a security policy that blocks pings. The security policy will *ultimately* be applied to traffic attempting to ping devices within the WEB VMs security group, but we're not that far. At this point, we are simply creating the policy, not assigning it to a specific security group yet.

We have chosen Policy's Security Groups as the destination. For now, think of Policy's Security Groups as a variable: "Block pings to security group X." This policy could later be applied to the WEB VMs security group (which is what we will be going for) or the APP VMs security group or any other group we create. Because "security group X" is listed as the *destination*, from the perspective of the group, it will be applied inbound. Traffic entering a VM belonging to security group X will be examined for echo messages. If found, they will be blocked.

Now imagine a policy that says, "Block security group X pings to any." For that policy, "security group X" would be the *source*. From the perspective of the group, that rule would be applied outbound. Traffic exiting a VM in security group X would be examined for echo messages. If found, they would be blocked.

Don't worry about memorizing which causes inbound traffic to be examined and which causes outbound traffic to be examined. Why? Because the informational note that NSX displays dynamically changes to tell you exactly that (incoming or outgoing) based on what you choose for source and destination. Look again at the note. Notice it says that the *current* selection is incoming?

12. Now with that covered, click OK and the Firewall Rules window will appear, showing the rule created in step 3 (see Figure 10.28).

FIGURE 10.28 Firewall rule created within the security policy

Firewall Rules

☐ Enable User identity at source ☐ Enabled TCP strict ☐ Enabled stateless firewall

+ ADD | EDIT | ↑ MOVE UP | ↓ MOVE DOWN | ✓ ENABLE | DISABLE | DELETE

	Name	Source	Destination	Services	Action	Enable
○	block pings to security group	Any	Policy's Security Groups	ICMP Echo	Block	Enabled

CANCEL | BACK | NEXT | FINISH

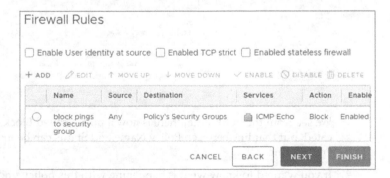

13. Since we are skipping step 4, Network Introspection Services, click Finish.

Enforcing Policies

To apply the policy to a security group:

1. Select the policy you just created and click the Apply link.

   Another window appears (see Figure 10.29).

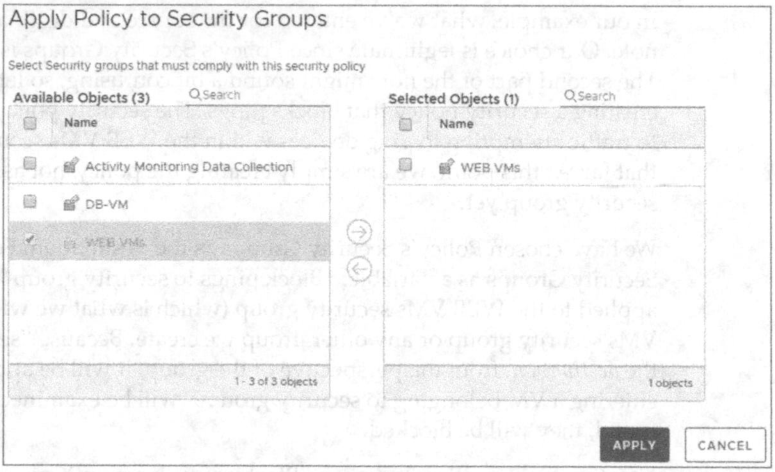

FIGURE 10.29 Applying the policy (finally!)

Apply Policy to Security Groups

Select Security groups that must comply with this security policy

Available Objects (3)

Name

Activity Monitoring Data Collection

DB-VM

WEB VMs

1 - 3 of 3 objects

Selected Objects (1)

Name

WEB VMs

1 objects

APPLY

CANCEL

2. Place a check mark next to the WEB VMs security group, and click the right arrow to move it to the Selected Objects pane.
3. Click the Apply button.

   The window shown is a list of your Service Composer security policies (see Figure 10.30).

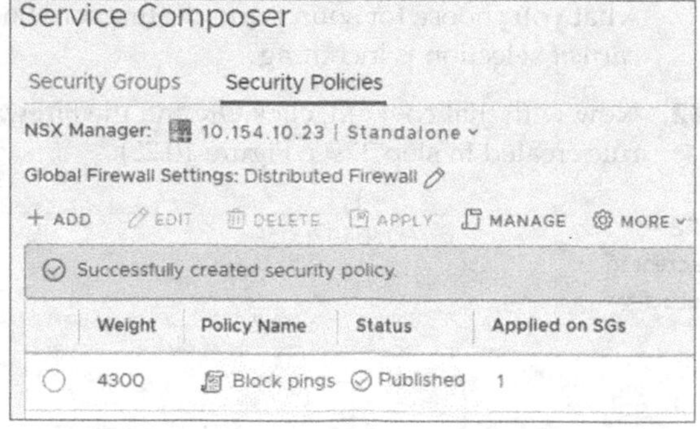

FIGURE 10.30 Security policy created and applied

We see from the output that there is now a policy called Block pings. It's actually truncated, but that line between Policy Name and Status can be moved to view the entire name.

4. If you wanted to know what is happening with this policy under the hood (firewall rules, guest inspection, and network inspection) simply click the name itself.

   We can also see in the same line that the security policy has been applied on 1 SG (security group).
5. To find out which group, click on the number to get the details.

The Bottom Line

Dynamic Inclusion Service Composer allows you to provision and assign security services within the virtual environment using security groups and to apply security policies. Group membership can be accomplished statically or dynamically.

Master It When creating a new security group, you will see these listed as steps:

Step 1. Name and description

Step 2. Define dynamic membership

Step 3. Select objects to include

Step 4. Select objects to exclude

Step 5. Ready to complete

What parameter is not valid criteria to match on when dynamically assigning a member to a security group?

1. Computer OS name
2. VM name
3. vNIC
4. Computer name
5. Security tag

Inbound vs. Outbound You create a firewall rule within a Service Composer security policy. The source is Any. The destination is Policy's Security Groups. VM-6 is a member of a security group with this policy applied.

Master It When Policy's Security Groups is set as the destination in a Service Composer firewall rule, which traffic will be examined based on the security policy?

1. Incoming traffic
2. Outgoing traffic

Default Policy Priority Service Composer can create a single policy that includes firewall rules, guest introspection services, and network introspection services. When multiple security policies are listed, priority is based on a weight value.

Master It After creating a new security policy, it is added to the existing list of policies. By default, how will the order of the policies be affected?

1. The new policy will have top priority
2. The new policy will have the lowest priority
3. The new policy is not published until a weight is entered.

Chapter 11

vRealize Automation and REST APIs

vRealize Automation (vRA) is a cloud automation platform. It allows end users to quickly provision IT services through a self-service web portal catalog. Think of it as a vending machine for provisioning applications and infrastructure that can leverage resources located on-premises and in the cloud. It allows DevOps engineers, developers, IT operations, and business teams to get what they need when they need it. vRA simplifies the combination of these diverse environments, creating a hybrid cloud platform (also known as a Cloud Management Platform, or CMP). Security and control are maintained by IT, and developers can roll out new application features and patches very quickly in production, often with no downtime.

REST APIs, or Representational State Transfer Application Program Interfaces, provide a way to interact with NSX programmatically through command scripts or by being incorporated in an application.

IN THIS CHAPTER, YOU WILL LEARN ABOUT:

- vRealize Automation for on-demand provisioning
- vRealize Automation endpoints
- Associating NSX with vRA
- Three types of vRA network profiles
- vRealize Orchestrator
- Creating blueprints for the vRA catalog
- Configuring entitlements
- Using REST APIs

vRealize Automation Features

Before drilling down into the combination of vRA with NSX, let's look at the big picture key features.

Manage and Go

- vRA makes it easy to manage multi-cloud environments.

  This includes not only managing on-prem and VMware Cloud on AWS (VMC on AWS), but extending to public native clouds as well, such as Google Cloud Platform, Amazon Web Services, and Microsoft Azure.

- vRA is easy to set up.

  VMware has even automated the initial legwork in getting vRA up and running by creating vRealize Easy Installer, which sets up vRealize Suite Lifecycle Manager (for DevOps to automate pipeline management of applications), VMware Identity Manager (for admins to have granular control of available services in a catalog based on *who* is accessing it), and of course, vRealize Automation itself (see Figure 11.1). The installer is provided as an ISO file with support for installation on Windows, Linux, or macOS. To deploy vRealize Automation, you can find the necessary files on the my.vmware.com download page.

FIGURE 11.1 vRealize Easy Installer components

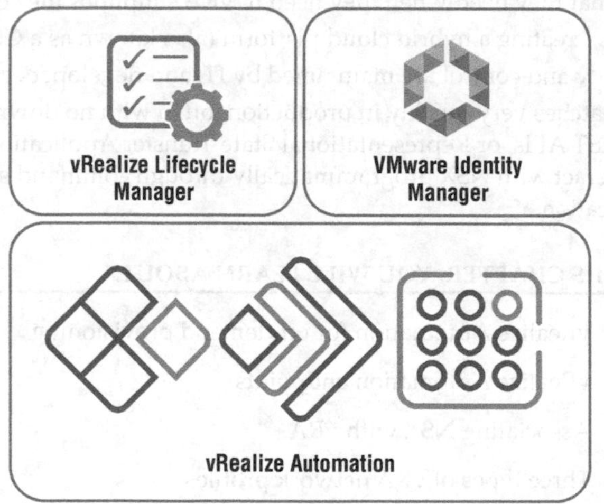

- vRA provides automated lifecycle management.

  vRealize Suite Lifecycle Manager covers the life of an application from start to finish including the installation, configuration, upgrading, and patching, all of which is based on VMware Validated Designs (VVD) and best practices.

Security across Environments

- vRA creates an aggregated portal of services.

  The catalog creates a single portal of services and images available to the end user instead of having one portal for on-prem, one for each private cloud, and one for each public cloud. vRA makes it easy for IT to control access across clouds.

  Admins have granular control over what each user can provision from the self-service portal by applying policies. For example, one of the choices in the catalog might be for a three-VM cluster. Instead of implementing a generic one-size-fits-all deployment of the virtual machines (VMs), each user can receive a personalized version of the service. Differences from user to user could include the guest operating system, applications pre-installed and configured, deployed load balancers for the cluster, on-prem vs. off-prem, and the like.

For example, a data engineer that frequently uses company-confidential datasets wants to deploy a cluster of VMs to build a machine learning model to analyze the data. The cluster is deployed within the data center. A developer chooses the same three-VM cluster from the catalog to test an application, but the VMs are deployed on AWS. Both users request the same service, but based on the policies applied by the administrator, the service is personalized to the user.

- vRA integrates identity services.

  For a complete identity management solution, vRA can be integrated with Active Directory.

Consistency

- vRA makes iterative development easy with blueprints.

  Blueprints are one of vRA's most important tools and are usually what you spend the most time working with when using vRA. Blueprints define the items that users request from the catalog.

- vRA includes a visual blueprint designer.

  Combining application and infrastructure services is easy and intuitive using a drag-and-drop tool that allows blueprints of these combinations to be created.

- vRA blueprints are portable.

  A blueprint, once created, can be deployed across different cloud environments instead of having to create different variations of the same blueprint. This means you can run any app on any cloud. Build it once, deploy it anywhere.

DevOps Agility Means Faster Time to Market

- vRA release automation pipeline management integrates with developer tools.

  VMware Code Stream allows developers to leverage the same tools they have been using by integrating them with vRA.

- vRA provides DevOps with an end-to-end pipeline view.

  The status and visualization of all active pipelines makes them easier to troubleshoot.

vRA Editions

vRA 8.0 is available in Advanced and Enterprise editions. This chapter is focusing on Enterprise features, but in a nutshell, the Advanced edition allows for Infrastructure as a Service (IaaS) across a hybrid environment that includes on-prem private cloud and VMC on AWS.

The Enterprise edition is for infrastructure and applications management across a multi-cloud environment that includes DevOps configuration tools and support for native public cloud services (see Figure 11.2).

FIGURE 11.2
vRA Advanced and Enterprise editions compared

	vRealize Advanced Edition	vRealize Enterprise Edition
IT Services	Infrastructure only	Infrastructure and Applications
Clouds	On-prem and VMware Cloud	Any cloud
Resource Lifecycle Management	✓	✓
Native public cloud services		Can embed native public cloud services in blueprints
Integration with configuration management tools		✓
Kubernetes support		✓
Cloud-agnostic blueprints		✓
VMware Code Stream		✓

Integrating vRA and NSX

While both vRA and NSX increase business agility, the combination of the two is like a superpower. An entire virtual network with VMs, routing, firewall rules, load balancing, Logical Switches, and so forth can be created by the consumer with a mouse click. That network can be isolated (which is great for development or testing) or have all the necessary connections to interact with the production environment and external networks.

vRealize Automation Endpoints

vRA requires that we have endpoints specified. An endpoint is basically anything that vRA utilizes to complete the provisioning process. For example, public clouds like Google Cloud Platform and Amazon Web Services are endpoints. A private cloud created on vSphere is an endpoint. NSX is an endpoint.

Once installed, you can access vRA by opening a browser and entering the fully qualified domain name of the virtual appliance: `https://vrealize-automation-FQDN/vcac`. vCloud Automation Center (VCAC) was the name of the product before it was changed to vRealize Automation. To create an endpoint for vSphere:

1. Go to the Infrastructure tab, click Endpoints from the left menu, and then click Endpoints again (see Figure 11.3).
2. Click the + New icon, and you will find categories of endpoints.
3. Click the category Virtual, and select vSphere (vCenter) (see Figure 11.4).

   A new window appears in which to configure the details of the vSphere endpoint including the name, description, the address in the format of `https://vcenter-FQDN` with `/sdk` added, and credentials. Our example is shown in Figure 11.5.

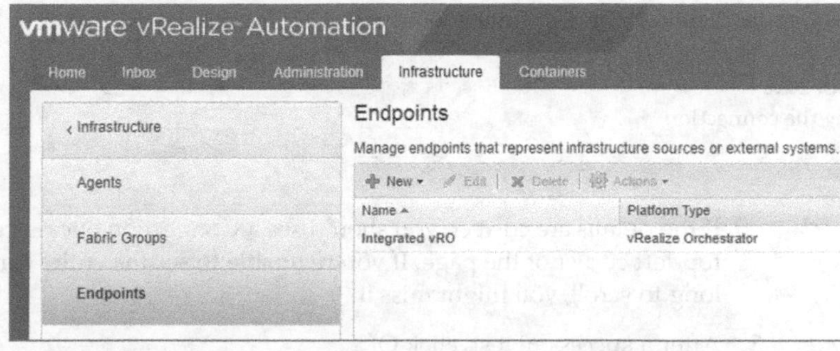

FIGURE 11.3
Accessing the vRealize Automation console

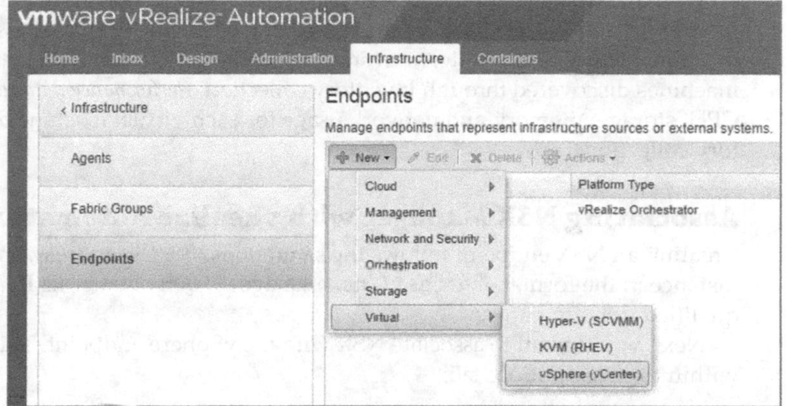

FIGURE 11.4
Selecting vSphere as the endpoint

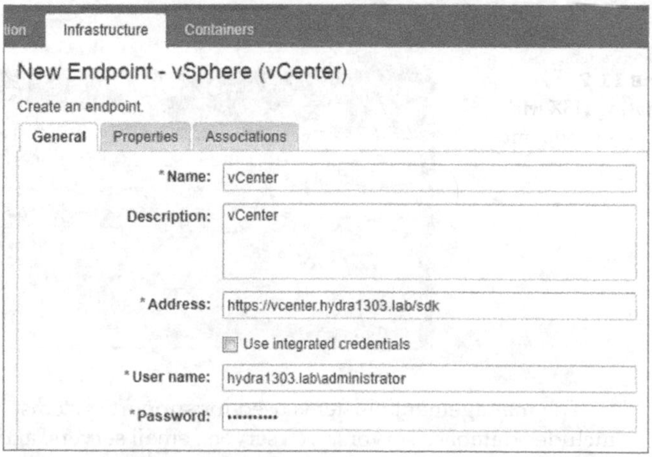

FIGURE 11.5
Entering general details for the endpoint

4. Click the Test Connection button in the bottom-right corner of the page (see Figure 11.6).

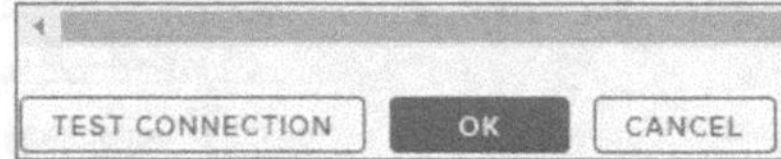

FIGURE 11.6
Testing the connection

If the details are correct, you should see a Connection Successful message briefly in the top-left corner of the page. If you're unable to see the entire console page and take too long to scroll, you might miss it.

5. After a successful test, click OK.

With a vSphere endpoint, we can perform data collection of inventory, state, and performance. *Inventory data collection* updates the record of the specific resources associated with each virtual machine including compute, network, and storage. *State data collection* records the power state of machines discovered through inventory collection. *Performance data collection* records the average CPU, storage, memory, and network usage for each virtual machine discovered through inventory collection.

Associating NSX Manager with vRealize Automation

Creating an NSX endpoint follows the same steps. For the address, enter the URL of the NSX instance in the format of `https://nsx-manager-FQDN` or enter its IP address instead of the fully qualified domain name.

Next, you'll want to associate NSX with the vSphere endpoint. This can be accomplished within the Associations tab:

1. Click the + New icon and select vCenter from the drop-down.
2. Click OK (see Figure 11.7).

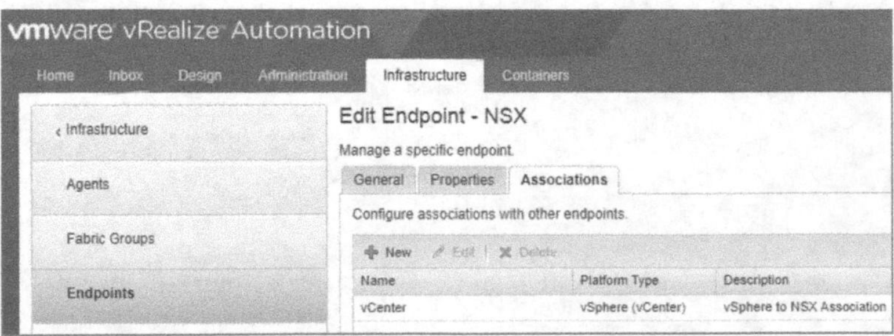

FIGURE 11.7
Associating NSX with the vCenter endpoint

The management cluster is used for support systems. Normally, the management cluster includes database servers, web servers, email servers, and any other system used to provide infrastructure support for vRealize Automation.

A production management cluster also hosts the following servers:

- vRealize Automation appliance servers
- VMware vRealize® Orchestrator™ servers

- VMware vRealize® Log Insight™ server
- NSX Manager server
- VMware vRealize® Business™ server
- vRealize Automation Infrastructure-as-a-Service (IaaS) servers
- Microsoft SQL Server database servers
- Email servers
- Network load-balancer servers

Network Profiles

Network profiles provide the network settings for vRA to use when provisioning VMs. They contain all the IP information that will be assigned including an address range, the default gateway, and the subnet mask. They also include configuration settings for the deployment of NSX Edges, depending on the network profile type.

There are three network profile types in vRA: external, NAT, and routed, as explained in the following sections.

External Network Profile

Let's say you already have a network segment with VMs up and running in production and you want vRA to provide the ability to create new VMs automatically configured to belong to the same segment. To coexist, the new VMs need to be on the same subnet. They would use the same gateway. They would have the same subnet mask. This is an example of when to use an external network profile. For now, if you're getting hung up on the word *external*, substitute it with *existing*. To add a VM to an existing network/subnet, you use an external (existing) network profile. More on this in a bit.

Within the profile, you can statically define the specific starting and ending IP range to assign to the newly created VMs. It's also possible to have this range pulled from an IP Address Management (IPAM) endpoint, but to implement either of the other two types of profiles (NAT or routed), the external network profile must use a static IP range.

NAT Network Profile

When we've asked students what Network Address Translation (NAT) does, the answer given most often is that it translates private to public IP addresses, but it turns out that simplification is more of an example than a definition. At its core, NAT is about fixing a routing problem. The private addresses can't be routed over a public network, so NAT does its translation magic to solve the issue.

NAT often comes to the rescue for another routing problem: dealing with overlapping address space on different segments. For example, you have a VM with the address 10.1.1.1 on segment A. It needs to communicate with a VM on segment B. To go from one segment to another, routing is involved. No problem. But what if the VM on segment B has the address 10.1.1.2? That's a problem. The 10.1.1.1 VM thinks that the 10.1.1.2 VM is on the same segment; therefore, it will not send the traffic to its gateway (the router). In other words, the traffic is *not routable*. So, we use NAT to solve the problem by translating in both directions. Because of the need for both sides to be translated in a one-to-one fashion, the external network profile providing the addresses on the other side of translation must use a static IP range for the NAT network profile to work.

If the term *external* in "external network profile" is still a bit confusing and you're wondering, "Why didn't they just call it *existing* network profile in the first place?" it might be easier to understand when comparing the external network profile with the NAT network profile. With NAT, instead of characterizing the groups as public vs. private, think of them as external vs. internal, and the idea of an external network profile might start to make more sense as you read the following paragraphs.

Consider this example. We have an existing upstream external network. Using vRA, we want to create a blueprint for a separate *internal* network to be used for development testing. We don't want this newly created network to be completely isolated. We want it to have connectivity with the rest of the network and the Internet. However, inside the development space, we want to use our own IP scheme and not have to worry if it conflicts with the production subnets. Our goal is to be able to ultimately click a button and have this test environment created in a way that is *completely* portable. We should be able to deploy it to a public cloud, a private cloud, or anywhere. A NAT network profile will allow that to be possible.

But you can't create a NAT network profile in complete isolation. There must be an *external* network to translate with. That external network is defined by the external network profile and the example development network is defined by the NAT network profile. When configuring a NAT network profile, it requires you to specify an external network profile so that it knows which existing network it should be translating with.

Under the hood, when you use a NAT network profile, vRA tells NSX to deploy the networks, it tells NSX to deploy an NSX Edge to do the translation, and it tells the DLR to route the networks to the upstream gateway.

Routed Network Profile

The routed network profile is another profile that can't exist in isolation. When you configure a routed network profile, it will also require that you specify an external network profile. So, what is a routed network profile? Let's say you want vRA to create a three-tiered application with multiple subnets (multiple *routed networks*, because routing is necessary to get from one subnet to another). So in addition to vRA creating these three segments, you also need the DLR to route the application traffic from segment to segment, which vRA is happy to take care of as well (see Figure 11.8).

Figure 11.8
Three subnets in blocks of 16 for the three-tiered application

Application VMs	network 10.1.1.0 255.255.255.240
Database VMs	network 10.1.1.16 255.255.255.240
Web VMs	network 10.1.1.32 255.255.255.240

For this, we use a routed network profile. It defines a routable space and the available subnets. Under the hood, when you use a routed network profile, vRA tells NSX to deploy the networks and it tells the DLR to route the traffic from the networks to the upstream gateway. Once deployed, the segments have connectivity with each other as well as the external network.

vRA External, Routed, and NAT Network Profiles

Let's compare the configurations for these three network profile types. For the external network profile:

1. Open the vRA console and go to Infrastructure ➢ Network Profiles.
2. Click the + New icon and choose External from the list (see Figure 11.9).

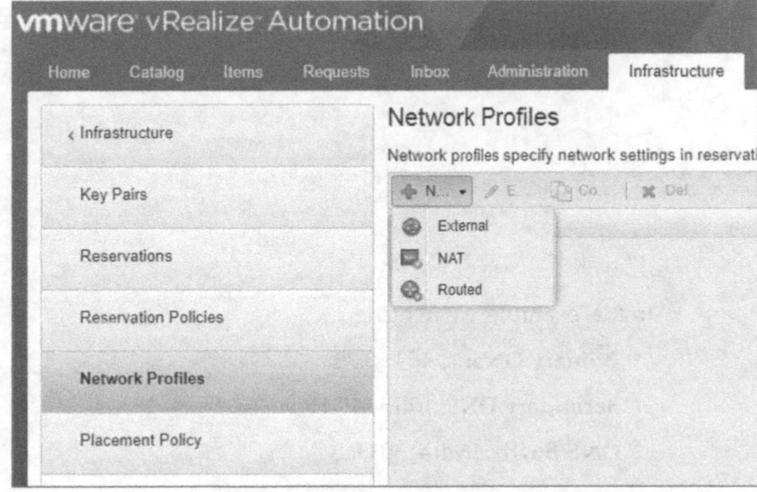

FIGURE 11.9 Selecting the network profile type

3. Enter a name for the profile, a subnet mask, and a gateway under the General tab.

   In this example, as you can see in Figure 11.10, we are using:

   Name: External Transit Network Profile

   IPAM endpoint: vRealize Automation IPAM

   Subnet Mask: 255.255.255.0

   Gateway: 10.154.41.1

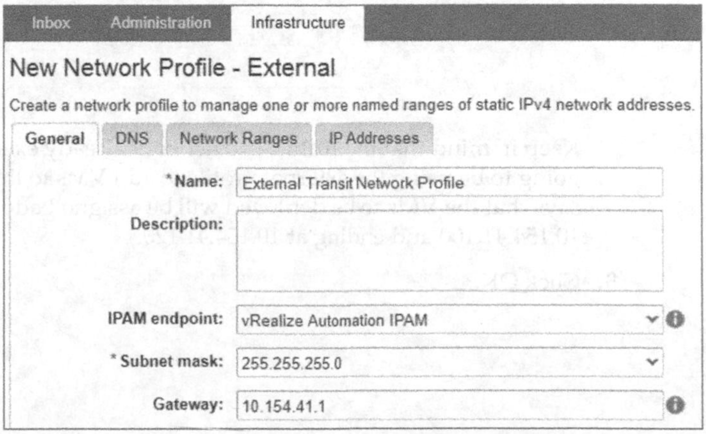

FIGURE 11.10 Configuring an external network profile

Inbox | Administration | Infrastructure

New Network Profile - External

Create a network profile to manage one or more named ranges of static IPv4 network addresses.

General | DNS | Network Ranges | IP Addresses

* Name: External Transit Network Profile

Description:

IPAM endpoint: vRealize Automation IPAM

* Subnet mask: 255.255.255.0

Gateway: 10.154.41.1

4. Under the DNS tab, add the IP address of your primary and secondary DNS servers, along with a DNS suffix, as shown in Figure 11.11.

FIGURE 11.11
Configuring supporting DNS information

Edit Network Profile - External
Create a network profile to manage one or more named ranges of static IPv4 network addresses.
General | DNS | Network Ranges | IP Addresses
Primary DNS: 10.154.10.35
Secondary DNS: 10.154.10.11
DNS suffix: hydra1303.lab
DNS search suffixes:
Preferred WINS:
Alternate WINS:

In this example, we're using:

Primary DNS: 10.154.10.35

Secondary DNS: 10.154.10.11

DNS Suffix: hydra1303.lab

5. Under the Network Ranges tab, click the + New icon and enter a name along with the start and end IP address to specify the range (see Figure 11.12).

FIGURE 11.12
Configuring the start and end IP range within the existing network

Inbox | Administration | Infrastructure
New Network Profile - External
Create a network profile to manage one or more named ranges of static IPv4 network addresses.
General | DNS | Network Ranges | IP Addresses
+ N... E... Del... Import from C...

Name	Description	Start IP	End IP
Engineering App IP range		10.154.41.100	10.154.41.120

OK Cancel

Keep in mind that the 10.154.41.0 network already exists. It's up and running. We are going to be using the external profile to add VMs to this network. The range we defined says that the VMs to be deployed will be assigned addresses from that range starting at 10.154.41.100 and ending at 10.154.41.120.

6. Click OK.

When configuring a NAT network profile, the DNS and Network Range tabs are the same as what we just saw with an external network profile, but let's look the General tab for a NAT network profile to spot the differences (see Figure 11.13).

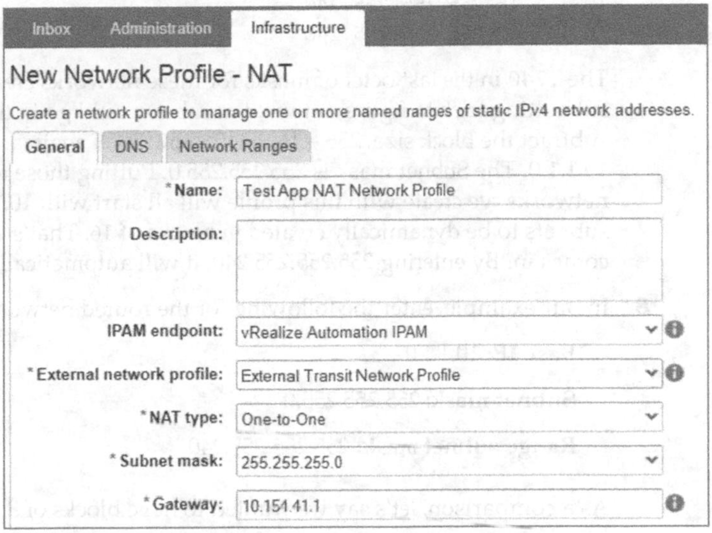

FIGURE 11.13
Under the General tab of a NAT network profile

Inbox | Administration | Infrastructure

New Network Profile - NAT

Create a network profile to manage one or more named ranges of static IPv4 network addresses.

General | DNS | Network Ranges

*Name: Test App NAT Network Profile

Description:

IPAM endpoint: vRealize Automation IPAM

*External network profile: External Transit Network Profile

*NAT type: One-to-One

*Subnet mask: 255.255.255.0

*Gateway: 10.151.41.1

7. Here, use the drop-down menu to select the external network profile we created.

   The asterisk in front of this field indicates that you must select a previously defined external network profile. Another difference is that a NAT type is selectable in this profile.

   Now let's look at the General tab for a routed network profile (see Figure 11.14).

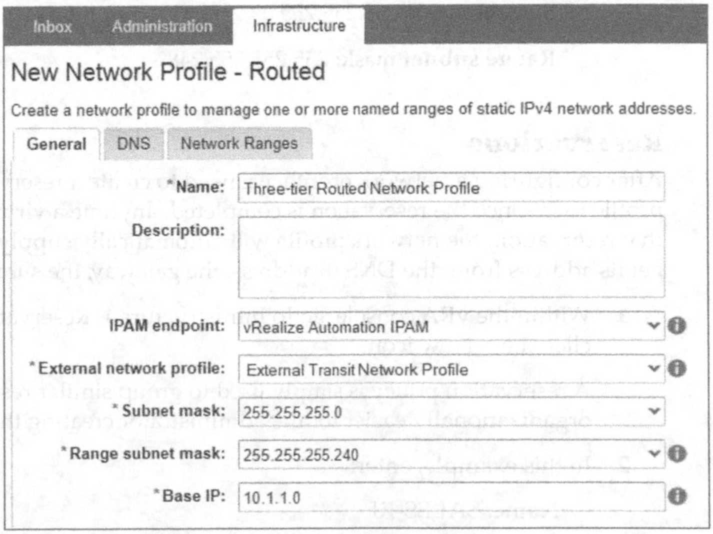

FIGURE 11.14
Under the General tab of a routed network profile

Inbox | Administration | Infrastructure

New Network Profile - Routed

Create a network profile to manage one or more named ranges of static IPv4 network addresses.

General | DNS | Network Ranges

*Name: Three-tier Routed Network Profile

Description:

IPAM endpoint: vRealize Automation IPAM

*External network profile: External Transit Network Profile

*Subnet mask: 255.255.255.0

*Range subnet mask: 255.255.255.240

*Base IP: 10.1.1.0

Recall the example we used for a routed network profile. It supported a three-tier application by creating these networks:

```
10.1.1.0 255.255.255.240
10.1.1.16 255.255.255.240
10.1.1.32 255.255.255.240
```

The `.240` in the last octet of masks for these networks creates blocks of 16. A common subnetting trick to figure out what number would go in that octet is to take 256 and subtract the block size. 256 – 16 = 240. Now, look again at Figure 11.14. The Base IP is 10.1.1.0. The Subnet mask is 255.255.255.0. Putting those together, it simply means that the networks we create with this profile will all start with 10.1.1.x. But we want each of these subnets to be dynamically created in blocks of 16. That's where the range subnet mask comes in. By entering 255.255.255.240, it will automatically carve out those blocks.

8. In our example, enter the following for the routed network profile:

   Base IP: 10.1.1.0

   Subnet mask: 255.255.255.0

   Range subnet mask: 255.255.255.240

   As a comparison, let's say we wanted to have blocks of 8 instead. 256 – 8 = 248:

   ```
   10.1.1.0 255.255.255.248
   10.1.1.8 255.255.255.248
   10.1.1.16 255.255.255.248
   ```

9. To accomplish this in the routed network profile, enter the following:

   Base IP: 10.1.1.0

   Subnet mask: 255.255.255.0

   Range subnet mask: 255.255.255.248

Reservations

After configuring a network profile, we need to create a reservation and assign the network profile to it. Once the reservation is completed, anytime a virtual machine is provisioned using that reservation, the network profile will automatically supply the IP information: the IP range to get its address from, the DNS IP address, the gateway, the subnet mask, and so forth.

1. Within the vRA console, go to Infrastructure ➢ Reservations ➢ Reservation Policies and click the + New icon.

   A reservation policy is simply used to group similar reservations together, making things organizationally easier for the administrator creating the blueprint.

2. In this example, enter:

   Name: SALES-RP

   Type: Reservation Policy (see Figure 11.15)

FIGURE 11.15
Creating a reservation policy

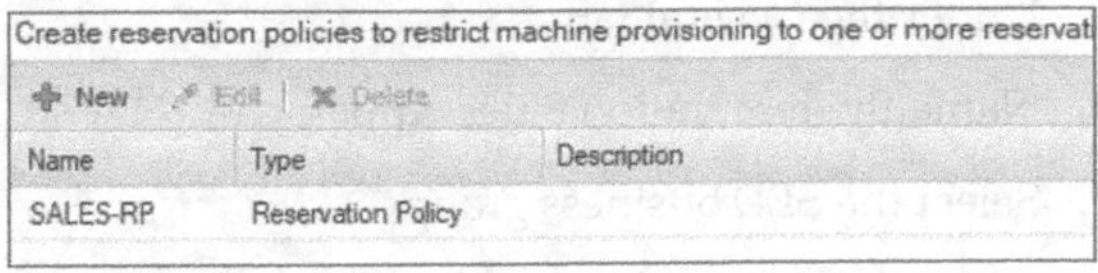
Create reservation policies to restrict machine provisioning to one or more reservat

New Edit Delete

Name	Type	Description
SALES-RP	Reservation Policy	

3. Click OK.
4. With the reservation policy created, select Reservations from the menu on the left (see Figure 11.16).

FIGURE 11.16
Creating a vRA reservation

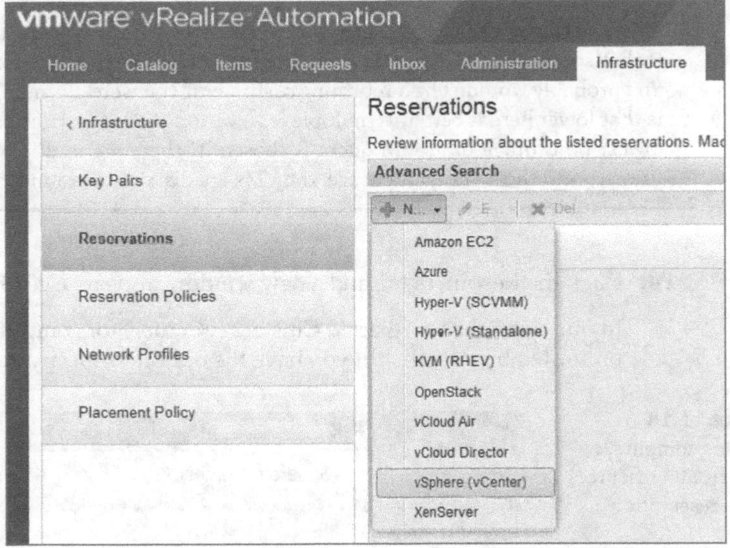

5. Click the New + icon to add a new reservation, and choose vSphere (vCenter) from the drop-down box.

   A new window appears (see Figure 11.17).

FIGURE 11.17
Configuring the General tab of a new reservation

Inbox Administration Infrastructure

New Reservation - vSphere (vCenter)

Create a reservation to allocate provisioning resources to a business group in a tenan

General | Resources | Network | Properties | Alerts

*Name: Sales App

Tenant: vsphere.local

*Business group: SED

Reservation policy: SALES-RP

*Priority: 1

Enable this reservation

Under the General tab:

6. Name the reservation **Sales App**.
7. Select the SED business group.
8. Select the SALES-RP reservation policy.
9. Set the priority to 1.

UNDERSTANDING PRIORITY

A reservation with a lower priority value is selected before a reservation with a higher priority value. If that sounds backwards, think of it like this. At Hydra 1303, customers are our number 1 priority. You probably wouldn't be a returning customer if you were our number 74 priority. The bottom line is that lower here is better. If multiple reservations have the same priority, the reservation with the lowest percentage of its VM quota is chosen. If there are multiple reservations all with the same priority and the same quota usage, the VMs are distributed round-robin among the reservations.

10. Click the Resources tab and a new window appears (see Figure 11.18).

    In our example, we selected Cluster2 (vCenter) for compute. The machine quota is unlimited by default, but you have the option to specify hard quotas.

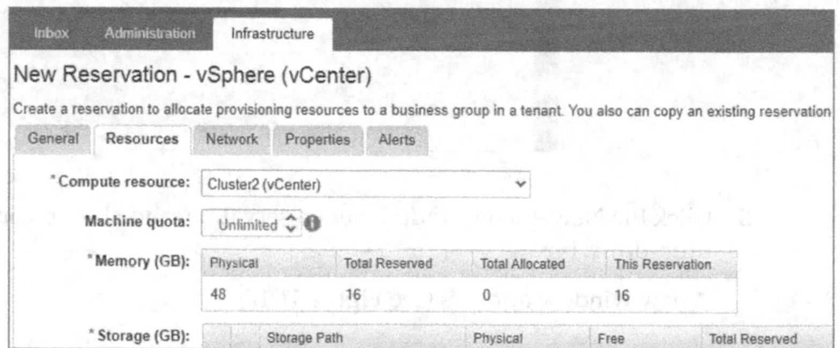

FIGURE 11.18 Selecting compute, memory, and resources for the reservation

11. Within the Memory block, click the This Reservation field and enter **16** to add 16 GB of memory to this reservation.
12. Within the Storage block, click the Storage Path to select what storage to choose from.
13. In our example, set the This Reservation Reserved column to **20** and change the Priority column to 1.
14. Click the Network tab.
15. Here you select the virtual wire segment to be used and the network profile.

    Scrolling down, you will find Advanced Settings where the transport zone can be selected.

vRealize Orchestrator Workflows

vRealize Orchestrator (vRO) is the engine that helps us to automate workflow processes and allows us to integrate third-party tools. It can be installed as a virtual appliance, as a vCenter server add-on, or as a standalone Windows server. It has a whole library of ready-made workflows to choose from, but it also gives us the ability to create highly customized workflows with a drag-and-drop tool for linking the actions together.

Creating a Blueprint for One Machine

Within the vRA console:

1. Click the Design tab, select Blueprints from the left menu, and click the + New icon (see Figure 11.19).

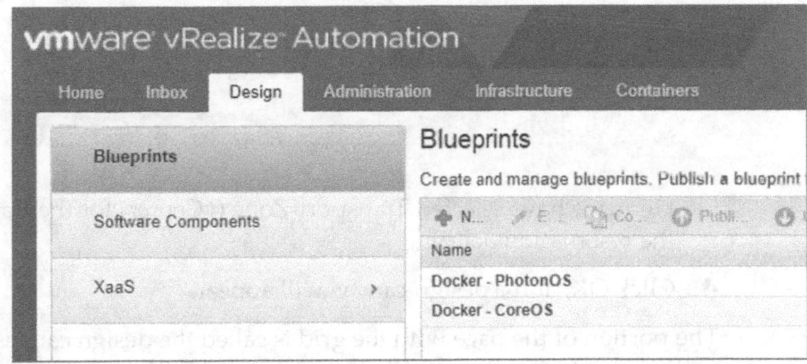

FIGURE 11.19 Creating a blueprint

The Design tab is only available to users that have one of the Architect roles associated with them: Application Architect, Infrastructure Architect, Software Architect, or XaaS Architect.

A new window appears (see Figure 11.20).

FIGURE 11.20 Blueprint general configuration settings

New Blueprint

General | NSX Settings | Properties

*Name: SALES-Srvr

*ID: SALESSrvr

Assign a permanent, unique ID to this blueprint.

Description: Linux Server for SALES

Deployment limit:

Minimum | Maximum

Lease (days):

*Archive (days): 0

Propagate updates to existing deployments

OK

2. Under the General tab, configure the following:

   Name: SALES-Srvr

   ID: (the ID text box auto-populates)

   Description: Linux Server for Sales

3. Click the NSX Settings tab (see Figure 11.21).

FIGURE 11.21 Configuring NSX settings within the blueprint

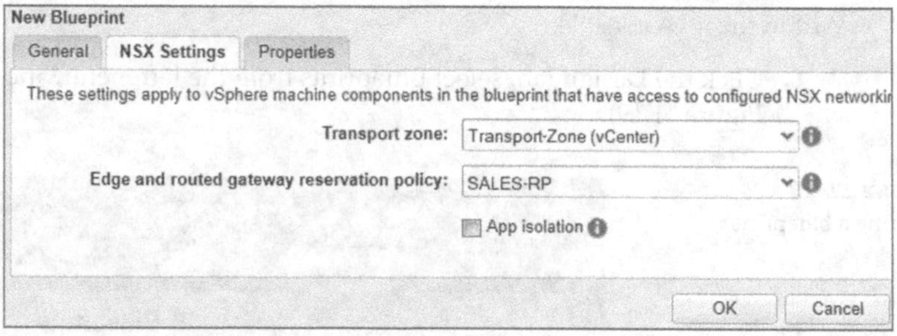

   Here, we have selected Transport-Zone (vCenter) for the transport zone and SALES-RP for the reservation policy.

4. Click OK, and a design canvas will appear.

The portion of the page with the grid is called the design canvas. You can drag components from the left side and drop them on the canvas. Multiple categories are found in the upper-left pane. Within each of these categories, there are numerous objects to choose from that you can drag to the design canvas. The objects are found in the lower-left pane. For example, with the category Machine Types selected (top-left pane), we see a list of 11 machine types to choose from (bottom-left pane, below the search bar), as shown in Figure 11.22.

To complete the blueprint design, follow these steps:

1. With Machine Types highlighted from the Categories pane, drag the vSphere (vCenter) Machine component to the design canvas grid on the right (see Figure 11.23).

2. In the ID text box that appears below the component, replace the text with **SALES-Srvr** (see Figure 11.24).

3. In the Description text box, enter **Server for SALES**.

4. From the Reservation Policy drop-down menu, select SALES-RP.

5. From the Machine prefix drop-down menu, select SALES-Linux.

   This prepends "SALES-Linux" to the VMs created by this blueprint.

6. In the Maximum box, set Instances to 2.

7. Click the Build Information tab.

8. From the Action drop-down menu, select Clone.

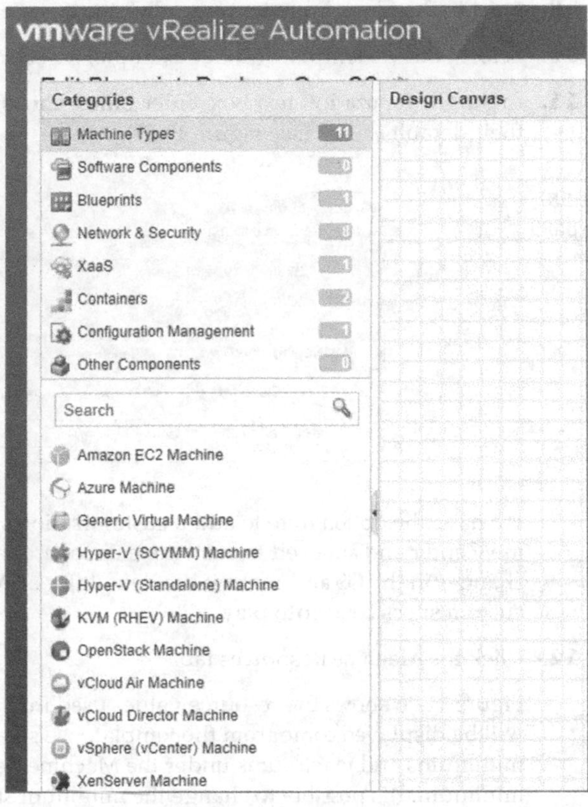

FIGURE 11.22 Drag objects from the left to the design canvas grid on the right.

FIGURE 11.23 vSphere (vCenter) component placed on the design canvas

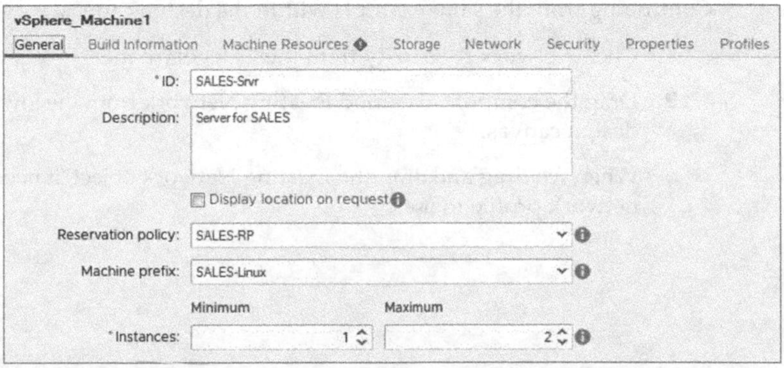

vSphere_Machine1

General | Build Information | Machine Resources | Storage | Network | Security | Properties | Profiles

*ID: SALES-Srvr

Description: Server for SALES

Display location on request

Reservation policy: SALES-RP

Machine prefix: SALES-Linux

Minimum | Maximum

*Instances: 1 | 2

FIGURE 11.24 Configuring the design canvas component

9. Next to the Clone From text box, click the browse ellipsis.
10. Select your OS template (in our example, we selected CentOS610) and click OK.
11. In the Customization text box, enter **Linux-Custom** and leave the remaining fields with their default entries (see Figure 11.25).

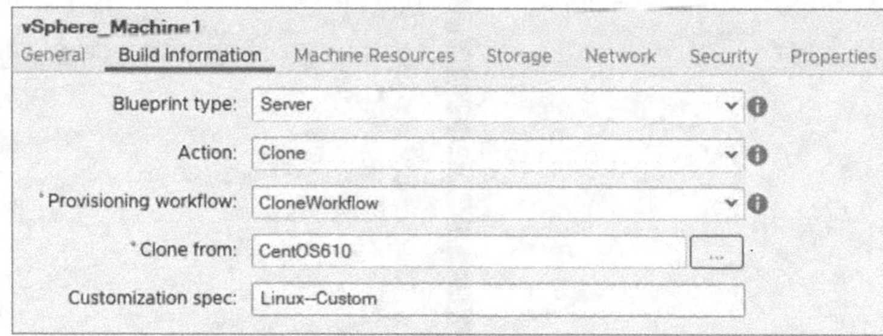

FIGURE 11.25 Adding the build information

We have the option here to add a customization spec. Customization specs are configured in vCenter and are used to customize the operating system. When you want to make changes in the OS and make it the default for all VMs being provisioned, this is when custom specs come into play.

12. Click the Machine Resources tab.

Figure 11.26 shows the resource values used in this example. The minimum numbers that will be displayed come from the template we selected. You can change any of these minimums and maximums under the Machine Resources tab except for the storage minimum. It's possible to change the minimum storage, just not here.

FIGURE 11.26 Configuring CPU, memory, and storage for the VMs

Options	Action
CPU	Enter **1** in the Minimum box and **2** in the Maximum box.
Memory (MB)	Enter **1024** in the Minimum box and **1056** in the Maximum box.
Storage (GB)	Enter 7 in the Maximum box.

13. Click Save.

Adding NSX Workflow to a Blueprint

Continuing from the same example within the design canvas:

1. Click Network & Security from the Category pane.
2. Drag the component named Existing Network from the lower-left pane to the design canvas.

When we drag and drop the Existing Network object, it needs to know which specific network profile to use.

3. Click the browse ellipsis to choose from the available network profiles.

   As soon as you select a network profile, you'll notice that the IP information associated with it is filled in automatically.

4. In our example, select External Transit Network Profile and click OK.
5. Click a blank spot on the design canvas to close the network dialog box.
6. On the design canvas, click the SALES-Srvr component (see Figure 11.27) .

FIGURE 11.27 Clicking the component brings up the configuration panel.

   The vSphere Machine component is selected, and the design configuration panel appears.

7. Click the Network tab.
8. Click the + New icon.
9. From the Network drop-down menu, select Test App NAT Network Profile, a profile we created for our example.
10. Click the OK button located on the next line down. Do not set an IP address.
11. Click Save and then Finish.

    When you click Finish, you'll see the blueprint has been saved to the Draft state. To make this a catalog item, we need to publish it.

12. In the Blueprints pane, highlight SALES-Srvr by clicking a blank space within the same row.
13. Click Publish.
14. Verify that the status of the blueprint has changed to Published.

Creating a Request Service in the vRA Catalog

A catalog item is a published blueprint that can be entitled to users. Entitlement is simply what a user is permitted to provision. For a catalog item to appear in the service catalog, it needs to be associated with a service and entitled to users.

Defining a Service

Using the vRA console:

1. Go to the Administration tab, select Catalog Management from the left menu, and choose Services (see Figure 11.28).

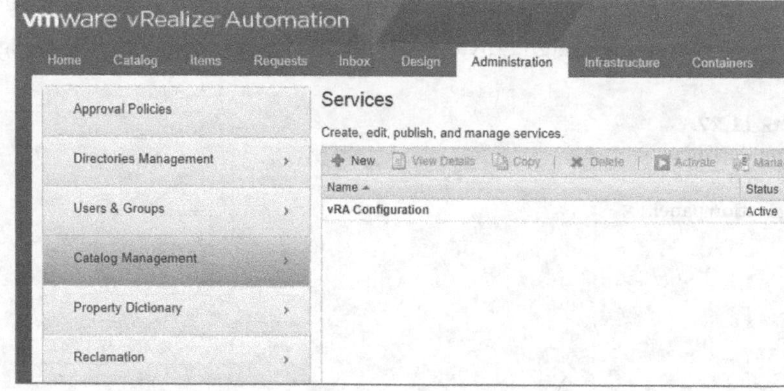

Figure 11.28 Creating a new service for the catalog

2. Click the + New icon, and the New Service configuration window will appear (see Figure 11.29).

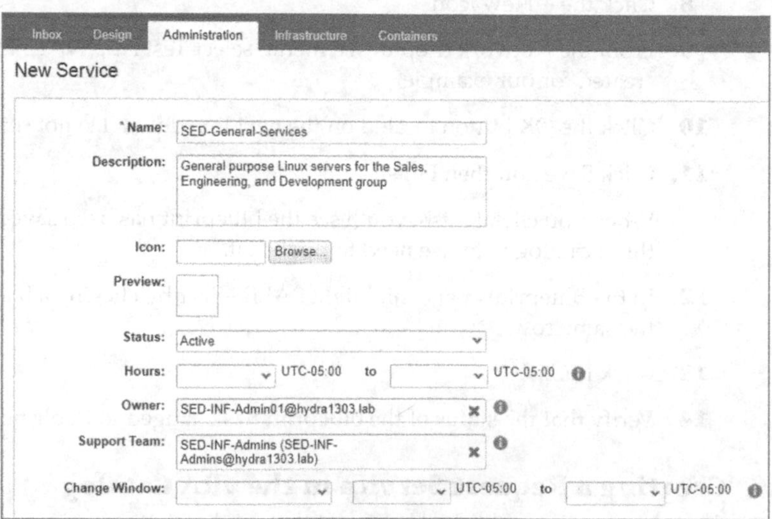

Figure 11.29 Configuring a new service for the catalog

3. In our example, enter the following:

   Name: SED-General-Services

   Description: General purpose Linux web servers for the Sales, Engineering, and Development group

Status: Active

Owner: SED-INF-Admin01@hydra1303.lab

Support Team: SED-INF-Admins (SED-INF-Admins@hydra1303.lab)

The owner and support team fields are initially blank with a search icon within the field. You can use this to easily find users and groups by entering only a partial name. For example, since members of the Sales, Engineering, and Development (SED) group all have usernames starting with SED, as shown in Figure 11.30, entering SED and clicking the search icon lists all users and groups with those characters, regardless of where the string of letters occurs in the username.

FIGURE 11.30 Using search to find matching users and groups

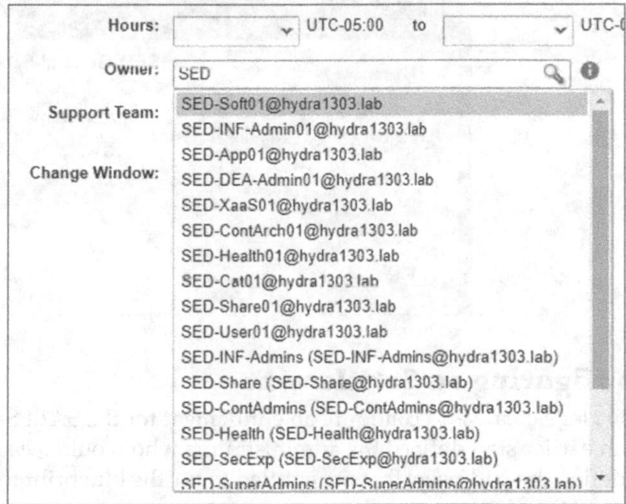

4. After entering the information, click OK.

ADDING CATALOG ITEMS TO A SERVICE

Continuing within the Service window for our example:

1. Click a blank space within the SED-General-Services row.

   This allows you to select it so that you can then choose one of the menu options. Once selected, the Manage Catalog Items menu will no longer be grayed out (see Figure 11.31).

2. Click Manage Catalog Items.
3. When a new window appears, click the green + sign and place a check mark next to the SALES-Srvr blueprint.
4. Click OK (see Figure 11.32).

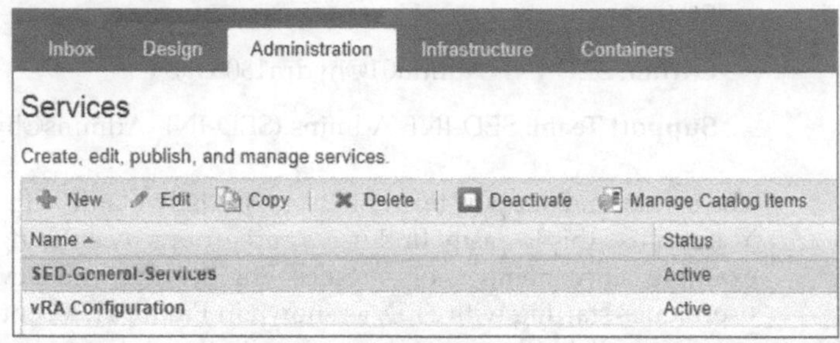

Figure 11.31 Enabling the Manage Catalog Items option

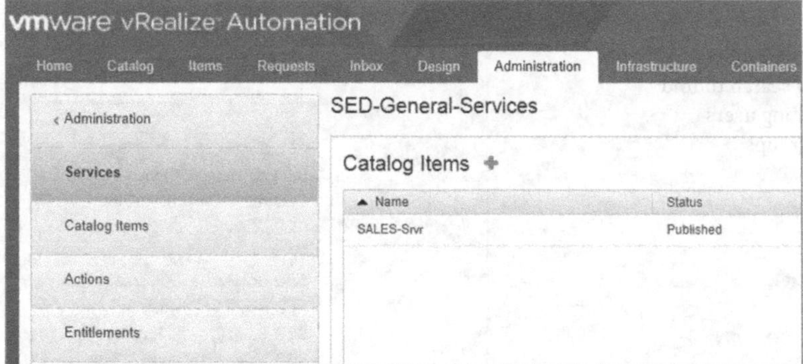

Figure 11.32 Catalog item published after clicking OK

Configuring an Entitlement

Now, let's create and configure an entitlement for the SALES-Srvr service. The users we specified in an earlier step defined the administrators who would *own or support* the service. We still need to define the end users that are entitled to *use* the blueprint to provision the server, which brings us to entitlement:

1. Select Entitlements from the left menu and click the + New icon.

   A new window appears (see Figure 11.33).

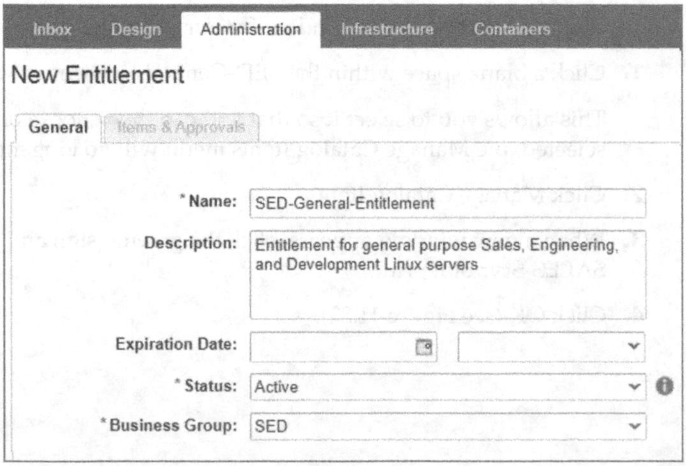

Figure 11.33 Creating a new entitlement

Inbox Design Administration Infrastructure Containers

New Entitlement

General | Items & Approvals

*Name: SED-General-Entitlement

Description: Entitlement for general purpose Sales, Engineering, and Development Linux servers

Expiration Date:

*Status: Active

*Business Group: SED

2. In our example, configure the following:

   Name: SED-General-Entitlement

   Description: Entitlement for general purpose Sales, Engineering, and Development Linux servers

   Status: Change to Active

   Business Group: SED

   On the right side of the same window is a section for Users & Groups (see Figure 11.34).

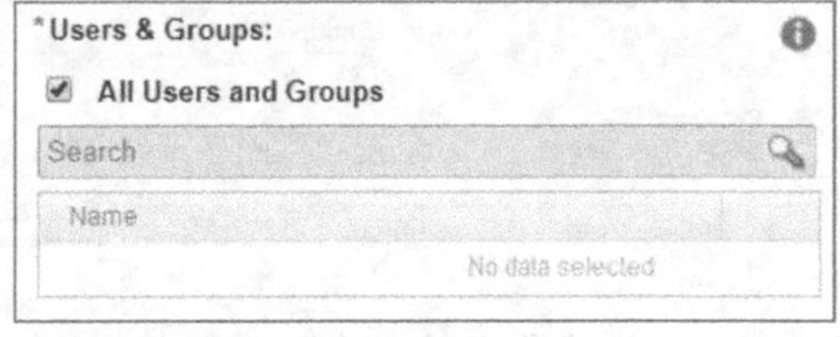

FIGURE 11.34
Users & Groups pane

3. Uncheck the box for All Users and Groups.

   This allows the search field to become available instead of grayed out. For this example, we want to entitle regular end users from the SED group that have no special vRA admin roles.

4. To find the name of that group, type in **sed** and click the search icon.

   Note that your search string is not case-sensitive. Therefore, entering lowercase **sed** would find users and groups containing the string for both cases. Entering **SED** would give the same results.

   This brings up all users with SED in their usernames (see Figure 11.35).

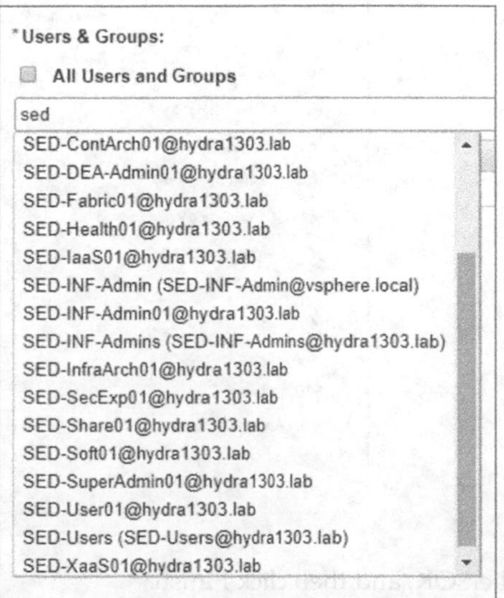

FIGURE 11.35
Using the search function to find the SED general users group

The next-to-last entry is what we are looking for: SED-Users (`SED-Users@hydra1303.lab`).

5. Select this group to add them to the entitlement, and click Next.
6. To the right of Entitled Services, click the green + sign (see Figure 11.36).

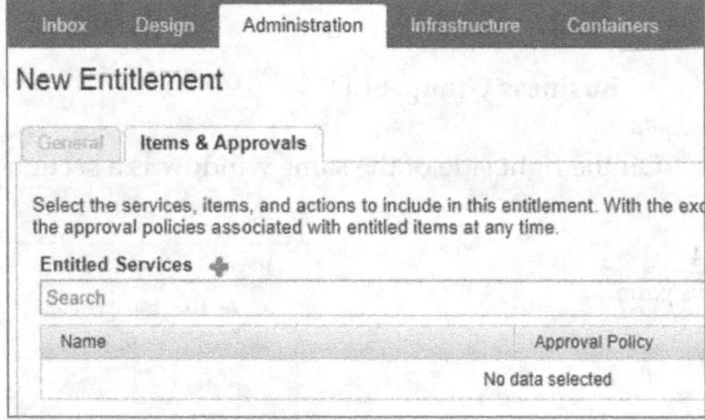

FIGURE 11.36 Defining entitled services, items, and actions

Now we can define what the group is entitled to do. This includes services to access, blueprints that will appear in the catalogs of the group members, and actions they are permitted to perform.

a. **Entitled Services:** Select SED-General-Services from the list of services and click OK.
b. **Entitled Items:** Select SALES-Srvr from the list of blueprints and click OK.
c. **Entitled Actions:** Select the top check box to allow all actions for this example.

Actions include abilities such as taking snapshots, rebooting, deleting, and shutting down the VM (see Figure 11.37).

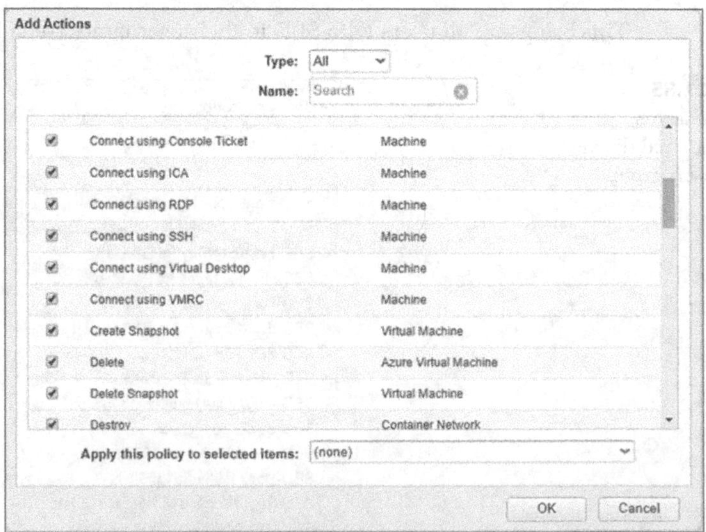

FIGURE 11.37 Defining what actions can be taken by the end user

7. Click OK, and then click Finish.

Deploying a Blueprint that Consumes NSX Services

The blueprint should now be available in the end user's catalog. Log out of vRA as an administrator and log back in with credentials of an SED user that does not have an administrator role. Here we are accessing the vRA console as SED-User01 (see Figure 11.38):

FIGURE 11.38 Verifying the catalog with a non-admin account

1. Click the Catalog tab (see Figure 11.39).

   We see the SALES-Srvr blueprint under the heading of SED-General-Services.

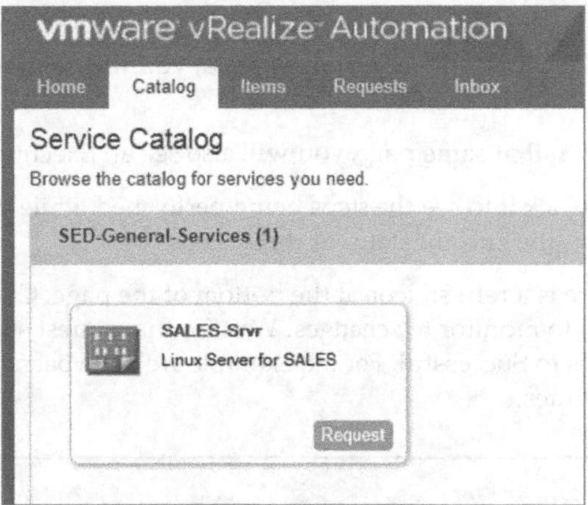

FIGURE 11.39 Catalog view using a vanilla user account

2. Click the Request button, and a request form will be generated.
3. Fill out a description of what you are requesting, the reason for the request, and the number of deployments (see Figure 11.40).

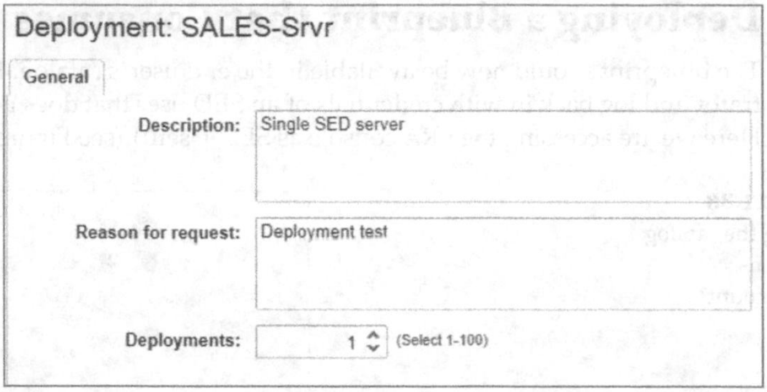

FIGURE 11.40 Entering the request form to provision

Deployment: SALES-Srvr

General

Description: Single SED server

Reason for request: Deployment test

Deployments: 1 (Select 1-100)

4. Click the Submit button, and you will get a confirmation message that your request has been submitted.
5. After submitting a request, you will obviously want to track it. To do this, click the Requests tab (see Figure 11.41).

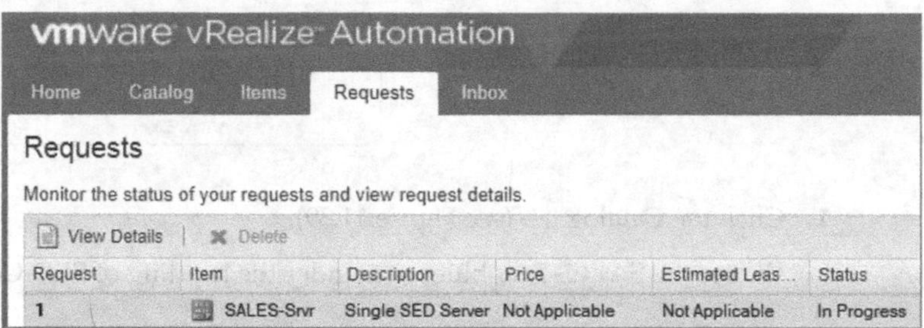

FIGURE 11.41 Tracking the progress of requests

6. To the left of each request listed, you will see a request number. Click that number to see the request details.

   On that same page, you will also see an Execution Information link on the far right.
7. Click it to see the steps being performed while your machine is being provisioned, as well as the current status of those steps.

There is a refresh icon at the bottom of the page. Click it periodically and check the Status column to monitor for changes. Wait for the request status to change from Submitted to In Progress to Successful. For the example we have been working on, the process will take 3–5 minutes.

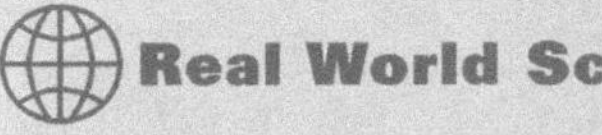

USE CASES FOR vRealize AUTOMATION

vRA is being used by some of our customers to meet Service-Level Agreements (SLAs) that deal with performance and security. Most are using vRA to speed up the process for application delivery by their development teams. Instead of being held up by governance issues and control, these necessities can be handled in the background by vRA without disrupting the productivity of the development team.

Customers have given us examples of how they've used vRealize Automation to allow their developers to configure and provision their own infrastructure. IT still controls all the security aspects and the resources, but instead of being inundated with tickets, they define the blueprints up front and much of their former legwork is now automated, resulting in increased productivity and agility for both administrators and end users.

REST APIs

An *Application Program Interface* (API) provides a simple interface for independent applications to exchange information, while hiding the underlying complexities. Most interfaces simplify connections. When you plug a toaster into an electrical outlet (a physical interface), you don't need to have a degree in electrical engineering to provide the power to make waffles. No soldering is involved. It's a simple interface that taps into electric power, but you need to follow a set of rules for it to work. The toaster plug must conform to the receptacle. The toaster must conform to the same voltage standard. The same standard is used throughout the country, so when you need to buy a new toaster, your choice is simplified to the point that you probably don't bother looking at any of the details relating to electricity.

With an API, it's a software interface. If you built an application that makes cartoon images of Facebook photos, for example, the application would use Facebook's API to retrieve the pictures. The API specifies the set of rules dictating how the requests should be structured. A developer can write code to send simple commands to the API and retrieve the requested content without needing to know the complexities that sit behind the interface.

Most of the time, when someone mentions a company's API, they are referring to Representational State Transfer Application Program Interfaces. That's a mouthful, so we just refer to them as either REST APIs or RESTful APIs. The format of a conversation between an application and a REST API is basically the same as what is going on when you're browsing the Internet. Your browser is the client. You use it to make calls to a web server, and it returns the results. REST APIs use HTTP GET commands to read or retrieve objects, just like your browser does when it is retrieving a web page. It also uses HTTP PUT or POST commands to create or update objects, as well as HTTP DELETE commands to remove objects. These identical HTTP commands are also used by your web browser under the hood when you're filling out an online form or deleting a blog post.

The URL (Uniform Resource Locator) of an object allows you to locate it. If you know the URL, an HTTP GET request can be issued to retrieve the properties of that object, its current state. Those properties are in a specific format (in XML or HTTP response code) and provide a *representation* of the *state* of the object. For example, you can issue an HTTP GET request to NSX to retrieve a list of ESXi hosts, VMs, data centers, VXLANs, etc. Of course, we don't want just anyone to be able to retrieve this information, so authentication would also be included with the request.

The HTTP requests make remote procedure calls that can create, delete, or modify objects depending on how the API is defined. This means that by using a RESTful API, a client can take actions on resources, such as creating a new user or increasing storage for a VM. The NSX API can be accessed with a web browser, allowing you to manually paste in instructions, or it can be used programmatically with scripting tools. VMware also uses the NSX API to integrate other VMware products like the one we've focused on in this chapter, vRealize Automation. The NSX API requires an authenticated SSL encrypted connection over port 443 to work. This same requirement is in play when checking your bank account with a web browser. The URL changes to HTTPS, using port 443, and the conversation is encrypted.

To use your browser as a REST client, simply do an Internet search for "REST API Client extension" and add it. Or for more bells and whistles allowing for cloud saves, workspaces, and monitoring, download a full client (available for Windows, Linux, or macOS). Currently, one of the most popular full-blown RESTful clients is Postman, which is what we are using as an example here (see Figure 11.42).

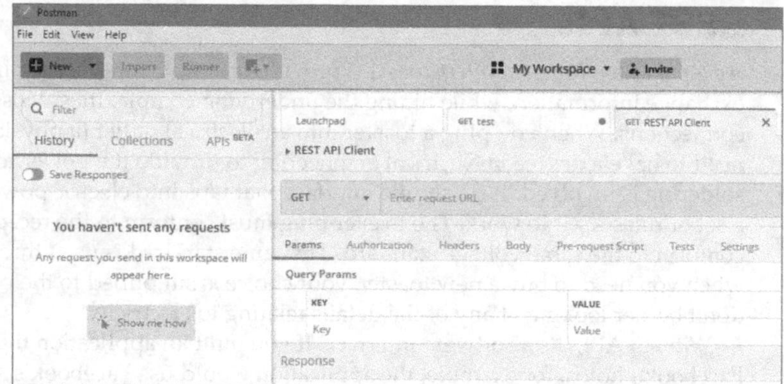

FIGURE 11.42 Postman desktop REST API client

Regardless of the client you choose, one of the first things you'll want to do is select Basic Authentication and add the NSX Manager credentials. In Postman, you can find this under the Authorization menu. Entering the credentials here will automatically add them to the request header (see Figure 11.43).

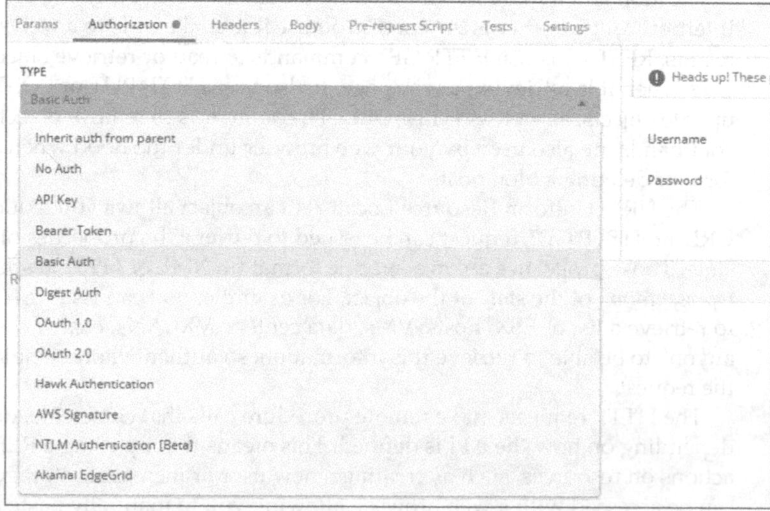

FIGURE 11.43 Adding NSX Manager credentials to the REST API header

NSX REST API GET Request

In this example, the NSX API is used to retrieve details and the runtime status of the NSX controller. Within the REST API client, add the following GET command, shown here and in Figure 11.44:

```
GET https://nsx-mgr.hydra1303.lab/api/2.0/vdn/controller
```

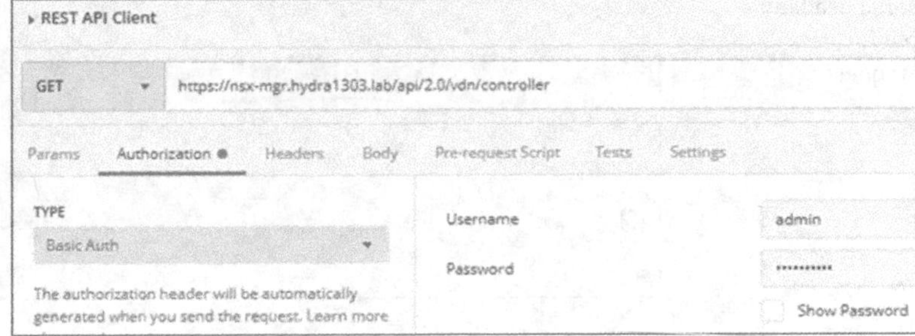

FIGURE 11.44 Issuing a GET request to retrieve controller status

The returned response looks like this:


```
<?xml version="1.0' encoding="UTF-8"?>
<controllers>
   <controller>
      <revision>0</revision>
      <clientHandle></clientHandle>
      <id>nsx-controller</id>
      <ipAddress>10.154.10.35</ipAddress>
      <status>RUNNING</status>
      <version>6.4.41119</version>
      <virtualMachineInfo>
          <objectID>VM-06</objectId>
          <objectTypeName>VirtualMachine</objectTypeName>
          <vsmUuid>4336654AB-EA01-06F9-5531-29AE84F0985</vsmUuid>
          <revision>22</revision>
          ...
```


From the output, we can determine that the status is RUNNING, the IP address is 10.154.10.35, and the version is 6.4.

NSX REST API POST Request

When we send an API POST command to make a configuration change, this requires more than just a single line to be entered. It is made up of two parts:

- **The Request:** The POST request command followed by the URL.
- **The Request Body:** An XML request message body in RAW format that includes the specific configuration options.

In order to also send the XML request body, an additional key-value header must be added (see Figure 11.45):

- **KEY:** Content-Type
- **VALUE:** application/xml

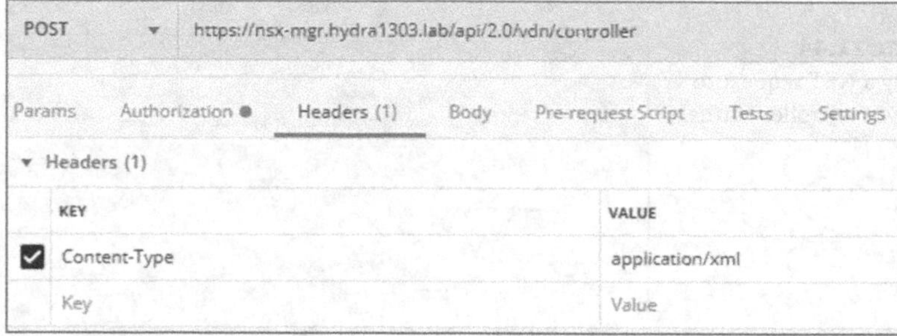

FIGURE 11.45 Additional header required for POST request

Sometimes, you may find that a response from a POST message is not received despite everything else being configured properly. If this is the case, add a second header with the key-value pair:

- **KEY:** Accept
- **VALUE:** application/xml

For this example, we want to add an additional NSX controller.
The Request:

```
POST https://nsx.mgr.hydra1303.lab/api/2.0/vdn/controller
```

The Request Body:

```
<controllerSpec>
    <id>nsx-controller3</id>
    <description>nsx-controller</description>
    <ipAddress>10.154.10.36</ipAddress>
    <resourcePoolId>domain-c4</resourcePoolId>
    <hostId>ESXi07</hostId>
    <datastoreId>VSAN-MGMT</datastoreId>
    <deployType>medium</deployType>
    <networkId>dvportgroup-1</networkId>
    <password>ScoobySnax336!</password>
</controllerSpec>
```

NSX REST API DELETE Request

To delete an object, a Request Body isn't necessary. It is a simple, one-line DELETE command similar in syntax to the GET command used for status information:

```
DELETE https://nsx-mgr.hydra1303.lab/api/2.0/vdn/controller/nsx-
controller3?forceRemoval=true
```

The Bottom Line

vRA Network Profile Network profiles contain specific network settings to use when provisioning VMs with vRealize Automation. The profiles contain IP address ranges, the gateway to use, the subnet mask to apply, and the ability to deploy NSX Edges if required.

Master It You want to create a vRA catalog item that allows the user to provision a VM that will be placed on an existing network segment. Which network profile type should you use?

1. External network profile
2. Internal network profile
3. NAT network profile
4. Routed network profile

Routed Network Profiles A routed network profile can create multiple subnet segments with connectivity through a Distributed Logical Router. The ranges (blocks) of the subnets are based on the subnet mask specified in the profile.

Master It A routed network profile is configured with the following information:

Base IP: 172.16.1.0

Subnet mask: 255.255.0.0

Range subnet mask: 255.255.255.224

The first subnet assigned would be 172.16.1.0 255.255.255.224. What would be the address and mask of the second subnet?

1. 172.16.2.0 255.255.255.224
2. 172.16.2.0 255.255.255.255
3. 172.16.1.32 255.255.255.224
4. 172.16.1.8 255.255.255.224

REST APIs REST APIs are used to allow different applications to easily communicate with one another by presenting a software interface that other applications can essentially plug into. This obviates the need for companies to have to realign code on both sides to provide inter-application communication. It also means that the tasks we complete using a GUI can be turned into code or automated as a script.

Master It The NSX API requires that a client connecting to it must be authenticated and the messages secured through encryption. What port is required to accomplish this?

1. 80
2. 8080
3. 443
4. 224

Appendix

The Bottom Line

Chapter 1: Abstracting Network and Security

SDDC Virtualization Software Defined Data Centers are possible due to decoupling physical hardware from software. VMware changed the game by first virtualizing compute resources. VMware virtual machines are operating systems that have been separated from the physical server by a hypervisor abstraction layer, called ESXi.

Master It VMware extended the same concepts to the other major infrastructure services including storage, networking, and security. What is the name of the hypervisor abstraction layer that VMware developed for networking and security?

Solution NSX

NSX Prerequisites NSX re-creates traditional physical network components such as routers, switches, ports, and firewalls in software. You manage the vSphere team for your organization and are considering NSX. Which additional physical components are required before NSX can be deployed? (Choose all that apply.)

Master It

1. Firewall virtual appliance
2. Distributed Resource Scheduler (DRS)
3. SDDC-compatible servers
4. None

Solution 4. NSX is a software overlay that runs over the existing physical network created by adding components to the ESXi hypervisor. No additional physical devices are needed.

NSX Kernel-Embedded Firewall By moving firewall services to the kernel, which of the following is *not* true?

Master It

1. An embedded firewall only increases resource utilization by a negligible amount.
2. Bandwidth is conserved due to the elimination of hairpinning.
3. Firewall rules are distributed and are the same on every ESXi host.
4. VM-to-VM traffic is easier to secure.

Solution 1. By embedding the firewall in the kernel, it *decreases* resource utilization, avoiding the need to send every packet to an external firewall.

Chapter 2: NSX Architecture and Requirements

Planes of Operation Traditional network devices operate autonomously, having the management, control, and data planes all contained within each. NSX moves the management plane to NSX Manager and the control plane to NSX Controllers.

Master It What NSX component provides the data plane?

1. NSX Data Appliance
2. NSX Virtual Switch
3. ESXi Host
4. NSX Edge

Solution 2. NSX Virtual Switch

NSX Controllers Instead of an active/backup design, each NSX Controller in a cluster is always active. This is so that they can slice and share the workloads.

Master It When deploying NSX Controllers in production, how many should a cluster contain?

Solution Three

Software-Defined Data Center Terminology It's commonly thought that most data center traffic is between the data center and outside networks, when in reality, it is from one VM to another within the data center. Both types of traffic have specific SDDC terms to describe each.

Master It East-West traffic refers to:

1. Traffic within the data center
2. Traffic between the data center and outside networks
3. Traffic between the virtual and physical networks

Solution 1. Traffic within the data center. This includes traffic from VM to VM within the same ESXi host and traffic between VMs located on different hosts.

Chapter 3: Preparing NSX

Deploying NSX Manager When deploying the NSX Manager, rather than cloning an existing instance, it is recommended to deploy it from an OVA file.

Master It The primary reason for deploying from an OVA file is so that NSX Manager gets its own what?

Solution UUID (Universally Unique Identifier)

Deploying an NSX Controller A secure password must be configured when deploying an NSX Controller.

Master It Which of the following is not a listed requirement for the NSX Controller password to be accepted?

1. At least one uppercase letter
2. At least one lowercase letter
3. At least one special character
4. At least eight characters
5. At least 12 characters

Solution 4. At least eight characters. The minimum password size for the NSX Controller is 12.

Connectivity between Multiple vCenter Domains Cross-vCenter can allow multiple data centers to be managed from a central point.

Master It Your Cross-vCenter design will include one primary NSX Manager and four secondary NSX Managers. How many vCenter Servers are required to support this configuration?

Solution Five. There is a one-to-one relationship between an NSX Manager and a vCenter Server. This holds true even when the design includes a primary NSX Manager and several secondaries.

Chapter 4: Distributed Logical Switch

Address Resolution Protocol Address Resolution Protocol (ARP) is used to discover the MAC address of the next hop along the path.

Master It You are troubleshooting a connectivity issue (see Figure 4.28). In one of your tests, you ping the server on the right from the PC on the left. Using a packet sniffer, you examine the packet received on the server. If everything is working as it should, what source MAC address do you expect to see in the Layer 2 header?

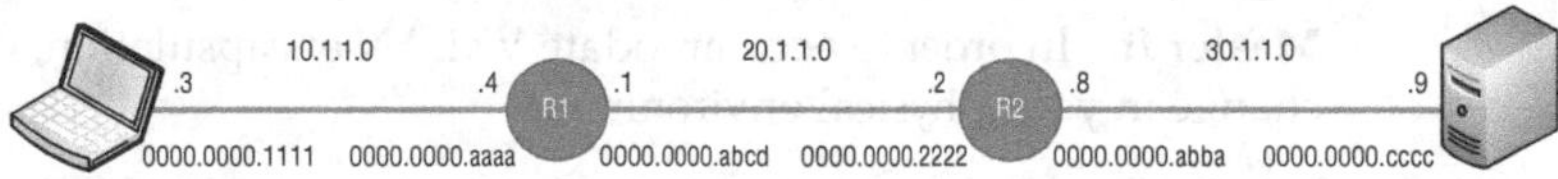

FIGURE 4.28 Troubleshooting connectivity

Solution 0000.0000.abba

Source and destination MAC addresses are used to cross each local link. Once received, the Layer 2 header is discarded and a new Layer 2 source and destination are filled in for the next link. The server would have seen the source MAC to be that of R2 (0000.0000.abba), not the PC's MAC address (0000.0000.1111), and it would have seen the destination MAC to be its own (0000.0000.cccc). The Layer 3 header is different. It doesn't change from end to end. The server would still see the L3 source as 10.1.1.3 and the L3 destination as itself, 30.1.1.9.

VTEP Table The Virtual Tunnel Endpoint can be thought of as a door or subway stop on the ESXi host to the VMs behind it. The VTEPs store the information for every VNI and VM that is local to the host. This information is then sent to the Controllers, which are responsible for distributing the information to all of the other ESXi hosts.

Master It You are troubleshooting an issue and need to verify that the mappings are correct. You issue the following command:

```
show logical-switch controller master vni 5001 vtep
```

What do you expect to see?

1. VNI 5001, the VTEP IP, and the VTEP MAC
2. VNI 5001, the VTEP IP, and the VM MAC
3. VNI 5001, the VM IP, and the VM MAC
4. VNI 5001, the VTEP IP, and the VM IP

Solution 1. VNI 5001, the VTEP IP, and the VTEP MAC.

The MAC table tells you where the VM lives; which door to go through. It maps the VM's MAC address (what you're trying to find) to the VTEP's IP address (the door).
The ARP table tells you the MAC address of the VM.

It maps the VM's IP address to its MAC address.

The VTEP table, which is what this question was asking about, tells you the MAC address of the VTEP.

It maps the VTEP's IP address to the VTEP's MAC address.

VXLAN Encapsulation NSX is a virtual overlay that exists on top of your physical network, the underlay. Once implemented, it's possible to greatly simplify your data center L2 design and quickly deploy a VM to attach to any segment regardless of its location within the data center. This is possible due to VXLAN encapsulation, which allows the traffic from the NSX virtual environment to be tunneled through the physical environment. Doing so adds an additional 50 bytes to your Ethernet headers.

Master It In order to accommodate VXLAN encapsulation, what might you need to change in your physical environment?

1. Enable trunking on the physical switches
2. Install hardware VTEPs
3. Change the MTU size
4. Suppress ARP broadcasts

Solution 3. Change the MTU size

By default, Ethernet has a Maximum Transmission Unit size of 1500 bytes. This means that any traffic larger than the set maximum will either be fragmented, or depending on the configuration, dropped. VMware recommends that the MTU size be changed to at least 1600 bytes. If your network is using jumbo frames (9000+ bytes), it will depend on what is running in your physical network.

The maximum MTU for Arista is 9214 bytes. The maximum for Cisco is 9216, and the maximum for Juniper is 9192.

Chapter 5: Marrying VLANs and VXLANs

Creating a Layer 2 Bridge Getting VM 172.16.1.5 on ESXi Host1 to communicate with VM 172.16.1.7 on ESXi Host9 can be easily accomplished in NSX using a VXLAN. The X is for eXtensible. You can use it extend your Layer 2 domain across any of your hosts, regardless of where they are located in your data center. NSX provides the virtual overlay network, and it's easy to have virtual talk to virtual. But we often want to be able to just as easily have virtual talk to physical: VXLAN to VLAN.

Master It You are configuring a Layer 2 Bridge to connect the VMs on VXLAN 5005 to the physical servers on VLAN 20. You're logged in to vSphere and you go to Menu ➤ Networking & Security (see Figure 5.31).

FIGURE 5.31 Network And Security (NSX) menu options

To create a Layer 2 Bridge, what do you click next?

1. Dashboard
2. Installation and Upgrade
3. Logical Switches
4. NSX Edges

Solution 4. NSX Edges

The first step is to create a Distributed Logical Router. DLRs and ESGs are two flavors of NSX Edges.We need to use the DLR as a Control VM to create a Layer 2 Bridge.

To do this, you will need to go to:

NSX Edges ➤ Add ➤ Distributed Logical Router

Hardware VTEP NSX provides several ways to bridge a VXLAN with a VLAN sharing the same IP subnet. You could create a Layer 2 Bridge (software bridge), use a hardware VTEP, or configure a Layer 2 VPN.

Master It You have been tasked with choosing a solution to bridge a workload on VXLAN 5005 with VLAN 15 on the physical network. Which of the following reasons might you give for implementing a hardware VTEP?

1. Least cost
2. Lowest latency
3. Single vendor solution
4. Services embedded in the VMkernel have a negligible impact

Solution 2. Lowest latency

Hardware VTEPs provide the lowest latency of the three choices. The higher cost of a physical switch supporting a hardware VTEP is a factor, and if troubleshooting support is needed, it may involve both VMware and the physical switch vendor. Also note that the hardware VTEP is not a service embedded in the VMkernel.

To Bridge or Not to Bridge Virtualization involves abstraction, and abstraction is all about hiding the underlying complexities. Moving workloads into the virtual environment provides options for simplification, including the ability to have single subnets that span the data center vs. lots of smaller individual domains to manage.

Some situations don't allow you to move workloads from the physical network to the virtual overlay in their entirety. When faced with this issue, knowing how to bridge the two can help to solve the problem with minimal effort.

Master It In which of the following situations would bridging *not* be considered?

1. Servers attached to a VLAN need to communicate at Layer 2 with VMs attached to a Logical Switch.
2. You are unable to virtualize an application due to licensing costs.
3. A VLAN port group on vDS-1 needs to communicate at Layer 2 with a VXLAN Logical Switch on vDS-2 in the same data center.
4. A legacy server can't be virtualized.

Solution 3. A VLAN port group on vDS-1 needs to communicate at Layer 2 with a VXLAN Logical Switch on vDS-2 in the same data center.

The VLAN port group and VXLAN Logical Switch must be connected to the same vDS in order to bridge them.

Chapter 6: Distributed Logical Router

Forwarding Address vs. Protocol Address The control and data planes are separate in NSX. The separation allows for higher availability since it's possible for the control plane to fail, while the data plane continues to route traffic.

Master It Because of the dichotomy of routing functions, there is a protocol address and a forwarding address assigned to learn routes and to route traffic. Which component would be assigned the forwarding address?

1. DLR
2. ESG

3. LR Control VM
4. UWA

Solution 1. DLR

The LR Control VM doesn't route any traffic, but it requires an IP address to be able to peer with the ESG to exchange routing information. That address is the protocol (routing protocol) address. The forwarding address is used by the DLR, not to exchange routing information, but to route the traffic to the ESG.

North-South East-West NSX handles VM-to-VM (East-West) traffic as well as NSX-to-physical (North-South) traffic. By a large margin, most traffic flows in a data center are made up of East-West traffic.

Master It What component specializes and is optimized for East-West traffic?

1. ESG
2. DLR
3. Layer 2 Bridge
4. Internal LIF

Solution 2. DLR

Because the DLR is a distributed router across all ESXi hosts in a transport zone, routing decisions do not have to be looked up on a routing device outside the host, causing the conversation to hairpin. Instead, the routing information is distributed to the host itself, in the kernel.

OSPF Design Rules OSPF is one option to use as a dynamic routing protocol for NSX. OSPF implementations require adhering to rules designed for scalability and stability. OSPF can operate in a single area, but convergence can be optimized by subdividing OSPF into multiple areas.

Master It If your OSPF design has multiple areas, which of the following is true?

1. All LSAs are Type 7 NSSA.
2. One area must be numbered 0.
3. No areas can be numbered 0.
4. Adding areas reduces scalability.

Solution 2. One area must be numbered 0.

Area 0 is the backbone area. If you only have one area, you are free to choose any number, but as soon as a second area is added, one must be Area 0. All other areas, by OSPF design, should directly connect to Area 0.

DLR Minus a LR Control VM When installing a DLR, a Logical Router Control VM is also deployed, by default. However, it's possible to deploy the DLR without the Control VM.

Master It Which could be a valid reason for purposefully choosing not to deploy the LR Control VM with the DLR?

1. You are only using the DLR to route North-South traffic.
2. You don't need the Control VM with OSPF.

3. You don't need the Control VM with static routes.

4. The LR Control VM is only necessary if the DLR is supporting multiple routing protocols simultaneously.

Solution 3. You don't need the Control VM with static routes.

The LR Control VM is used to peer with the ESG to exchange routes dynamically using a routing protocol. If you are only using static routes, it isn't necessary; however, you may want to add it anyway in case you change your mind later and want to enable a dynamic routing protocol. Also, the LR Control VM can only run a single routing protocol at a time.

Chapter 7: NFV: Routing with NSX Edges

Virtualization Terminology NSX is VMware's Software-Defined Network solution for network virtualization and security. Network Function Virtualization (NVF) is often mentioned when discussing SDN, but they aren't synonymous terms.

Master It NFV and SDN go hand-in-hand, but they have different objectives.

Which of the following is an objective of NFV?

1. Abstracting network functions from physical to virtual
2. Abstracting the control plane from the data plane
3. Abstracting routing functions from the kernel
4. Abstracting routing protocols

Solution 1. Abstracting network functions from physical to virtual

Network Function Virtualization focuses on taking network functions that have traditionally been supplied by physical devices, such as a physical firewall, and virtualizing the function. SDN's focus is on abstracting the control plane from the data plane to provide centralized control.

DLR Routing Restrictions Physical routers can easily run multiple routing protocols simultaneously and often support proprietary routing protocols like Cisco's EIGRP as well. They take a "ships in the night" approach with each protocol keeping track of its own information independently. With an NSX DLR, the supported routing options are different.

Master It Which of the following can a DLR support?

1. Only one routing method: BGP, OSPF, or static routes
2. BGP and OSPF simultaneously
3. BGP and static routes simultaneously
4. BGP, OSPF, IS-IS, and static routes

Solution 3. BGP and static routes simultaneously

A DLR can run a single dynamic routing protocol (BGP or OSPF) and static routes at the same time. BGP and OSPF cannot be run simultaneously and IS-IS is not supported by the DLR at all.

Configuring BGP on a DLR or ESG BGP comes in two flavors: internal BGP (iBGP) and external BGP (eBGP). Both are supported by the DLR and the ESG.

Master It The ESG is using BGP to exchange routes with the DLR. Examining the configuration, you find that the DLR uses AS number 65000 and the ESG is configured with AS 65001. Which statement is true?

1. iBGP is configured.
2. eBGP is configured.
3. 65000 is not a valid AS number.
4. The AS number must match to exchange routes.

Solution 2. eBGP is configured.

External BGP implies that your BGP neighbor does not share the same AS number. With Internal BGP, the AS numbers match. Either iBGP or eBGP could be used between the DLR and ESG. BGP AS numbers have a private range from 64512 to 65535. Therefore, 65000 is a valid AS number.

Justifications for Enabling ECMP Equal Cost Multi-Path (ECMP) routing is a mechanism for routing packets over parallel links all having the same cost. Because they are both parallel and equivalent in terms of routing characteristics, the protocol allows the links to act as if they were bundled together.

Master It Which of the following would *not* be a valid reason for enabling ECMP for connections between NSX and the external network?

1. To increase scalability
2. To increase availability
3. BGP does not load balance by default
4. OSPF does not load balance by default

Solution Virtually every dynamic routing protocol load balances across equal cost paths by default (OSPFv2, IS-IS, RIP, RIPv2, EIGRP as well as their IPv6 cousins OSPFv3, IS-IS for IPv6, RIPng, and EIGRP for IPv6). BGP is the exception in its attempt to be overly cautious about preventing routing loops. ECMP provides a way to allow multiple BGP equal cost routes to coexist in the routing table. The benefits outweigh the risks here, since you are trading what might be considered an excessive precaution for the benefits of increased bandwidth, fault tolerance, load balancing, and the ability to reduce failover time to zero in the case of a single path failing.

Chapter 8: More NVF: NSX Edge Services Gateway

Matching VPN Solution to Use Case The NSX Edge Services Gateway supports several types of VPNs to support different use cases. When choosing a VPN solution, factors to consider include temporary vs. permanent and mobile vs. fixed locations.

Master It Your organization has contractors based in different countries who travel to customer sites. To access resources within the corporate data center in New York, which type of VPN would you configure for these workers?

1. Site-to-site VPN
2. Layer 2 VPN
3. Layer 3 VPN
4. SSL VPN

Solution 4. SSL VPN

The SSL VPN is a user VPN allowing the user to initiate a connection and form a secure tunnel to the destination.

Benefits in Balancing Availability and scalability are always a concern in any network. Load balancing provides both. For example, if you are load balancing traffic across four servers, availability is not affected if one server needs to be taken down for maintenance. The other three continue working and the service remains available. Or say you are load balancing across four web servers. You can scale up and add more servers to improve performance when needed or scale down by removing servers when overall utilization decreases.

Master It Which of the following is *not* a valid load balancer configuration choice when specifying how the ESG will split the incoming traffic to connected servers?

1. Weighted round-robin
2. IP hash
3. Least used connection
4. Most used connection

Solution 4. Most used connection

There is no option for most used connection. The least used connection algorithm takes into consideration the server load. It checks to see which server has the least number of active sessions and sends the traffic to that server.

Choosing the Right Interface to Relay An Amazon delivery driver places a package on your porch and rings the doorbell. The bell rings throughout the house but no one is home to hear it. This is analogous to a DHCP Discover message. It's a broadcast intended for the local segment, which is fine if you have a DHCP server on that segment (or for the analogy, that someone is home). DHCP Relay is like having a smart doorbell connected to the cloud. When the doorbell button is pressed, it sends live video to your phone allowing you to communicate with the delivery driver. Similarly, DHCP Relay forwards the message to the ESG, which responds with an offer.

Master It In Figure 8.50, the admin configured a DHCP Relay Agent so that VM-B could successfully receive an IP address from the ESG. On which interface did the admin configure DHCP Relay to get this to work?

1. 192.168.1.1
2. 192.168.1.2
3. 10.30.8.1
4. 10.10.1.1

Solution 3. 10.30.8.1

The question was specifically referring to VM-B. VM-B is on the 10.30.8.X segment. If the DLR's internal interface, 10.30.8.1, is configured as a DHCP Relay Agent, the interface will actively listen for and intercept DHCP messages on that connected segment and will forward them to the DHCP server, which in this example is the ESG, 192.168.1.1. To make it easier to remember where to configure the agent, DHCP Relay is almost always configured on the interface used as the default gateway for the VMs.

Chapter 9: NSX Security, the Money Maker

IOChain Gang NSX uses a set of IOChain slots to handle how packets are processed at the kernel level. The first four are reserved for NSX and some slots are available to integrate third-party solutions into the process, giving NSX greater functionality.

Master It Instead of having antivirus software installed internally on a VM, you want to insert a third-party antivirus solution into the IOChain. Which would be a valid slot number within the IOChain to accomplish this?

1. Slot 1
2. Slot 2
3. Slot 4
4. Slot 16

Solution 3. Slot 4

Slots 4–12 are available to add Guest Introspection services from third-party vendors that have partnered with VMware to use their proprietary solutions to extend NSX functionality. The first slot is slot 0, the last slot is slot 15.

Matching on Access Lists NSX firewall rules can match on things like partial VM names, operating systems, security tags, data center, and so forth, making rules easy to understand and implement.

Master It In addition to the ability of firewall rules matching on various object types and labels, NSX also supports the traditional IP 5-tuple categories. Which of the following is *not* a 5-tuple variable?

1. Source IP address
2. Source port
3. Protocol
4. Subnet mask

Solution 4. Subnet mask

The 5-tuple values are source IP address, destination IP address, source port, destination port, and protocol.

IP Discovery If you specify a vCenter object in your DFW rule, like a VM name, NSX needs a way to discover the IP address of that VM before the rule can be enforced, or the mapping must be done statically.

Master It Which of the following is *not* a valid option for NSX to discover the IP address of a VM based on the name referenced in a DFW rule?

1. DHCP snooping
2. ARP snooping
3. Gratuitous snooping
4. SpoofGuard

Solution 3. Gratuitous snooping

Gratuitous snooping is a method employed by parents of teenagers acting suspiciously, but there's no such thing in NSX.

Chapter 10: Service Composer and Third-Party Appliances

Dynamic Inclusion Service Composer allows you to provision and assign security services within the virtual environment using security groups and to apply security policies. Group membership can be accomplished statically or dynamically.

Master It When creating a new security group, you will see these listed as steps:

Step 1. Name and description

Step 2. Define dynamic membership

Step 3. Select objects to include

Step 4. Select objects to exclude

Step 5. Ready to complete

What parameter is not valid criteria to match on when dynamically assigning a member to a security group?

1. Computer OS name
2. VM name
3. vNIC
4. Computer name
5. Security tag

Solution 3. vNIC

It is possible to add a *specific* vNIC to a security group, but it wouldn't be done dynamically. It would be configured under the step to select objects to include.

Inbound vs. Outbound You create a firewall rule within a Service Composer security policy. The source is Any. The destination is Policy's Security Groups. VM-6 is a member of a security group with this policy applied.

Master It When Policy's Security Groups is set as the destination in a Service Composer firewall rule, which traffic will be examined based on the security policy?

1. Incoming traffic
2. Outgoing traffic

Solution 1. Incoming traffic

An easy way to approach this is to look at the rule from the perspective of the members within the security group. VM-6 belongs to the group listed as the destination. Traffic forwarded to this destination would therefore be incoming from VM-6's perspective. If this example had Policy's Security Groups specified as the source, VM-6 is sourcing traffic that would be examined as it travels outbound to the destination.

Default Policy Priority Service Composer can create a single policy that includes firewall rules, guest introspection services, and network introspection services. When multiple security policies are listed, priority is based on a weight value.

Master It After creating a new security policy, it is added to the existing list of policies. By default, how will the order of the policies be affected?

1. The new policy will have top priority
2. The new policy will have the lowest priority
3. The new policy is not published until a weight is entered

Solution 1. The new policy will have top priority.

The higher the weight, the higher the priority. By default, the new policy will have top priority with a weight value that is automatically set by NSX at a value 1000 greater than any other existing policy. This default behavior places the policy at the top of the list. The weight value can be manually changed to customize the order.

Chapter 11: vRealize Automation and REST APIs

vRA Network Profile Network profiles contain specific network settings to use when provisioning VMs with vRealize Automation. The profiles contain IP address ranges, the gateway to use, the subnet mask to apply, and the ability to deploy NSX Edges if required.

Master It You want to create a vRA catalog item that allows the user to provision a VM that will be placed on an existing network segment. Which network profile type should you use?

1. External network profile
2. Internal network profile
3. NAT network profile
4. Routed network profile

Solution 1. External network profile

The external network profile is used when you want to add VMs to an existing segment.

Routed Network Profiles A routed network profile can create multiple subnet segments with connectivity through a Distributed Logical Router. The ranges (blocks) of the subnets are based on the subnet mask specified in the profile.

Master It A routed network profile is configured with the following information:

Base IP: 172.16.1.0

Subnet mask: 255.255.0.0

Range subnet mask: 255.255.255.224

The first subnet assigned would be 172.16.1.0 255.255.255.224. What would be the address and mask of the second subnet?

1. 172.16.2.0 255.255.255.224
2. 172.16.2.0 255.255.255.255
3. 172.16.1.32 255.255.255.224
4. 172.16.1.8 255.255.255.224

Solution 3. 172.16.1.32 255.255.255.224

The base IP 172.16.1.0 and subnet mask 255.255.255.0 determine the entire range of addresses that can be used for the deployment. You read this as, "All subnets created from this profile will start with 172.16.1.x"

The range subnet mask indicates how to subdivide this 172.16.1.x range. Since the last octet of the mask is 224, we can use a shortcut to avoid binary hell and take 256 minus 224, resulting in blocks of 32 in the last octet. All of the created networks would have the mask of 255.255.255.224 and the first four blocks would look like this:

172.16.1.0

172.16.1.32

172.16.1.64

172.16.1.96

REST APIs REST APIs are used to allow different applications to easily communicate with one another by presenting a software interface that other applications can essentially plug into. This obviates the need for companies to have to realign code on both sides to provide inter-application communication. It also means that the tasks we complete using a GUI can be turned into code or automated as a script.

Master It The NSX API requires that a client connecting to it must be authenticated and the messages secured through encryption. What port is required to accomplish this?

1. 80
2. 8080
3. 443
4. 224

Solution 3. 443

Specifically, it uses TCP port 443, the standard for SSL connections.

Index

E

F

G

H

I

K

L

M

N

O

P

R

S

T

U

V

W–Z